CRUISERS
OF THE US NAVY
1922–1962

△ This attractive but undated aerial photograph
was taken during *Pittsburgh*'s period of service,
1952–54. Her crew is mustered on deck. In the
autumn of 1955, one year before her final
decommissioning, *Pittsburgh* is said to have her
40mm AA replaced by twenty 3in/50 Mk 22, but
sadly no photograph exists to prove this. (USN)

CRUISERS
OF THE US NAVY
1922–1962

Stefan Terzibaschitsch
Translated by Harold Erenberg

Naval Institute Press

LIST OF ABBREVIATIONS

Published and distributed in the United States of America by the Naval Institute Press, Annapolis, Maryland 21402

Library of Congress Catalog Card No. 88–61640

ISBN 0–87021–974–X

First published 1984 as *Kreuzer der U.S. Navy* by Koehlers Verlagsgesellschaft mbH, Herford, West Germany.

Jacket illustrations: front, USS *Long Beach* (CGN-9); back, USS *Little Rock* (CLG-4).

The illustrations in this book have been collected from many sources, and vary in quality owing to the variety of circumstances under which they were taken and preserved. As a result, certain of the illustrations are not of the standard to be expected from the best of today's equipment, materials and techniques. They are nevertheless included for their inherent information value, to provide an authentic visual coverage of the subject.

Designed and edited by DAG Publications Ltd. Designed by David Gibbons; edited by Michael Boxall; layout by Anthony A. Evans; typeset by Typesetters (Birmingham) Ltd and Ronset Typesetters Ltd; camerawork by M&E Reproductions, North Fambridge, Essex; printed and bound in Great Britain by The Bath Press, Avon.

AN/SPC– The full designation of detection radar installations on US warships. Mostly abbreviated with 'SPS–' and used always in combination with a number.

ASROC Rocket-guided anti-submarine torpedo or depth-charge; also the designation for the launcher itself.

BPDMS Abbreviation for short-range defensive guided weapon installations with (at the time) Sea Sparrow missiles.

CA Designation for heavy cruisers.

CAG Designation for guided weapon cruisers that retain part of their main gun armament (8in).

CB Designation for large cruiser.

CG Designation for cruisers with main armament of guided weapons only.

CGN Designation for guided weapon cruisers with nuclear propulsion.

CIWS Overall term for fully electronically guided quick-firing gun installations serving as the last, close-in defence against approaching aircraft and missiles.

CL Designation for light cruisers.

CLG Designation for guided weapon cruisers that retained part of their 6in main gun armament.

CRUDESFLOT A flotilla made up of cruisers and destroyers; now called 'Cruiser-Destroyer Group' (CRUDESGRU).

CRUDIV Cruiser Division; an old term used when cruisers were organized in divisions.

DASH Unmanned remote-controlled helicopter drone used in the 1960s for submarine hunting.

DL Designation for large destroyers.

ESM Electronic counter-measures (passive).

ECM Electronic counter-measures (active).

ECCM Defence consisting of electronic counter-measures.

FLG Fire-control instrument.

FLR Fire-control radar.

FK Missile (collective term for all unguided rockets).

FRAM Comprehensive ship modernization programme dating from the early 1960s.

IFF Electronic installation for the differentiation between friend and foe.

IX Designation for 'any kind of auxiliary ship', quite often test ships.

LAMPS Submarine-hunting system on cruisers, destroyers and frigates, based on helicopter types SH-2 (LAMPS I) and SH-60 (LAMPS III).

Mack Current abbreviation for the use of a mast/funnel combination on modern ships.

NTDS Introduced from 1960 for a data-based command and evaluation instrument on larger ships.

PIRAZ Abbreviation for radar control stations on warships.

SAR Abbreviation for general term for search and rescue operations needed by ships in distress when carried out by ship or helicopter and/or aircraft.

SUM A below-surface missile used by ships to combat submarines.

Sonar Below-surface detection by radio means.

SPS– Standard prefix in detection radio instruments from about 1950.

SPG–, SPQ– Standard prefix in gun and guided weapon fire-control instruments.

SRN– Standard prefix in TACAN aerials.

TACAN Ship-carried navigational aids for aircraft and helicopters.

TACTAS Abbreviation for depth-adjustable towed sonar installations SQR-18 and SQR-19.

TR Torpedo tube, long ship-torpedo es for use against other ships.

URN– Standard prefix in TACAN aerials.

UTR Torpedo tube, short anti-submarine torpedoes or long torpedo tubes Mks 24 and 25 for wire-guided long anti-submarine torpedoes.

VDS Designation for older depth-adjustable sonar installations.

CONTENTS

PREFACE

This book covers the classes of cruisers built for the United States Navy from the 1920s and 1930s under the restrictions of the various international treaties, those built for service in the Second World War and immediately thereafter, and concludes with *Long Beach* (CGN-9). In 1975, the existing guided missile frigates (DLG/DLGN) were redesignated CG/CGN – guided missile cruisers – and the old era of ship classification and construction ended.

The book begins with the seven pre-war (1922–41) classes totalling 37 ships – 19 light and 18 heavy cruisers. For war purposes, 42 light and 20 heavy cruisers were built from 1942 until 1948. A further 37 were projected, but when the war ended their construction was suspended; in some cases it had already been halted. Of 62 cruisers completed during the war, 11 were converted during the mid-1950s to carry guided missiles. The year 1961 saw completion of what, in terms of design and displacement, may be considered the last 'real' cruiser: the nuclear cruiser *Long Beach*. At the time of writing, this ship is the last survivor of those described in this book.

I should like to thank all those who, in recent years, have offered me critical appraisal of my earlier books. I have found that US naval experts in the Federal Republic of Germany, Austria and Switzerland possess a profound knowledge of their chosen subject, and several of them have collaborated with me on this book – which has benefitted greatly from their assistance. In particular I should like to express my debt to the following individuals and institutions:

Eberhard Kaiser of Reinbek, who drew the line illustrations; Elmar Vitt of Berg, Gladbach, for his painstaking research into weaponry, electronics and ship camouflage during the Second World War, and for revising manuscripts and offering invaluable advice; Jurg Kürsener of Lohn in Switzerland, for exploratory work in the Naval History Division, Washington, DC, and for providing background information concerning the organization of cruiser formations; Heinz O. Vetters of Meersburg; H. K. Rudolf of Rodenbach; David Kimble of Seward, Nebraska; Willi Dunko of Scharding; Robert Heller of San Brino, California; Professor Dr Jürgen Rohwer of Stuttgart; the staff of the Chief of Naval Information, Washington, DC; and Bob Lawson (Tailhook Association) of Bonita, California.

Stefan Terzibaschitsch

INTRODUCTION

The US Navy between the Wars

The scope of US Navy planning, from the end of the First World War to the establishment of the two-ocean navy brought about by the vision of President F. D. Roosevelt, embraced not only the number of ships built, but also the administrative disposition of the fleet. The old European pattern had dictated the disposition of important fleet ships. Battleships were deployed in the battle fleet, the navy's principal striking force. In peacetime, cruisers and destroyers were allotted to this main fleet. There was a secondary formation, the scouting force, later known as the scouting fleet, which was a reconaissance fleet made up mainly of heavy cruisers, but also with destroyers. The results of the Battle of Jutland prompted a re-thinking, and the British gave up the concept of scouting immediately after the end of the war; the Americans retained both categories until 1939.

The United States has two long coastlines, open to attack from east and west. The US Navy saw its main tasks as being to protect the USA's coasts, to keep open seaways to any allies in Europe and the Far East, and to keep any sea battles as far away from the USA as possible. This was the theory, based on the fact that, during the First World War, Germany was the main enemy, with a large battle fleet, while Japan was numbered among the Allies. The end of the war brought a very different situation. After the Allied victory, there were, in effect, no potential enemies in the Atlantic. On the other hand, it was quite feasible that the increasing political and military strength of Japan would ultimately make it an enemy. So the battle fleet was concentrated in the Pacific, where Pearl Harbor became the most important US naval base. Guam and Wake Islands were successively set up as depot stations. To protect the Atlantic, a large number of heavy cruisers, destroyer flotillas and other ships were allotted to the east coast. The cruisers were deployed in the scouting fleet.

The long period of economic depression obliged the US Congress to curtail expenditure. The Navy was hardly in a position to convince Congress that approximately half the fleet should be stationed on the east coast where there was no apparent enemy. So for fiscal reasons, a US fleet (which, with its large number of battleships was essentially the battle fleet) was deployed in the Pacific, while the scouting fleet, which should really have been an important adjunct of it, was far away on the east coast. The scouting fleet was known as the Atlantic Squadron, a modest description for an east coast formation deploying many ships. In 1939 when, as had been predicted, Germany and Italy were seen as potential enemies, expenditure was provided for an Atlantic and a Pacific Fleet, and the concepts of battle fleet and scouting fleet disappeared.

Even when the battle fleet and scouting fleet were one body, their effective mutual functioning had been very questionable given existing conditions. A confrontation with the two potential enemies could never have taken place in the 1920s because: the range of battleships and certainly that of cruisers was inadequate; intermediate US Navy bases were still in the course of construction; the support ship fleet was quite undeveloped and no effective refuelling at sea could ever have been undertaken. Overall distances were enormous. It is approximately 4,700 miles from the Panama Canal to Pearl Harbor and 2,000 miles from San Diego to Pearl Harbor. (The Panama Canal was of great significance given the considerable distance separating the fleets. The heavy cruisers were often switched to the west coast were they operated from San Pedro in California, making passage to Pearl Harbor for extended manoeuvres. From there they were obliged to return to the east coast for refitting.) The shortest route from Halifax, Nova Scotia, to the British Isles is approximately 2,400 miles. If one accepts that a set-piece sea battle in the middle of the Pacific simply could not take place, the traditional concepts of a battle fleet and a scouting fleet were surely obsolete. Yet another reason for maintaining the scouting fleet was lost when aircraft became essential in battleships and cruisers, and when radar technology, tracking and surveillance became standard practice.

In peacetime it was also the task of American cruisers to protect American interests overseas, particularly in the Far East, in the disturbed South China Sea and in South American waters. An independent Asiatic Fleet, consisting of one to three cruisers and a small number of destroyers, was detached and managed by the scouting fleet, although from time to time light cruisers of the *Omaha* class were at hand.

The Evolution of US Cruiser Types

At the end of the First World War the US Navy had an operational cruiser fleet of light, relatively thinly armoured and slow vessels, all built between 1892 and 1907. To these could be added a number of heavy units that were better armed and better protected. Without exception, all these older ships lacked an adequate turn of speed and were unable to keep up with fleet torpedo-boats and destroyers. Even the newest of them was at least ten years old. It was apparent, therefore, that the obsolete ships needed to be replaced by suitable designs, able to match the new Japanese construction that was beginning to emerge. In 1918 cruiser duties were categorized as:
- Protection of the battle fleet against torpedo-boats and destroyers
- Protection of its own torpedo-boats and destroyers against superior surface ships
- Providing reconnaissance for the battle fleet
- Providing flagships for destroyer flotillas, etc.

The Washington Fleet Conference was to make the programme of modernization difficult, one of its clauses dividing cruisers into light or heavy – depending on gun calibre – not displacement. A maximum displacement of 10,000 tons was accorded to both categories. As with the other classes of warship covered by the treaty, the Americans adhered to the treaty restrictions until the end of the 1930s.

In their intention of building light, fast and well-armed ships, capable of carrying aircraft, the Americans had an immediate success with the

Omaha class. By extending the original design, the number of 6in guns was increased from eight to twelve; however, this meant that the ships were basically over-weaponed, and problems of stability resulted, which may be why the class received hardly any modification or modernization during the Second World War, although two of the 6in guns were removed from most of them. The relatively short endurance of the *Omaha*s restricted their deployment to protecting destroyer formations, which was what they had been designed for.

The position was different in the heavy cruiser category; these ships were classified as such until later, but they were given 8in guns from the outset. Although constructed in accordance with the Washington Treaty, they did measure up to new Japanese construction; indeed, they were impressive in terms of range, speed and heavy armament, although their armour left something to be desired. Some improvement in protection was effected in later ships. The ten 8in guns given to the *Penascola*s were unique to that class, as were the five 6in triple turrets of the *Brooklyn*-class light cruisers. (This later class was the very considerable reply to the Japanese *Mogami*-class cruisers.)

The comparative lack of range of the *Omaha*-class cruisers was rectified in the larger, heavy cruisers. This, coupled with their longer-range 8in guns, made them suitable to escort otherwise unaccompanied aircraft carriers. In this one sees even at this early stage a parallel with the task force concept, which originated and flourished during the Second World War. The later *Brook-lyn*-class ships were planned to have a greater radius of action because they were intended for fleet support roles, their fire being more effective against fast destroyers, especially at night and in bad weather. The rate of fire of 8in and 6in guns was in the ratio 3:9 shells per minute. Thus a heavy cruiser could fire a broadside of 27 shells in one minute, while a *Brooklyn* cruiser with its five turrets could achieve 135 – in other words, could fire off more weight of shell than a heavy cruiser, albeit to a lesser range. In the light of this argument it makes perfect sense that so many ships of the *Cleveland/Fargo* class were constructed. They had one turret less than the *Brooklyn*s, but this was compensated by the greater number of ships. A balance in the firing rates of both calibres was finally to be achieved with the introduction of automatic 8in Mk 16 turrets in the *Des Moines* class, although these came at a time when the old-fashioned sea battle

had passed into history. Experiences in the Solomon Islands of the inadequate firing rate of the 8in guns expedited development of this fully automatic triple turret; but the size of the turret and its magazine necessitated an increase in dimensions and displacement.

The tendency in the 1930s to build heavier cruisers because they had a greater radius of action was against the dictates of the London Naval Treaty of 1936, which lowered cruiser displacement to 8,000 tons maximum. At this weight, it was thought they would best be equipped with five 6in twin turrets. These, however, would not be available in the requisite time. To make the most of the situation and also to make the best use of allotted tonnage, a decision was made for a 6,000-ton ship with five armoured 5in twin mountings (in effect, light turrets). This lead to the *Atlanta* class, which were unpopular at first with the naval commanders, but which proved themselves notably in the course of the war. While there had been no positive experience of the type as a guide to the future, a further quartet – the *Oakland* class – were ordered, perhaps so as to have as many units as possible of a thoroughly planned design available for fleet use. These cruisers could be built at yards that were too small for the construction of the *Cleveland* class. No construction of 8,000-ton ships with 6in twin turrets was ever undertaken, the outbreak of war rendering treaty restrictions irrelevant. Instead, a start was made on the construction of larger light cruisers with an extended radius of action and increased armament.

Just before the end of the 1930s a building concept for 'large' cruisers appeared. This would seem to have been a reaction to reports that the Japanese were planning such ships, something that never happened. What the Navy was aiming at was the construction of a cruiser with 12in guns that could match enemy cruisers for speed and excel them in range and firepower. There were a number of designs on this theme, culminating in the *Alaska* class.

The emerging use of aircraft carried on board for reconnaissance purposes altered the shape of cruisers on commissioning. There was a twofold argument for abandoning visual reconnaissance: the aircraft carried on board could do the job more quickly and accurately from their higher vantage-point; there was no longer (as will be explained later) a real battle fleet for which to reconnoitre. Reconnaissance aircraft simplified the task of locating armed merchant-ship raiders,

a task which usually fell to cruisers. That their value was recognized is evidenced by the fact that most cruisers were designed to accommodate at least four aircraft in an enclosed hangar, exemplified very clearly in the *Brooklyn*s, which had a spacious hangar aft. Rather different was the task allotted to aircraft aboard battleships: their main function was to observe the accuracy of the parent ship's gunfire. From the outset, the perceived importance of aircraft prompted increasing endeavour to ship as many of them as possible, perhaps in 'flight deck cruisers', but for various reasons nothing came to a design-planning stage.

Just before the outbreak of war, it became apparent that the *Baltimore* and *Cleveland* classes could not all be built at the same time, given existing yard capacity. As escorts for aircraft carriers, light cruisers were preferred because of their greater firing rate, so they received priority construction. This decision shows clearly that, before the war, the concept of the carrier strike force (a carrier fleet) totally dictated the size and disposition of the cruiser fleet. It was, therefore, deemed necessary to withdraw nine units from the urgently required *Cleveland* class for replanning and converting to light aircraft carriers. From 1943 these light carriers strengthened the US carrier fleet which heavy losses early in the war had depleted. The construction of the heavy *Baltimore* class was likewise only initiated when an adequate number of *Cleveland*s had left the slips.

Light cruisers were also preferred because more of them could be built. At all times the

US CRUISER CLASSES BUILT OR CONVERTED FROM 1922 TO 1962

Inter-war period		Baltimore	14
Class	Number	Oregon City	3
Omaha	10	Worcester	2
Pensacola	2	Des Moines	3
Northampton	6	Alaska	2
Portland	2	Total	63
New Orleans	7		
Wichita	1		
Brooklyn	9	**New and guided missile**	
Total	37	**coversions of 1950s and**	
		1960s	

Built during Second World War		Class	Number
Class	Number	Boston	2
Atlanta	4	Galveston	2
Cleveland	26	Little Rock	4
Oakland/Juneau	7	Albany	3
Fargo	2	Long Beach	1
		Total	12

threat posed by Japanese aircraft was paramount, and from 1943/44 ships were packed with light AA guns – almost to the point at which stability was threatened. This was why, the *Omaha*s apart, most of the cruisers in service underwent considerable modification, during which efforts were made to reduce top-heaviness. On the other hand, it was not widely known that the Navy failed to make good its intention about 1941 to reconstruct the *Omaha* class as anti-aircraft cruisers.

The proven value of small anti-aircraft cruisers meanwhile led to the development of the *Worcester* class whose ships were twice as heavy. In them it was possible to realize what had not been permissible under treaty restrictions, namely the fitting of six fully automatic 6in twin turrets in ships with an extensive range. Once again, the end of hostilities curtailed construction and only two remained; the emergence of guided missiles rendered these obsolete.

US Cruisers Today

The modern cruisers built in the 1960s and 1970s have three things only in common with their predecessors: they retained their status as secondary ships of the surface-fleet; their size, to some extent; they maintained their traditional role as protection for carrier formations. When one examines the sizes of old and modern cruisers discrepancies become apparent. The modern ones are smaller; this is clear if we look at *Long Beach* (CGN-9), which can also to be regarded as the last 'true' cruiser to be planned and built. Subsequent ships officially allocated until 1975 to the (large) 'frigate' category were really inflated destroyers whose displacement had grown from approximately 3,500 tons in the Second World War to approximately 8,000 tons. That these 'frigates' were supposed to have a special value is deduced from the fact that they were too heavy to be destroyers and too light to be cruisers; but it can be said that, in contrast to their predecessors, they were multi-purpose ships with emphasis on surface-to-air missile capacity and an abundance of submarine-hunting devices. Obviously they needed to be heavier than destroyers if they were to fulfil both these different tasks effectively.

Later came the possibility of fitting surface vessels with nuclear propulsion with its manifold advantages; but this demands at the present time a displacement of at least 9,000 tons. Furthermore, the two recent classes with this propulsion, *California* (CGN-36) and *Virginia* (CGN-38) had

been planned as DLGNs before they were raised to their new level in 1975. This step enabled the then Chief of Naval Operations (CNO), Admiral Holloway, to achieve, among other matters, a balance between the numbers of Soviet and American cruisers. In all respects the Russians had at all times more cruisers than the US Navy, even if they were not as effective.

Just to what extent currently the term 'cruiser' is linked to the function and degree of activity in fleet use and how little to displacement is illustrated clearly by comparing the *Ticonderoga* class (CG-47) with the *Spruance* class (DD-963) from which it evolved. One sees certainly a displacement increase of approximately 20 per cent, but the dimensions remain the same. *Ticonderoga* owes its classification as a cruiser above all to the great importance of its two AEGIS battle installations. Very significant in this case is the doubled capacity and degree of resistance to missile hits (if one battle installation is put out of action, there remains a second). Double installations require double missile magazines with an obvious need for space and this is a reason for building large ships. Further good reasons for the increased displacement of current vessels over wartime types is that modern types now have to accommodate a host of large, heavy electronic installations, as well as the enhanced habitability requirements of the modern, all-volunteer navy. One should not lose sight of the fact that cruisers are not *just* container vessels for complex battle systems; to some extent they must, like destroyers and frigates, remain silent when stalked by nuclear submarines. Modern cruisers are distinguished by the following main factors: high firepower; capability to operate independently in high-threat situations, without protection of carrier-borne aircraft; capacity to serve as lead ships of a task force and direct and coordinate air defence, surface and underwater offensive operations – in all of which one notes possible

ACTIVE CRUISER CLASSES IN THE US NAVY IN THE MID-1980s

Designation	Class	No. Ships	Displacement
CGN-38	*Virginia*	4	11,260 tons
CGN-36	*California*	2	10,150 tons
CGN-35	*Truxton*	1	9,200 tons
CGN-25	*Bainbridge*	1	8,580 tons
CGN-9	*Long Beach*	1	17,350 tons
CG-47	*Ticonderoga*	2(+24)	9,600 tons
CG-26	*Belknap*	9	7,930 tons
CG-16	*Leahy*	9	7,800 tons
Total		29(+24)	

parallels with the bringing back into service of battleships.

One reason why operating costs have been kept fairly low is that, because of the great degree of automation in the almost totally computerized combat systems, modern cruisers (and for that matter all new types of fighting ships) require smaller crews than in the past.

The US Navy currently refuses to implement the construction of nuclear cruisers of the CGN-42 class, costing approximately 1.5 billion dollars. In line with what may be budgeted, the construction of the *Ticonderoga* class is to be continued, involving about three ships per year. To this end Bath Iron Works will serve as the second yard to Ingalls. Construction contracts have already been awarded for 13 of the 26 planned ships of this class. The Navy admits its inability to cope without these ships. Leaving aside the last six CGNs, all other CG/CGNs have served half of their normal active life. Even after all possible means of prolonging their lives have been carried out, 35 years remains the utmost active service span. If nothing happens to alter the picture, their work will not be undertaken by additional cruisers, but rather by guided missile destroyers of the *Arleigh Burke* class (DDG-51) which are smaller than CG-47 class ships and have a rather smaller AEGIS installation into the bargain. They are lacking in helicopter hangars. In the assumption that events will continue to unroll in this way, one can forecast that new cruiser construction will cease to exist by at least the end of the century.

Classification and Nomenclature

The US Navy first attempted to classify and categorize ship designations by means of letters of the alphabet in the eighteenth century; since then the various combinations of letters have been as numerous as the very many types and categories of ships developed over two hundred years. The history of ship classification is both a constituent part and supplementary documentation of the types, categories and individual ship classes. The US Navy tightened up its classification procedure in 1920. At that time a basis was formulated for a division into types and categories and these are in principle still applicable, even though classification lists were always being expanded or brought up to date. Currently there is a division of:

- Types, i.e., ships for a particular purpose, built to conform to that purpose.

- Categories, which are part of a definite type, but destined for particular roles.

Since 1920, US Navy classification has continued to develop. Its present shape is one that has been adopted as the basis for general classification in all NATO countries, certainly for those types that have been allotted one or two letters. We can therefore make the following current division:

B Battleship
CV Aircraft carrier (US)
R Aircraft carrier (non-US)
C Cruiser
D Destroyer
F Frigate
S Submarine
P Patrol vessel
L Amphibious warfare ship
M Mine warfare ship
A Auxiliary ship
Y Harbour service craft and Depot ships

In each type there are always one or more categories to which two or more letters are allotted. These categories form the basis of the American ship classification method. A US vessel does not necessarily have a name, but it will always have a designation made up of letters of its category and a numeral according to a series allocated once only in each category. Individual ships show their numerals, not their letters; auxiliary ships and harbour craft are an exception to this rule. Clearly, on account of the multiplicity of categories, many diverse ships carry the same numerals on their bows. As, therefore, one cannot identify a type precisely from bow numeral alone, other criteria are of special importance. It is easier to classify and identify ships of other NATO navies because they have a letter prefixed to the numeral.

As a departure point from type letter C (for cruiser), the two most important categories are designated:

CL Light cruiser
CA Heavy cruiser

But, this generic division holds true only for the period the 1920s to the 1940s, these abbreviations having been used during an earlier era, but with a different meaning. There had been some ships with CL designation that were 'protected cruisers', and long before the introduction of the *Pensacola* class there were vessels with CA designation signifying 'armoured cruisers'. It is outside the scope of this book to deal with these earlier vessels, but a list is appended. (It will be noticed that certain designating numbers were never allotted.) The matter becomes even more complicated when it is realized that very old heavy cruisers were unofficially designated ACR; some were merely designated C followed by a numeral. Moreover, CAs and CLs were allotted numbers in sequence; but such rules were not adhered to strictly. Ships CL-1 to CL-3 were initially classified as scout cruisers and designated accordingly with the prefix CS. To explain this apparent jumble of letters, the tables present cruiser-category designations prior to the *Omaha* class.

From the outset US cruisers were named after American cities. (One exception was *Canberra* (CA-70) which, on the orders of President

CATEGORY LETTER SYMBOLS

Letters	Designation	Notes
ACR	Armoured Cruiser	Not an official symbol; brought in later.
C	Cruiser	Symbol applied subsequently to designate protected and unprotected cruisers.
CA	Cruiser, First line	—
CA	Heavy Cruiser	Used in 1920 as a distinction from CL in terms of size and importance; from 1931 for cruisers with 8in guns.
CAG	Guided Missile Heavy Cruiser	Symbol for guided missile cruisers also equipped with 8in guns.
CB	Large Cruiser	Used only for *Alaska* class.
CBC	Large Tactical Command Ship	Provided from 1952 for *Alaska* class conversions that did not take place.
CC	Battler Cruiser first line	1920–1928 reserved for battle-cruisers of the *Lexington* class that were not built.
CC	Command Ship	Introduced in 1952 for *Northampton* as follow-up symbol for CLC; from 1952 used appropriately to designate other types; LCC = Command Ship of the Amphibious Force.
CF	Flying Deck Cruiser	Reserved during 1930s for Flight Deck Cruisers (which were not proceeded with).
CG	Guided Missile Cruiser	1958. Symbol for cruiser conversions that had guided missiles but no heavy armament; during the 1970s the symbol for all guided missile conversions that were still in use; from 1 July 1975 for all former DLGs with the

Letters	Designation	Notes
		exception of the *Farragut* class; later on for the *Ticonderoga* class.
CGN	Guided Missile Cruiser, Nuclear Powered	Initially, from 1962 as CG(N) for *Long Beach*; from 3 October 1967 as CGN; from 1 July 1975 for former DLGNs and all new constructions.
CL	Light Cruiser	See remarks re CA; used from 1931 to designate cruisers with 6in guns or smaller.
CLAA	Anti-Aircraft Light Cruiser	1949 to 1968 designation for *Atlanta* and *Oakland* classes.
CLC	Task Fleet Command Ship	Until 1952, symbol for *Northampton* as counterpart to CBC.
CLG	Guided Missile Light Cruiser	Counterpart to CAG, re cruiser conversions which have also 6in guns; replaced by CG in the 1970s.
CLGM	Guided Missile Light Cruiser	Not used by the US Navy; symbol for non-American ships equipped with an assortment of SAM and SSM weapons.
CLK	Cruiser Hunter Killer	Intended after Second World War for submarine-hunters of cruiser size, which later became 'Frigates' (DL).
CM	Minelayer, First line	Used until the end of the 1920s for cruisers, then applied to mine ship types.
CS	Scout Cruiser	Symbol applied retrospectively to scout cruisers dating back to the pre-1920s.
CV	Aircraft Carrier, First line	Carrier cruisers were so designated originally when these were thought of as scouting ships; from 6 June 1928, only carriers in the true sense were CV.

Roosevelt, was named after the Australian city of Canberra in order to honour the Australian heavy cruiser of that name which fought with, and was sunk in company with, three American heavy cruisers off Savo Island on 9 August 1942.) The last cruiser to be named according to this traditional method was *Long Beach* (CGN-9). On 1 July 1975, wide-reaching changes were made to the overall system of classifying ships and the following deviations from the hitherto common practice were made:

- Certain DLG/DLGNs reclassified to CG/CGNs kept names that honoured meritorious sea officers.
- From the *California* class (CGN-36), CGNs were given names of Federal States in the USA; these were capital ships, and it was in line with the naming of the SSBNs of the *Ohio* class (strategic submarines).
- From the *Ticonderoga* class (CG-47), those cruisers which had the AEGIS combat system were given the names of historic places or the traditional names of previous warships.

Organization and Deployment

For as long as cruisers have existed in the US Navy they have been organized in cruiser divisions (CRUDIV). During the years preceding the Second World War this was the only disposition, although not all units of a CRUDIV necessarily operated together. It could happen that one particular cruiser was used for administrative roles in its division, or could serve as flagship to a superior division or in a quite different formation. Hence, for example, *Indianapolis* (CA-35), which had long belonged to CRUDIV 4 and 6, was almost constantly in use as a flagship for all cruisers in the Pacific, and later, just before its tragic loss, flagship of Fifth Fleet. The smaller cruisers were sent to the Far East either singly or in a formation with the Asiatic Fleet, or they were used as flagships for destroyers, destroyer flotillas or large submarine groups. As more and more cruisers were built, the number of divisions rose. A division would consist of either light or heavy cruisers only. The number of ships in a division varied between two and six, four being the general rule. Logistics dictated that, if possible, ships of identical class be contained in one division; if this were impossible, then ships of a kindred class.

Organization was eased by the fact that up to 1940 the bulk of the fleet was stationed in the Pacific. There was concentrated the battle fleet with all the battleships and aircraft carriers. Other groups were: Submarines, US Fleet, Atlantic Squadron, US Fleet, Asiatic Fleet and, lastly, Base Force, US Fleet, with its auxiliaries. As long as the US Fleet was in being, each cruiser division was given a formation affiliation, e.g., CRUDIV 2, Battle Force. At that time, the US Fleet implied the bulk of the fleet, which was in the Pacific and distributed among the bases of Pearl Harbor, San Diego, San Pedro and others. The relatively few naval forces in the Atlantic were grouped together as the Atlantic Squadron, from which units could be dispatched as required to Britain, to South America or to the Mediterranean. In 1940 with the growth of the fleet under way, President Roosevelt established his two ocean navy, and a greater balance was achieved between the US Pacific Fleet and the US Atlantic Fleet. At this time the Asiatic Fleet, nominally became disestablished.

Just before the USA entered the war an operational chain of command (Task Fleet Organization) was introduced to supplement the administrative organization. Operational fleets were formed, from which operational formations could be drawn for a particular strategic purpose; these would make up a Task Force. Among them were numbered 'Carrier Task Forces', consisting of one or more aircraft carriers with escorts of cruisers and destroyers; and Fire Support Task Forces with battleships, cruisers and destroyers. Additionally there were task forces consisting of submarines only and others with landing craft or transport vessels. Even those aircraft formations that were not based on ships but were at the disposal of a fleet commander were formed by him into their own task forces. The abbreviation for task force was TF; the subordinate smaller formations were task groups (TG) and task units (TU). The Task Force Organization is still in being today, particularly when a unit is assigned to the fleet, when the commander of an administrative formation is simultaneously TF and TG commander.

Occasionally a CRUDIV operated within the framework of a TF. In the post-war period the number of cruisers was drastically run down and so, of course, was the number of CRUDIVs. In 1961 and 1962 a general reorganization of administration in the Pacific and Atlantic Fleets took place as a consequence of the great reduction in cruiser numbers; these were then grouped with destroyers in Cruiser-Destroyer Flotillas (CRUDESFLOT) and later Cruiser-Destroyer Groups (CRUDESGRU). This meant that each group constituted one or two cruisers (one of

ADMINISTRATIVE DISTRIBUTION OF US CRUISERS

Abbreviations

Before the PAC-/LANTFL separation

FLAGSHIPS:

FS	Flagship, Scouting Force, US Fleet
FAS	Flagship, Aircraft Scouting Force, US Fleet
F/AS	Flagship, Asiatic Fleet
F/SA	Flagship, South Atalantic Force
FSUB	Flagship, Submarine Force, US Fleet
FCB	Flagship, Cruisers Battle Force, US Fleet
FCS	Flagship, Cruisers Scouting Force, US Fleet
FDB	Flagship, Destroyers Battle Force, US Fleet
FDPAT	Flagship, Destroyers Patrol Force, US Fleet
FDFL1B	Flagship, DESFLOT 1 Battle Force, US Fleet
F3B	Flagship, CRUDIV 3 Battle Force, US Fleet
F4S	Flagship, CRUDIV 4 Scouting Force, US Fleet
F7LANTSQ	Flagship, CRUDIV 7 Atlantic Squadron

OTHER CRUISER AFFILIATIONS:

3/AS	CRUDIV 3, Asiatic Fleet
3B	CRUDIV 3 Battle Force, US Fleet
4S	CRUDIV 4 Scouting Force, US Fleet
PATFOR	Patrol Forces, US Fleet (later designation for the former 'Atlantic Squadron')
7PATFOR	CRUDIV 7, Patrol Force

After the PAC-/LANTFL separation

FLAGSHIPS:

FS/PAC	Flagship, Scouting Force, Pacific Fleet
FCB/PAC	Flagship, Cruisers Battle Force, Pacific Fleet
FCS/PAC	Flagship, Cruisers Scouting Force, Pacific Fleet
FC/PAC (/LANT)	Flagship, Cruisers, Pacific (Atlantic) Fleet
FDB/PAC	Flagship, Destroyers Battle Force, Pacific Fleet
F9B/PAC	Flagship, CRUDIV 9, Pacific Fleet
F4/PAC	Flagship, CRUDIV 4, Pacific Fleet

OTHER CRUISER AFFILIATIONS:

4S/PAC	CRUDIV 4 Scouting Force, Pacific Fleet
8/LANT	CRUDIV 8, Atlantic Fleet

them serving as flagship) and several destroyer squadrons (DESRON).

The lists on these pages (which are based on official documents) show the nominal affiliation of each cruiser, its deployment (in dock or temporarily detached) notwithstanding. Many cruisers served the entire war in one CRUDIV; others served in several or were even transferred from the Pacific to the Atlantic Fleet. When hostilities ceased, cruisers still far from completion or commissioning were nevertheless given CRUDIV identity.

ADMINISTRATIVE DISTRIBUTION OF US CRUISERS, 1925–1937

1925

FDB	CL-4 Omaha
2/LANT	CL-9 Richmond (F), -5 Milwaukee, -6 Cincinnati, -11 Trenton
3S/LANT	CL-8 Detroit, -12 Marblehead, -7 Raleigh, -13 Memphis
FDFL/LANT	CL-10 Concord

1927

FDB	CL-4 Omaha
3/AS	CL-9 Richmond (F), -6 Cincinnati, -12 Marblehead
FDFL/LANT	CL-10 Concord
2S/LANT	CL-11 Trenton (F), -5 Milwaukee, -7 Raleigh, -13 Memphis

1928

FDB	CL-4 Omaha
3S/LANT	CL-9 Richmond (F), -6 Cincinnati
FDFL/LANT	CL-10 Concord
2/AS	CL-11 Trenton (F), -5 Milwaukee, -13 Memphis, -7 Raleigh (in Europe)

1929

FDFL/PAC	CL-4 Omaha
2S/LANT	CL-9 Richmond, -11 Trenton, -12 Marblehead, -13 Memphis
3S/LANT	CL-6 Cincinnati, -5 Milwaukee, -7 Raleigh, -8 Detroit
FDFL/LANT	CL-10 Concord

1931

FS	CA-31 Augusta
2S	CL-13 Memphis, -9 Richmond, -11 Trenton, -12 Marblehead
3S	CL-10 Concord, -5 Milwaukee, -4 Omaha, -6 Cincinnati
4S	CA-26 Northampton, -24 Pensacola, -27 Chester
5S	CA-29 Chicago, -25 Salt Lake City, -29 Louisville
F/AS	CA-30 Houston

1933

2B	CL-11 Trenton (F), -12 Marblehead, -13 Memphis
3B	CL-10 Concord (F), -6 Cincinnati, -5 Milwaukee, -4 Omaha
FDFLB	CL-8 Detroit
FS	CA-35 Indianapolis
4S	CA-26 Northampton (F), -24 Pensacola, -33 Portland
5S	CA-29 Chicago (F), -28 Louisville, -25 Salt Lake City

FDFLS	CL-7 Raleigh

1934

2B	CL-13 Memphis (F), -12 Marblehead, -9 Richmond
3B	CL-10 Concord (F), -6 Cincinnati, -5 Milwaukee, -4 Omaha
FDFLB	CL-8 Detroit
FS	CA-35 Indianapolis
4S	CA-26 Northampton (F), -25 Pensacola, -25 Salt Lake City
5S	CA-29 Chicago, -27 Chester, -35 Indianapolis
6S	CA-30 Houston, -28 Louisville, -33 Portland
FDFLS	CL-7 Raleigh
F/AS	CA-31 Augusta
F/SA	CL-11 Trenton
FDB	CL-8 Detroit

1935

2B	CL-11 Trenton (F), -12 Marblehead, -9 Richmond
3B	CL-10 Concord (F), -6 Cincinnati, -5 Milwaukee, -4 Omaha
FDB	CL-8 Detroit
FS	CA-35 Indianapolis
4S	CA-26 Northampton (F), -27 Chester, -24 Pensacola, -25 Salt Lake City
5S	CA-29 Chicago (F), -33 Portland, -30 Houston
6S	CA-28 Louisville (F), -35 Indianapolis, -32 New Orleans, -38 San Francisco
7S	CA-34 Astoria, -36 Minneapolis, -37 Tuscaloosa
FDS	CL-7 Raleigh
FAS	CA-31 Augusta
F/SA	CL-13 Memphis

1936

2B	CL-11 Trenton (F), -12 Marblehead, -13 Memphis, -9 Richmond
3B	CL-10 Concord (F), -6 Cincinnati, -5 Milwaukee
FDFLB	CL-8 Detroit
FS	CA-35 Indianapolis
4S	CA-26 Northampton (F), -24 Pensacola, -25 Salt Lake City
5S	CA-29 Chicago (F), -27 Chester, -30 Houston
6S	CA-28 Louisville, -35 Indianapolis, -33 Portland

7S	CA-34 Astoria (F), -36 Minneapolis, -32 New Orleans
8S	CA-38 San Francisco, -39 Quincy, -37 Tuscaloosa
FDFLS	CL-7 Raleigh (at that time in Europe).
FAS	CA-31 Augusta
F/SA	CL-4 Omaha

1937

2B	CL-11 Trenton (F), -12 Marblehead, -13 Memphis, -9 Richmond
3B	CL-10 Concord (F), -6 Cincinnati, -5 Milwaukee, -4 Omaha
8B	CL-41 Philadelphia (F), -40 Brooklyn
FDFL1B	CL-7 Raleigh (at that time in Europe)
FDFL2B	CL-8 Detroit
FS	CA-35 Indianapolis
4S	CA-26 Northampton (F), -30 Houston, -24 Pensacola, -25 Salt Lake City
5S	CA-29 Chicago (F), -27 Chester, -28 Louisville, -33 Portland
6S	CA-36 Minneapolis (F), -34 Astoria, -32 New Orleans, -35 Indianapolis
7S	CA-38 San Francisco (F), -39 Quincy, -37 Tuscaloosa, -44 Vincennes
F/AS	CA-31 Augusta

1939

FCB	CL-48 Honolulu (In the Atlantic)
FDB + FDFL2B	CL-10 Concord
FDFL1B	CL-7 Raleigh
2B	CL-11 Trenton (F), -13 Memphis
3B	CL-8 Detroit, -6 Cincinnati, -5 Milwaukee
8B	CL-41 Philadelphia, -40 Brooklyn, -42 Savannah, -43 Nashville
9B	CL-48 Honolulu (F), -46 Phoenix, -47 Boise, -49 St. Louis
FS	CA-35 Indianapolis
4S	CA-26 Northampton (F), -30 Houston, -24 Pensacola, -25 Salt Lake City
5S	CA-29 Chicago (F), -27 Chester, -28 Louisville, -33 Portland
6S	CA-36 Minneapolis (F), -34 Astoria, -32 New Orleans, -35 Indianapolis
7S	CA-38 San Francisco (F), -39 Quincy, -37 Tuscaloosa, -44 Vincennes (all in the Atlantic)
FSUB	CL-9 Richmond
AS	CA-31 Augusta (F), CL-12 Marblehead

ADMINISTRATIVE DISTRIBUTION OF CRUISERS, 1939–45 (PACIFIC)

Pennant No.	Name	30 June 39	30 Sept 39	6 Jan 40	1 Feb 40	1 July 40	15 Aug 40	15 Oct 40	26 Dec 40	27 Jan 41	Remarks
CL-4	Omaha	3B	3B	3B	3B			F DES-PATFOR	F DES-PATFOR +FDFL9/ PATFOR		
CL-5	Milwaukee	3B	3B	3B	3B	3B	3B	3B	3B		
CI-6	Cincinnati	3B	3B	3B	3B	3B	3B	3B	3B		
CI-7	Raleigh	FDFL1/B	FDFL1/B	FDFL1/B	FDFL1/B	FDFL1/B	FDFL1/B	FDFL1/B	FDB+ FDFL1/B	FDFL1/B	
CL-8	Detroit	FDB+ FDFL2/B	FDB+ FDFL2/B	FDB+ FDFL2/B	FDB+ FDFL2/B	FDB+ FDFL2/B	FDB+ FDFL2/B	FDB+ FDFL2/B	FDFL2/B	FDB+ FDFL2/B	
CL-9	Richmond	FSUB	FSUB	FSUB	FSUB	FSUB	FSUB	FSUB	FSUB/S	FSUB/S	
CL-10	Concord	F3B	F3B	F3B	F3B	F3B	F3B	F3B	F3B	F3B	
CL-11	Trenton		3B	3B			/LANT*	3B	3B	3B	*temporary
CL-12	Marblehead										
CL-13	Memphis	FAS	FAS	FAS	FAS	FAS		PATFOR	FDFL8/ PATFOR		
CA-24	Pensacola	4S	4S	4S	4S	4S	4S	4S	4S	5S	
CA-25	Salt Lake City	4S	4S	4S	4S	4S	4S	4S	4S	5S	
CA-26	Northampton I	F4S	F4S	F4S	F4S	F4S	F4S	F5S	F5S	F5S	
CA-27	Chester	5S	5S	5S	5S	5S		7/PATFOR	7/PATFOR	5S	
CA-28	Louisville	5S	5S	5S	5S	5S		7/PATFOR	7/PATFOR	4S	
CA-29	Chicago I	FCS+F5S	FCS+F5S	FCS+F5S	FCS+F5S	FCS+F5S		F4S	FCS+F4S	FCS+F4S	
CA-30	Houston I	4S	4S	4S	4S*	4S**	4S**	4S**	**	**	*Replacement flagship CINCUSFL **Designated Flagship, Asiatic Fleet, Nov 1940
CA-31	Augusta						4S	PATFOR	PATFOR*	*	*From 1 May 1941 F PATFOR
CA-33	Portland	5S	5S	5S	5S	5S		5S	5S	4S	
CA-35	Indianapolis	FS+6S	FS+6S	FS+6S*	FS+6S	FS+6S	FS+6S	FS+4S	FS+4S	FS+4S	*CA-30 FS up to 4 Feb 1940
CA-32	New Orleans	6S	6S	6S	6S	6S	6S	6S	6S	6S	
CA-34	Astoria I	6S	6S	6S	6S	6S	6S	6S	6S	6S	
CA-36	Minneapolis	F6S	F6S	F6S	F6S	F6S	F6S	F6S	F6S	F6S	
CA-37	Tuscaloosa	7/LANT	7/LANT	7/LANT	7/LANT	7/LANT	7/LANT	7/PATFOR	7/PATFOR		
CA-38	San Francisco	F7/LANT	F7/LANT	F7/LANT	6S	6S	6S	6S	6S	6S	
CA-39	Quincy I	7/LANT	7/LANT	7/LANT	7/LANT	7/LANT	7/LANT	7/PATFOR	7/PATFOR		
CA-44	Vincennes I	7/LANT	7/LANT	7/LANT	7/LANT	7/LANT	7/LANT	7/PATFOR	7/PATFOR		
CA-45	Wichita	7/LANT	7/LANT	7/LANT	F7/LANT	F7/LANT	F7/LANT	F7/PATFOR	F7/PATFOR		
CL-40	Brooklyn	8B	8B	8B	8B	8B	8B	8B	8B	8B	
CL-41	Philadelphia	F8B	F8B	F8B	F8B	F8B	F8B	F8B	F8B	F8B	
CL-42	Savannah	8B	8B	8B	8B	8B	8B	8B	8B	8B	
CL-43	Nashville	8B	8B	8B	8B	8B	8B	8B	8B	8B	
CL-46	Phoenix	9B	9B	9B	9B	9B	9B	9B	9B	9B	
CL-47	Boise	9B	9B	9B	9B	9B	9B	9B	9B	9B	
CL-48	Honolulu	FCB+F9B	FCB+F9B	FCB+F9B	FCB+F9B	FCB+F9B	FCB+F9B	FCB+F9B	FCB+F9B	FCB+F9B	
CL-49	St. Louis	9B	9B	9B	9B	9B	/LANT*	9B	9B	9B	*temporary
CL-50	Helena I				9B	9B	/LANT*	9B	9B	9B	*temporary

Pennant No.	Name	3 April 41	27 June 41	1 Oct 41	23 Mar 42	6 May 42	8 Aug 42	20 Jan 43	31 Mar 43	28 April 43	Remarks
CL-7	Raleigh	FDFL1B/PAC	FDFL1B/PAC	FDFL1B/PAC	FDFL1B/PAC	FDFL1B/PAC	*	1/PAC	1/PAC	1/PAC	*Not given CRUDIV-appointment

Pennant No.	Name	3 April 41	27 June 41	1 Oct 41	23 Mar 42	6 May 42	8 Aug 42	20 Jan 43	31 Mar 43	28 April 43	Remarks
CL-8	Detroit	FDB/PAC+ FDFL2B/PAC	FDB/PAC+ FDFL2B/PAC	FDB/PAC+ FDFL2B/PAC	FDB/PAC+ FDFL2B/PAC	FD/PAC+ FDFL2B/PAC	*	1/PAC	1/PAC	1/PAC	*Not given CRUDIV-appointment
CL-9	Richmond	FSUBS/PAC	3B/PAC	3B/PAC	3B/PAC			F1/PAC	F1/PAC	F1/PAC	
CL-10	Concord	F3B/PAC	F3B/PAC	F3B/PAC	F3B/PAC						
CL-11	Trenton	3B/PAC	3B/PAC	3B/PAC	3B/PAC						
CA-24	Pensacola	5S/PAC	5S/PAC	5S/PAC	5S/PAC	5/PAC	5/PAC	5/PAC	5/PAC	5/PAC	
CA-25	Salt Lake City	5S/PAC	5S/PAC	5S/PAC	5S/PAC	5/PAC	5/PAC	5/PAC	5/PAC	5/PAC	
CA-26	Northampton I	F5S/PAC	F5S/PAC	F5S/PAC	F5S/PAC	F5/PAC	F5/PAC				
CA-27	Chester	5S/PAC	5S/PAC	5S/PAC	5S/PAC	5/PAC	5/PAC	F5/PAC	F5/PAC	F5/PAC	
CA-28	Louisville	4S/PAC	4S/PAC	4S/PAC	4S/PAC	F4/PAC	F4/PAC	F4/PAC	F4/PAC	F4/PAC	
CA-29	Chicago I	F4S/PAC	F4S/PAC	F4S/PAC	FCS/PAC+ F4S/PAC			4/PAC			
CA-33	Portland	4S/PAC	4S/PAC	4S/PAC	4S/PAC	4/PAC	4/PAC	4/PAC	4/PAC	4/PAC	
CA-35	Indianapolis	FS/PAC +4S/PAC	FS/PAC +4S/PAC	FS/PAC +4S/PAC	FS/PAC +4S/PAC	FC/PAC +4/PAC	FC/PAC +4/PAC	FC/PAC +4/PAC	FC/PAC +4/PAC	FC/PAC +4/PAC	
CA-32	New Orleans	6S/PAC	6S/PAC	6S/PAC	6S/PAC	6/PAC	6/PAC	6/PAC	6/PAC	6/PAC	
CA-34	Astoria I	6S/PAC	6S/PAC	6S/PAC	6S/PAC	6/PAC	6/PAC				
CA-36	Minneapolis	F6S/PAC	F6S/PAC	F6S/PAC	F6S/PAC	F6/PAC	F6/PAC	F6/PAC	F6/PAC	F6/PAC	
CA-38	San Francisco	6S/PAC	6S/PAC	6S/PAC	6S/PAC	6/PAC	6/PAC	6/PAC	6/PAC	6/PAC	
CA-39	Quincy I						6/PAC				
CL-40	Brooklyn	8B/PAC									
CL-41	Philadelphia	F8B/PAC									
CL-42	Savannah	8B/PAC									
CL-43	Nashville	8B/PAC					9/PAC	9/PAC	9/PAC	9/PAC	
CL-46	Phoenix	9B/PAC	9B/PAC	9B/PAC	9B/PAC						
CL-47	Boise	9B/PAC	9B/PAC	9B/PAC	9B/PAC	9/PAC	9/PAC				
CL-48	Honolulu	FCB/PAC+ F9B/PAC	FCB/PAC+ F9B/PAC	FCB/PAC F9B/PAC	FCB/PAC+ F9B/PAC	F9/PAC	F9/PAC	F9/PAC	F9/PAC	F9/PAC	
CL-49	St. Louis	9B/PAC	9B/PAC	9B/PAC	9B/PAC	9/PAC	9/PAC	9/PAC	9/PAC	9/PAC	
CL-50	Helena I	9B/PAC	9B/PAC	9B/PAC	9B/PAC	9/PAC	9/PAC	9/PAC	9/PAC	9/PAC	
CA-44	Vincennes I					4/PAC	4/PAC				
CA-45	Wichita							6/PAC	6/PAC	6/PAC	
CL-51	Atlanta I						F11/PAC				
CL-52	Juneau I						11/PAC				
CL-53	San Diego						11/PAC	F11/PAC	F11/PAC	F11/PAC	
CL-54	San Juan						11/PAC	11/PAC	11/PAC	11/PAC	
CL-55	Cleveland						12/PAC	12/PAC	12/PAC	12/PAC	
CL-56	Columbia						12/PAC	12/PAC	12/PAC	12/PAC	
CL-57	Montpelier						F12/PAC	F12/PAC	F12/PAC	F12/PAC	
CL-58	Denver						12/PAC	12/PAC	12/PAC	12/PAC	
CL-60	Santa Fe								F13/PAC	F13/PAC	
CL-62	Birmingham								13/PAC	13/PAC	
CL-63	Mobile								13/PAC	13/PAC	
CA-68	Baltimore							F10/PAC	F10/PAC	F10/PAC	
CA-69	Boston							10/PAC	10/PAC	10/PAC	
CA-70	Canberra								10/PAC	10/PAC	
CL-95	Oakland								11/PAC	11/PAC	

Pennant No.	Name	20 July 43	15 Oct 43	1 Jan 44	1 Mar 44	1 July 44	1 Oct 44	1 Feb 45	1 May 45	1 July 45	Remarks
CL-7	Raleigh	F1/PAC	1/PAC	1/PAC	1/PAC						
CL-8	Detroit	1/PAC	1/PAC	1/PAC	1/PAC			1/PAC	1/PAC	1/PAC	
CL-9	Richmond	1/PAC	F1/PAC	F1/PAC	F1/PAC	F1/PAC	F1/PAC	F1/PAC	F1/PAC	F1/PAC	
CL-10	Concord					1/PAC	1/PAC	1/PAC	1/PAC	1/PAC	
CL-11	Trenton					1/PAC	1/PAC	1/PAC	1/PAC	1/PAC	
CA-24	Pensacola	5/PAC	5/PAC	5/PAC	5/PAC	5/PAC	5/PAC	5/PAC	5/PAC	5/PAC	
CA-25	Salt Lake City	5/PAC	5/PAC	5/PAC	5/PAC	5/PAC	5/PAC	5/PAC	5/PAC	5/PAC	

Pennant No.	Name	20 July 43	15 Oct 43	1 Jan 44	1 Mar 44	1 July 44	1 Oct 44	1 Feb 45	1 May 45	1 July 45	Remarks
CA-27	Chester	F5/PAC	F5/PAC	F5/PAC	F5/PAC	F5/PAC	F5/PAC	F5/PAC	F5/PAC	F5/PAC	
CA-28	Louisville	F4/PAC	F4/PAC	F4/PAC	F4/PAC	F4/PAC	F4/PAC	F4/PAC	F4/PAC	F4/PAC	
CA-33	Portland	4/PAC	4/PAC	4/PAC	4/PAC	4/PAC	4/PAC	4/PAC	4/PAC	4/PAC	
CA-35	Indianapolis	FC/PAC +4/PAC	FC/PAC +4/PAC	FC/PAC +4/PAC	FC/PAC +4/PAC	FC/PAC +4/PAC	FC/PAC +4/PAC	FC/PAC +4/PAC	FC/PAC +4/PAC	FC/PAC +4/PAC	
CA-32	New Orleans	6/PAC	6/PAC	6/PAC	6/PAC	6/PAC	6/PAC	6/PAC	6/PAC	6/PAC	
CA-36	Minneapolis	F6/PAC	F6/PAC	6/PAC	6/PAC	6/PAC	6/PAC	6/PAC	6/PAC	6/PAC	
CA-37	Tuscaloosa						4/PAC	6/PAC	6/PAC	6/PAC	
CA-38	San Francisco	6/PAC	6/PAC	6/PAC	6/PAC	6/PAC	6/PAC	F6/PAC	F6/PAC	F6/PAC	
CL-42	Savannah								9/PAC	9/PAC	
CL-43	Nashville	9/PAC				15/PAC	15/PAC	15/PAC	15/PAC	15/PAC	
CL-46	Phoenix					F15/PAC	F15/PAC	F15/PAC	F15/PAC	F15/PAC	
CL-47	Boise					15/PAC	15/PAC	15/PAC	15/PAC	15PAC	
CL-48	Honolulu	F9/PAC	F9/PAC	F9/PAC	F9/PAC	F9/PAC	F9/PAC	F9/PAC	F9/PAC	F9/PAC	
CL-49	St. Louis	9/PAC	9/PAC	9/PAC	9/PAC	9/PAC	9/PAC	9/PAC	9/PAC	9/PAC	
CL-53	San Diego	F11/PAC	F11/PAC	F11/PAC	F11/PAC	F11/PAC	F11/PAC	F11/PAC	F11/PAC	F11/PAC	
CL-54	San Juan	11/PAC	11/PAC	11/PAC	11/PAC	11/PAC	11/PAC	11/PAC	11/PAC	11/PAC	
CL-95	Oakland	11/PAC	11/PAC	11/PAC	11/PAC	11/PAC	11/PAC	11/PAC	11/PAC	11/PAC	
CL-96	Reno	11/PAC	11/PAC	11/PAC	11/PAC	11/PAC	11/PAC	11/PAC	11/PAC	11/PAC	
CL-97	Flint					11/PAC	11/PAC	11/PAC	11/PAC	11/PAC	
CL-98	Tucson						11/PAC	11/PAC	11/PAC	11/PAC	
CA-45	Wichita	6/PAC	6/PAC	F6/PAC	F6/PAC	F6/PAC	F6/PAC	4/PAC	F4/PAC	4/PAC	
CL-55	Cleveland	12/PAC	12/PAC	12/PAC	12/PAC	12/PAC	12/PAC	12/PAC	12/PAC	12/PAC	
CL-56	Columbia	12/PAC	12/PAC	12/PAC	12/PAC	12/PAC	12/PAC	12/PAC	12/PAC	12/PAC	
CL-57	Montpelier	F12/PAC	F12/PAC	F12/PAC	F12/PAC	F12/PAC	F12/PAC	F12/PAC	F12/PAC	F12/PAC	
CL-58	Denver	12/PAC	12/PAC	12/PAC	12/PAC	12/PAC	12/PAC	12/PAC	12/PAC	12/PAC	
CL-60	Santa Fe	F13/PAC	F13/PAC	F13/PAC	F13/PAC	F13/PAC	F13/PAC	13/PAC	13/PAC	13/PAC	
CL-62	Birmingham	13/PAC	13/PAC	13/PAC	13/PAC	13/PAC	13/PAC	F13/PAC	F13/PAC	F13/PAC	
CL-63	Mobile	13/PAC	13/PAC	13/PAC	13/PAC	13/PAC	13/PAC	13/PAC	13/PAC	13/PAC	
CL-64	Vincennes II		F14/PAC*	F14/PAC	F14/PAC	F14/PAC	F14/PAC	F14/PAC	F14/PAC	F14/PAC	*From 1 Nov 1943
CL-65	Pasadena					F17/PAC	F17/PAC	F17/PAC	F17/PAC	F17/PAC	
CL-66	Springfield					17/PAC	17/PAC	17/PAC	17/PAC	17/PAC	
CL-67	Topeka					18/PAC	F18/PAC	F18/PAC	F18/PAC	F18/PAC	
CA-68	Baltimore	F10/PAC	F10/PAC	F10/PAC	F10/PAC	F10/PAC	F10/PAC	F10/PAC	F10/PAC	F10/PAC	
CA-69	Boston	10/PAC	10/PAC	10/PAC	10/PAC	10/PAC	10/PAC	10/PAC	10/PAC	10/PAC	
CA-70	Canberra	10/PAC	10/PAC	10/PAC	10/PAC	10/PAC	10/PAC	10/PAC	10/PAC	10/PAC	
CA-71	Quincy II			10/PAC	10/PAC	10/PAC	10/PAC	10/PAC	10/PAC	10/PAC	
CA-72	Pittsburgh					F19/PAC	F19/PAC	F19/PAC	F19/PAC	F19/PAC	
CA-73	St. Paul					19/PAC	19/PAC	19/PAC	19/PAC	19/PAC	
CA-74	Columbus							F21/PAC	F21/PAC	F21/PAC	
CL-80	Biloxi		13/PAC	13/PAC	13/PAC	13/PAC	13/PAC	13/PAC	13/PAC	13/PAC	
CI-81	Houston II		14/PAC*	14/PAC	14/PAC	14/PAC	14/PAC	14/PAC	14/PAC	14/PAC	*From 1 Nov 1943
CL-82	Providence						20/PAC	F20/PAC	F20/PAC	F20/PAC	
CL-86	Vicksburg					14/PAC	14/PAC	14/PAC	14/PAC	14/PAC	
CL-87	Duluth						18/PAC	18/PAC	18/PAC	18/PAC	
CL-89	Miami		14/PAC*	14/PAC	14/PAC	14/PAC	14/PAC	14/PAC	14/PAC	14/PAC	*From 1 Nov 1943
CL-90	Astoria II			14/PAC	14/PAC	17/PAC	17/PAC	17/PAC	17/PAC	17/PAC	
CL-91	Oklahoma City						F20/PAC	20/PAC	20/PAC	20/PAC	*Ship did not come into service during the Second World War, later reclassified GLG-3.
CL-92	Little Rock						20/PAC	20/PAC	20/PAC	20/PAC	
CL-101	Amsterdam						20/PAC	20/PAC	20/PAC	20/PAC	
CL-102	Portsmouth									22/PAC	
CL-93 (later 66)	Galveston									22/PAC*	
CL-103	Wilkes Barre					17/PAC	17/PAC	17/PAC	17/PAC	17/PAC	
CL-104	Atlanta II					18/PAC	18/PAC	18/PAC	18/PAC	18/PAC	

Pennant No.	Name	20 July 43	15 Oct 43	1 Jan 44	1 Mar 44	1 July 44	1 Oct 44	1 Feb 45	1 May 45	1 July 45	Remarks
CL-105	Dayton					18/PAC	18/PAC	18/PAC	18/PAC	18/PAC	
CL-106	Fargo									F22/PAC	
CL-107	Huntington									22/PAC	
CA-130	Bremerton					19/PAC	19/PAC	19/PAC	19/PAC	19/PAC	
CA-131	Fall River					19/PAC	19/PAC	19/PAC	19/PAC	19/PAC	
CA-132	Macon							21/PAC	21/PAC	21/PAC	
CA-135	Los Angeles							21/PAC	21/PAC	21/PAC	
CA-136	Chicago II							21/PAC	21/PAC	21/PAC	
CB-1	Alaska					F16/PAC	F16/PAC	F16/PAC	F16/PAC	F16/PAC	
CB-2	Guam					16/PAC	16/PAC	16/PAC	16/PAC	16/PAC	

ADMINISTRATIVE DISTRIBUTION OF CRUISERS, 1939—45 (ATLANTIC)

Pennant No.	Name	1 Feb 41	1 April 41	6 Oct 41	29 Jan 42	26 April 42	5 Aug 42	16 Nov 42	15 Mar 43	15 July 43	Remarks
CL-4	Omaha	FD/LANT+ FDFL8+9/ LANT	FD/LANT+ FDFL9/LANT	2/LANT	2/LANT	2/LANT	2/LANT	2/LANT	F2/LANT	F2/LANT	
CL-5	Milwaukee	2/LANT	2/LANT	2/LANT	2/LANT	2/LANT	2/LANT	2/LANT	2/LANT	2/LANT	
CL-6	Cincinnati	2/LANT	2/LANT	2/LANT	2/LANT	2/LANT	2/LANT	2/LANT	2/LANT	2/LANT	
CL-12	Marblehead						2/LANT	2/LANT	2/LANT	2/LANT	
CL-13	Memphis	F2/LANT	F2/LANT	F2/LANT	F2/LANT	F2/LANT	F2/LANT	F2/LANT	2/LANT	2/LANT	
CA-28	Louisville	7/LANT									
CA-31	Augusta	*	*	F/LANT	F/LANT +7/LANT	F/LANT +7/LANT	F/LANT +7/LANT	F/LANT +7/LANT	F/LANT +7/LANT	F/LANT +7/LANT	*Acting F/LANT
CA-37	Tuscaloosa	7/LANT	7/LANT	7/LANT	7/LANT	7/LANT	7/LANT	7/LANT	F7/LANT	F7/LANT	
CA-39	Quincy I	7 LANT	7/LANT	7/LANT	7/LANT	7/LANT		7/LANT			
CL-40	Brooklyn			8/LANT	8/LANT	8/LANT	8/LANT	8/LANT	8/LANT	8/LANT	
CL-41	Philadelphia		FC/LANT+ F8/LANT	FC/LANT+ F8/LANT	FC/LANT+ F8/LANT	FC/LANT+ F8/LANT	FC/LANT+ F8/LANT	FC/LANT+ F8/LANT	F8/LANT		
CL-42	Savannah			8/LANT	8/LANT	8/LANT	8/LANT	8/LANT	8/LANT	8/LANT	
CL-43	Nashville			8/LANT	8/LANT						
CA-44	Vincennes I			7/LANT	7/LANT						
CA-45	Wichita	FC/LANT+ F7/LANT	FC/LANT+ F7/LANT	F7/LANT	F7/LANT	F7/LANT	F7/LANT	F7/LANT			
CL-47	Boise								8/LANT	8/LANT	
CL-51	Atlanta I			F10/LANT	F10/LANT						
CL-52	Juneau I			10/LANT	10/LANT	8/LANT	8/LANT				
CL-53	San Diego			10/LANT	10/LANT						
CL-54	San Juan			10/LANT	10/LANT						
CL-60	Santa Fe						F13/LANT	F13/LANT			
CL-62	Birmingham						13/LANT	13/LANT			
CL-63	Mobile							13/LANT			

Pennant No.	Name	4 Dec 43	6 May 44	5 Aug 44	1 Nov 44	1 Dec 44	5 Mar 45	27 Dec 45	Remarks
CL-4	Omaha	F2/LANT	F2/LANT	F2/LANT	F2/LANT	F2/LANT	F2/LANT		
CL-5	Milwaukee	2/LANT	2/LANT	2/LANT					
CL-6	Cincinnati	2/LANT	2/LANT	2/LANT	2/LANT	2/LANT	2/LANT		
CL-12	Marblehead	2/LANT	2/LANT	2/LANT	2/LANT	2/LANT	2/LANT		
CL-13	Memphis	2/LANT	2/LANT	2/LANT	2/LANT	2/LANT	2/LANT		
CA-31	Augusta		7/LANT	7/LANT	7/LANT	F7/LANT			
CA-37	Tuscaloosa		F7/LANT	F7/LANT	F7/LANT				
CL-40	Brooklyn	8/LANT	8/LANT	8/LANT	8/LANT	8/LANT	8/LANT		
CL-41	Philadelphia	F8/LANT	F8/LANT	F8/LANT	F8/LANT	F8/LANT	F8/LANT		
CL-42	Savannah	8/LANT	8/LANT	8/LANT	8/LANT	8/LANT			

Pennant No.	Name	4 Dec 43	6 May 44	5 Aug 44	1 Nov 44	1 Dec 44	5 Mar 45	27 Dec 45	Remarks
CL-81	*Houston II*							10/LANT	
CL-82	*Providence*							F10/LANT	
CL-92	*Little Rock*							10/LANT	
CL-102	*Portsmouth*							10/LANT	
CL-106	*Fargo*							F12/LANT*	*CRUDIV No. uncertain
CL-107	*Huntingdon*							12/LANT*	*CRUDIV No. uncertain
CL-145	*Roanoke*							12/LANT*	*CRUDIV No. uncertain
CA-71	*Quincy II*					7/LANT		12/LANT*	*CRUDIV No. uncertain
CL-144	*Worcester*								

COMPOSITION OF CRUISER DIVISIONS AT THEIR PEAK, END OF SECOND WORLD WAR

Pacific Fleet, as at 1 Oct 1945

CRUDIV 1
CL-8 *Detroit* F**
CL-11 *Trenton*

CRUDIV 4
CA-28 *Louisville* F
CA-45 *Wichita*

CRUDIV 5
CA-27 *Chester* F
CA-24 *Pensacola*
CA-25 *Salt Lake City*

CRUDIV 6
CA-38 *San Francisco* F
CA-32 *New Orleans*
CA-36 *Minneapolis*
CA-37 *Tuscaloosa*

CRUDIV 9
CL-49 *St. Louis*

CRUDIV 10
CA-68 *Baltimore* F
CA-69 *Boston*
CA-70 *Canberra*
CA-71 *Quincy*

CRUDIV 11
CL-54 *San Juan* F
CL-95 *Oakland*
CL-96 *Reno*
CL-97 *Flint*
CL-98 *Tucson*
CL-119 *Juneau II*

CRUDIV 12*
CI-57 *Montpelier* F
CL-55 *Cleveland*

CL-56 *Columbia*
CL-58 *Denver*

CRUDIV 13
CL-60 *Santa Fe* F
CL-63 *Mobile*
CL-62 *Birmingham*
CL-80 *Biloxi*

CRUDIV 14
CL-64 *Vincennes II* F
CL-86 *Vicksburg*
CL-89 *Miami*

CRUDIV 15
CL-43 *Nashville*

CRUDIV 16
CB-1 *Alaska* F
DB-2 *Guam*

CRUDIV 17
CL-65 *Pasadena* F
CL-66 *Springfield*
CL-90 *Astoria II*
CL-103 *Wilkes Barre*

CRUDIV 18
CL-67 *Topeka* F
CL-87 *Duluth*
CL-104 *Atlanta II*
CL-105 *Dayton*

CRUDIV 19
CA-73 *Saint Paul* F
CA-130 *Bremerton*
CA-131 *Fall River*

CRUDIV 20
CL-91 *Oklahoma City* F
CL-101 *Amsterdam*

CRUDIV 21
CA-74 *Columbus* F
CA-135 *Los Angeles*
CA-136 *Chicago II*

CRUDIV 23
CA-75 *Helena II*

CRUDIV 22
was apparently set up during this period, but there is no record of the ships involved

Atlantic Fleet, as at 27 Dec 1945

CRUDIV 10
CL-82 *Providence* F
CL-81 *Houston II*

CL-92 *Little Rock*
CL-102 *Portsmouth*

CRUDIV 12*
CL-106 *Fargo* F
CL-107 *Huntington*
CL-144 *Worcester*
CL-145 *Roanoke*

*The records are contradictory.
**F=Flagship.

AFFILIATION OF CRUISERS TO TASK FORCES, TASK GROUPS AND TASK UNITS DURING IMPORTANT OPERATIONS IN THE WAR

Atlantic

Date	Operation	Battle Unit	Cruisers involved
1 July 41	Iceland	TF19	CL-40 *Brooklyn*, -43 *Nashville*
Nov 41	Convoy WS-124	TG14.4	CA-39 *Quincy*, -44 *Vincennes*
July 42	Convoy PQ-17		CA-45 *Wichita*, -37 *Tuscaloosa*
Aug 42	Operation 'Easy-Unit'		CA-37 *Tuscaloosa*
Sept 41	South Atlantic Force	TF3	CL-13 *Memphis*, -6 *Cincinnati*, -4 *Omaha*, -5 *Milwaukee*,
March 43	4th Fleet		plus CL-12 *Marblehead* Flagship CA-31 *Augusta*
Nov 42	Operation 'Torch'	TF34 TG34.1	CA-45 *Wichita*, -37 *Tuscaloosa*

Date	Operation	Battle Unit	Cruisers involved
		TG34.8	CL-42 *Savannah*
		TG34.9	CA-31 *Aug*, CL-40 *Brooklyn*, CL-55 *Cleveland*
		TG34.10	CL-41 *Philadelphia*
10 July 43– 7 Aug 43	Capture of Sicily	TG86.1	CL-40 *Brooklyn*, -62 *Birmingham*
		TG81.5	CL-47 *Boise*, -42 *Savannah*
		TG85.3	CL-41 *Philadelphia*
9 Sept 43– 13 Oct 43	Salerno landing	TG81.5	CG-41 *Philadelphia*, -42 *Savannah*, -47 *Boise*, -40 *Brooklyn*
22 Jan 44	Landing at Anzio	TG81.8	CL-40 *Brooklyn*

Date	Operation	Battle Unit	Cruisers involved
6 June 44	Landings in Normandy	TF122 / TF125 / TF129	CA-31 Augusta, CA-37 Tuscaloosa, -39 Quincy
15 Aug 44	Operation 'Dragoon' (Landings in South of France)	TF86	CA-31 Augusta, CL-4 Omaha, -6 Cincinnati
		TF84	CA-71 Quincy
		TF85	CL-41 Philadelphia
		TF87	CL-37 Tuscaloosa, CL-40 Brooklyn, -12 Marblehead

Pacific

Date	Operation	Battle Unit	Cruisers involved
7 Dec 41	At Pearl Harbor		CL-7 Raleigh, -8 Detroit, -46 Phoenix, -50 Helena, -48 Honolulu, CA-32 New Orleans, -38 San Francisco
8 Dec 41	In the Philippines	TF5	Flagship CA-30 Houston, CL-47 Boise, CL-12 Marblehead
Jan-Feb 42	(Borneo area) 'ABDA-Command' (US Asiatic Fleet)	TF5	Flagship CA-30 Houston, CL-47 Boise, -12 Marblehead
27 Feb 42	Battle of the Java Sea		CA-30 Houston
28 Feb 42	Battle of Sunda Straits		CA-30 Houston +
13 April 42	'Tokyo-Raid'	TF16	CA-26 Northampton, -25 Salt Lake City, -44 Vincennes, CL-43 Nashville
May 42	Battle of the Coral Sea	TG17.2	CA-36 Minneapolis, -32 New Orleans, -34 Astoria, -27 Chester, -33 Portland
		TG17.3	CA-29 Chicago
June 42	Battle of Midway	TG17.2	CA-34 Astoria, -33 Portland
		TG16.2	CA-32 New Orleans, -36 Minneapolis, -44 Vincennes, -26 Northampton, -24 Pensacola, CL-51 Atlanta
May 42	Aleutian Islands	TG8.6	CA-35 Indianapolis, -28 Louisville, CL-43 Nashville, -49 St. Louis, -48 Honolulu
15 June 42	After reorganisation of the carrier battle groups following arrival of 10 ships from the Atlantic	TF11	CA-36 Minneapolis, -32 New Orleans, -34 Astoria
		TF16	CA-28 Louisville, -33 Portland, -27 Chester, CL-51 Atlanta
		TF17	CA-26 Northampton, -25 Salt Lake City, -24 Pensacola, CL-53 San Diego
		TF18	CA-39 Quincy, -44 Vincennes, -38 San Francisco, CL-54 San Juan
June-Aug 42	South Pacific Force Landings on Tulagi and Guadalcanal; night battle Savo Island	TG61.1	CA-36 Minneapolis, -32 New Orleans, -33 Portland, CL-51 Atlanta
		TG62.2	CA-29 Chicago
		TG62.3	CA-44 Vincennes, + -39 Quincy, + -34 Astoria +
		TG62.4	CL-54 San Juan
24 Aug 42	See battle off eastern Solomons	TF11	CA-36 Minneapolis, -32 New Orleans
		TF16	CA-33 Portland, CL-51 Atlanta
		TF18	CL-54 San Juan, CA-38 San Francisco, -25 Salt Lake City
11-12 Oct 42	Night battle off Cape Esperance	TF64	CA-38 San Francisco, -25 Salt Lake City, CL-47 Boise, -50 Helena
26-27 Oct 42	Sea battle Santa Cruz	TF17	CA-33 Portland, CL-54 San Juan
		TF17	CA-26 Northampton, -24 Pensacola, CL-53 San Diego, -52 Juneau
		TF64	CA-38 San Francisco, CL-50 Helena, -51 Atlanta
12-15 Nov 42	Night battles off Guadalcanal	TG67.4	CA-38 San Francisco, -24 Pensacola, -33 Portland, CL-50 Helena, -52 Juneau +
		TG62.4	CL-51 Atlanta +
		TF16	CA-26 Northampton, CL-53 San Diego
30 Nov 42	Battle of Tassafaronga	TG67.2	CA-36 Minneapolis, -32 New Orleans, -24 Pensacola, -26 Northampton, + CL-48 Honolulu
29-30 Jan 43	Skirmish off Rennel Island	TF18	CA-45 Wichita, -29 Chicago, + -28 Louisville, CL-57 Montpelier, -55 Cleveland, -56 Columbia
5-13 July 43	Night skirmishes off Kula Gulf and Kolombangara	TG36.1	CL-48 Honolulu, -50 Helena, + -49 St. Louis
2 Nov 43	Skirmishes off Empress Augusta Bay	TF39	CL-57 Montpelier, -55 Cleveland, -56 Columbia, -58 Denver (CRUDIV 12)
7 Aug 43	Bombardment of Kiska (Aleutians)		CA-35 Indianapolis, -28 Louisville, CL-48 Honolulu, -43 Nashville, -49 St. Louis
18 Feb 43	Bombardment of Attu (Aleutians)		CL-7 Richmond, CA-35 Indianapolis

Date	Operation	Battle Unit	Cruisers involved
26 March 43	Skirmish off Komandorski Islands		CL-7 Richmond, CA-25 Salt Lake City
4-8 Dec 43	Assault against Kwajalein and Nauru	TG50.1	CA-68 Baltimore, -38 San Francisco, -32 New Orleans, -36 Minneapolis, CL-95 Oakland
		TG50.3	CA-33 Portland, CL-63 Mobile, -60 Santa Fe, -54 San Juan, -53 San Diego
11-29 May 43	Operation 'Landcrab' (Occupation of Attu)	TG16.6	CL-7 Raleigh, -8 Detroit, -9 Richmond, -60 Santa Fe
		TG16.7	CA-45 Wichita, -38 San Francisco, -28 Louisville
10 Nov- 10 Dec 43	Operation 'Galvanic' (Capture of Gilbert Islands)	TG52.2	CA-36 Minneapolis, -38 San Francisco, -32 New Orleans, -68 Baltimore
		TG53.4	CL-63 Mobile, -60 Santa Fe, CA-33 Portland, -35 Indianapolis
		TG50.3	CA-27 Chester, -24 Pensacola, -25 Salt Lake City
		TG50.4	CL-95 Oakland, CL-53 San Diego, -54 San Juan
29 Jan- 23 Feb 44	Operations 'Flintlock' and 'Catchpole' (Marshall Islands)	TG52.8	CA-36 Minneapolis, -32 New Orleans, -38 San Francisco
		TG53.5	CA-28 Louisville, CL-63 Mobile, -60 Santa Fe, CA-35 Indianapolis, CL-80 Biloxi
		TG58.1	CL-95 Oakland
		TG58.2	CL-53 San Diego
		TG58.3	CA-45 Wichita
		TG58.4	CA-69 Boston, -68 Baltimore, CL-54 San Juan
		TG50.15	CA-27 Chester, -24 Pensacola, -25 Salt Lake City
17-18 Feb 44	Truk	TG58.1	CL-60 Santa Fe, -63 Mobile, -80 Biloxi, -95 Oakland
		TG58.2	Cl-53 San Diego, CA-38 San Francisco, -45 Wichita, -68 Baltimore
		TG58.3	CA-36 Minneapolis, -32 New Orleans
22 April- 13 May 44	Hollandia	TF75	CL-46 Phoenix, -43 Nashville
June-Aug 44	Operation 'Forager' (Landings on Saipan and Tinian)	TG52.17	CA-35 Indianapolis, CL-62 Birmingham, CA-28 Louisville, CL-57 Montpelier, -55 Cleveland
		TG52.10	CL-48 Honolulu, CA-36 Minneapolis, -38 San Francisco, -45 Wichita, -32 New Orleans, CL-49 St. Louis
19-20 June 44	Battle of the Philippine Sea	TG58.1	CA-69 Boston, -68 Baltimore, -70 Canberra, CL-54 San Juan, -95 Oakland
		TG58.2	CL-60 Santa Fe, -63 Mobile, -80 Biloxi
		TG58.3	CA-35 Indianapolis, CL-96 Reno, -57 Montpelier, -55 Cleveland, -62 Birmingham
		TG58.4	CL-53 San Diego, -64 Vincennes, -81 Houston, -89 Miami
		TG58.7	CA-45 Wichita, -36 Minneapolis, -32 New Orleans, -38 San Francisco
21 July- 10 Aug 44	Capture of Guam	TG53.5	CL-48 Honolulu, CA-36 Minneapolis, -38 San Francisco, -45 Wichita, -32 New Orleans, CL-49 St. Louis, CA-35 Indianapolis
24-25 Oct 44	Battle of Surigao Strait	TG77.2	CA-28 Louisville, -33 Portland, -36 Minneapolis, CL-58 Denver, -52 Columbia, -46 Phoenix, -47 Boise
25-26 Oct 44	Battle of Cape Engaño	TG38.2	CL-80 Biloxi, -64 Vincennes, -89 Miami, CL-60 Santa Fe
		TG38.3	-63 Mobile, -96 Reno, CA-32 New Orleans
		TG38.4	-45 Wichita
17-25 Oct 44	Invasion of Leyte	TG77.1	CL-43 Nashville
		TG78.3	CL-58 Denver, -56 Columbia
		TG79.4	CA-28 Louisville, -33 Portland, -36 Minneapolis, CL-48 Honolulu, -58 Denver, -56 Columbia
		TG77.3	CL-46 Phoenix, -47 Boise
		TG38.1	CA-45 Wichita, -69 Boston, -70 Canberra, CL-81 Houston
		TG30.2	CA-27 Chester, -24 Pensacola, -25 Salt Lake City
		TG38.2	CL-64 Vincennes, -89 Miami, -53 San Diego, -95 Oakland

Date	Operation	Battle Unit	Cruisers involved	Date	Operation	Battle Unit	Cruisers involved
		TG38.3	CL-60 *Santa Fe*, -63 *Mobile*, -62 *Birmingham*, -96 *Reno*			TG58.3	CB-1 *Alaska*, -35 *Indianapolis*, CL-65 *Pasadena*, -103 *Wilkes Barre*, -90 *Astoria*
		TG38.4	CA-32 *New Orleans*, CL-80 *Biloxi*			TG58.4	CL-60 *Santa Fe*, -80 *Biloxi*, -53 *San Diego*
Jan 45	Invasion of Luzon	TG77.1	CL-47 *Boise*			TG58.5	CA-68 *Baltimore* CL-97 *Flint*
		TG77.2	CA-36 *Minneapolis*, -28 *Louisville*, -33 *Portland*, CL-56 *Columbia*	14 March-30 June 45	Capture of Okinawa	5FL. TF54	CA-35 *Indianapolis*, CA-37 *Tuscaloosa*, -38 *San Francisco*, -36 *Minneapolis*, CL-62 *Birmingham*, -49 *St. Louis*, CA-45 *Wichita*, -24 *Pensacola*, -33 *Portland*, CL-80 *Biloxi*, CA-25 *Salt Lake City*, -32 *New Orleans*, CL-63 *Mobile*
		TG77.3	CL-46 *Phoenix*, -57 *Montpelier*, -58 *Denver*				
1 Dec 44-23 Jan 45	Organization of 3rd Fleet	TG38.1	CA-38 *San Francisco*, -68 *Baltimore*, -69 *Boston*, CL-90 *Astoria*, -53 *San Diego*, -95 *Oakland*			TG58.1	CA-68 *Baltimore*, -72 *Pittsburgh*, CL-64 *Vincennes*, -89 *Miami*, -86 *Vicksburg*, -54 *San Juan*
		TG38.2	CL-65 *Pasadena*, -54 *San Juan*, -89 *Miami*, -103 *Wilkes Barre*			TG58.2	CL-60 *Santa Fe*
		TG38.3	CL-60 *Santa Fe*, -63 *Mobile*, -80 *Biloxi*, -64 *Vincennes*, -97 *Flint*			TG58.3	CA-35 *Indianapolis*, CL-65 *Pasadena*, -66 *Springfield*, -90 *Astoria*, -103 *Wilkes Barre*
Feb-April 45	Liberation of Philippines					TG58.4	CB-1 *Alaska*, -2 *Guam*, CL-49 *St. Louis*, -97 *Flint*, -95 *Oakland*, -53 *San Diego*
28 Feb 45	Palawan	TG74.2	CL-58 *Denver*, -57 *Montpelier*, -55 *Cleveland*				
10-18 March 45	Zamboanga	TG74.3	CL-46 *Phoenix*, -47 *Boise*				
18 March 45	Panay	TG74.2	CL-55 *Cleveland*				
29 March 45	Negros						
26 March 45	Cebu	TG78.2	CL-46 *Phoenix*				
17-18 April 45	Mindanao	TG74.2	CL-57 *Montpelier*, -58 *Denver*, -55 *Cleveland*				
10-18 Feb 45	Carrier raids against Japanese Islands	TG58.1	CL-64 *Vincennes*, -89 *Miami*, -54 *San Juan*				
		TG58.2	CA-38 *San Francisco*, -69 *Boston*				

+ = Sunk. From 7 April 1945 the allotment of ships to the TGs was changed.

War Losses, 1941–5

During the Second World War the US Navy lost ten cruisers in action:

- CA-26 *Northampton (Northampton* class), hit by torpedoes during Japanese destroyer attack 30 Nov 1942 off Tassafaronga.
- CA-29 *Chicago (Northampton* class), hit by Japanese aerial torpedoes off the Solomons 29/30 Jan 1943.
- CA-30 *Houston (Northampton* class), hit by gunfire and torpedoes from Japanese warships in Strait of Sunda, 1 March 1942.
- CA-34 *Astoria (New Orleans* class), hit by shells from Japanese warships off Savo Island, 9 August 1942.
- CA-35 *Indianapolis (Portland* class), torpedoed by Japanese submarine in the Philippines, 29 July 1945.
- CA-39 *Quincy (New Orleans* class), hit by shells and torpedoes from Japanese warships off Savo, 9 August 1942.
- CA-44 *Vincennes (New Orleans* class), torpedoed by Japanese warships off Savo, 9 August 1942.
- CL-50 *Helena (Brooklyn* class), torpedoed by Japanese warships in Gulf of Kula, 6 July 1943.
- CL-51 *Atlanta (Atlanta* class), torpedoed by Japanese warships off Guadalcanal, 13 Nov 1942.
- CL-52 *Juneau (Atlanta* class), same fate as *Atlanta*.

Severest losses were suffered among cruisers completed before 1942. It may well be that the improved quality of the new cruisers played a significant part in the fact that many of them, although badly damaged, managed to stay afloat. On the other hand, the losses among older ships is attributable to the fact that from the start of the war in the Pacific they had to bear the brunt of attacks from an as yet intact Japanese Fleet.

No American cruiser was lost during the subsequent wars in Korea and Vietnam.

Armament: Guns

During the Second World War, US cruisers had three main tasks: to combat enemy surface ships and convoys, to guard its own fleet formations from hostile air attacks, and to provide supporting fire in landing operations. Prior to the war, the main armament was considered to be the most important component. Anti-aircraft defence was not developed fully until during the course of the war when, to the limits of practicability (and stability), free deck space and any other possible spaces were utilized to accommodate AA guns.

NATALE S. NAPPI, P.E.
14104 PARKVALE ROAD
ROCKVILLE, MD. 20853

From the 1920s the main armament of heavy cruisers consisted of the 8in gun, while light cruisers carried the 6in, the lesser firepower of which was compensated by its higher rate of fire. The main armament of the *Atlanta* and *Oakland* class cruisers consisted only of 5in dual-purpose guns. Shortly after hostilities began it became apparent that 5in barrages were inadequate to deal with Japanese air attacks; it was necessary to be able to engage attacking aircraft directly and at shorter range, and this could only be accomplished by the use of quick-firing anti-aircraft guns.

Development of both main and anti-aircraft weapons continued throughout the war. Various versions of the 8in and 6in gun barrels and turrets were fitted at different times in new classes, so that by the end of the war the following had been introduced:

- fully automatic 8in triple turrets in the *Des Moines* class;
- fully automatic 6in twin turrets in the *Worcester* class;
- fully automatic 5in/54 Mk 42 single turret;
- the fully automatic 3in/70 Mk 23 twin turret; these last two being fitted chiefly in aircraft carriers and destroyers.

Development of AA weaponry was equally striking. The effectiveness of the .50 calibre AA machine-guns, dating back to the pre-war period, was minimal, and they disappeared from cruisers shortly after the beginning of hostilities. The water-cooled 28mm quadruple anti-aircraft gun Mk 2 (pom-pom), introduced at about the time war broke out, had what seemed to be a considerable range, but its performance fell far short of expectations in terms of service and maintenance. These were removed from cruisers in 1942, and fitted in destroyers and escort ships instead. The 20mm Oerlikon was meanwhile introduced and widely used until the end of the war. A significant contribution to the effectiveness of AA occurred in 1942/3 when the 40mm Bofors was introduced, cruisers having them, too, in twin and quadruple mountings. Huge numbers of these weapons were fitted in almost all surface ships. The 20mm and 40mm AA guns were the main defence against Kamikazes until the end of the war, but during the last two years of the conflict it was realized that even the 40mm Bofors could not stop a determined suicide bid. The Kamikaze had to be engaged at longer range, so work began on the development of the semi-automatic 3in Mk 22, which would use proximity-fuzed projectiles. This was not ready for service until after the war, and

GUNS FITTED IN US CRUISERS

Calibre	Designation	Range	Notes
12in	Mk 8	33,650m	Triple turret in *Alaska* class
8in	Mk 9	25,600m	Twin and triple turrets in *Pensacola* class
8in	Mk 14	29,000m	Triple turrets in *Northampton* and *Portland* classes
8in	Mk 12	27,800m	Triple turrets in *Wichita* and *New Orleans* classes
8in	Mk 15	27,800m	Triple turrets in *Baltimore* and *Oregon City* classes
8in	Mk 16	27,800m	Triple turrets in *Des Moines* class
6in	Mk 18	24,000m	Single mountings and twin turret in *Omaha* class
6in	Mk 16	23,800m	Triple turrets in *Brooklyn*, *Cleveland*, *Fargo* and twin turrets in *Worcester* classes
5in	Mk 13	13,200m	Single mountings in pre-war cruisers
5in	Mk 12	16,000m	Twin turrets in *St. Louis*, *Helena* and those built during the war
3in	Mk 22	13,300m	In various CA and CL in service after the war
3in	Mk 23	17,800m	In CLK-(DL-)1 *Norfolk*
40mm	Mk 2	10,000m	Quadruple mountings in most cruisers from 1942
40mm	Mk 1	10,000m	Twin mountings in a large number of cruisers from 1942
28mm	Mk 2	6,700m	Quadruple mountings in a large number of older cruisers up to 1942
20mm	Mk 2, Mk 4	4,400m	Single and twin mountings in all cruisers from 1942

The above data relate to guns fitted in US cruisers before 1975. Of cruisers completed before 1962, only *Long Beach* was fitted with two 20mm close-range defence installations, CIWS Mk 15 Phalanx, in 1962.

did not begin equipping the then active cruisers until the early 1950s, shortly before conventional weaponry began to be replaced by guided missiles. The accuracy of guns had increased, however, with a refinement of aiming techniques and, from 1942, the assistance of radar, especially for main armament and the heavy 5in AA. It was not possible to have all AA guns radar-controlled because of weight considerations, and fire control was inadequate to some extent until the end of the war. The 40mm Bofors was similarly handicapped until the introduction of the Mk 51 Mod. 3 and Mk 63 permitted blind firing.

Armament: Guided Weapons

Today the various cruiser classes are intimately involved with guided weapons; in effect they and the destroyers are the main guided-weapon carriers of the US Navy. Since the end of the 1970s ship-to-ship guided weapons have become increasingly important following constant ship-to-air weapon development together with the necessary electronics technology during the previous three decades. There are three basic categories of guided weapon today:

ICBM Ship to land (Strategic)
SAM Ship to air
SSM Ship to ship

After years of neglect, the SSM Harpoon system and the Tomahawk cruise missile play an ever-increasing role in the fleet and, once again, cruisers are the main users of them alongside old battleships that have been brought back into service.

At the beginning of the guided missile era only one attempt to provide a pilotless aircraft for attacking ships at long range was successfully completed. This was the Regulus programme of the 1950s. The first missile was the Regulus I with a range of about 500 miles and a weight of 4.7 tons. It was subsonic and, from 1953, was fitted in submarines. In 1957 it was fitted in the four heavy *Baltimore*-class cruisers *Helena* (CA-75), *Los Angeles* (CA-135), *Macon* (CA-132) and *Toledo* (CA-133). No major ship conversion work was involved. Aft and to starboard a platform projected over the ship's side from which the missile could be launched without the need for special release mechanism. Up to three Regulus I could be housed in the aircraft hangar. For guidance an improved Type SP radar aerial was used, which became known as SPQ-2. Ultimately only ten of these missiles were deployed for active purposes. They were not popular aboard ship, particularly in cruisers, where the requirements involved in the carrying of such a weapon clashed frequently with the ships' duties as flagships. A

MISSILES FITTED IN US CRUISERS

Latest Designation	Type	Length (m)	Range (miles)	Weight (kg)
RIM-2	Terrier BW-0	4.5	10	1,362
RIM-2	Terrier BT-3	4.1	20	1,362
RIM-8	Talos	10.1	50	3,175
RIM-24A	Tartar	4.6	7.5	590
RIM-24B	Tartar (improved)	4.7	17.5	595
RIM-66	Standard SM-2 (MR)	4.3	40	636
RIM-67	Standard SM-2 (ER)	7.9	75	1,316
RGM-6	Regulus I	10.2	500	4,680
RGM-84	Harpoon	4.6	75	694
RGM-15	Tomahawk	6.2	300/500/2000	1,452
RWR-5	ASROC	4.6	6	450

projected follow-up system, Regulus II, which was to have a range of 1,000 miles did not get under way and was dropped totally in 1958. It had been intended to fit Regulus II in CGN-9 *Long Beach*, in the three CGs of the *Albany* class and in DL-1 *Norfolk*.

The Regulus programme was discontinued in favour of the Polaris system (intercontinental ballistic missile) even though the applications of the two systems were basically different. The Polaris system was essentially intended for submarines, but it had been planned to equip freighters with Polaris firing tubes, operated by multi-national crews of the various NATO nations. There had also been a plan for the three *Albany*-class cruisers to be equipped with eight Polaris firing tubes amidships, utilizing the space occupied by Regulus II. However, it was then decided definitely that only submarines (SSBN) would carry the ICBM, and the *Albany*s were given ASROC only, as was *Long Beach*.

Apart from the experimental ships *Mississippi* (AG-128), *Norton Sound* (AVM-1) and *Gyatt* (DDG-1, ex-DD-712), the cruisers were the first to be fitted with the SAM installations, Talos, Terrier and Tartar, which had been introduced in the 1950s. This came about through the partial conversion of eight currently available heavy and light cruisers from the *Boston*, *Galveston*, and *Little Rock* classes; through the total conversion of the heavy cruisers, *Albany*, *Chicago* and *Columbus*; through new construction (*Long Beach*); and then as time went on through the new constructions of the *Farragut* class (DLG-6) and the *Charles F. Adams* class (DDG-2). It was applied also to all successive DLG/DLGN classes

that were 'promoted' to cruiser status from mid-1975. Further development meant that two of the '3 Ts' were replaced by the standard missiles, Tartar by Standard Medium Range, Terrier by Standard Extended Range. Talos had no direct successor. Technical information was released to the Press revealing that consideration was being given to converting the *Cleveland*, *Worcester*, *Baltimore*, *Oregon City* and *Des Moines* classes for guided missile use, installing a combination of Talos, Terrier and Tartar. Ultimately, however, only the eleven conversions named above and the new *Long Beach* came into fleet use, further conversions being deferred in the light of new developments. It could also well be that the extremely high conversion costs were an inhibiting factor.

Armament: Anti-Submarine Weapons

During the Second World War, cruisers were not used to hunt submarines, nor was this the task of certain cruisers operating during the 1960s and 1970s, the *Boston*, *Galveston* and *Little Rock* classes, which carried guided weapons. These ships needed to be protected from submarines. It was a different matter with the guided missile cruisers *Albany* and *Long Beach*, which accompanied carriers as general-purpose ships: their size enabled them to house complete ASW installations, which consisted, from time to time, of:

- SQS-23 hull sonar installation,
- appropriate weapon control system,
- ASROC eight-charge launcher with

submarine-hunting rocket-propelled torpedoes and/or a nuclear depth-charge, and
- two triple sets of A/S tubes Mk 32 for short torpedoes Mk 44 and later Mk 46.

This is the fighting potential the modern US cruiser still largely commands. Apart from the *Albany*s and *Long Beach*, cruisers designed specifically for ASW, *Norfolk* (CLK-1, later DL-1), had an assortment of currently available weapons:

- four anti-submarine rocket-launchers Mk 108 'Weapon Alfa'
- eight Mk 24 torpedo tubes for wire-guided long torpedoes
- a then-current sonar installation
- later even an ASROC installation, and
- 6 Mk 32 torpedo tubes linked with the abandonment of the Mk 24 tubes.

Electronic Installations

Before the introduction of electronic fire control by radar, the only systems in large ships were optical base rangefinders which were an integral part of some, or in certain cases, all turrets. These were precision instruments and, within their limited range, made good shooting possible. The radar systems fitted from about 1942 were not confined to ship and aircraft detection; some instruments could be used for direct fire control, which meant that for the first time guns could be directed to fire at a point beyond the horizon with relative accuracy – and also during the hours of darkness. Many different radar aerials were developed and these were installed as complete systems (e.g., Mk 3/FC) either in front of existing fire control gear (e.g., Mk 4/FD), or positioned on top of them (e.g., Mk 12/22). From the beginning of the Second World War and during the period immediately following, an ever-increasing number of fire control systems became available. The lists on these pages present a summary of five control systems fitted in US Navy cruisers, together with a list of the equally important search radars fitted.

RADARS FITTED IN US CRUISERS

Fire control instruments for main armament

Mk 6 Mod. 8
The fire control system for 6in guns of the *Omaha* class which possibly also had Mk 8 and Mk 16.

Mk 18
The first fire control system for the 8in guns of the

Pensacola class in the main lift of both ships. It was later replaced by Mk 35.

Mk 24

The fire control system for the main armament in ships of the *Northampton* class. It was later replaced by Mk 31.

Mk 27

Controlled the main armament of the *Portland* class; during the war it was replaced by Mk 34 and was paired with Mk 3.

Mk 31

A replacement for Mk 24 in the *Northampton* class and also fitted in the *New Orleans* class. During the war it was paired with Mk 3.

Mk 34

Introduced with the *Brooklyn* class. It was used for the 6in guns of all light cruisers exept the *Omaha*, *Atlanta*, *Oakland* and *Roanoke* classes. and for the 8in guns of the *Wichita*, *Baltimore* and *Oregon City* classes. During the war Mk 34 replaced older instruments in other cruisers. Mk 34 was used for the main armament (14in and 16in) in the battleship total conversions *California*, *Tennessee* and *West Virginia*. In the first years of the war Mk 34 was coupled with radar: Mk 1 (in *Wichita*), with Mk 3 (infrequently), with Mk 8 Mod. 3 and Mk 13. Both the last named radar antennae were so alike that it was not possible to distinguish between them.

Mk 35

Replaced Mk 18 in the *Pensacola* class and was also intended for the *New Orleans* class.

Mk 38

A large-base rangefinder for the main armament in battleships of the *North Carolina*, *South Dakota* and *Iowa* classes and in the CBs of the *Alaska* class; it can still be found in two places on board; on the forward conning tower and on the after superstructure. During the war Mk 3 was added – in a separate position. Later on, Mk 8 and Mk 13 were fitted directly on top of Mk 38. Independently of these, many battleships (at about the end of the war) were fitted with the small radar Mk 27 on top of the armoured bridge where the Mk 3 had formerly been positioned. The *Iowa*-class battleships, brought back into service in 1982, still show this combination; Mk 38/Mk 13.

Mk 54

Only used for 8in guns in the three ships of the *Des Moines* class. This FCG is easily recognized by its long, conical (in plan) extended sub-structure. The appropriate FC radar for this was Mk 13. For a long time this system was referred to as Mk 39.

Fire control gear for anti-aircraft guns

Mk 19

Introduced in 1927; used for the 5in/25 guns in the

Pensacola class (replaced in 1943 by Mk 33), *Northampton* class and *Portland* class (in this case fitted laterally to the bridge and replaced later by Mk 33).

Mk 28

Interim model before Mk 33. Introduced in the first five ships of the *New Orleans* class for the 5in/25. Later replaced by Mk 33.

Mk 33

Widely used fire control gear for the 5in AA guns in older aircraft carriers, cruisers and destroyers. It was developed in parallel with Mk 28, but ended up as the better equipment. It was used widely until the end of the war in cases where it was not possible to make use of the heavier Mk 37. There were two versions of Mk 33; one was open at the top, the other totally enclosed. In both versions the computer was in the instrument itself. Its format dictated to some extent whether the radar Mk 4 introduced early in the war was extended from the front of the equipment or mounted on its roof. The radar antenna Mk 28 (used to some extent at the end of the war) was always positioned on the front edge, but the radar combination Mk 12/22 was too heavy to be used on top of a Mk 33.

Mk 37

Introduced in 1939, mainly in destroyers, for the control of 5in/38 AA. It was to give almost forty years of good service in various versions, often modified and improved, and it did not disappear until the beginning of the 1980s when the last FRAM-I-destroyers were detached from the fleet. During the war Mk 37 was used in all types of ship, even auxiliaries. In contrast to Mk 33 the appropriate computer was housed not in the FCG itself but elsewhere in the ship. Mk 37 was the first system designed to be used with fire control radar. It was paired successively with radar Mk 4/FD, Mk 12/22 and Mk 25, but not often with Mk 28. There was a special version of Mk 37 which appeared with radar Mk 25 Mod. 7 aboard the weapons ships *Mississippi* (AG-128) and the guided missile cruiser *Boston* (CAG-1) as a predecessor of SPQ-5.

Mk 44

A small simple visual apparatus for the 28mm quadruple AA. With such equipment one could control several similar mountings sited nearby.

Mk 50

Similarly, a visual equipment for 3in AA in the *Omaha* class.

Mk 51

Introduced in 1942; it included the by now proven visual equipment Mk 14 (this being coupled with 20mm AA). Mark 51 was intended for use with 40mm AA. In those ships too lightly constructed to receive Mk 37, Mk 51 could also be used to control the 5in AA. Mk 51 Mods. 1 and 2 still had small fire control

radar; Mod. 3 on the other hand was paired with Mk 28 which meant that the radar antenna could not be mounted on the apparatus itself, but was mounted directly on the gun mounting. As a matter of policy a Mk 51 gear was apportioned to each 40mm mounting. After the introduction of fire control radar in 1944, an additional Mk 51 was apportioned to every two or three 5in/38 guns which were thus enabled to carry out radar-directed blind firing in conjunction with Mk 37.

Mk 56

Introduced shortly after the Second World War, mainly for the guidance of the then new 3in/50 Mk 22. This equipment was very versatile; with its radar Mk 35 (later SPG-35) it could also be used for control of the 40mm AA guns. The four battleships of the *Iowa* class were fitted after the war with Mk 56 FCG, but not with the 3in/50 which belonged to it. In the 1960s the Mk 56 was coupled with the 5in/38 in frigates of the *Garcia* and *Brooke* classes. The development of Mk 56 began in 1942; at the end of the 1970s, it was removed from all auxiliary and amphibious ships with the exception of the frigates named above.

Mk 57

Introduced from October 1944 in *Alaska* and *Guam* and from the very beginning was coupled with radar Mk 29 to enable blind firing to be carried out by 40mm AA guns.

Mk 58

A transition gear approaching Mk 63, intended for the 40mm AA guns in the cruisers *Mobile* and *Oakland*. The equipment actually installed in these ships was the rather more developed Mk 63.

Mk 63

Introduced at the end of 1944 as a radar supported FCG; it was intended for use with 40mm and later for 3in/50 AA guns; initially, radar Mk 28 (mounted on the guns) was used and later Mk 34 – given the later designation SPG–50. Mk 63 enabled the guns to fire blind. These were small devices which were very difficult to identify and it made the observer's task of differentiating between Mk 51 Mod. 3 and Mk 57 Mod. 2 and 4 most difficult. The ship spotter had the following alternatives: either one noted a 3in/50 AA with radar screen and that would be one of the aforementioned FCG; or there might be no radar screen in which case a Mk 56 could be deduced, and certainly clearly visible.

Mk 67

The first specially designed control gear for the new 5in/54 Mk 42. It was coupled with Mk 25 fire control radar and only installed in a few cases; namely in *Mississippi* class. However, it was too heavy and was replaced.

Mk 68

From the onset this was taken in with fire control

radar SPG-53 and coupled as a series with the Mk 42 cannon. Apparently it is still the main instrument for the Mk 42 cannon but will be replaced from 1982 partly by the Mk 86 (for example in three ships of the DDG-2 class).

Mk 86

Developed principally for fire control of the lightweight 5in/54 Mk 45 gun. Among the exterior main components may be counted the surface radar aerial SPQ-9 and the radar scanner SPG-60 (STIR), which permits also the control of guided missiles. An electro-optical sensor is also fitted. Mk 86 exists in several versions. Mod. 9 (fitted to OG-47 class) dispenses with SPG-60. This can be done because, in ships of the *Ticonderoga* class, the Mk 99 contains four radar arrays SPG-62. Mk 86 was introduced in 1970.

Mk 92

Not installed in cruisers. It is one of the HSA installations M25 and M27 adapted for the US Navy as fire control systems for frigates and smaller ships. Mk 92 Mod. 2 includes also SPG-60 STIR, which, for example, belongs to the standard fire control of guided missile frigates of the FFG-7 class. From the mid-1980s measures are to be taken to improve the general performance of this system.

Fire control installations for guided missiles

The following designations are valid for the whole fire control system to which special radar arrays belong.

Mk 71

Appeared in a version suitable for the Terrier guided missile in the first two guided missile cruisers *Boston* CAG-1 and *Canberra* CAG-2; in *Boston* it was paired at first with Mk 25 Mod. 7, and later, in the case of both ships, with SPQ-5.

Mk 73

Likewise compatible with the fire control of the Terrier guided missile and installed in CLG-6 – 8 and in (formerly) DDG-6 – 8, to work in conjunction with SPQ-5. In the last of these ships it was replaced by Mk 76.

Mk 74

Available in two installations – initially for the Tartar missile – in the three CGs of the *Albany* class paired with radar arrays SPG-51. Further models are to be seen in ships of the DDG-2, DDG-993, CGN-36 and CGN-38 classes which all have the shorter Standard Missile 'Medium Range'.

Mk 76

Intended for the long Standard missile version 'Extended Range'; it was fitted earlier in CV-63, -64 and -66, and is currently fitted to ships of the classes DDG-37, CG-16, CG-26, CGN-9, CGN-25 and CGN-35. They are always used in conjunction with two radar arrays type SPG-55.

Mk 77

A Talos fire installation always used with two each of radar arrays SPG-49 and SPW-2. They were installed in CGN-9, CG-10 – 12 and CLG-3, -4 and -5 until the final withdrawal of these in 1981. At the end of the 1960s the SPG-49 gear were to have been replaced by SPG-61, but this did not take place on account of high costs involved and because of the very considerable weight of a complete Talos launching installation.

Mk 91

Should be considered in connection with the Mk 29 launching system of the NATO Sea Sparrow short-range close defence system BPDMS. Its installation has been mainly in destroyers, aircraft carriers and large auxiliary vessels. The appropriate radar arrays are apparently also designated Mk 91, but it is possible that they may have their own separate designation. Mk 91 is the successor to Mk 115.

Mk 99

To be found in the AEGIS ships of CG-47 class where they control the 'Medium Range' guided missile Type Standard SM-2. Each AEGIS cruiser has two such installations which always work in conjunction with two SPG-62 fire control radar arrays.

Mk 115

The older fire control installation for the BPDMS system alternate with Mk 25 launcher which from the beginning of the 1980s was being increasingly replaced by Mk 29. The appropriate fire control gear has the designation Mk 76.

Mk 114, Mk 116 and Mk 117

Anti-submarine fire control installations which are used in conjunction with different sonar systems and also with the ASROC anti-submarine system and are consequently to be found also in modern cruisers.

Fire control radar for guns

Mk 1 (CXAS)

Introduced initially under the designation FA. The prototype was first seen in June 1941 in *Wichita* (CA-45). The detection range was approximately 38 miles. Only ten installations were built and were used chiefly in conjunction with Mk 34. It was soon superseded by Mk 3.

Mk 3

Also introduced with the designation FC. This was the first noteworthy fire control radar antenna and it is also one which was rewarding to the ship spotter. It appeared in two different forms; an antenna in the shape of a cylinder cross-section (Mk 3 Mods. 1 and 3) with dimensions 1.8 × 1.8m and the more widely used and therefore better known antenna Mk 3 (Mods. 0 and 2) with dimensions 3.7 × 0.9m. The latter was fitted – in some cases separated from any FCG, and was always used in action in two antennae in battleships and cruisers where they controlled the

firing of the main armament. The first models, with a long antenna were fitted in October 1941 in the light cruiser *Philadelphia*. With an antenna placed at a height of 24m, a Mk 3 could detect an approaching 16in shell at a range of approximately 18km, a submarine on the surface at 11km and a bomber flying at 3000m at 41km. A total of 139 Mk 3s had been delivered by 1944. The replacement for this was FC radar antenna Mk 8.

Mk 4

This was introduced under the alternative designation FD. Mark 4 came in at the same time as Mk 3, in September 1941. This was the radar of the systems Mk 33 and Mk 37, which were intended for fire control of the 5in guns. The Mk 4 aerial consisted of two half segments of the aerial Mk 3 Mod. 2 set at an angle of 90°. The detection ranges were:

5in shell falling in water	up to 11.0 km
Battleship	up to 27.0 km
Destroyer	up to 18.3 km
Submarine	up to 11.0 km
Bomber	up to 36.5 km

The results obtained in blind firing and in detection of low-flying aircraft left something to be desired and, in consequence, a later replacement was the radar combination Mk 12/22 and of Mk 33 by Mk 28. In all, from 1941 to 1944, 667 installations were delivered.

Mk 8 (CXEM)

This was chosen to follow Mk 3 in battleships and cruisers. The antenna was set on top of the Mk 38 or Mk 34 and consisted of a box sloping forwards, measuring 1.0 × 3.0m, on the front of which 3 × 14 radiators were fitted so that, from the front, a certain similarity could be discerned with a hedgehog or porcupine. Selected detection ranges were:

Battleship	up to 36.5 km
Destroyer	up to 28.3 km
Submarine	up to 9.1 km
Bomber	up to 27.4 km

By 1943, 205 installations had been delivered of which some were modified to become Mk 8 Mod. 3; in these the antenna corresponded more closely with that of Mk 13, which was later to replace them.

Mk 10

Was combined as a fire control radar with Mk 50, and was intended for the fire control of 3in guns in light cruisers of the *Omaha* class. Mk 10 Mod. 3, of which only twenty installations were completed, was a narrow mesh, parabolic reflector. It was followed in 1944 by a further 37 installations of Mod. 5, which consisted of parabolic reflectors with a diameter of approximately 1.15m.

Mk 12

The replacement installation for Mk 4 on the Mk 37. The antenna resembled that of Mk 4. Deliveries began in 1943. A total of 801 sets had been delivered by the end of the war, latterly mostly combined with Mk 22 height-finder radar. This combination was too heavy to be paired with Mk 33 and therefore this gear was used with radar Mk 28.

Mk 13

Replaced Mk 8 radar in battleships and cruisers during the war. In place of the 'porcupine', an antenna consisting of a 2.40 × 0.60m half-cylinder was fitted. Many Mk 8 radar antennae had been modified as Mod. 3 versions by the end of 1945 and were given the same altered antenna. Mk 13 was the last fire control radar to be developed for fire control of large calibre guns. It is still to be seen in the battleships of the *Iowa* class that have been brought back into service.

Mk 22

Developed as a 'height-finder', in other words a radar for the detection at upper altitudes, and had a parabolic section ('orange peel') measuring 1.80 × 0.45m. A total of 995 units were delivered from 1943. As far as is known Mk 22 was used almost exclusively in combination with Mk 12 and only rarely with Mk 4.

Mk 25

The first fire control radar equipment to be produced after the war. From the outset it was to be used with Mk 37 as a replacement for Mk 12/22. The antenna consisted of a narrow-mesh, parabola of 1.5m diameter. With 50kW of power, the range was quite impressive, initially more than 45km and later twice that distance. Development began in March 1944 and finally the Mod. 2 version came to production status; from May 1947 more than 400 were delivered for fleet use. Later followed Mod. 3 with 250kW of power and a range of approximately 137km. At this stage various Mod. 2s produced for 1952 were modified as Mod. 3s. With this version it was possible to follow one's own projectiles during their flight.

Mk 25 Mod. 7

Fitted with a larger parabolic reflector and was the first radar designed for Terrier missiles. It was used in *Mississippi* (AG-128) and *Boston* (CAG-1).

Mk 27

Stand-by radar for fire control of the main armament in battleships and cruisers. In most cases it replaced Mk 3 on the armoured bridge. It used the detection radar aerial SJ, measuring 1.5 × 0.9m. This installation was introduced in 1944, but only 41 antennae were delivered.

Mk 28

The FL radar for those fire control units that were too light to be given Mk 12/22; they were thus used with Mk 33 with the aerial projecting from the front side. There were also relatively few instruments Mk 37 for which the combination Mk 28/22 was suitable because they were not compatible with Mk 12. In

performance value, Mk 28 stood between Mk 4 and Mk 12. The later version Mk 28 Mod. 2 was coupled with the optical aiming device Mk 63 in which case the parabolic aerial was fitted to the mounting of the twin or quadruple 40mm Bofors. A total of 550 installations were supplied in 1944 and 1945. Production continued from July 1945 in the form of Mk 34 Mod. 2. Detection ranges were:

Bomber	18.3 km
Fighter	13.7 km

Mk 32

In effect the IFF component for the radar installations Mk 3, Mk 4 and Mk 12.

Mk 34

The successor to Mk 28, and was coupled with the lighter visual instruments Mk 63 Mods. 1 and 2, and Mk 57 Mods. 3 and 4. The parabolic reflectors had a diameter of 90cm. This enabled a bomber to be detected at a range of approximately 23km. Mk 34 was developed and introduced after the Second World War. A later version, Mk 34 Mod. 17, was given the designation SPG-34; this installation had a parabolic antenna made of glass fibre with a diameter of 1m. It was intended for use with 3in/50 guns as the current Mk 63 optical equipment was too small and weak for this purpose.

Mk 35

The fire control radar for the Mk 56 and with it controlled the fire of 3in/50 and 5in/38 guns. Series production followed in the early 1950s. The parabolic antenna had a diameter of 1.2m.

SPG-50

A refurbished SPG-34 for optical gear Mk 63. This antenna too had a diameter of 1m and was for use with 3in guns. The installation could track aerial targets moving at a speed of 800km per hour. Delivery began in 1956 and ended after 196 units had been produced.

SPG/53

The fire control radar for the Mk 68, and is used in many modern cruisers for the 5in/54 Mk 42 guns. In the course of time versions A to F have been developed. The antenna consists similarly of a parabolic reflector and is set on top of the Mk 68.

SPG-60 STIR

An integral part of the Mk 86 FC system which, unusually, has been adapted for use with the lightweight 5in Mk 45 guns, but also for the older and heavier Mk 42. The additional designation STIR means 'Separate Tracking and Illuminating Radar'. SPG-60 can be used in guided missile ships as an additional radar illuminator for the guidance of missiles (e.g., Standard or Sea Sparrow). SPG-60 is found in all cruisers built since 1970 and also in the *Ticonderoga* class.

SPQ-9

The second fire control radar antenna belonging to

the Mk 86. It is intended for surface use and, in this connection, has a radar dome which is a distinguishing mark in all cruisers built since 1970. One version is for limited air surveillance; here the aerial is exposed. Up to now this version has not been observed in US ships. The antenna rotates at 60rpm and is said to be able to cope with up to 120 targets. SPQ-9 consists of both IFF and ECCM components.

Phalanx–Radar

Phalanx is certainly the current designation for the whole spectrum of short-range defence installations against low-flying aircraft; strictly speaking Phalanx is only the fire control radar belonging to this system, and is positioned over the 6-barrelled 20mm Vulcan gun. When used operationally against missiles. Phalanx can work completely independently in a pre-selected range; it can, however, be linked with other systems aboard and used against surface targets, for example fast patrol boats, hovercraft or even against low-flying aircraft. Phalanx radar does not have a Mk – or SPG designation. Before its introduction the two BPDMS installations, whose launcher carries the designations Mk 25 or Mk 29, were the only defence against small warships and low-flying aircraft. Each of these installations has its own fire control radar. Neither of the two systems is currently operational in cruisers.

Fire control radar for guided missiles

Mk 25 Mod. 7

The first radar for Terrier missiles. This was a parabola with a diameter larger than that of the normal Mk 25 model. It was sited in a relatively high position on a Mk 37. It was fitted in the 1950s, only in the weapons test ship *Mississippi* (AG-128, ex-BB-41) and for a time in *Boston* (CAG-1), and was ultimately replaced by SPQ-5.

SPQ-5

The first follow-up radar developed for the Terrier system. It has considerable similarities with SPQ-49 which was used for Talos. SPQ-5 was installed in all cruisers of the *Boston*, *Little Rock* and *Galveston* classes that had Terrier installations. This applied at this time to the four ships of the *Farragut* class (formerly DLG-6, today known as DDG-37). In the changeover from Terrier I to Terrier II, all SPQ-5s were replaced by the rather lighter – radar antennae SPG–55. The prototype of SPQ-5 was tried out in *Norton Sound* (AVM-1), and the first series installation was put into *Canberra* (CAG-2).

SPQ-2

The designation for a modified radar antenna for missile guidance. It was used to guide the Regulus I missile and was installed in 1958/59 in the four heavy cruisers that carried Regulus I.

SPG-49

The control radar for the Talos system. It was introduced in 1962 and functioned always in conjunction with SPW-2 (described later in this chapter). In exterior appearance the very extensive antennae resembled considerably that of SPQ-5. Originally, SPG-49 was conceived in 1947 as a combined radar for missile control. The aerial was to be set up on a base of Mk 37. Under certain conditions the overall performance of SPG-49 left much to be desired, and this was the main reason why, as early as 1979, the Talos installations were removed from fleet use. The detection range of an object of 5m^2 was approximately 270km.

SPW-2

The computer guided radar array for Talos. Each Talos installation had two SPG-49 instruments with two associated SPW-2s.

SPG-51

Should be considered in connection with the guided missile installation Mk 74 and is the radar array for Tartar and certain follow-up models of Standard MR types which are found in cruisers of the *Albany*, *California* and *Virginia* classes, and also in many American and foreign guided missile ships (DDG and FFG). There are many versions of SPG-51 in existence and all have a parabolic antenna with a diameter of 2.40m. Development started in 1952 with a series production following a good ten years later in classes CG-10 and DDG-2.

SPG-55

Operates in conjunction with the guided missile installation Mk 76 and has a range of approximately 180km. There are various versions in existence, all intended for Terrier ER. They can all control both 'beam riding' and the 'semi-active' Terrier and also all follow-up models of Standard ER type – even in their nuclear version. SPG-55 is found in ships of the classes CGN-9, CG-16, -26, CGN-25 and -35 and DDG-37.

SPG-62

The radar which followed SPG-51, but can only be used with FC system Mk 99 in AEGIS cruisers. The parabolic antenna is very similar to SPG-51. In AEGIS cruisers it controls missiles of Standard MR type but only in the last phase of the projectile's approach to its target.

Mk 115

The radar system for the older BPDMS system, around the launcher Mk 25. This uses a twin antenna – one for transmitting and one for reflecting impulses. Mk 115 has been developed since 1963 and was installed from 1967. Its range is four miles. The Mk 25 launcher was installed in 1967, initially in aircraft carriers, being replaced in the 1980s by Mk 29, and also in frigates of the *Knox* class, where they

were similarly replaced in the 1980s by CIWS Mk 15 Phalanx. The control gear for this was Mk 76 Mod. 0.

Mk 91

This is, in contrast, the radar for the newer NATO Sea-Sparrow system with the launcher Mk 29. Two versions are produced:

Mk 0 with a single antenna, used in American ships,

Mk 1 with a twin antenna, used in friendly navies which use the Mk 29 system. In American ships Mk 91 formerly worked in conjunction with close-range detection radar systems SPS-58/65 and at present with IPD/TAS Mk 23.

Search radar installations

CXAM

After a few experimental types, CXAM appeared as the first efficient larger ship's radar aerial in mid-1940 when it was fitted in six fleet ships: BB *California*, CV *Yorktown*, CA *Pensacola*, *Northampton*, *Chester* and *Chicago*. *California*'s antenna, which was badly damaged at Pearl Harbor, was recovered and fitted to CV *Hornet* in 1942. The dimensions of the aerial were 5.2 × 5.5m. Performance in a vertical mode was fairly poor, but moderate in a horizontal direction. Some range details are:

Battleship or cruiser	up to 16 miles
Destroyer	up to 12 miles
Flying-boat at a height of 3,300m	up to 70 miles
Fighter at a height of 3,300m	up to 50 miles

CXAM-1

At the end of 1941, fourteen antennae of this type, with better all-round performance, came into operational use; they were retained until the end of 1943. They were installed in: CV *Lexington*, *Saratoga*, *Ranger*, *Enterprise* and *Wasp*; BB *Texas*, *Pennsylvania*, *West Virginia*, *North Carolina*, *Washington*; CL *Cincinnati*; AV *Curtiss* and *Albermarle*.

SC, SC-1 (XAR*)

This was a misguided attempt to attain the performance of CXAM with a smaller antenna measuring 2.3 × 2.6m. In actual fact the detection ranges were smaller:

for a bomber	30 miles
for a fighter	23 miles
for a battleship	10 miles
for a destroyer	3 miles

SC was introduced from the end of 1941, but, as early as the beginning of 1942, the SC-1 followed, with twice the range. This led to all SC sets being converted to SC-1. In all, approximately 400 units were delivered.

*Those older designations which date back to the early development phase of radar detection are given once again in brackets: CXAM was the first version of them to be introduced.

SC-2, 3, 4, 5

SC-2 was an improved SC-1 installation with a right-angled antenna measuring 1.4 × 4.6m, which had an IFF component. Ranges were:

for a bomber at a height of 3,300m	80 miles
for a fighter at a height of 3,300m	40 miles
for a large ship	20 miles

After delivery of 415 SC-2s, there followed from December 1943 production of 200 slightly improved SC-3s and 250 SC-4s, production ceasing at the end of 1944. In 1945 the production of 100 SC-5s took place; all these installations made use of the right-angled antenna as used in SC-2 with only superficial variations. SC-2 to 5 were usually destroyer installations, but they were found occasionally in battleships and cruisers and especially in aircraft carriers (in this case invariably with two antennae). The last SC-5 installations were removed from fleet use in 1963.

SG, SG-1 (SXGR)

This was the first pure surface detection installation in the US Navy, tested as early as June 1941 in the destroyer *Semmes*. The first production model was fitted in April 1942 in the cruiser *Augusta*. By November 1943 a total of 955 SGs and SG-1s had been produced. To the end of the war SG was the standard radar equipment of all ships larger than destroyers. Many ships – including cruisers – had two SC aerials on board to give full coverage of 360°. Some ranges were:

For a bomber at a height of 150m	15 miles
For a battleship	22 miles
For a destroyer	15 miles

SK (SXFA)

The most powerful of the airsearch installations used by the US Navy during the second half of the war, it was essentially a SC-2 installation with a 15.2m^2 antenna with an additional IFF beam. Large numbers were installed in battleships and those auxiliary ships larger than destroyers. A medium bomber at a height of 3,000m could be detected at a range of approximately 100 miles. A total of 250 installations were delivered from January 1943 to April 1944.

SK-2

Based on the previously described SC-3, it had a circular antenna with a diameter of 5.2m; this was essentially a direct successor to SK, but only 75 of them were produced, from April to December 1944. Both SK and SK-2 showed inadequacies in the detection of very high-flying aircraft, something that was later improved by a rather better version of the SK-3 antenna.

SM (CXBL)

The first radar installation destined to control a ship's own aircraft. The circular antenna with a diameter of 2.4m, being combined with IFF bars BO or BL, weighed approximately 2 tons and initially could only be used in aircraft carriers. A bomber could be detected at a height of 3,000m at a distance of 50 miles, or a battleship at 25 miles. The first installation was made in March 1943 in *Lexington* (CV-16). A total of 23 installations had been delivered by October 1944.

SP (CXDT)
The installation that followed SM; its chief virtue was that it was lighter and had a smaller circular aerial with a diameter of 1.8m. Performance details corresponded to those of SM, but were improved subsequently. SP was also installed after the war in a few cruisers and radar destroyers, but most of those delivered after the autumn of 1944 were fitted in aircraft carriers. During the 1950s SP was used as a base for the fire control radar installation SPQ-2 which was used in the guidance of Regulus I.

SR-2
In April 1945 the prototype of this installation was tested; originally it had been intended for use in escort ships, but its antennae proved to be too heavy. Moreover there was no integrated IFF component and a separate rotating IFF antenna was necessary. The performance was totally unsatisfactory and by the end of the war only eighteen installations had been delivered out of 200 ordered; the remainder were cancelled. Among other installations these were fitted in the three then new aircraft carriers of the *Midway* class, in the light aircraft carrier *Saipan* and in one heavy and seven light cruisers, two destroyers and four radar submarines. In all larger ships it was soon replaced by SPS-6.

SR-3, 6
The designation of this installation's antenna has proved absolutely impossible to identify; a narrow rotating aerial, the IFF component of which was almost as long as the aerial itself. The performance of this installation, which was planned as a replacement for SK and SK-2, was – not just because of the too low number of revolutions of the antenna – so unsatisfactory that production ceased after 22 units had been installed. Nevertheless, SR-3 was found after 1948 in all three cruisers of the *Midway* class, in two battleships, eleven cruisers and five light cruisers, and in the test ship *Mississippi* (AG-128). A lightweight version, SR-6, was provided for one light cruiser. Subsequently all these installations were given the SPS-6A or SPS-6B antennae which did increase performance significantly.

SX (SXHR)
The first real 'height-finder', a transitional installation for controlling one's own aircraft, which led to the development of SPS-8. SX had an irregular working double antennae, both parts of which could be displaced around 90° on a vertical axis. SX was the follow-up installation of SM and SP in this particular area. In 1945 there were two prototypes. A total of

45 installations was manufactured, of which the first four were fitted to the three CVBs of the *Midway* class and in CV *Tarawa*. In 1948, 25 of these installations were still in use. SX was to be seen in *Mississippi* (AG-128) and in all active aircraft carriers at that time: *Boxer*, *Leyte*, *Antietam*, *Princeton*, *Valley Forge* and *Philippine Sea*. This installation was not given to cruisers.

SPS-2
By far the largest ship-carried radar antenna, much value being placed on an extended range, but this worked to the detriment of detection accuracy. It was intended to be able to detect missiles then in existence, such as the German V2 and similar weapons, over a distance of 300 miles. The eccentric-looking antenna measured 6.1×12.2m and weighed 23 tons. Obviously the support provided by a normal mast was insufficient and a solid substructure was necessary. In fact a heavy bomber could be detected at 300 miles and an airborne object with a surface of $1m^2$ detected at 165 miles. The range achieved did not come up to expectations. SPS-2 had, however, considerable influence on the later installations SPS-11, 13, 34 and 44, yet they were not fitted systematically in ships for operational duties. SPS-2 itself was only found in CLC-1 *Northampton* and in CLG-4 *Little Rock*. It was planned to install it in both CAGs of the *Boston* class and in CLG-3 *Galveston*, but because of its extreme weight and probably because of its lack of accuracy this was abandoned; ultimately both these installations were removed from their ships. The direct successor to SPS-2 as a 'height-finder' was SPS-30, but also all the three-dimensional installations known by the collective term FRESCAN.

SPS-3 (XDK)
Found in only one instance – in about 1954 in CLC-1 *Northampton*; this was the first experiment with a hemispheric radar installation which was not proceeded with because of its weak performance (a fighter aircraft flying at 12,200m at 10 miles range). CXRX, a modified SPS-8 antenna which displayed a better performance, served for some time as a hemispheric radar.

SPS-6, 6A, 6B, 6C, D and E
After SPS-6 had been tested in 1948 in Macon (CA-132) as the successor to SR-3 and SR-6, a decision was made in favour of installations SPS-6B and C which were very widely used, and soon their 1.5×5.5m antennae were to be seen in large numbers. They were in fact fitted in all kinds of ships. They were the first air surveillance antennae and they are currently found in certain former American ships that are now serving with friendly nations. As an indication of the detection range, with an SPS-6B aerial a heavy bomber could be detected at a height of 9,500m and at a distance of 145 miles. 25 SPS-6, 45 SPS-6A and 110 SPS-6B were delivered, all

between 1948 and 1952. After this latter date large numbers of versions C, D and E were produced, the antennae of which could not be distinguished from SPS-6B. After a small number had been replaced by SPS-12, full replacement was made in about 1958 by the large series of 'Mattress' antennae SPS-17, 28, 29 and 37.

SPS-8, CXRX, SPS-8A, -8B
Also a 'height-finder' developed in effect from SX and with similarly eccentric-looking antennae. Their principal duty was to control their own fighter aircraft. A fighter could be detected with SPS-8A and B over a range of 72 miles. SPS-8, the earliest installation, which had weaker detection ranges, was delivered from 1952. SPS-8 and 8A had the same antenna. SPS-8B was tried out in AG-128 *Mississippi* and was introduced from 1959, being fitted in *Independence* (CV-62) and *Kitty Hawk* (CV-63), and others. It was planned to introduce versions SPS-8C and D using these antennae, but at about this time development work on SPS-30 materialized. CXRX was a modified version of SPS-8 with a modified antenna which could pick up a bomber at 20 miles. In 1955 single test installations were fitted in the first guided missile cruisers *Boston* and *Canberra* (CAG-1 and 2) and remained installed for some years. The dimensions of the antennae were approximately 3.4×5.2m. If series production had commenced it would have had the designation SPS-27, but CXRX was replaced by SPS-30.

SPS-10
Was introduced in October 1953 and has proved to be the most reliable surface detection aerial to the present time. After it had been shown that a submarine periscope projecting only 1m out of the water could be detected at a range of approximately 9,200m, SPS-10B was immediately fitted in warships of all descriptions and later on even in minesweepers and auxiliary ships. The aerial was 3.1m long and up to the present time, versions E, F and G are available. There was no replacement until 1982 when installation SPS-67 succeeded SPS-10, but it retained the antenna that SPS-10 had used.

SPS-12
With SPS-29/37, SPS-12 was the first replacement for SPS-6B, certainly in larger ships, but also in certain Canadian, Japanese and Italian frigates and this remains so to the present time. The antenna weighed approximately 550kg and measured 2.4×7.6m. Delivery of SPS-12 began in September 1953. A bomber could be detected at a range of approximately 60 miles. In the USA a total of 139 were delivered as a series; others were built under licence in Italy.

SPS-13
Had a certain similarity to SPS-2, but it was smaller and the detection range was only just over 200 miles. It could receive warning of aerial targets at a

height of approximately 29km and a distance of 140 miles. The antenna weighed approximately 5 tons and measured 2.8 × 6.1m and was therefore too heavy to be used in destroyers. It was to have been the replacement for SPS-8 and 12 in the Terrier guided missile ships at the beginning of the 1960s, and an advanced programme involving large numbers had been mapped out when the various advantages presented by the FRESCAN development of SPS-39 were made known, and this resulted in the fact that only one example of SPS-13 was installed, in Canberra in January 1958.

SPS-17

Was the first installation of what were to become later SPS-28, 29 and 37. SPS-17 had a right-angled 3.0 × 5.3m antenna. A fighter could be detected at a height of 12,000m and a range of approximately 200 miles. This was the first installation to be positioned on the forward mast of the guided missile conversions of the CLG-3 and CLG-4 classes. The equipment was developed in 1952/53 and was tested in the former destroyer leader *Willis A. Lee* (DL-4) from February to April 1957. Twenty installations were ordered in 1956 for use in the ocean radar station ships (AGR). In view of development work in connection with SPS-28 and 29 further orders did not materialize. There was also a version SPS-17A using a large, 12.8m antenna, later known as SPS-37A and SPS-43A. This was also installed on AGRs.

SPS-26

The first installation in the FRESCAN series. The antenna was similar to that of the later SPS-39. Only one test specimen was installed, in August 1957 in *Norfolk* (DL-1). She was used as a test ship in many areas at that time. Maximum ranges were: an aircraft at 160 miles and at approximately 23,000m. It was found, however, that SPS-26 was not suitable as the main installation in ships, but was best considered in conjunction with other long-range air/surface observation installations. As it did not prove to be particularly reliable it did not go into series production, but underwent development to become SPS-39.

SPS-28

The lightweight version of SPS-17 using the same antenna. The first delivery was made at the beginning of 1957 and the installation was found principally in the radar early warning escort ships (DER), and in destroyers.

SPS-29

Suceeded SPS-28 and was produced in very large numbers for cruisers and destroyers. Its weight was the same at that of SPS-28, its 3.4 × 5.5m antenna being only slightly altered, least of all in the first three versions. SPS-29D had, in contrast to the other altered antennae, one that consisted of angle-segments, which were chiefly fitted in the larger US coastguard vessels. It had a similar profile to the SPS-37A/43A antenna later introduced. SPS-29 had a range of approximately 270 miles. From 1959 to 1960 a total of 89 installations were delivered.

SPS-30

The last 'height-finder' in US ships, and replaced SPS-8A and 8B from May 1962; it was to remain until the end of the 1970s without replacement – the performance of SPS-48 making this unnecessary. The irregular antenna (3.7 × 4.6m) made detection possible at a range of up to 240 miles. A total of 57 installations were delivered and fitted in carriers, cruisers, radar early warning destroyers and amphibious flagships. It was removed from cruisers and aircraft carriers at the end of the 1970s.

SPS-32/33

This functioned in accordance with the SCANFAR principle; surface aerials in pairs were positioned on the four surfaces of the bridge house; their measurements and weights were very considerable. Dimensions: SPS-32 6.1 × 12.2m; SPS-33 6.1 × 7.6m. This combination allowed detection ranges of approximately 400 miles; however this did not justify such an installation and certainly not its total weight. The equipment was not adjudged to be too successful and this is shown in the fact that only two units were installed, in the aircraft carrier *Enterprise* (CVN-65) and in the guided missile cruiser *Long Beach* (CGN-9). During modernisation, halfway through ship service time, these installations were removed from both ships in 1980/81 and SPS-48 and 49 were fitted in their place.

SPS-37

Represents a further development of SPS-29 in that the same right-angled antenna was retained. The detection range in this case amounted to approximately 233 miles. Installations were fitted in many cruisers, destroyers and aircraft carriers. Using the 12.8m antenna (the one that had been developed for SPS-17A!) the version was known as SPS-37A and the range was now increased to approximately 300 miles. A total of 46 installations of SPS-37 were delivered, the first one in the cruiser *Los Angeles* (CA-135) in September 1960.

SPS-39

Belonged to the three-dimensional FRESCAN detection installations. It was introduced from January 1960 for guided missile cruisers and destroyers; with it was fitted the same antenna as had been given to SPS-26. It was shaped in the form of a slightly inclined cylinder housing and weighed 1.3 tons. This allowed a detection range of approximately 160 miles. The SPS-39 installations remained for quite some time in guided missile cruisers of the USN and other navies, with most of them (roughly from 1963) having the antennae replaced by a rather smaller surface array as was used later automatically with the SPS-52 installation. The detection range was approximately 145 miles. For a long time – and this applies today – it was hardly possible to judge by the antenna alone whether an SPS-39 or SPS-52 was in a ship – a problem which one finds all the time with other electronic installations. Apart from these smaller antenna there was – though only one was produced – SPS-39B, similar to the original aerial of SPS-39, but essentially a larger antenna which allowed detection at approximately 175 miles. It was installed in CLG-3 *Galveston*. In the intervening time most of the old SPS-39 antennae were replaced by SPS-52 or SPS-48. There was an alternative to SPS-39, the SPS-42, an installation using the same aerial, but manufactured to work with the Information Representation Installation NTDS ('Naval Tactical Data System'). SPS-42 was found chiefly in Terrier guided missile cruisers.

SPS-40

Installed for fleet use from June 1961 and subsequently fitted in all other kinds of ship. SPS-40 was effectively the successor to the SPS-17/28/29/37 radar groups and in some respects to SPS-6 and SPS-12. SPS-40 was developed from installation SPS-31 which in just one case had been fitted experimentally between 1958 and 1962 in the radar early warning destroyer *Furse* (DD-887, ex-DDR-882). The testing of SPS-40 was made in *Richard E. Kraus* (DD-849). It had been intended to fit this installation only in destroyers, but as it performed well it became the standard lightweight installation in many different kinds of ship to the present time and was adopted by many non-US ships. This delayed the introduction of SPS-49 for all of a decade. Version SPS-40B was given a better IFF component. From 1978 versions SPS-40 C and D represented a 40 per cent improvement in performance, and destroyers and frigates have subsequently received SPS-40E.

SPS-43

A further improvement on SPS-37 which was made more resistant to ECM interference. It uses the smaller antenna as was used in SPS-37 (mainly in those missile cruisers which were formerly designated as DLG/DLGN!) and, in the case of SPS-43A, the prominent 12.8m long antenna which had been used in SPS-17A and 37A. SPS-43A was used mainly in aircraft carriers where, from the beginning of the 1980s, they began gradually to be replaced by SPS-49. From their introduction in March 1961 a total of 49 installations was delivered.

SPS-48

Of the series of three-dimensional FRESCAN detecting installations, SPS-48 was for a time the most effective variant. The need for its development was apparent in 1959 when it was realized that the performance of SPS-39/42 was unsatisfactory for use in the long-range Talos guided missile system. By 1960 an order for the construction of the first two installations had been placed. It required only three years before the first tests took place in USS *Preble* (then DLG-15). The first production model was apparently installed in March 1965 in *Worden* (DLG-18). At that time the range was approximately 230 miles. The antenna is a rectangular shape measuring 5.2 × 5.3m, weighing something over 2 tons. When installed its performance was compared with that of ten SPS-8s or with that of two SPS-2s. Certain SPS-48A installations were subsequently upgraded as SPS-48Cs. The most modern version SPS-48E is involved in the programme 'New Threat Upgrade' for Standard-SM-2-ER installations. Together with SPS-49, SPS-48 could be considered (at the beginning of the 1980s) one of the best standard installations and this is valid not just for guided missile ships but for other ships as well.

SPS-49

A two-dimensional air search system which appeared from the end of the 1970s parallel with SPS-40. The first designs for this item date back to the early 1960s. Tests took place in USS *Gyatt* (DD-712, ex-DDG-1) from July 1964 to January 1965. At that time, however, the improved version of SPS-40 was given

preference as it represented better value. The introduction, therefore, of a by then much improved SPS-49 was delayed until 1976 when the first production model was installed in USS *Dale* (CG-19). Subsequently SPS-49 was fitted in cruisers of the CG-47 class and in guided missile frigates of the FFG-7 class. The thirty-first unit of the *Spruance* class, *Hayler* (DD-997) was also supplied with SPS-49, the first ship of this class to receive it. In aircraft carriers SPS-49 replaced SPS-43A from the beginning of the 1980s. The range then was 250 miles; it could well now be greater. The antenna has an outer dimension of 7.3 × 4.3m and weighs approximately 1.4 tons.

SPS-52

A development of SPS-39 in the chain of 3-D systems which more recently has been fitted not just in guided missile ships but also in amphibious multi-purpose ships (LHA). The SPS-52 antenna, which is considerably lighter than the SPS–48, works in conjunction with the old SPS-39 installation. It permits a small aircraft to be detected at 60 miles, and its maximum range is 245 miles. SPS-52C, with its somewhat modified antenna, is the most important sensor for the SYS-1 installation which is part of the LADT System ('Integrated Automatic Detection Tracking System').

SPS-67

A new surface search radar which was first introduced in *Long Beach* (CGN-9) after she was converted in 1981-82. Essentially SPS-67 corresponds with the old SPS-10 installation the antennae of which it uses; its interior design is more modern, however, and it is more economic to maintain.

SPY-1

The newest multi-function radar of the air defence system AEGIS in (initially) guided missile cruisers of the CG-47 class. Each installation has four 3.7 × 3.7m surface arrays (which do not rotate) arranged in phase, which can be set to cover the entire 360° horizon in four different directions. Development began in 1965. AEGIS functions with guided missile fire control system Mk 99, responsible for fire control of the standard SM-2 in ships of the *Ticonderoga* class. AEGIS itself comprises detection, tracking, IFF, ECM and ECCM functions. SPY-1 can detect, track and attack simultaneously hundreds of aerial targets at distances of several hundred miles. AEGIS ships can integrate their system with those of other air defence systems carried by other ships in their formation. The complete AEGIS system was tested in *Norton Sound* (AVM-1) at sea from 1974. The first production model was fitted in USS *Ticonderoga* (CG-47) from 1982.

Aircraft

Experience gained during the first war proved the value of aircraft for spotting and reconnaissance, and after the war all battleship and cruiser classes (except *Atlanta*) were designed to carry as many aircraft as possible. Light cruisers of the *Omaha* class carried two aircraft. All other cruisers, with or without a hangar, normally carried two to four. In flagships a fifth 'personal' aircraft for the admiral was usually stowed. Recent evidence shows that there was a fifth aircraft in the cruisers *Chicago* (CA-29), *Indianapolis* (CA-35) and *San Francisco* (CA-38), and possibly in some other ships. Stowage of additional aircraft depended on whether the ship had a hangar or not. The *Omaha*s and *Pensacola*s did not have one. One or two additional aircraft, with wings folded, could be stowed between the two catapults, but this left the aircraft on the catapults very exposed to the weather. In the *Cleveland* and *Baltimore* classes 'parking space' on the after deck was wider. The *Alaska* class and other pre-war classes all had hangars. Theoretically the *New Orleans* class could take up to eight aircraft: four with folded

wings in the hangar; two with folded wings on deck between the catapults; and two on the catapults in a state of readiness. The hangar in the *Brooklyn* class, situated aft, was unusually roomy, extending forward to the barbette of the after triple turret. This could house in dry conditions: six Type SOC aircraft with folded wings; one further dismantled aircraft; and several piston engines. Aircraft were brought into the hangar by a deck crane. Theoretically it was possible to accommodate eleven aircraft, but this was never attempted. The normal practice was to carry four, at most five aircraft, which were sufficient for a continuous scouting operation.

As aircraft became increasingly heavier, take-off assistance from a catapult became necessary, and battleships and cruisers were equipped with one or more catapults for use in favourable weather. Normally two catapults were fitted in cruisers. In *Brooklyn*, *Wichita* and the later classes, the catapults were right aft on the quarterdeck; in the *Alaska* class and other pre-war cruisers they were amidships, paired with a

powerful crane. In the latter classes there was a high, roomy turntable of approximately 4m diameter, which turned a track of approximately 21 metres in length. Inside this turntable were stores, workshops and even a dark-room for developing film. If it was required to launch an aircraft while the ship was under way, the catapult cantilever would be pointed to port or starboard and the ship turned into the wind. The 'dolly', i.e., the set of rails on which the aircraft's main float rested, was hurled forward by the impetus of an explosive charge to the end of the cantilever, the aircraft, with its throttle open, receiving sufficient momentum (approx. 70mph) to enable it to take off. The catapult cantilever was in a relatively high position so as to ensure that the aeroplane took off well clear of the water.

Recovery was attended by considerable dangers for both ship and aircraft, especially if the sea was rough. The ship would turn into the wind and slow down, to achieve a zone of calm water on which the seaplane would settle. Matting was let down from the ship on to the surface of the water in front of the aircraft. The upper surface of the mat had a net of cordage containing a hook which would catch the underside of the main float. The aircraft's engine would then be switched off and the aircraft was hauled in by the slowly travelling ship until it could be lifted by crane either to its catapult or to the hangar deck. This method of recovery required a well-trained crew, but the ship could at least remain under way, which was of great importance if enemy aircraft or submarines were in the vicinity. The total shutting down of a ship's engines during a recovery took much too much time and rendered the ship helpless.

Prior to July 1937 aircraft were organized as Observation Squadrons (VO) for battleships and Scouting Squadrons (VS) for cruisers. These squadrons were orientated according to the existing BATDIV and CRUDIV. Each ship division had a VO or VS squadron. From July 1937 a squadron apportioned to a cruiser division received the designation VCS (Cruiser Scouting Squadron), and its designation number corresponded to the number of the cruiser division. If a ship were switched to another CRUDIV the corresponding squadron section would be given the new number and its aircraft would be given new markings. Squadron strength varied proportionately the composition of the division. VCS 2 and VCS 3 had, for example, usually six to eight machines, while VCS of the divisions with the *Brooklyn* cruisers had 16 to 20 machines. In 1939 there were in all, 124 aircraft in the active cruisers and 38 in the battleships. From mid-1941 there was a total of 2,000, most of them stationed on land bases. All the reconnaissance types were convertible, i.e., their undercarriage could be replaced fairly easily by floats. At the end of the war there were still 1,093 VO/VS aircraft; through the construction of more battleships and cruisers,

the percentage figure for aircraft carried aboard ships had become greater, while the requirement for corresponding land-based aircraft had become rather smaller.

For a short period between 1939 and 1941, aircraft of VO and VCS squadrons could be distinguished by the appearance of the tail fin: in VO squadrons it was painted in stripes. At about the time the USA entered the war, all such distinguishing marks were removed.

The manufacturing companies of Curtiss and Chance Vought were responsible for the planning, development and production of a total of seven different types of aircraft installed in battleships and cruisers from the mid-1920s until the end of the war. Many of these types, for example the SOC Seagull and OS2U Kingfisher, were produced in large numbers and were installed over a long period of time.

By the time the war ended in 1945, the seaplane had long been in decline. From the few battleships and cruisers remaining in active service, as, for example, the *New Orleans* class, one or two aircraft cranes had been removed even during the war on the grounds of weight. From the end of the war the installation of aircraft ceased totally, and catapults were removed. The roomy hangars were mostly used to stow picket boats for which the remaining cranes could be well employed. Two reasons for the cessation of aircraft installations may logically be adduced: the reconnaissance and fire control roles that aircraft had carried out had been taken over by radar and electronic fire control; while at this time the first helicopters were being fitted aboard ships. Subsequently, helicopters would come to carry out utility roles aboard many types of surface ships.

In the mid-1960s an ambitious attempt by the US navy to install the helicopter drone anti-submarine system DASH (Drone Anti-

Submarine Helicopter) in many frigates (DLG/DLGN), destroyers (DD) and escort ships (DE), proved, apart from a few applications, a complete failure. It had been intended that the small drones should carry short anti-submarine torpedoes or drop depth-charges.

In 1971 the introduction of the LAMPS-1 weapon system (Light Aircraft Multi-purpose System) followed, the most important component being the relatively light helicopter SH-2D/F. This helicopter and its appropriate equipment in the ship provided an extended arm in the sphere of ASW. The LAMPS-I system was still in being thirteen years after its introduction, extended in fact by the introduction of a new SH-2. Originally LAMPS-I had been intended as an interim system until LAMPS-III was operationally ready, but LAMPS-III is proving to be so expensive that delivery – originally scheduled from 1984 – is proceeding very hesitantly and fewer ships will receive it than had been planned. LAMPS-III can be regarded as a profoundly wide-ranging development, having parallels with the aircraft from the era of the classic gun cruiser, bringing to modern cruisers an extensive airborne component for surface and ASW warfare. Both the LAMPS systems are fitted in, among other ships, those large guided missile ships which, in mid-1975, were 'promoted' from frigate (DLG/DLGN) rank to cruiser (CG/CGN).

▽ During the 1960s and 1970s helicopters were used as courier and flag transports. The photograph on the left shows a UH-2B Seasprite about to land on *Albany* (CG-10) on 21 April 1972. On the right is an H-19 aboard *Newport News* (CA-148) at Hamburg in 1963.

AIRCRAFT CARRIED ABOARD US CRUISERS

Vought VE-9

The VE-9 was the naval version of the wheeled aircraft VE-7 introduced in 1918. As in all older models, the adaptation of an aircraft for naval use meant merely that the wheels were replaced by one main and two wing floats. This type appeared for the first time in June 1922 in *Nevada* (BB-36). In contrast to the original type VE-7, most VE-9s were unarmed. In all, twenty-one VE-9s were built. The last of the type disappeared from fleet use in September 1928. Its replacement was:

Vought UO

A total of 163 of these were built, in four marginally improved versions. Its air-frame was similar to that of VE-7, but its engine was more powerful by 200hp. Like VE-7, UO was also a biplane with a two-man crew, and was unarmed. It was introduced in June 1924 in *Tennessee* (BB-43), and remained in service until the end of 1929.

Vought 02U/03U Corsair

Planned from 1926, 02U was installed in battleships with squadrons VO-3B, -4B and -5B. This type had a fixed machine-gun and a twin machine-gun in the observer's position and could also carry small bombs under its lower wing. From 1930 an improved model, 03U-1, was introduced of which 87 were produced. This version was installed in battleships and cruisers, and – with wheels – in aircraft carriers. This type was not withdrawn from squadron use until mid-1941. During the intervening period came the:

Curtiss SOC Seagull

This was put into operational use from the autumn of 1935. Although production ceased in mid-1939, it remained a very successful biplane, chiefly on account of its folding wings, and it remained in some ships until the end of 1945. SOCs operated from battleships and cruisers, beginning with VS-5B from the end of 1935. Its service period was very extended. A total of 64 Seagulls were built in navy factories; they were designated SON.

Curtiss SO3C Seamew

This was a monoplane and was less successful. It first saw squadron use from mid-1942 with VCS-12 in *Cleveland* (CL-55). After the construction of 141 units, production ceased. It was withdrawn from squadrons from March 1944 while other deployed SOCs were still kept in use.

Vought OS2U Kingfisher

This, the most popular reconnaissance aircraft, was delivered to VO-4, i.e., to BATDIV 4 from August 1940. A total of 1,218 had been delivered by November 1942; 129 were built by the navy and were designated OS2N. A disadvantage was that the wings could not be folded, so it was installed initially in newer cruisers and battleships that did not have hangars. The older cruisers were unwilling to give up their SOCs because they allowed for easier stowage. Kingfishers remained in VO/VOC squadrons until 31 May 1946.

Curtiss SC Seahawk

This was the last reconnaissance type, introduced quite late in October 1944 in *Guam* (CB-2). Its wings could be folded. A total of 577 – not just for service aboard ship – were built before their service in squadrons was discontinued in October 1949.

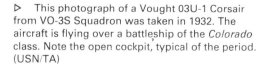

△ This Vought seaplane, Type VE-7G, was similar in appearance to the VE-9, the first series reconnaissance aircraft that was fitted in US battleships from 1922. The photograph was taken on 19 October 1922. (USN/TA)

▷ This photograph of a Vought 03U-1 Corsair from VO-3S Squadron was taken in 1932. The aircraft is flying over a battleship of the *Colorado* class. Note the open cockpit, typical of the period. (USN/TA)

◁ A UO-1 two-seater photographed in about 1931. As can be seen on the fuselage, this aircraft belonged to the battleship *Tennessee* (BB-43). (USN/TA)

◁ This Curtiss SOC-3 Seagull – seen here at Oakland airfield – belonged to the battleship *Pennsylvania* (BB-38) and was flown by VO-1 Squadron. For the first time one sees that the cockpit could be completely enclosed. This aircraft's tail fin is painted completely in red. The wings could be folded which meant that the aircraft could be stowed close together in narrow hangars. A Type SOC was tried out in about 1938/39 in the German light cruiser *Leipzig*. (USN/TA)

◁ The Curtiss SC-1 Seahawk was the US Navy's last reconnaissance aircraft and was installed in battleships and cruisers. It differed from the Kingfisher in having a thicker strut to the main float, a shorter, single-seat cockpit, by the pronounced forward slope to the tail fin and a more squat engine housing. The photograph was taken on 25 July 1947 over the Hawaii island of Oahu. The aircraft belonged to VO-1B Squadron.

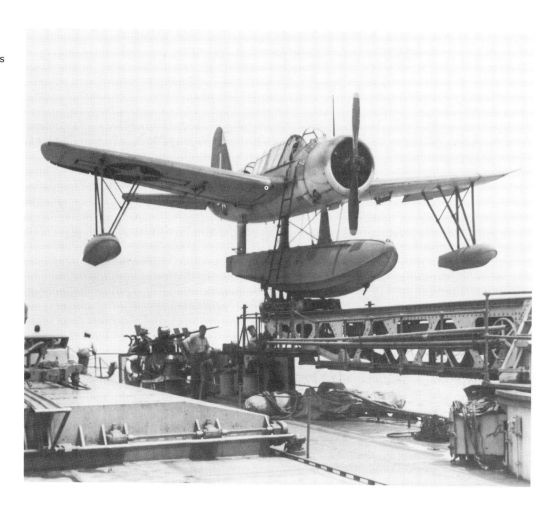

▷ A Vought OS2U-1 Kingfisher off Okinawa, 8 June 1945. The parent cruiser's port catapult, hangar mechanism and crane are clearly seen, as is the aircraft's long, two-seater cockpit with plexiglass hood. The airframe was supported on the main float by three struts. (USN/TA)

AIRCRAFT ON US CRUISERS: SUMMARY

Type	Name	Manufacturer	First employed	End of squadron service	Crew	Engine HP	Max weight Kg	Service ceiling m	Max range miles	Weapons	Remarks
VE-9		Vought	June 1922 in *Nevada*	30 Sept 1928	1	180	945	4,575	291	—	21 built
UO		Vought	14 June 1924 in *Tennessee*	31 Dec 1929	1	200	1,037	5,700	398	—	Versions UO-1, -2, -5; total of 163 built
02U/03U	Corsair	Vought	15 July 1930 in VO-3B	30 June 1941	2	450	1,635	5,700	608	three 0.30in MG	Versions 02U-1, -2, -3, -4; total of 291 built
SOC	Seagull	Curtiss	12 Nov 1935 in VS-5B	30 Nov 1946	2	600	2,446	4,544	675	two 0.30in MG two 150kg bombs	Versions SOC-1, -2, -3, SON-1; total 259 built
SO3C	Seamew	Curtiss	Sept 1942 in VCS-12 *Cleveland* (CL-55)	31 Mar 1944	2	600	3,150	4,819	1,150	One 0.30in and one 0.50in MG two 150kg depth-charges or two 45kg bombs	Versions SO3C-1, -2, -2C, -3; total 141 built
OS2U	Kingfisher	Vought	16 August 1940 in VO-4	31 May 1946	2	450	2,700	3,965	805	two 0.30in MG	Versions OS2U-1, -2, -3, OS2N-1; total 1,218 built
SC	Seahawk	Curtiss	22 Oct 1944 in VCS-16 *Guam* (CB-2)	1 Oct 1949	1	1,350	4,050	11,376	625	two 0.50in MG two 150kg bombs	Versions SC-1, SC-2, total 141 built

Colour Schemes and Camouflage

Even after the installation of radar detection equipment it was not possible to dispense with visual recognition of warships. Certainly, by radar one could establish exactly the distance of a ship or formation, but not what type of ship was involved. At best one could distinguish between large, larger and smaller ships. If it were essential to identify type or class, the only recourse was visual reconnaissance. Only rarely could this information be supplied by submarines; the task usually fell to spotter aircraft, but it was no means simple to identify a warship positively, and camouflage made the job even more difficult. Camouflage is, in effect, a term used to describe any measure that renders more difficult the estimation of distance, course or speed, and the identification of a ship's class. The ingenious use of sail cloth can make baffling changes to a ship's silhouette. Invariably auxiliary cruisers had dummy funnels, and mock superstructures were added to confuse or deceive the enemy. Even more than in the first war, the US Navy during the Second World War disguised their ships by means of paint camouflage. The guide lines for the use of diverse camouflage measures were constantly amended according to changing circumstances and newly acquired knowledge.

Until 1940, US cruisers were painted light grey. The shade of colour was known as 'light gray' and, from September 1937 as 'light gray a', designated as (applied colour: No. 5 'outside Navy gray'). This paint – not to be thought of in any sense as camouflage paint – had another name – 'peace gray'. Those ships' decks that were steel plated were painted dark grey (applied colour No. 20 'outside Deck gray'), while any wood planking was left in its natural colour. The boot topping and funnel caps were black. One should mention that different colour arrangements prevailed for other classes of ship, e.g., for submarines, and vessels of the Coast Guard Service (USCG) which were not under Naval control in peacetime. In January 1941 new guide lines for camouflage were published. Various systems of camouflage known as 'measures' were set out. The following were introduced for cruisers:

Measure 1 Dark Gray System. Vertical surfaces and steel decks were painted dark grey ('dark gray', 5-D) with only the superstructure and mast above the funnel caps in light grey ('light gray, 5-L). The wooden decks remained in their natural colour.

Measure 3 Light Gray System. This resembled the 'Peace gray' measure, but in a slightly different shade –'light gray'. Decks were logically painted as in Measure 1.

Measure 5 Painted Bow Wave. Used in conjunction with Measure 1 and characterized by a white artificial bow-wave on the ship's side ('white', 5-U). Although the previously prescribed measures had been rescinded by September 1941 and replaced by new ones, it took some time before all ships were painted in accordance with the new guide lines. To take an example, Measure 1 was in wide use in December 1941. It was still found in smaller ships as late as 1943.

The new measures as applied to cruisers were:

Measure 11 Sea Blue System. All vertical surfaces were sea blue ('sea blue', 5-S) with all deck surfaces (even those with wooden planking) blue-black ('deck blue', 20-B).

Measure 12 Graded System. All vertical surfaces of the hull from the boot topping (this was, as always, black) up to the main deck were sea blue ('sea blue', 5-S), the superstructure ocean grey ('ocean gray', 5-O), the tops of the masts and topmost superstructure a misty grey ('haze gray', 5-H). The dividing line between sea blue and ocean grey followed the line of the main deck, even when this was not a straight but an irregular line. The deck colour was similar to Measure 11.

Measure 12 'splotch' As a variant from Measure 12, irregular patterns of spots replaced the sharp dividing lines on the hull - sea blue with ocean grey blurs on the upper portion and ocean grey with misty grey patches on the superstructure.

Measure 12 'mottled' A further variation from Measure 12 and similar to it, but with a dappling pattern effect.

Measure 14 Ocean Gray System. Vertical surfaces ocean grey ('ocean gray', 5-O), mast tops and topmost superstructure mist-grey ('haze gray', 5-H). Decks as in Measure 11. In June 1942, the camouflage systems were altered once again. Officially only Measure 14 remained unchanged, the others being eliminated. However, it was to be some time before all ships could be repainted. For example, Measure 12 'splotch' was seen on many ships until the end of 1942. The new directives were:

Measure 16 Thayer System. This and the following measure were intended for ships serving in northern waters in long daylight periods. Vertical surfaces were white ('white', 5-U) and light blue ('Thayer blue', 5-B), the dividing line followed certain geometric figures which were different on port and starboard sides of the ship.

Measure 17 Was an experimental system to try out 'dazzle patterns' later to be introduced. Vertical surfaces were apparently navy blue ('navy blue', 5-N), ocean grey ('ocean gray', 5-O) and mist-grey ('haze gray', 5-H) in a geometrical pattern, identical on port and starboard sides – something that was peculiar to this measure only.

Measure 21 Navy Blue System. This was the measure most commonly used. All the vertical surfaces were of the same navy blue ('navy blue', 5-N).

Measure 22 Graded System. Vertical surfaces of the hull from waterline to an imaginary line parallel to the waterline through the deepest part of the main deck were painted navy blue; everything above this including the rest of the hull and superstructure were ocean grey. In contrast with Measure 12 the dividing line ran parallel with the waterline.

All the previous described measures had these in common: boot topping black ('dull black', BK), deck dark blue ('deck blue', 20-B) and lower surfaces of the overhangs white ('white', 5-U).

In March 1943, new directives were promulgated, and further systems of camouflage were introduced. On this occasion, while Measure 17 was eliminated; the others currently in use (14, 16, 21 and 22) were retained. Now were introduced the so-called 'dazzle patterns', systems with patterns designed to confuse. The 'dazzles' were made up from many colours and consisted of very carefully determined geometric figures. The measure suggested only the basic shades of colour to be used. The separations into colours were to be made according to fixed colour plans which were called 'designs' (patterns). These were provided with a number/letter combination with the letter determining the ship's class for which the pattern had originally been designed. Hence 'a' denoted aircraft carrier, 'b' battleship, 'c' cruiser, 'd' destroyer and so on. It is noteworthy that most cruisers carried patterns that had been intended for destroyers.

The schematic ideas ('measures') and the patterns ('designs') could now be combined with one another in any way imaginable. Measure '32/10c' indicated therefore that the colour tones of Scheme 32 were combined with the colour patterns of Design 10c. In all these dazzle measures the colours were either dark blue, or the decks could be painted in a pattern of dark blue and ocean grey. There were new introductions from March 1943:

Measure 31/ . . . Dark Pattern System. This

system relied heavily on dark colours; there is to date no positive proof that it was used on cruisers.

Measure 31a/ . . . Medium Pattern System, Low Contrast. This involved medium colour tones with little contrast to one another. The two-colour patterns were navy blue and mist grey. In the three-colour patterns, ocean grey was added to these two. These colours were applied only to vertical surfaces. The decks were painted as already described.

Measure 32/ . . . Medium Pattern System, High Contrast. This system used strongly contrasting colours. The overall impression was 'medium light'. Two-colour patterns used light grey ('light gray, 5-L) and black ('dull black', BKO; in three-colour patterns; ocean grey was added.

Measure 33/ . . . Light Pattern System. This was a measure based on lighter colours. In two-colour patterns ocean grey and light grey were used; in three-colour patterns navy blue, mist grey and pale grey ('pale gray', 5-P). As an indicaton of how these worked out in practice, one should note that in aircraft carriers for example the 'dazzle pattern' camouflage paints might be applied in as many as six different shades of a colour.

The next directives for camouflage changes came in March 1945. As the 'dazzle' schemes (31 to 33) made vessels very visible from the air, they were dispensed with in view of the growing threat from Kamikaze aircraft. But Measures 14, 21 and 22 were retained even though it was rare at this time to see a cruiser using Measure 14. What was new was a modification of the well-tried Measure 12 and Measure 13. This last named had been made available as early as September 1941, but came into use only towards the end of the war.

Measure 12 modified Modified Graded System. Ships' hulls from the boot topping to the main deck line painted either in navy blue ('navy blue', 5-N) or navy grey ('navy gray', 5-N). Everything above the main deck line was ocean grey with the deck surfaces blue-black. This measure could be distinguished from Measure 22 in that the dividing line followed the line of the main deck. Furthermore, there was less contrast between the vertical surfaces of the hull and superstructure than in Measure 22.

Measure 13 Haze Gray System. In this all vertical surfaces were mist grey and the deck surfaces blue-black. As far as is known this meaure was not introduced until after the end of the war; there is no evidence of its being used on cruisers before then. Measure 13 then became the standard camouflage system until 1953 when new

guide lines were made known.

Many cruisers started and ended the war with multi-coloured 'dazzle' camouflage patterns. Only *Pensacola* (CA-24) was given two such patterns, one after the other; all other ships received only one in the course of their period in service. It is noteworthy that cruisers mostly carried camouflage patterns that had been intended originally for destroyers, as will be seen from the next summary. Certain of these patterns were combined with different camouflage measures.

Systems introduced since March 1953 are:

Measure US 17 This corresponds to the earlier Measure 14. All vertical surfaces are ocean grey ('ocean gray, no. 17), decks in dark grey ('dark gray', A/B). As far as is known, this measure was not applied to cruisers.

Scheme US 27 Corresponds to the earlier Measure 13: vertical surfaces are mist grey ('haze gray', no. 27), the decks dark grey.

As far as is known there were no special directives as to camouflage colours for cruisers during either the Korean or Vietnamese Wars.

COLOUR SCHEMES IN VO/VCS SQUADRONS BETWEEN 1939 AND 1941

VO BATDIV	VCS CRUDIV	Colour scheme
1		red
2		white
3		blue
4		black
5		yellow
	2	
	3	red double-stripes
	4	blue stripes
	5	yellow stripes
	6	black stripes
	7	green stripes
	8	black double-stripes
	9	green double-stripes
	CL-7 +8	blue double-stripes

THE MATT BLUE-GREY CAMOUFLAGE COLOUR SPECTRUM

White, 5-U	Sea blue, 5-S
Thayer blue, 5-B	Navy blue, 5-N
Pale gray, 5-P	Dark gray, 5-D
Light gray, 5-L	Deck blue, 20-B
Haze gray, 5-H	Dull black, BK
Ocean gray, 5-O	

The above listed colours are only those which applied to cruisers. There were many additional colours, applied, for example, to battleships, smaller warships, landing craft and auxiliary vessels.

CAMOUFLAGE PATTERNS USED ON US CRUISERS DURING THE SECOND WORLD WAR

Pattern	Cruisers
11a	CL-57, 87
2c	CL-48, 49
7c	CB-2
10c	CL-101
1d	CL-7, 56, 81, 89, CB-1
3d	CL-8, 9, 58, 64
5d	CL-46
6d	CA-28, CL-62, 80, 86
7d	CA-33, 35
9d	CA-27
10d	CA-24
13d	CA-37, 38
14d	CA-24, 25
16d	CA-68
18d	CA-70, 71, 72
22d	CL-54, 97
24d	CL-53, 65, 66, 67, 90, 96, 103, 104

Two other 'dazzle' designs were not designated numerically; these were used in conjunction with special, seldom-used camouflage measures: Measure 16 ('Thayer System') on CL-43; and Measure 17 on CA-31.

APPLICATION OF 'DAZZLE' SCHEMES TO US CRUISERS (BY CLASS)

Pennant No.	Camouflage design	Pennant No.	Camouflage design
CL-7	32/1d	CL-56	33/1d
CL-8	33/3d	CL-57	32/11a
CL-9	32/3d	CL-58	33/3d
CL-11	32/2f	CL-62	33/6d
CA-24	33/10d	CL-64	33/3d
CA-24	32/14d	CL-65	32/24d
CA-25	33-14d	CL-66	33/24d
CA-27	32/9d	CL-67	33/24d
CA-28	32/6d	CL-80	32/6d
CA-31	17 dazzle	CL-81	32/1d
CA-33	33/7d	CL-86	33/6d
CA-35	32/7d	CL-87	32/11a
CA-37	33/13d	CL-89	32/1d
CA-38	33/13d	CL-90	33/24d
CL-43	16 Thayer dazzle	CL-101	31a/10c
CL-46	32/5d	CL-103	32/24d
CL-48	32/2c	CL-104	33/24d
CL-49	32/2c	CA-68	32/16d
CL-53	33/24d	CA-70	32/18d
CL-54	32/22d	CA-71	32/18d
CL-96	31a/24d	CA-72	32/18d
CL-97	33/22d	CB-1	32/1d
		CB-2	32/7c

For information on other camouflage measures, see comprehensive summary on page 317.

OMAHA CLASS

This was the US Navy's first class of what could be called 'true' light cruisers, designed on the basis of experience gleaned during the First World War. In combination with destroyers, which even then attained respectable speeds, these ships were to form the fast scouting vanguard of the fleet. They would also be superior to enemy destroyers and able to attack them with their 6in guns. Their development owes something also to the lessons learned by the British and Germans during the war.

With their four narrow funnels set in pairs, the *Omaha*-class ships had a strong resemblance to the much smaller, four-funnel destroyers which preceded them. They were the first American ships to have a tripod mast forward and – with the exception of the *Atlanta/Oakland* class – were the only American cruisers to carry torpedo tubes during the Second World War.

Specially noteworthy was the arrangement of the 6in main armament. Originally it was proposed to fit only eight 6in guns, in casemates (four on each side), but the final design had an additional 6in twin turret forward and another one aft, both on the centre-line, which from a weight point of view made the ship somewhat over-weaponed. Later, because of the weight factor in five ships the number of 6in guns was reduced and the rather deeper positioned casemate tubes were removed aft. These were the first American ships to have an alternative arrangement of boiler and turbine compartments, which was subsequently adopted in other cruiser classes. At the time of their completion these ships, with their speed of approximately 32 knots, were the fastest cruisers in the US Navy.

The fitting of two aircraft catapults, one on each side, increased the weight problem even more, and during the Second World War the catapults were removed from several ships. Apart from this, they did not undergo any extensive modernization during the war. The anti-aircraft weaponry was increased by the addition of 20 and 40mm guns and radar installations were later fitted. No ship of the class was lost during the war.

Milwaukee was lent from 1944 to 1949 to the Soviet Navy where she operated under the name *Murmansk*. Shortly after the end of the war all ships of this class were decommissioned and scrapped.

Omaha

1923 24 Feb Commissioned in Atlantic Fleet.
  Routine training with numerous visits to foreign ports, including Mediterranean and Caribbean.
1939–40 Neutrality patrols in mid-Atlantic.
1941 7 Dec Patrolled South Atlantic, hunting German blockade-runners.
1944 March To Naples in preparation for landings in South of France.
19–25 Aug Bombardment of Toulon. Returned to South Atlantic. Patrol duty until end of war.
1945 15 Aug Returned to east coast
1 Nov Decommissioned.

△ *Omaha* off Toulon, 20 March 1939. All twelve 6in guns are still in position. Two SOC scout aircraft are on their catapults. (MB)

▷ Dated 28 August 1943, this yard photograph was taken aboard *Milwaukee* looking forward. The most important explanatory numbers indicate: (3) platform for the newly fitted SK radar antenna; (7) newly fitted torpedo fire control; (8) 40mm twin Bofors with splinter screen; (9) newly fitted 20mm AA gun. (USN)

Milwaukee

1923 20 June Commissioned. Shake-down cruise to Australia. During the two decades between the world wars mainly on operations in the Pacific.

1938 3 Jan Cruising in Far East until

27 April then east coast.

1939 14 Feb Measured greatest depth of Atlantic – approximately 9220m; this position hence-forth known as 'Milwaukee depth'.

1941 7 Dec At New York Navy Yard.

31 Dec Departed for convoy duties in Caribbean.

1942 31 Jan Via Panama Canal; convoy duties to Society Islands; returned via the Panama Canal.

7 March South Atlantic Patrol Force operating out of Recife for next two years.

1944 8 Feb Left Bahia for New York Navy Yard until

27 Feb Convoy escort to Belfast.

29 March Convoy escort to Murmansk.

20 April Lent to Soviet Navy and served as *Murmansk*. In this capacity convoy escort in North Atlantic until end of war.

1949 16 March Handed back to USN.

◁ *Omaha* at New York Navy Yard, 10 February 1943. Only ten 6in guns remain, both the aftermost guns having been removed. Note how the camouflage Measure 22, combined with the very low freeboard aft gives the illusion that the darker painted area represents a much greater height of boot topping. (USN)

Cincinnati

1924 1 Jan Commissioned. Shake-down cruise to South America.

June With Scouting Force via east coast and Caribbean.

1925 Manoeuvres in Panama Canal·area, operations off east coast.

1927 17 Feb Left for Shanghai and Manila.

1928 April Returned to east coast. Manoeuvres off Hawaii.

25 July Arrived Newport, R.I.; operations off east coast.

1932 Transferred to Pacific Fleet, joining Battle Force.

1934 April–July With fleet, cruised to east coast.

1934 31 May Fleet review off New York; returned to west coast.

1935–38 Training cruises with naval reservists.

1939 Transferred to Atlantic Fleet.

1940 April Stationed once more at Pearl Harbor, visited Guam and the Philippines.

1941 March Returned to Atlantic. On entry of USA into the war, patrols and convoy escort in West Atlantic; blockaded Martinique and hunted German blockade-runners.

1944 Yard refit at New York.

March–July Convoy escort New York to Belfast.

28 July Left Norfolk for Mediterranean, took part in landings in South of France.

9 Sept Returned to New York for refit.

17 Nov Joined 4th Fleet at Recife, Brazil; patrol duties until end of war.

1945 summer Two midshipman training cruises.

1 Nov Decommissioned.

△ *Milwaukee* at the end of the 1930s. The forward upper starboard casemate gun has been swung out and is facing aft. The two after funnels are surrounded by four searchlights. Easily identified is the Mk 16 range-finder on the bridge housing. (USN)

▷ *Cincinnati* leaving New York Navy Yard pre-war. Typical in ships of this class is the rather pointed stern section. The lower after pair of 6in casemate guns have already been removed. (USN)

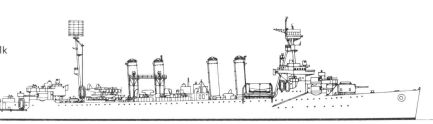

Cincinnati (CL-6) in July 1942. CXAM-1 radar is positioned on the top of the after mast. Mk 16 fire control can be seen above the row of bridge windows and abaft the housing of the torpedo tubes. There is only one SG radar antenna and Mk 3 radar on the forward mast. She still has two 28mm AA quadruple mountings with Mk 44 fire control.

∇ ▷ *Cincinnati* with Measure 12 camouflage, 8 July 1942. Even before the fitting of the heavy CXAM-1 radar antenna the after mast was tensioned with steel cables, and the funnels are also braced. There are 28mm quadruples forward and aft, 20mm Oerlikons and a 3in gun aft. On the forward masthead can be seen the Mk 3 and SG radar antenna. (USN)

F644 C2346 NAVY YARD, N.Y. JULY 8-42
USS CINCINNATI

Raleigh

1924 6 Feb Commissioned. Completing at New York Shipbuilding Crpn.

16 April Shake-down cruise off Virginia Capes.

30 July With Light Sea Cruiser Division, Scouting Fleet in northern European waters (Iceland, Greenland).

3 Sept Repairs at New York.

16 Oct Manoeuvres off east coast, west coast and Hawaii.

1925 13 July At Boston Navy Yard. For next two years operations off east coast.

1927 5 Feb Landed Marine Corps troops in Nicaragua.

1928 During first half of year operations off California and Hawaii.

15 April Flagship of Commander Naval Forces, Europe; visited several European ports.

26 June Returned to Boston.

1929 4 Sept Returned to Norfolk; with Light Cruiser Division 3, Scouting Force; operated for several years from Boston on east coast operations.

1973 15 August West coast, based on San Diego.

1936 27 April Transferred to east coast.

15 June At Norfolk Navy Yard.

27 Sept Security operations during Spanish Civil War.

1938 28 April Relieved by *Omaha*.

13 May At the Norfolk Navy Yard.

16 August With Flotilla 1, Destroyer Squadrons, Battle Force, then transferred to west coast.

5 Sept Arrived San Diego; several cruises to Caribbean and Hawaii as flagship, Flotilla 1.

1941 7 Dec Damaged by torpedoes in Pearl Harbor.

1941–42 Dec–Feb Repairs at Pearl Harbor; convoy escort to San Francisco.

1942 March–July Repairs at Mare Island Navy Yard.

23 July Joined TF 15; convoy escort to Hawaii, Samoa and Fijian Islands

24 Nov Arrived Dutch Harbor, Alaska.

1943 10 Jan Joined TG 8.6; occupation of Amchitka.

23 Mar At Puget Sound Navy Yard.

22 April Joined TG 16.6 at Adak.

Feb–12 August Bombarded Kiska.

August–Sept At Mare Island Navy Yard.

15 Sept Once again off Aleutians.

1944 1 Feb TG 94.6, bombarded Kurile Islands.

March–May At Puget Sound Navy Yard.

6 June Joined TF 94, suffered failure of half the engine installation; repairs at Puget Sound; transferred to east coast.

July Two midshipmen training cruises in Caribbean and off east coast.

2 Nov Decommissioned.

◁ This is how *Raleigh* appeared in July 1942 after work at Mare Island Navy Yard. One sees quite clearly the effect of the dark paint used in Measure 21. She has 40mm twin AA guns in addition to the 20mm AA machine-guns. SC radar can be seen on the after mast. There are still four searchlights in the area of the after funnel group.

There is only one Mk 3 fire control radar. (USN)

▽ After her refit at Puget Sound Navy Yard *Raleigh* appears on 25 May 1944 camouflaged according to Measure 32/1d. A second Mk 3 fire control radar has been added and two searchlights removed. A deck house between both groups of

funnels has been extended in size. Changes are visible in the area of the forward masthead: the Mk 3 radar has been moved forward to make way for the SK antenna; a further addition is the support bar on the mast which carries the SG radar. (USN)

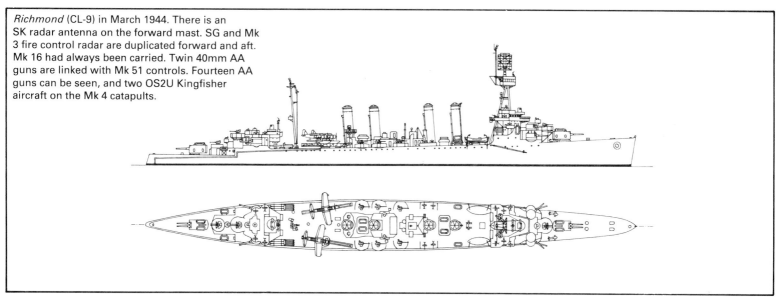

Richmond (CL-9) in March 1944. There is an SK radar antenna on the forward mast. SG and Mk 3 fire control radar are duplicated forward and aft. Mk 16 had always been carried. Twin 40mm AA guns are linked with Mk 51 controls. Fourteen AA guns can be seen, and two OS2U Kingfisher aircraft on the Mk 4 catapults.

△ *Detroit,* February 1942. This interesting detailed photograph of the forward mast bridge section shows that a fire control position has been installed over the upper casemate gun, and awaits the appropriate fire control equipment when the 40mm twins have been stripped. (USN)

▽ *Detroit,* seen on completion of work at Mare Island Navy Yard, 16 August 1942. Clearly, the bridge section has been somewhat modified. (USN)

Detroit

1923 31 July Commissioned; shake-down cruise in Mediterrean; with Scouting Force exercises in Mediterrean and along east coast.

1924 Sept–Oct Relay ship used in round-the-world flights of units of US Army Air Force.

23 Nov Flagship, Commander, Light Cruiser Divisions.

1924–25 Dec–Jan At Boston Navy Yard.

1925 2 Feb Transferred to Pacific Fleet; manoeuvres in Hawaiian waters.

10 July Returned to east coast.

1925–26 July–March and July–Dec Flagship, Light Cruiser Division 3; operations along east coast and in Caribbean.

1927 March–April Security duties off Nicaragua during unrest there.

16 June Flagship, Commander, Naval Forces Europe; goodwill visits to Europe, North Africa and eastern Mediterranean.

12 Sept Returned to Norfolk; flagship, Commander, Light Cruiser Divisions from 6 July to 29 September 1930.

1931 Jan Manoeuvres in Panama Canal area.

19 March Flagship, Commander, Destroyer Squadrons, Battle Force; at San Diego for several years.

1934 Manoeuvres in Atlantic.

1941 Returned to home base at Pearl Harbor.

1941 7 Dec At Pearl Harbor; immediately after Japanese attack, protection of Oahu Island and search for Japanese fleet formation.

10 Dec Convoy duty between Pearl Harbor and west coast. On one convoy 9 tons of gold and 13 tons of silver transported to San Francisco, from Corregidor in USS *Trout* (SS-202).

1942 August At Mare Island Navy Yard.

Sept Two convoys to Samoa.

10 Nov Left San Francisco for Kodiak, Alaska, to become flagship, TG 8.6. Protection of Aleutians until 1 January 1943.

1943 Feb–March At Bremerton yard.

April Bombardment of Attu.

August Bombardment of Kiska; remained in Alaska area until taking part with TF 94 in bombardment of Kurile Islands.

1944 25 June Left Adak for a yard period at Bremerton.

9 August Arrived Balboa; for a time flagship South East Pacific Fleet; cruises off South American west coast until December.

1945 16 Jan Left San Francisco for Ulithi.

4 Feb Duty there with 5th Fleet; flagship, Replenishment Group.

1 Sept Tokyo Bay.

15 Oct Sailed for USA, bringing troops home.
1946 11 Jan Decommissioned.

Richmond
1923 2 July Commissioned. Shake-down cruise to
Europe, Africa, South America. At end of year
Flagship, Scouting Force.
1925 Jan Flagship, Light Cruiser Division, Scouting Fleet. Cruises and manoeuvres along Californian coast and off Hawaii; goodwill cruise to
Australia and New Zealand.
1925–27 Nov–Feb Operations off east coast.
1927 Feb China Station for one year.
1928 July East coast for next six years.
1934–37 Oct–Dec Operations off west coast.
1937 21 Dec Flagship, Submarine Force, US
Fleet, until Dec 1940, then transferred to Pearl
Harbor.
1940 Jan–June Flagship, CRUDIV 3, Scouting
Force.
Nov Neutrality Patrol along Pacific coast of North
and South America.
7 Dec En route for Valparaiso, Chile.
1942 Escort duties, Pacific.
1942–3 Dec–Jan Mare Island Navy Yard.
1943 Jan Aleutians; Flagship, TG 16.6.
May Occupation of Attu.
Aug Bombardment of Kiska.
Aug–Sept Mare Island Navy Yard, remainder of
year patrolling Aleutians.
1944 4 Feb Bombardment of Kurile Islands until
end of war, then occupation of Northern Japan.
1945 14 Sept Returned to east coast via Pearl
Harbor and Panama Canal.
21 Dec Decommissioned.

△ *Detroit,* camouflaged according to Measure 33/3d, after completion of yard work at Bremerton, mid-1944. The number of searchlights has been reduced. SK radar has been added forward, and two SG and two Mk 3 antennae. (USN)

▽ *Richmond* in 1946, before her armament had been removed prior to being scrapped. Various light weapons and electronic installations have already been removed. (RPh)

◁ *Richmond* presumably in the 1920s. The primitive radio-telegraphy of the time made such long masts a necessity. She still has all twelve 6in guns and all ten torpedo tubes in four groups. (USN)

▽ *Richmond,* at the end of 1942. She has darker camouflage paint; both the aftermost 6in guns have been removed. (USN)

▽   An undated photograph of *Concord,* probably at the end of the thirties when her tall main top-mast had already been removed and the forward mast had been converted to a tripod with mast-head. All the 6in guns are still on board. (USN)

△ *Concord,* after November 1942, camouflaged according to Measure 22. Only ten 6in guns are shipped, the other two having been replaced by depth-charge rails in the stern. These had to be supported against the outer plating as the hull is very narrow at this point. On both catapults can be seen the latest reconnaissance aircraft, the Kingfisher. (USN)

Concord

1923 3 Nov Commissioned.

1923–24 23 Nov–9 April Shake-down cruise to Mediterranean. To Cape of Good Hope via Suez Canal, then flagship, Destroyer Squadrons Scouting Force.

1924–25 Transferred to Pacific; then returned to Atlantic.

1927 4 June Took part in fleet parade reviewed by President Hoover.

1932–34 Operated from San Diego as flagship, CRUDIV 3, Battle Force; manoeuvres in Panama Canal area and Caribbean.

1935 30 Sept and 1938 12 July Took part in fleet review in honour of President F. D. Roosevelt.

1938–39 winter Returned to Pacific, training cruises based on Pearl Harbor.

1941 7 Dec In yard at San Diego.

1942 Feb Escort duties in south-east Pacific, occasionally as flagship, South East Pacific Force.

1943 5 Sept–24 Nov Rear-Admiral R. E. Byrd on board to establish value of certain south-east Pacific islands for national defence. During this cruise aviation fuel explosion on board killed

22; damage repairs carried out at Balboa, Panama Canal area.

1944 March After completion of yard work sailed for Northern Pacific Force at Adak, arriving there on

2 April As flagship, TF 94; bombardment of Kurile Islands; remained in this area until end of war; from

1945 31 August Played a part in occupation of Japan.

14 Sept Returned to east coast via Pearl Harbor and Panama Canal.

12 Dec Decommissioned.

▽ *Trenton* at the end of the thirties, firing saluting salvoes. Twelve 6in guns are in place, but no catapults. (USN)

Trenton

1924 19 April Commissioned.

24 May Shake-down cruise to Mediterranean; through Suez Canal into Persian Gulf, returned via Mediterrean to east coast.

29 Sept At Washington Navy Yard.

mid-Oct Explosion in forward turret, all turret crew killed; until mid-Feb 1925 operations off east coast.

1925 Feb Transferred to Pacific fleet via Panama Canal; manoeuvres, some in mid-Pacific.

7 June Returned to east coast.

1 July–9 Nov With Light Cruiser Division 2 involving an extended cruise with Battle Force to Australia and New Zealand.

1928 Jan Landed Marine Corps unit in Nicaragua.

March With *Memphis* on Asiatic station.

1922–33 Operations off east coast and Central America; early in 1933 until September 1934 Pacific fleet, flagship, Cruisers, Battle Force, then returned to east coast.

1936 Jan Once more with Pacific fleet; at Mare Island Navy Yard, then with Battle Force, then in winter 1937–38 second cruise to Australia.

1939 May Atlantic fleet; with Squadron 40-T in Iberian waters until mid-July 1940 returned to USA.

1940 Nov With Pacific fleet, CRUDIV 3, Battle Force.

1941 Dec Balboa, Panama Canal area.

1942–44 Operations in south Pacific.

1944 August At yard, San Francisco.

2 Sept Transferred to Aleutians; patrol duties in the Aleutians, Kurile Islands and Alaska until end of war.

1945 1 August At Mare Island Navy Yard.

18 Nov To east coast via Panama Canal.

20 Dec Decommissioned.

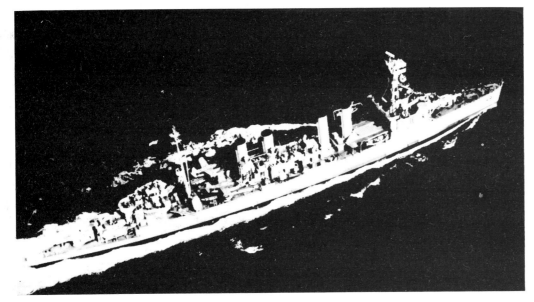

◁ Aerial view of *Trenton,* May 1943. The contrast between the two colours used in camouflage Measure 22 is very indistinct. The two sets of torpedo tubes are swung outwards. Cruisers without hangars shipped the Kingfisher. The older SOCs were retained mostly by ships that had a hangar, the folding wings allowing under-cover stowage. (USN)

▽ *Trenton* in San Francisco Bay, 11 August 1944. The starboard camouflage is Measure 32/2f. It is remarkable that all four searchlights are still in their peacetime position around the after funnel group. A Kingfisher aircraft is in position. (USN)

△ *Trenton circa* 1945, shortly before being decommissioned. She is camouflaged to Measure 21. The searchlight arrangement had not been reduced by August 1944. (Cas)

Marblehead

1924 8 Sept Commissioned; shake-down cruise to England and Mediterranean.

1925 Cruise to Australia; beginning of

1927–28 surveillance of political events and elections in Nicaragua; then to Shanghai with *Richmond* and *Trenton*, operating on River Yangtze until

1928 March Sailed to Boston with a tour in Nicaragua.

1928–33 August–Jan Operations along east coast.

1933–38 Feb–Jan Operations along west coast.

1938 Jan Detached to Asiatic Fleet based on

Cavite, Philippines.

1941 24 Nov With TF 5 departed for Philippines.

7 Dec There at outbreak of hostilities; convoys and patrols with Dutch and Australian ships in Dutch East Indies.

1942 Jan Covered withdrawal of Allied ships following attack on Japanese convoy off Balikpapan.

4 Feb Badly damaged from air by two Japanese bombs; 15 dead, 34 badly injured.

△ *Marblehead* in New York Navy Yard, 5 May 1944. Midships details of catapult installation on the starboard side, tensioned after mast and aftermost of the four funnels. (USN)

◁ The upper of the two detailed photographs of *Marblehead* shows details of the weaponry, i.e., the after 6in twin turret, an open and one uncovered twin 40mm and a Mk 51 fire control gear. The lower photograph is a view from the narrow quarterdeck of the after 6in turret, of the 20mm and 40mm AA guns (together with Mk 51 fire control) and one of the two range-finders and the Mk 3 and SK radar antennae. Both photographs were taken in New York Navy Yard on 5 May 1944. (USN)

13 Feb Began difficult passage with intermediate stop at Ceylon on 21st, where adequate repairs could not be carried out; left for South Africa.

24 March Arrived Simonstown; repair work until

15 April Departed for east coast USA.

4 May Refit at New York Navy Yard.

15 Oct Sent to South Atlantic Fleet; operations based on Recife and Bahia until February 1944. Five months of operations on convoy routes in North Atlantic, then departure for Palermo, Sicily.

1944 August New York Navy Yard.

29 July Preparation for landings in South of France.

15–17 August Fire-support of landings then returned to the USA; summer training cruise with midshipmen of Naval Academy.

1945 1 Nov Decomissioned.

△   *Marblehead* off New York Navy Yard, 6 May 1944, still camouflaged in Measure 22. There is a new deck-house between the funnels, a splinter screen for the 3in guns, and comprehensive radar equipment. There are only two searchlights on the third funnel which has not been lowered as in the other ships. Note the strong tensioning of the after mast. (USN)

▽   A very interesting photograph of *Marblehead* dating from the second half of 1944. (USN)

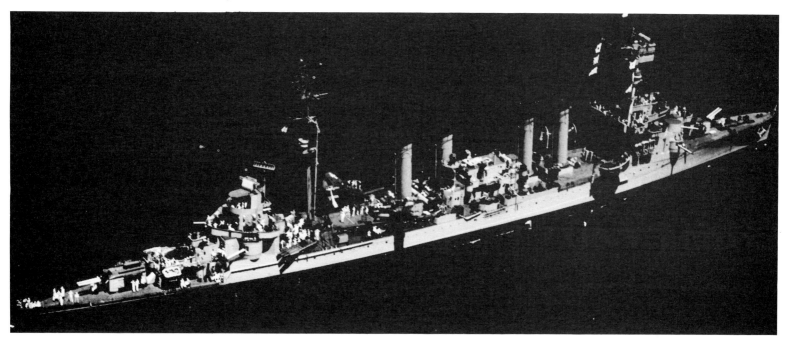

Memphis

1925 4 Feb Commissioned; shake-down cruises in Caribbean.

June Sailed from Honolulu with Scouting Force to South Pacific, visiting Australia and New Zealand until September 1925. Operations in West Indies from October 1925 until April 1926, then returned to New York. Sailed for France, arriving there 26 February 1926.

4 July Flagship, Commander, USN Forces Europe.

1926 4 July In European waters until 1927.

31 July–31 August At Santander, Spain.

3 June Took Charles A. Lindbergh and his 'The Spirit of St. Louis' aboard at Southampton and returned him to Washington on 11 June.

1928 Jan Accompanied President Coolidge to West Indies; four months of operations in Carribean; transferred to east Pacific.

1928–30 August–May On Asian station; operations along Central American coast, particularly off Nicaragua; approximately five years of operations in this area and along the west coast of USA.

1938 Jan Goodwill cruise to Australia.

1 April At Honolulu.

1939 12 July Took part in fleet parade off San Francisco.

August Sailed for Alaska, remained there until beginning of 1941.

1941 24 April Left Newport on neutrality patrol; arrived Recife on 10 May 1941. Operations in South Atlantic throughout most of Second World War.

1942 Nov Completed refit at New York Navy Yard.

1943 Jan President F. D. Roosevelt on board during Casablanca Conference.

Feb–Sept Further operations in South Atlantic until end of 1944.

1945 16 Jan Arrived Naples.

27 Jan Flagship, Commander, USN Forces Europe.

18 Feb At Algiers, while President F. D. Roosevelt attends last Allied Conference.

27 Oct Participated in Navy-Day festivities at Naples.

17 Dec Decommissioned.

△ *Memphis* off New York Navy Yard, 2 November 1942. Noteworthy are the deck-house between the funnels, and the very low line separating the colours as prescribed by Measure 22. Signalling flags are hanging out to dry. CXAM-1 radar is positioned on the after mast, here positioned laterally. (USW)

▽ *Memphis* in June 1945. Two Kingfisher aircraft are on their catapults. The Mk 3 fire control radar has its own mast. (USN)

PENSACOLA CLASS

This first class of US heavy cruisers was – until just before commissioning – given the same CL designation as had been given to the *Omaha* class. At that time light and heavy cruisers were differentiated on the basis of gun calibre not displacement. It was also the first US cruiser class to be developed in accordance with the terms of the Washington Treaty. Strict adherence to the treaty made it difficult to reconcile the conflicting requirements for firepower, armour and speed. The 'Washington Cruiser' could not exceed 10,000 tons standard, so designers were preoccupied with the following considerations:

It would not be possible to provide adequate armour protection against close-range 8in guns.

It did not become apparent until later that a ship's own 8in guns could keep an opponent of equal size at a range such that its own armour was sufficient protection against long-range hits by 8in shells. This view was to be overturned very decisively in the later generation *New Orleans* class.

8in guns were superior to 6in guns, so a light cruiser could be kept at a distance where its gunfire would be ineffectual.

The outcome was armour that could not withstand a direct hit from anything larger than a destroyer's 5in guns.

Distribution of the 8in turrets was quite remarkable: two twin and two triple turrets, as fitted in the *Nevada*-class battleships. But in these cruisers the two twin turrets were positioned lower than the two triple turrets; heavier weights above lighter ones. The reason for this was that at the point of installation the hull was too narrow to accommodate the sub-structure of the wider triple turret. Because the triple turrets were sited two decks higher than the twin turrets, not surprisingly the ships were top-heavy and rolled considerably in heavy seas. It was intended to relieve this condition by adding hull bulges at a later date. The two ships carried more 8in guns than any other class of US cruisers.

▽ *Pensacola,* the first cruiser to be completed in the 1930s. This photograph dates from that period. Note the tripod mast whose supports reach down to the main deck, and the rather high bridge construction reaching up to two decks. The very high position of No. 2 turret and the very high and heavy masthead contributed to a grave degree of top-heaviness. Torpedo tubes are still shipped. (L. L. von Münching Collection)

The class inherited the alternating arrangement of boilers and turbines of the *Omaha* class, so as to reduce the effect of damage from hits in the engine installation. If a boiler or turbine installation were put out of action by gunfire, a second one would be available.

The six torpedo tubes fitted originally were removed before the Second World War, when it was realized that it was unlikely that ships of this type would have an opportunity to carry out surface torpedo attacks. The tubes were fitted subsequently in the escort ships (DE). Two further measures to reduce top-heaviness were the removal in 1945 of the heavy tripod mast forward, and removal of the starboard catapult from *Pensacola*. Both ships had had the after tripod mast considerably shortened in 1941; a thinner, single pole mast was added behind the after funnel. These measures were applied effectively to *Pensacola* in 1945 and were to have been carried out in *Salt Lake City*, but the yard date allotted to this work was cancelled in view of the impending end of the war.

The peace-time armament was strengthened during the war by the addition of many 20 and 40mm AA machine-guns as photographs and the data tables show. Just before war began the number of 5in/25 AA guns was increased from four to eight. This was, incidentally, the only pre-war class of heavy cruiser not to have a hangar, consequently each catapult could only handle a light scout aircraft. Two more aircraft could have been stored on deck between the funnels. In the view of naval experts the *Pensacola* class was not an effective design. They can be seen as over-weaponed, inadequately armoured and not particularly seaworthy, this latter not solely on account of a too low freeboard. Yet both ships survived the war and, even after being used as test ships in the atom bomb tests off Bikini, they remained afloat.

Pensacola

1930 6 Feb Commissioned.
24 March–5 June Cruised along west coast of South America.

1930–34 Operations off east coast with occasional manoeuvres off Hawaii and California.
1935 15 Jan Transferred to Pacific Fleet.
3 Jan Arrived at San Diego; operated in Pacific until
5 Oct Stationed at Pearl Harbor.
1941 29 Nov Left Pearl Harbor in convoy to Manila.
7 Dec Diverted to Australia.
1942 5 Feb From Pearl Harbor to Samoa.
17 Feb Joined TF with *Lexington* (CV-2).
6 Mar With *Yorktown* (CV-5); Coral Sea.
21 April Returned to Pearl Harbor; sailed to New Hebrides with VMF-212.
4 June Participated in Battle of Midway.
13–22 June At Pearl Harbor, then transport of MAG-22 to Midway; patrols off Hawaii.
7 August Departed for Guadalcanal.
26 Sept Noumea, New Caledonia.
26 Oct Took part in Battle off Santa Cruz; took on 188 survivors of *Hornet* (CV-8).
12–13 Nov Battle of Guadalcanal; joined TF 67.
30 Nov Battle of Tassafaronga; badly damaged by

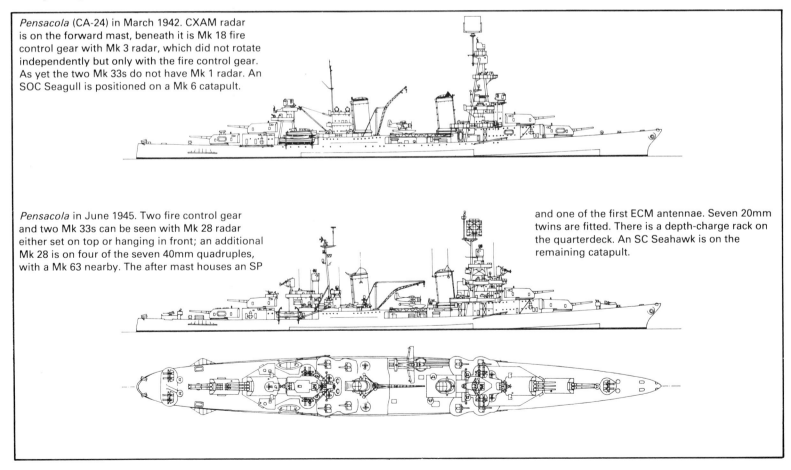

Pensacola (CA-24) in March 1942. CXAM radar is on the forward mast, beneath it is Mk 18 fire control gear with Mk 3 radar, which did not rotate independently but only with the fire control gear. As yet the two Mk 33s do not have Mk 1 radar. An SOC Seagull is positioned on a Mk 6 catapult.

Pensacola in June 1945. Two fire control gear and two Mk 33s can be seen with Mk 28 radar either set on top or hanging in front; an additional Mk 28 is on four of the seven 40mm quadruples, with a Mk 63 nearby. The after mast houses an SP and one of the first ECM antennae. Seven 20mm twins are fitted. There is a depth-charge rack on the quarterdeck. An SC Seahawk is on the remaining catapult.

a torpedo from destroyer; 125 dead, 68 wounded; provisional repairs at Tulagi.

1942–43 6 Dec–7 Jan Further repair at Espiritu Santo, left for Pearl Harbor 7 January.

1943 27 Jan–Nov Yard repairs at Pearl Harbor Navy Yard, given new superstructure aft.

1943 19 Nov Bombarded Tarawa.

1944 29 Jan Operations off Marshall Islands.

1 Feb Occupation of Roi and Namur.

30 March–1 April Carrier escort to Palau, Yap, Ulithi and Woleai.

25 April Left Majuro via Pearl Harbor.

May Mare Island (short yard stay); left for North Pacific.

27 May Arrived Bay of Kulak.

13–28 June Bombarded Kurile Islands.

13 August Arrived Pearl Harbor.

3 Sept Bombarded Wake Island.

9 Sept Bombarded Marcus.

16 Oct Liberation of Philippines.

20 Oct Invasion of Leyte.

25 Oct Battle of Cape Engaño.

11 Nov Bombarded Iwo Jima.

22 Nov At Saipan preparing for invasion of Iwo Jima.

1945 24 Jan Bombarded Iwo Jima.

16 Feb Repeated bombardment of Iwo Jima.

17 Feb Hit six times by shore battery, 17 dead, 119 wounded; short repairs.

19 Feb Once more off Iwo Jima.

5–20 March Repairs at Ulithi.

25 March Bombarded Okinawa.

15 April Left for west coast.

7 May–3 August At Mare Island Navy Yard for conversion. Until end of the war at Adak, Alaska; then with CRUDIV 5 occupation of North Honshu.

14 Nov Left Japan via Okinawa and Pearl Harbor for west coast.

3 Dec Arrived San Francisco.

1945–46 8 Dec–9 Nov 'Magic Carpet' cruise to Guam.

1945 29 April Left for San Pedro.

29 May Arrived Bikini Atoll; target ship for atomic bomb tests on 25 July 1946.

26 August Decommissioned.

△ *Pensacola* in Hawaiian waters in August 1942, while serving as a unit of the aircraft carrier *Hornet*'s task force. The difference in width of the double and triple turrets is very evident. The secondary armament of 5in/25 guns, which had been increased to a total of eight, have splinter screens. The old tripod main mast shows the Mk 35 rangefinder; this does duty as a base for Mk 3 fire control radar. Above it is the CXAM radar antenna. One can make out the 28mm quadruples and, near them, the 20mm Oerlikons. The Mk 33 fire control gear supports Mk 4 radar. (USN)

▷ *Pensacola* on 17 December 1942 in Espiritu Santo Bay, beside a tender while provisional repairs are being carried out for the torpedo damage sustained at the Battle of Tassafaronga on 30 November 1942. The CXAM radar can no longer be seen. (USN)

◁ During her short stay at Mare Island Navy Yard in May 1944, *Pensacola* was camouflaged in Measure 32/14d. This photograph was taken at that time. SK radar had been fitted a year earlier and the after superstructure had already been re-shaped. (USN)

▷ *Pensacola* was converted during her three months' stay at Mare Island Navy Yard in the summer of 1945. The photograph taken on 29 June 1945 shows how she looked after this conversion, painted in accordance with Measure 21. The shortening of the forward mast was the most effective measure in reducing top-heaviness. Note the roomy propeller guard which can be seen below the after 8in twin turret. (USN)

▷ This detailed photograph of *Pensacola* taken at Mare Island Navy Yard on 3 July 1945 shows clearly the position of Mk 28 fire control radar on the fire control gear Mk 33, on the Mk 35s and on four quadruples. At this time a total of eight Mk 28 radar antennae were shipped. Aircraft control radar SP was also fitted. Note the twin 20mm AA guns. (USN)

△ This is how *Pensacola* looked three months later on 18 October 1945 in Omnato, during the occupation of North Honshu. A Seahawk scout plane is on the single remaining port catapult. (USN)

△ This peace-time photograph of *Salt Lake City* dates from the first half of the 1930s and shows clearly the harmonious lines of the two ships of the *Pensacola* class. The torpedo tubes aft of the catapults were removed in May 1934 at a time when the Japanese were strengthening the torpedo armament of their own heavy cruisers. (USN)

▽ *Salt Lake City* on 21 June 1944 after she had been camouflaged in accordance with Measure 33/14d at Mare Island. Mk 4 radar is suspended in front of the two Mk 33s. As the after part of the ship's hull was painted in a light colour the designation number '25' was painted in a darker colour. It should be pointed out that – in contrast to the custom in German ships during the Second World War – American ships continued to carry their designation number quite visibly. (USN)

Salt Lake City
1929 11 Dec Commissioned as CL-25.
1930 20 Jan Shake-down cruise along the coast of Maine.
Feb–March Cruised to South America.
31 March Assigned to CRUDIV 9, Scouting Force.
12 Sept With CRUDIV 5.
1931 1 July Reclassified as CA-25.
1932 Fleet manoeuvres off west coast, remaining with Pacific Fleet.
1933 Jan–Feb To Pearl Harbor.
Sept Assigned to CRUDIV 4.
1933–34 Oct–Jan At Puget Sound Navy Yard.
1934 May Took part in fleet review off New York.
18 Dec Returned to San Pedro.
1935–38 Operations off west coast.
1939 13 Jan–7 April Short cruise to Caribbean.
1939–40 Oct–June Cruises to Hawaii, Wake, Guam.
1941 August Visited Australia.
7 Dec Accompanied by *Enterprise* (CV-6) returned from Wake; searched in vain for the Japanese attack formation.
15 Dec Pearl Harbor.
Dec Bombardment support with TF 8 at Wake, Midway, Samoa.
1942 Feb Marshall Islands.
3 April Marcus.

▽ *Salt Lake City* retained her Measure 21 camouflage for quite a long time, as can be clearly seen in this photograph of 10 May 1943; in other words, after the damage suffered in the Aleutians had been made good. Note the two 40mm Bofors quadruples with the splinter screens which project somewhat over the ship's side, and the fire control positions in front of them carrying Mk 51. Twelve smoke-generating canisters are housed aft. Mk 4 fire control radar is to be seen on the Mk 33. (USN)

4 April With CV-6 and CV-8 'Tokyo Raid'.
May With *Enterprise*, in a superfluous cruise, to the Coral Sea.
June Support duties at Midway.
August Landings on Tulagi and Guadalcanal.
15 August Took on survivors from *Wasp* (CV-7).
11/12 Oct The Solomons; Battle of Cape Esper-ance, hit three times by Japanese surface ships.
1942–43 Nov–March In yard at Pearl Harbor.
1943 March Aleutians with TF 8; badly damaged by Japanese surface ships.
23 Sept Departed for yard repairs in San Francisco.
14 Oct Arrived Pearl Harbor.
Nov In company with fleet carriers attacked Wake, Rabaul, Tarawa.
1944 29 Jan–17 Feb With TG 50.15 operations in Marshall Islands; Wotje, Majuro, Eniwetok, Kwajalein.
30 March–6 April Paiau, Yap, Ulithi, Majuro, Woleai (West Carolines).

△ *Salt Lake City*, without her starboard catapult, seen on 31 December 1945 in San Francisco Bay, having returned from a 'Magic Carpet' cruise bringing home military personnel from the combat areas of the Pacific. She was to have been converted in a similar way to *Pensacola*, but the end of the war rendered this intention superfluous. (Cas)

◁ The catapult installations and other details of the midships section of *Salt Lake City*, Mare Island, June 1944. (USN)

30 April Pearl Harbor, then to west coast.
7 May–1 July at Mare Island Navy Yard.
8 July Adak (Alaska).
13 August Returned to Pearl Harbor.
29 August Departed for Wake; fire support on 3 September.
1944 Sept–Oct Saipan, Marcus.
Oct Protected carrier groups during Second Battle of Philippines.
1944–45 Oct–Feb With CRUDIV 5 (TF 54) supporting carriers.

1945 March–May First operations off Iwo Jima and Okinawa.
8 August To Aleutians via Saipan.
31 August Occupation of Honshu.
29 Oct Transported military personnel to west coast; one catapult having been removed.
1946 March To Pearl Harbor to prepare for atomic bomb tests.
July At Bikini; survived both tests.
29 August Decommissioned.
1948 25 May Used as target ship and sunk.

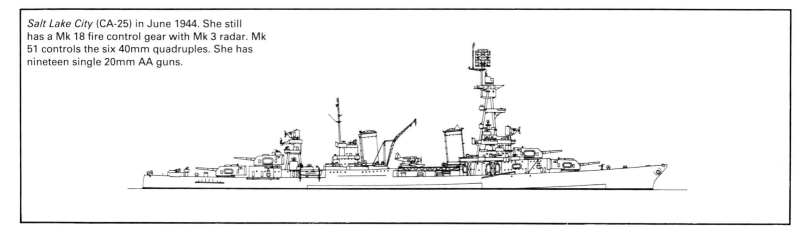

Salt Lake City (CA-25) in June 1944. She still has a Mk 18 fire control gear with Mk 3 radar. Mk 51 controls the six 40mm quadruples. She has nineteen single 20mm AA guns.

NORTHAMPTON CLASS

This design, dating from 1926, differed from the *Pensacola* class in having three 8in gun turrets instead of four, which was to be the armament in all future heavy cruisers. Dispensing with one gun gave advantages in weight. The two boiler compartments were separated by a bulkhead. Seaworthiness was improved with the fitting of a higher *forecastle*. *Augusta*, *Chicago* and *Houston* were built as flagships, the extra space to accommodate staff being achieved by extending the forecastle deck and its outer plating off to a point level with the catapults. Some sections of armour plating was stronger than in the previous class. In 1935 the six torpedo tubes were removed and the number of 5in/25 guns doubled. The forward funnel of *Northampton* was made taller in a rather unsightly manner; later during the war the forward funnel in all ships of the class were given a 'half' funnel capping to keep the bridge superstructure free of exhaust gases.

Northampton, *Chicago* and *Houston* were lost in the first years of war; the remaining three ships were subsequently modified.
Chester from 1945: A short mast forward, a new lattice mast aft.
Louisville from 1943: A half-height mast forward, a new lattice mast aft.
Augusta from 1943: A half-height mast forward, the old mast aft. From 1945: A half-height mast forward, a new lattice mast aft.

The complete superstructure behind the after funnel served as a base for many 20mm AA guns and for the fire control gear. The elimination of the original main mast gave the AA much more favourable arcs of fire. As the war continued the three remaining ships – as had been done previously with *Chicago* – were fitted with 40mm AA and a further two fire control instruments installed. Certain lateral openings on the main deck were plated over. From the outset, the installation of aircraft had been managed better than in *Pensacola;* four scout aircraft could be protectively housed. The two catapults, one on each side in the space between the funnels, were mounted high on turntables, the forward end of the catapult platforms projecting above the extended forecastle deck. This relatively high positioning was intended to help the aircraft to take off successfully whatever the weather. The ships were more stable and gave much better seakeeping than the *Pensacola*s.

Northampton
1930 17 May Commissioned as CL-26. Shakedown summer cruise to Mediterranean.
1931 Reclassified as CA-26.
1932–41 Mainly in the Pacific, first operating from San Pedro, then from Pearl Harbor.
7 Dec At sea with *Enterprise* (CV-6); searched for Japanese fleet.

1942 1 Feb Bombarded Wotje.
24 Feb Bombarded Wake.
4 March Attack on Marcus.
April 'Tokyo Raid' with *Hornet* and *Enterprise*, then departed to take part in Battle of Coral Sea, but arrived too late.
4–5 June Battle of Midway.
13 June Returned to Pearl Harbor.
August Operations off Guadalcanal.
5 Oct Carrier protection off Bougainville.
26 Oct Battle of Santa Cruz.
30 Nov Sunk by two torpedo hits during Battle of Tassafaronga.

▽ This historic photograph shows *Northampton* entering Pearl Harbor on 8 December 1941. The air is still thick with smoke as a consequence of the Japanese air attacks which had taken place the day before. Despite its poor quality the photograph shows two things clearly: the unattractive aspect of the funnel which had been heightened just before the war, and the combination of the two camouflage Measures 1 and 5, the latter being carried out in a bow-wave. One year later this name ship of the class was sunk by Japanese torpedoes. (USN)

△ *Northampton* during her first operational period at the beginning of the thirties. The overall harmonious lines of the ship should be noted. The torpedo tubes seen here were removed in the mid-thirties. At that time she had only four 5in/25 AA guns. (USN)

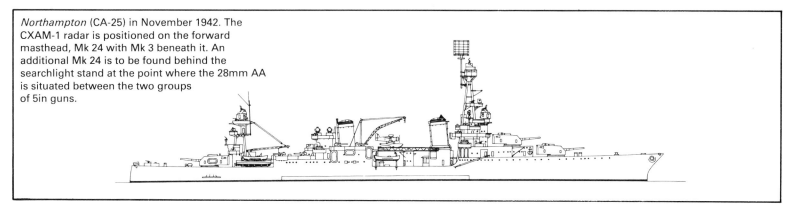

Northampton (CA-25) in November 1942. The CXAM-1 radar is positioned on the forward masthead, Mk 24 with Mk 3 beneath it. An additional Mk 24 is to be found behind the searchlight stand at the point where the 28mm AA is situated between the two groups of 5in guns.

Chester

1930 24 June Commissioned as CL-27.

1 July Reclassified as CA-27.

13 August Departed for Europe.

1931 March Manoeuvres in Panama Canal zone.

April At New York Navy Yard, including fitting of a catapult.

1932 31 July Departed for west coast; operations with Pacific Fleet from San Pedro.

1934 9 April Departed for east coast.

31 May Took part in fleet parade off New York.

9 Nov Returned to San Pedro.

1935 25 Sept Took Secretary of War to Philippines.

15 Nov Took part in Inauguration of the President of the Philippines.

14 Dec Returned to San Francisco, operated with CARDIV 4.

1936 28 Oct Left for east coast, departed Charleston, South Carolina accompanying *Indianapolis* (CA-35) carrying President F. D. Roosevelt; Goodwill Tour to South America.

24 Dec Returned to San Pedro.

1937 Operations off west coast, Hawaiian waters and Alaska.

1940–41 Sept–Jan At an east coast yard.

1941 3 Feb New home base at Pearl Harbor.

May–June Cruised to west coast.

10 Nov Escorted troop transport to Manila.

7 Dec Off Wake Island with TF 8, with *Enterprise* (CV-6) and *Northampton* (CA-26).

1942 18–24 Jan Supported landing on Samoa.

1 Feb With TG 8.3 attacked Taroa, suffered damage from aerial bombs, 8 dead, 38 wounded.

Feb Yard repairs at Pearl Harbor; then convoy escort to San Francisco with TF 17.

1942 4 May Attacked Guadalcanal – Tulagi.

8 May Participated in Battle of Coral Sea.

10 May Rescued 478 crew members of the sunken *Lexington* (CV-2).

June–August At a west coast yard.

21 Sept Arrived at Noumea to join TF 62.

20 Oct In Solomon Islands, hit by torpedo, 11 dead, 12 wounded, provisional repairs at Espiritu Santo from 23 October.

29 Oct Left for Sydney for additional repair work.

25 Dec Left for Norfolk for yard refit.

1943 13 Sept Returned to San Francisco, and

from there carried out escort duty to Pearl Harbor until 20 October.

8 Nov Left Pearl Harbor for invasion of Marshall Islands.

1944 25 April Departed for a short period at a yard from 6–22 May.

27 May At Adak, Alaska to join TF 94; bombarded Kurile Islands 13–26 June.

13 August Arrived Pearl Harbor.

29 August With TG 12.5.

3 Sept Bombarded Wake.

9 Oct Bombarded Marcus; joined TG 38.1.

25–26 Oct Escorted carriers and took part in Battle of Leyte.

1944–45 8 Nov–21 Feb Patrol duties around Ulithi and Saipan, including bombardment of Iwo Jima and Bonin Islands.

1945 March-June At a west coast yard for conversion.

21 June returned to Ulithi.

27 June Observation duties off Okinawa, with TG 95.2 to Yangtze Delta; protection of minesweepers until end of July.

August Operational cruise to Aleutians.

31 August Left to take part in occupation of various Japanese islands.

9 Oct Transported military personnel from Iwo Jima.

2 Nov Left for San Francisco.

18 Nov Arrived San Francisco.

Nov–Dec 'Magic Carpet' cruise to Guam.

1946 14 Jan Transferred to east coast.

30 Jan Arrived at Philadelphia.

10 June Decommissioned.

▽ *Chester* seen in the late thirties, when she still had only four 5in guns. The 0.5in machine-guns are on platforms on the forward mast. (USN)

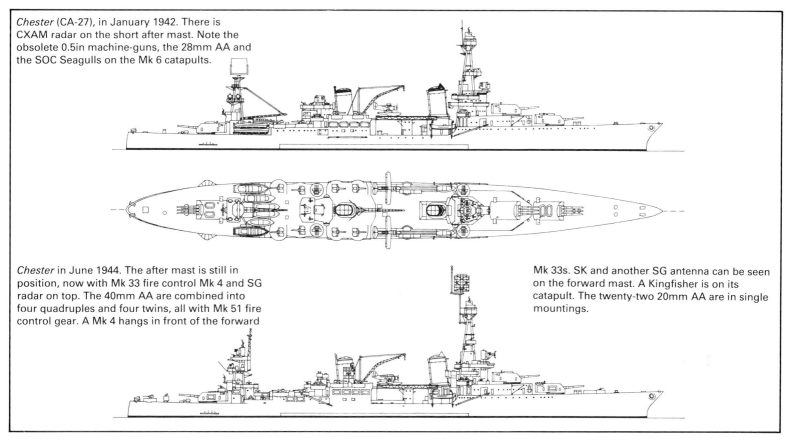

Chester (CA-27), in January 1942. There is CXAM radar on the short after mast. Note the obsolete 0.5in machine-guns, the 28mm AA and the SOC Seagulls on the Mk 6 catapults.

Chester in June 1944. The after mast is still in position, now with Mk 33 fire control Mk 4 and SG radar on top. The 40mm AA are combined into four quadruples and four twins, all with Mk 51 fire control gear. A Mk 4 hangs in front of the forward

Mk 33s. SK and another SG antenna can be seen on the forward mast. A Kingfisher is on its catapult. The twenty-two 20mm AA are in single mountings.

▽   *Chester* in October 1942, camouflaged according to Measure 21 (later 11). One can see clearly the additional 5in AA near the after funnel,

the 28mm quadruples, some 20mm AA and CXAM radar. The forward funnel has a half-cap.

Numerous survival rafts have been provided in addition to the ship's boats. (USN)

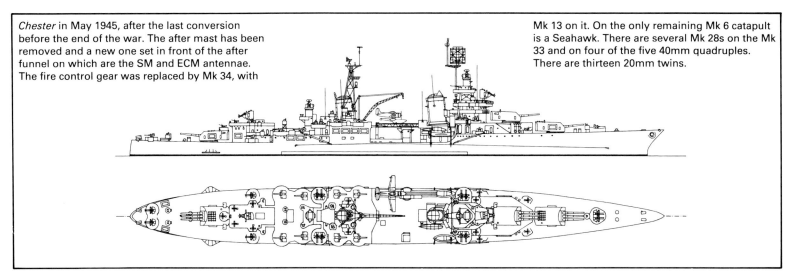

Chester in May 1945, after the last conversion before the end of the war. The after mast has been removed and a new one set in front of the after funnel on which are the SM and ECM antennae. The fire control gear was replaced by Mk 34, with Mk 13 on it. On the only remaining Mk 6 catapult is a Seahawk. There are several Mk 28s on the Mk 33 and on four of the five 40mm quadruples. There are thirteen 20mm twins.

▽ During her yard refit in the first half of 1943, *Chester* was given her 40mm Bofors installation. She is seen here in July 1943. The CXAM radar was later removed and replaced by SK. (USN)

▷ *Chester* as she appeared in October 1943, now with SK radar. One sees clearly the different arrangement of Mk 4 radar on both the Mk 33s. She is still camouflaged in Measure 21. (USN)

◁ *Chester* in dockyard hands in November 1944. She has a new camouflage Measure, 32/9D, and a modified bridge. (USN)

△▽ During a short yard stay in May 1944, *Chester* was repainted, this time in Measure 32/9d. These two photographs show the starboard and port patterns of this Measure. Note the Kingfisher scouts on both the catapults; only aircraft with folding wings could be accommodated in the two hangars. Most of the lateral openings have been enclosed. (USN)

◁ At the end of a 'Magic Carpet' cruise to Guam, *Chester,* lying high in the water, anchors in San Francisco Bay on 18 November 1945. This was the end of operational cruises for this ship and she was decommissioned approximately six months later. (Cas)

◁ △ *Chester* at Mare Island Navy Yard early in 1945 when a relatively quick, fundamental conversion was carried out which caused considerable change in her appearance. These three photographs illustrate the scope of the changes. The new tripod lattice mast has SM radar and ECM antennae TDY and DBM. There is a twin fire control combination Mk 34-13. Mk 63 is now installed together with Mk 28 fire control radar with the Mk 33, and there are also some 40mm Bofors mountings. In the interest of weight, one catapult has been removed. (USN)

△ *Louisville* in the early 1930s. Then, as now, ships carried the letter 'E' on the funnel or on another easily visible place as proof of the attainment of a performance level, something that had to be won each year. The 'E' appears very large. Note the considerable number of portholes, many of which were plated over during the Second World War. (USN)

▽ May 1942 saw *Louisville* in Mare Island Navy Yard. This photograph taken on 26 May shows relatively few changes: there is a new mast aft, a half-cap on the forward funnel, the camouflage is that of Measure 21, the fire control radar is Mk 3 and Mk 4, and she has shipped 28mm AA, and SC-1 radar. (USN)

△ *Louisville* in mid-November 1942. The crane has now been removed, and the Mk 44 have been replaced by Mk 51 on the 28mm quadruples. (USN)

Louisville

1931 15 Jan Commissioned; shake-down cruise from Bremerton to New York via Panama Canal.

1932 Operations and manoeuvres off west coast.

1934 April Left San Diego on a nine month long cruise of Central American states in Caribbean and along east coast.

1935 Cruised to Alaska; Pearl Harbor man-oeuvres.

1936–37 Operations and manoeuvres off west coast.

1938 Jan Pacific cruise extended to include Hawaii, Samoa and Australia; exercises in Caribbean winter of 1939 until May 1940; returned to west coast in autumn.

1940 Panama Canal; cruised along east coast of South America; then from Brazil to Simons-town, South Africa; transported $148,000,000 in British gold to New York; returned to Pacific.

1941 7 Dec En route to Borneo, diverted to Pearl Harbor; from there to San Diego to join TF 17;
1942 16 Jan Took troops to Samoa.
March With TF 11 in the Solomons.
May At Mare Island Navy Yard.
31 May Left for Aleutians to join TF 8; bombarded Kiska.
11 Nov Left San Francisco via Pearl Harbor for South Pacific.
1943 29 Jan With TF 67 took part in battle off Rennell.
April To the Aleutians via Pearl Harbor.
11–30 May Occupation of Attu.

July Bombarded Kiska; convoy escort in North Pacific.
Dec At Mare Island Navy Yard for refit and conversion.
1944 Jan Returned to South Pacific.
29 Jan Bombarded Wotje.
3 Feb Bombarded Roi and Namur.
22 Feb Bombarded Eniwetok, from then with TF 58.
March Bombarded Palau Islands.
April Bombarded Truk and Satawan.
June Bombarded Saipan, Tinian and Guam.
Sept Bombarded Peleliu.

18 Oct In the Philippines; after the Leyte operations joined TF 38 off Luzon.
1945 5/6 Jan En route to Lingayen suffered considerable damage by two Kamikaze attacks; left for repair at Mare Island. Returned to Pacific to join TF 54.
May–June Suffered Kamikaze damage once again.
15 June Left for repairs at Pearl Harbor.
16 August Cruised to Guam and Manchuria, Tsingtau, Inchon, then to China once again; then returned to USA.
1946 17 June Decommissioned.

△ Overall view of *Louisville* on 10 November 1942 (USN)

◁ ▷ Two more yard photographs of *Louisville* dated 26 May 1942 showing many details of equipment. The 28mm and 20mm AA, the Mk 44 (then over the quadruples) and the 5in/25 guns. (USN)

◁ The comprehensive conversion of *Louisville,* which took a slightly different shape from the later conversion of *Chester,* took place at the end of 1943 when, additionally, 40mm AA were installed – four quadruples and two twins. The narrow stern section allowed the fitting of twins only instead of, for example, in the case of *Pensacola,* quadruples. In this conversion SK radar and Mk 8 were installed and camouflage according to Measure 32/6d was applied. The photograph below was taken at Mare Island on 17 December 1943. (USN)

▷ The spring of 1945 saw CA-28 again in the hands of Mare Island Navy Yard. The starboard catapult was removed, and the Mk 8 fire control radar was replaced by Mk 8 Mod. 3. (USN)

△ This overall photograph of *Louisville* was taken at the conclusion of yard work in April 1945 when she was painted according to Measure 22 which can be clearly seen, and received Mk 28 fire control radar. Seen here she seems at first glance to have much in common with *Indianapolis* after her last conversion. (USN)

▽ Characteristic in units of the *Northampton* class that served as flagships was the 'extended forecastle', with its outer plating extending almost to the catapult, a measure taken to obtain more space for crew. *Chicago* was one of these units, as is exemplified in this photograph taken apparently at the end of the 1930s. The torpedo tubes had already been removed and the lateral openings plated over. As can be clearly seen, *Chicago* had a half-cap on her forward funnel before the beginning of the war. (USN)

Chicago

1931 9 March Commissioned; shake-down cruise to Honolulu, Tahiti and Samoa; transferred to east coast.

15 August Arrived; flagship of Commander, Cruisers, Scouting Force (remained with this formation until 1940!). with PACFL; operations in west coast area/Alaska/Panama Canal zone/Hawaii, February 1932 until April 1934.

1934 May Took part in fleet parade off New York; remained on east coast.

Oct Returned to San Pedro, operated from there.

1940 29 Sept Cruised to Pearl Harbor; operated from there for next 14 months; became first cruiser to receive CXAM radar in September 1940.

1941 7 Dec At sea with TF 12 in unsuccessful search for Japanese fleet.

12 Dec Returned to Pearl Harbor; patrol duties.

1942 2 Feb Left Pearl Harbor sphere of operations for newly organized 'Allied Naval Force'.

March–April Fire support operations off New Guinea and New Caledonia.

4 May Accompanied by *Yorktown* (CV-5) attacked Japanese forces on Tulagi, the Solomons.

June–July Further operations in south-west Pacific.

7–9 August Supported first landings on Guadalcanal and other islands in Solomons archipelago.

9 August Took part in Savo Island battle; damaged by Japanese destroyer torpedoes; first repairs at Noumea and Sydney; left for west coast.

13 Oct Arrived San Francisco; yard repairs.

1943 Jan Departed for Noumea.

27 Jan Convoy escort to Guadalcanal.

29 Jan Took part in battle off Rennell, hit twice by aerial torpedos.

30 Jan Sunk by four more aerial torpedos.

▽   One month before her sinking, *Chicago* on 20 November 1942 at Mare Island. She has CXAM radar and other installations appropriate to cruisers of this class at that time. There is SG radar on the forward mast beneath the fighting masthead. (USN)

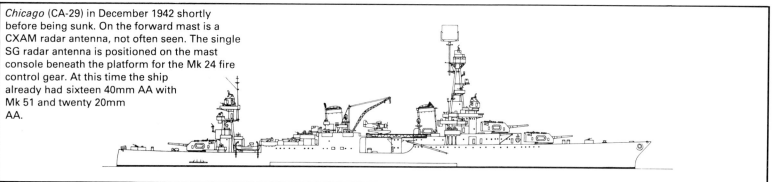

Chicago (CA-29) in December 1942 shortly before being sunk. On the forward mast is a CXAM radar antenna, not often seen. The single SG radar antenna is positioned on the mast console beneath the platform for the Mk 24 fire control gear. At this time the ship already had sixteen 40mm AA with Mk 51 and twenty 20mm AA.

Houston

1930 17 June Commissioned as CL-30.

1 July Reclassified as CA-30; shake-down cruise
  in Atlantic.

1931 10 Jan Left New York for Pacific.

22 Feb Arrived Manila, Philippines; flagship,
  'Asiatic Station'; remainder of year training
  cruises in Far East.

1932 31 Jan Represented American interests at
  Shanghai; remained there until relieved by
  Augusta (CA-31).

1933 17 Nov Departed for San Francisco; re-

△   This detailed photograph of *Houston* dates
from the mid 1930s. The deck space around the
after funnel, where later four additional 5in/25s
were fitted, is at this time occupied by two Corsair
aircraft. The ship still has many boats, and the
torpedo tubes are still fitted. (USN)

▽   *Houston* in the 1930s. (USN)

▷   A photograph of *Houston* which has passed
into history, taken in October 1935 off San Diego
when President F. D. Roosevelt was on board. The
forward mast shows the command pennant of the
Fleet Commander, Admiral Reeves; the
President's standard flies from the after mast. This
picture shows the extended hull armour covering
the section where there are no portholes. (USN)

mained on west coast during the inter-war years.

1934 1 July Took President F. D. Roosevelt on a 12,000-mile cruise from Annapolis; returned to San Diego.

1935 15 May Cruised to Hawaii with SECNAV H. L. Roosevelt.

3 Oct Departed from Seattle on second cruise with President F. D. Roosevelt.

1937 28 May Took part in opening of Golden Gate bridge at San Francisco.

1938 14 July President F. D. Roosevelt aboard again for fleet review off San Francisco.

19 Sept Flagship, US Fleet.

28 Dec Returned to Scouting Force in Atlantic.

1939 4 Jan Departed for exercises off east coast.

30 May Returned to Seattle; berthed at yard until December 1939.

1940 17 Feb At Mare Island.

Oct Left for Philippines.

19 Nov Became Flagship, Commander, Asiatic Fleet.

1941 7 Dec Left Panay Island for Darwin, Australia.

28 Dec Arrived Darwin; joined American-British-Dutch-Australian formation (ABDA) at Soerabaya.

1942 4 Feb Damaged off Balikpapan, after 8in turret out of action.

15 Feb Left Australia on convoy escort, heading for Timor.

26 Feb Battle of Java Sea; took part in attempt to prevent the occupation of Java by Rear-Admiral Karel Doorman.

27 Feb Sunk by torpedoes.

△ One of a series of US Navy photographs used for ship recognition training. *Augusta* is seen here on 31 March 1941 at Mare Island. As a flagship she had the extended forecastle. The original torpedo openings have already been sealed, the additional 5in guns have been installed near the after funnel. Note the proximity of the rangefinder on the platform behind the after funnel and the foremast extension which will serve for installation of CXAM-1 radar. (USN)

◁ This photograph is an oddity. Dated 1 December 1942, it is a portion of a very big enlargement of a photograph of a formation of ships. A further unusual feature is that this ship is painted in camouflage Measure 17 which was not used for cruisers other than *Augusta.* The camouflage was identical on port and starboard sides. As with certain other sister ships the forward funnel has a half-cap. (USN)

◁ This detailed photograph dates from April 1942 and shows the upper section of *Augusta*'s forward mast. There is a Mk 24 control gear, topped by radar Mk 3 for the 8in guns. Behind this can be seen the tall antenna for CXAM radar, the texture of which shows clearly. (USN)

Augusta

1931 30 Jan Commissioned as CL-31, served with LANTFL.

1 July Reclassified as CA-31.

1932 March Transferred to PACFL.

1933 9 Nov transferred to Asiatic Fleet as Flagship, Asiatic Station, representing American interests at Shanghai.

1940 Nov Returned to west coast; berthed at yard.

1941 April Transferred to LANTFL as flagship.

Dec Carrier escort operating from Bermudas.

1942 August–11 Nov North Africa landings.

1942–43 Dec–Jan At New York Navy Yard.

1943 August With Royal Navy at Scapa Flow for Murmansk convoy duties.

Nov Yard modernization in USA.

1944 April Returned to England.

June Supported landings in Normandy.

July Transferred to Mediterranean.

15 August–25 Sept Landings in South of France.

1944–45 Oct–Feb Yard modernization and conversion at Philadelphia.

1945 7 July Took President Truman to Antwerp and returned to Newport News after Potsdam Conference.

7 August 'Magic Carpet' cruises between Europe and east coast.

1946 16 July Decommissioned.

△ The final comprehensive conversion of *Augusta,* in line with that given to *Chester* and *Louisville,* took place in 1944/45. She is seen here in July 1945 when President Truman was taken to the Potsdam Conference. One can see clearly the platform fitted between both the after fire control gear on which many AA guns and a Seagull reconnaissance aircraft are positioned. Despite her additional wartime fittings and conversion, *Augusta* had lost very little of her rakish appearance. (IWM)

▷ *Augusta* on 4 February 1946 in English waters, probably on one of her 'Magic Carpet' cruises. By this time the impending decommissioning had already been indicated. The two catapults and SK radar are no longer aboard and it would seem that no SP had been fitted at all during the last conversion. The outer casing of the hangar shows signs of lengthy war usage. Various AA guns are covered by awnings. (WL)

PORTLAND CLASS

Both cruisers of this class corresponded basically with the *Northampton* design, but had an increased length of 3 metres. The Washington Treaty's permitted displacement of 10,000 tons had not been fully utilized in the *Northampton*s, but in these two ships it was, and opportunity was taken to improve the armour over magazines and engine compartments. Only CA-33 and 35 completed to this design. The projected CA-32, 34, 36 to 39 and 44 were due to be built to an improved design, with stronger armour. Many of the features that were later to be given to the *Northampton* class appeared here in embryo, e.g., the omission of torpedo tubes and the increase in AA armament to eight 5in/25. In their pre-war outline the two classes were easy to tell apart: *Portland,* to reduce top-heaviness had a

considerably lower tripod mast forward, and her after tripod was considerably lighter. Both units were built as flagships which was of great practical use; the *New Orleans* class which followed had no additional space for staff, the available tonnage having been used for other purposes.

As in *Northampton, Portland* had a taller forward funnel before the war, a temporary measure which was abandoned during the war to facilitate the fitting of light funnel cappings.

Both ships were modified in May 1943, in the light of battle experience and to the same degree as the surviving *Northampton*s were later to be converted. The last modification was made to *Indianapolis* in mid-July 1945, a bare fortnight before she became the last US capital ship to be lost in the war.

▷ This detailed photograph of *Portland* on 7 February 1942 shows clearly the appearance and distribution of her AA weapons at the beginning of the war. The searchlight base is clearly visible on the after funnel as is the second rangefinder behind it. (USN)

▽ An identification photograph of *Portland* in June 1942. As with *Northampton,* the higher forward funnel did nothing to enhance her appearance. At this time the 5in AA are protected by splinter screens. There is a scout aircraft SOC on the catapult. Degaussing loops run along the hull. With difficulty one can make out SC radar at the top of the mast. There are four 28mm quadruples. The two fire control Mk 33s are on platforms fitted on each side of the tripod mast. (USN)

Portland

1933 23 Feb Commissioned.

4 April Rescue of airship Akron.

1935 2 Oct Left San Diego on escort duty for President F. D. Roosevelt (in *Houston*).

1936 20 May Crossed Equator for first time, during Pacific manoeuvres: then with CRUDIV 5, Scouting Force until outbreak of war.

1941 7 Dec With a carrier group bound for Midway; operations between west coast, Hawaii and Fiji.

1942 May Took part in Battle of Coral Sea; picked up 722 survivors from *Lexington* (CV-2).

2–6 June With TF 17 at Battle of Midway.

7–9 August Landings on Tulagi and Guadalcanal.

23–25 August Battle off East Solomons.

26 Oct Battle off Santa Cruz, with *Enterprise* (CV-6).

12 Nov Battle off Guadalcanal, damaged by torpedo on 13th, could only steam in circles; despite loss of after 8in turret, sank a Japanese destroyer.

14 Nov Tulagi, first repairs; towed to Sydney for provisional repairs; left for west coast via Samoa and Pearl Harbor.

1943 3 March Repairs and conversion completed at Mare Island.

May Departed for Aleutians.

26 July Bombarded Kiska.

Sept–Oct Two passages to Pearl Harbor and one to San Francisco.

1943–44 Nov–Feb Gilbert and Marshall Islands.

1944 3 March–1 April Escorted carriers off Palau Islands, Yap, Ulithi, and Woleai.

21–24 April To New Guinea, landings at Hollandia.

May–August At Mare Island.

12–29 Sept Bombardment prior to landings on Peleliu, then to Manus.

17 Oct Arrived off Leyte, supported landings.

24 Oct Took part in night battle in Surigao Straits.

1945 3 Jan–1 March Lingayen and Corregidor.

26 March–20 April Bombarded Okinawa.

8 May–17 June Received capitulation of Japanese occupying the Carolines.

21 Sept–10 Oct 'Magic Carpet' cruise; then to east coast.

27 Oct 'Navy Day' at Portland, Maine, her name town.

1946 12 July Decommissioned.

▽ A comprehensive conversion of *Portland* was carried out in May 1943, together with *Pensacola*, *Indianapolis* and the three remaining units of the *Northampton* class. At this critical stage of the war cruisers were urgently needed and *Portland*'s conversion was completed in two months. The Mk 33s are now well separated along the ships's axis. The 'flying platform' for 20mm AA is a new addition. The new, solid tripod lattice mast supports only the small SG radar. The forward funnel was shortened to its original size and both funnels were given a half-cap. There is SK radar on the forward mast. (USN)

Portland (CA-33) in June 1942, still with the higher forward funnel which she had received before the war. There is SC radar on the top of the forward mast and SG below it. The two Mk 33 fire control gear with Mk 4 on them are positioned on consoles abeam the forward mast. The AA component consists of sixteen 28mm and there are also seventeen 20mm on board.

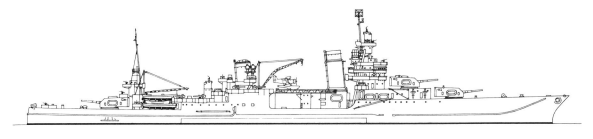

▷ Details of *Portland*'s
forward midships section,
as seen in May 1943 after
completion of the
conversion at Mare Island.
The old Mk 27 rangefinder
was still on board when this
photograph was taken.
(USN)

Indianapolis

1932 15 Nov Commissioned; shake-down cruise in Atlantic and off Cuba.

1933 Feb Training cruise in Panama Canal area and off coast of Chile.

1 July President F. D. Roosevelt aboard.

4 July At Philadelphia Navy Yard.

Sept–Oct With SECNAV C. A. Swanson on an inspection cruise of west coast and Hawaii.

1 Nov Flagship, Scouting Force.

1934 29 May Returned to New York; President F. D. Roosevelt aboard; took part in fleet review.

9 Nov Returned to Long Beach.

1936 18 Nov. Took President F. D. Roosevelt on Goodwill cruise to South America.

15 Dec Returned to Charleston, S.C.

1941 7 Dec With TF 12.

13 Dec Arrived Pearl Harbor; joined TF 11.

1942 Feb Operated with *Lexington* (CV-2) in South Pacific; with *Yorktown* (CV-5) operated off New Guinea.

April–July At Mare Island Navy Yard; then escort duties to Australia, Aleutians.

7 August Bombarded Kiska; occupied and set up a base on Adak.

1943 Jan Occupied and set up a base on Amchitka; operations in the Aleutians during spring and summer.

Sept Left for Mare Island.

Oct Pearl Harbor; Flagship, 5th Fleet (VADM Spruance).

10 Nov Left for invasion of Gilbert Islands.

19 Nov Bombarded Tarawa and Makin.

1944 31 Jan Left Tarawa for Marshall Islands; bombarded Kwajalein Islands.

March–April Once again, Flagship, 5th Fleet; operated in region of Palau; Yap, Ulithi, Woleai.

11 June Bombarded Saipan.

19–22 June Took part in Battle of Philippines.

23 June Bombarded Saipan again, then Tinian; operated for several weeks in the region of Marian Islands; reconquest of Guam.

12–29 Sept Bombarded Peleliu in West Carolines.

1944–45 Nov–Jan Refitting and conversion at Mare Island.

1945 14 Feb Operated with the VADM Mitscher's carrier fleet escorting carriers off Iwo Jima; Japanese mainland islands.

14 March Left Ulithi; carrier escort in operations off Japanese main islands.

24 March Beginning of bombardment of

▽ *Indianapolis* did great service as a flagship. On several occasions in peacetime she carried President F. D. Roosevelt whom she was to survive by only a few months. The photograph below was taken on 29 May 1934 during a fleet review off Ambrose Light. The President's colour flies from the after mast. One sees clearly how much lower the tripod mast is as compared with that of the *Northampton* class; the omission of torpedo tubes is also to be observed. From the very beginning she had all eight 5in/25 AA guns. (USN)

◁ *Portland* was once again at Mare Island Navy Yard from May to August 1944. This time she was painted in the camouflage of Measure 33/7d, the port side pattern of which is seen here. The AA platform against the after funnel, which now has no AA guns, has been given additional splinter protection, the old Mk 27 fire control gear has been replaced by the combination Mk 34, Mk 8 and both the Mk 33 fire control have been given Mk 28 radar. There are smoke canisters on the quarterdeck. (USN)

▷ This detailed photograph taken at Mare Island on 9 April 1942 shows clearly that *Indianapolis* had no Mk 33 at the beginning of the war; she had only two, older Mk 19, one on the front of the forward mast and one behind the second funnel. The 20 and 28mm AA can be seen. Beyond her is a ship of the *Omaha* class.

Okinawa; shot down six Japanese aircraft.

31 March Hit by aircraft bombs aft, suffered damage, particularly to propeller shaft; left for west coast.

June–July Repairs and modifications at Mare Island.

16 July Transported at top speed first two atomic bombs to Tinian.

26 July Arrived Tinian (5,000 nautical miles in ten days).

28 July Left Guam for Okinawa, but never arrived there.

30 July Hit by two torpedoes from *I-58*; sank within twelve minutes; 883 men died, only 316 saved after a search which had been too long delayed.

△ A navy recognition photograph of *Indianapolis* taken at Mare Island on 20 April 1942; from the dark camouflage one assumes she is painted according to Measure 11. (USN)

Indianapolis (CA-35) in May 1944, following her last substantial yard work. The mounting of the SK radar antenna on the after mast is peculiar only to this ship. The two Mk 33 fire control gear are unenclosed but have a tarpaulin covering. The Mk 4 is in an unusual position. She has 8in turrets Mod. 1 in which all three guns can be moved simultaneously in a vertical plane.

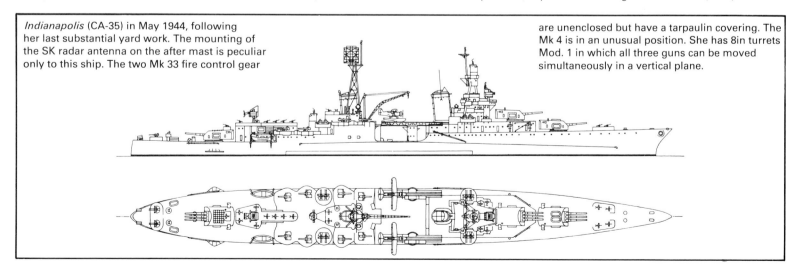

△ *Indianapolis* spent a complete month at Mare Island in September 1943 undergoing conversion, as had been carried out with *Portland*; and a similar period – for the penultimate time – in the winter of 1944/45. From May to November 1944 she was repainted in Measure 32/7d. She is seen here on 9 December 1944 wearing the Measure 22 camouflage which she retained until she was lost.

In contrast to *Portland*, the SK radar is positioned on the after mast.

▽ One of the best known and most attractive photographs of *Indianapolis*, taken on 10 July 1945, just before she carried the two atom bombs to Tinian. Her appearance had been little changed at her last Mare Island refit. Fire control radar Mk 8

Mod. 3 had been given to the Mk 34 fire control gear. Mk 28 fire control radar had been fitted earlier in December 1944. Twenty-one days after this photograph was taken, *Indianapolis* was sunk in tragic circumstances, just before the ending of the war. (USN)

NEW ORLEANS CLASS

The fact that the first US heavy cruisers (*Pensacola* and *Northampton* classes) were 1,000 tons lighter than they need have been did not become apparent until the ships were completed. In 1929 the naval authorities planned the building of three cruiser classes consisting of fifteen units. After the rather lightly and badly armoured *Northampton* class, the construction numbers 32 to 36 were to have been given to the rather better armoured *Portland* type. At about this time there was considerable concern in the navy for the provision of better armour. It was hoped to provide this in a new design of five ships, even if it meant doing without certain other features. In order to get quick results it was decided to use the construction numbers 33, 34 and 36, which had been reserved for the *Portland* class, in a new design with increased armour; this was not too difficult because all three ships were to be built at naval yards. For this reason the *Portland* class remained with only two ships.

From CA-37 on, new, lighter 8in triple turrets were fitted. The *New Orleans* class had a new profile which differed in some respects from that of the *Northampton*s. The forecastle deck reached back to the after funnel, and in general terms the ships were somewhat lower. The aircraft hangar was not built around the after funnel but placed on the rather over-large after superstructure. The two catapults were installed behind the group of funnels. In an attempt to reduce top-heaviness the lofty tripod mast was replaced by a single-pole mast on the turret-shaped bridge, compensating among other things for the weight of the fire-control gear in its rather high positioning. The stem was rather higher than in the preceding class. There were no torpedo tubes. Two of the ships, *Quincy* and *Vincennes*, both built at Bethlehem, Quincy, were 600 tons lighter than their sisters. The latter came very close to the Washington standard limits.

Changes made in the light of wartime experi-ence affected the bridge; removal of the armoured citadel; strengthening of the 1940/41 28mm AA with 20mm Oerlikons; removal of one aircraft crane and, later, temporary removal of one catapult and temporary fitting of a lighter capping on the forward funnel. As the war progressed 40mm AA was installed. It had been intended to install 40mm twin AA on 'B' 8in turret in *Minneapolis*, but this was not done.

The point must be made that, of this class on which so much emphasis had been laid concerning the provision of better armour, three ships *Astoria*, *Quincy* and *Vincennes*, were lost in the Battle of Savo, all through Japanese gunfire.

▽ *New Orleans* on 8 July 1942, camouflaged in Measure 11 or 21. There appears to be no fire control radar on the Mk 33. On the other hand the SC radar can be distinguished on the forward mast. All the 5in guns have been given splinter shields. (USN)

New Orleans

1934 15 Feb Commissioned.

May–June Shake-down cruise to northern Europe.

28 June Returned to New York.

5 July–2 August Cruise along California coast with President F. D. Roosevelt aboard.

1935 Operated in East Pacific with CRUDIV 6.

1935–6 20 August–7 Dec At New York.

1937 Once more in the Pacific; operated off west coast.

1939 10 Dec Detailed for 'Hawaiian Detachment'.

1941 7 Dec In yard for machine repairs; convoy duties to Palmyra and Johnston Islands.

1942 13 Jan Mare Island for machine repairs and installation of 20mm AA and radar.

12 Feb Convoy duties to Australia and Noumea, then returned to Pearl Harbor to join TF 11.

15 April With TF 11 and *Yorktown* (CV-5) sailed for New Hebrides.

7–8 May Battle of Coral Sea; took on 580 survivors from *Lexington* (CV-2).

28 May With *Enterprise* (CV-6) departed in direction of Midway.

4 June Battle of Midway;

7 July Departed for Fiji via Pearl Harbor for invasion of Solomons, provided escort protection for *Saratoga* (CV-3).

31 Aug Escort duty for torpedoed *Saratoga*.

21 Sept To Pearl Harbor.

Nov Departed for Fiji with *Saratoga*.

30 Nov Took part in the night Battle of Tassafaronga; heavily damaged, lost the bow section to a torpedo; made Tulagi under own proper; sailed on to Sydney for completion of preliminary repairs.

24 Dec Arrived Sydney.

1943 7 March Left for Puget Sound to have new bow section fitted.

31 August Returned to Pearl Harbor.

5–6 Oct Bombarded Wake.

20 Nov Bombarded Gilbert Islands.

4 Dec Carrier escort in East Marshalls.

1944 29 Jan Bombarded Kwajalein.

11 Feb Left the Carolines.

△ Forward section of *New Orleans* during her yard refit at Mare Island in March 1945. On that occasion the Mk 28 fire control radar was installed among other items. There are 20mm twins on the forecastle in a stepped arrangement. (USN)

17–18 Feb Carrier attacks on Truk and other targets.

April Landings on Hollandia.

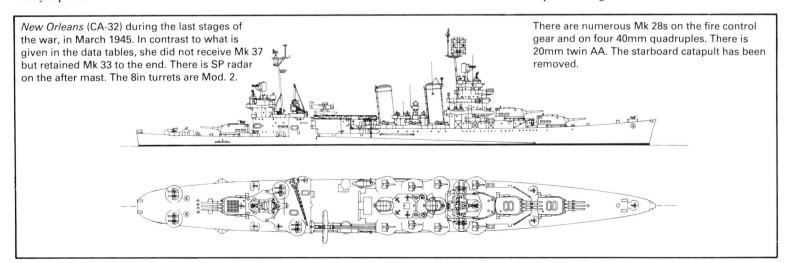

New Orleans (CA-32) during the last stages of the war, in March 1945. In contrast to what is given in the data tables, she did not receive Mk 37 but retained Mk 33 to the end. There is SP radar on the after mast. The 8in turrets are Mod. 2.

There are numerous Mk 28s on the fire control gear and on four 40mm quadruples. There is 20mm twin AA. The starboard catapult has been removed.

22 April One of own aircraft struck mast and damaged guns: one dead, one badly injured.
30 April Bombarded Truk and Satawan.
15–16 June Bombarded Saipan.
19–20 June Took part in Battle of Philippines.
August Bombarded Saipan and Tinian.
1–2 Sept Bombarded Iwo Jima.

Oct Took part in Battle of Leyte Gulf and Battle of Samar, then carrier protection off Mindoro.
Dec At Mare Island; then training cruises off Hawaii.
18 April Arrived Ulithi.
23 April Bombarded Okinawa during the next two months; in Subic Bay until end of the war.

28 August Received Japanese capitulation in Chinese and Korean harbours.
17 Nov Left River Peking for west coast with returning military personnel on board.
8 Dec Arrived San Francisco.
1946 Jan 'Magic Carpet' cruise to Guam.
10 Feb Decommissioned.

△ *New Orleans* leaving Mare Island after yard work that lasted until March 1945. She is camouflaged in Measure 22. The SP radar is on the after mast, and the starboard catapult has already been removed. Otherwise there was no major conversion as had happened with other classes. (USN)

▽ *New Orleans* in late 1945 or early 1946 in San Francisco Bay when she was undertaking a 'Magic Carpet' cruise to Guam. At some time during the intervening period the AA position had been removed from the forecastle as had the starboard catapult. Contrary to what one might expect of Measure 22, she has a black funnel cap. (USN)

◁ A peacetime photograph of *Astoria* taken in the mid-1930s. SOC reconnaissance aircraft are on the catapult. (AP)

Astoria

1934 28 April Commissioned.

1934–40 Scouting Fleet; Flagship, CRUDIV 7 and 6.

1941 7 Dec At sea with TF 12 (transport of USMC aircraft for Midway); vain search for Japanese combat fleet.

1942 Feb–June Among escort vessels for *York-town* (CV-5).

7–8 May Battle of Coral Sea.

3–6 June Battle of Midway.

7 August Supported landings on Guadalcanal.

8–9 August Battle of Savo Island; sank at 12.15 hours; after being hit by 65 shells. 238 dead, 142 wounded.

▽ *Astoria* seen presumably just a few weeks before she was lost on 9 August 1942 off Savo Island. Her many portholes have been plated over. (USN)

Minneapolis
1934 19 May Commissioned.
July–Sept Shake-down cruise to Europe.
1935 4 April Through Panama Canal to west coast.
18 April Arrived San Diego; joined CRUDIV 7, Scouting Force; permanent operations off west coast.
1939 One cruise in Caribbean.
1940 Pearl Harbor.

1941 7 Dec When the Japanese attacked she was only 20 miles from Pearl Harbor; patrol duties off Hawaii until end of January 1942.
1942 Feb–March With *Lexington* (CV-2) attacked Gilberts and Marshalls.
4–8 May Battle of Coral Sea.
3–6 June Battle of Midway.
July Repairs at Pearl Harbor Navy Yard.
August Carrier escort off Guadalcanal.
30 August Towed *Saratoga* (CV-3) after torpedo

damage.
Sept–Oct Landing support off Lunga Point and Funafuti.
29 Nov Flagship, TF 67, off Guadalcanal; hit by

▽ *Minneapolis* on 23 August 1935. It is clear that she had no splinter protection for the 5in AA at this time. In peacetime she carried numerous ship's boats on the hangar roof. (USN)

two torpedoes; reached Mare Island under own power.
1943 Sept In Pacific for 20 months.
1943 5 Oct Bombarded Wake.
20 Nov–4 Dec Occupation of Makin; Marshall Islands.
1944 Feb–April Marianas and Caroline Islands.
May At Majuro.
14 June Bombarded Saipan.

19–20 June With TF 58 in Battle of Philippine Sea.
8–9 August Re-occupation of Guam.
6 Sept–14 Oct Re-occupation of Palaus.
17 Oct Leyte Gulf.
24 Oct Battle in Surigao Straits.
1945 4–18 Jan Landings on Luzon.
13–18 Feb Landings on Bataan and Corregidor; preparations for Okinawa landings.
25 Feb Bombarded Okinawa until mid-April

when gun barrels were worn out.
12 April Departed for Bremerton. Puget Sound Navy Yard.
15 August In Subic Bay, the Philippines, at end of war.
9 Sept Received Japanese surrender in Korea.
1946 14 Jan Sailed from China to west coast with returning military personnel.
1947 10 Feb Decommissioned.

△ *Minneapolis,* probably at the end of 1942 or the beginning of 1943 when she arrived at Mare Island Navy Yard. One can see clearly what influence the hangar and the after superstructure must have had on the stability of ships of this class. The only radar antenna to be seen is a Mk 3; the SC-1 antenna had already been removed. (USN)

▽ *Minneapolis* as she appeared on 4 September 1943 after yard work at Mare Island. Her SG and SK radar have been installed and the fire control radar installation has been completed. Note the installation of a Mk 4 on the Mk 33. The installation of 40mm quadruples in the position they occupy aft meant that their bases projected out over the deck. Note the special camouflage which could well have led an observer to mistake the vessel for a destroyer. (USN)

△ *Tuscaloosa*, 23 August 1935. (USN)

Tuscaloosa

1934 17 August Commissioned; shake-down cruise to South America until Christmas 1934; at New York Navy Yard until March 1935.

1935 April Joined CRUDIV 6 at San Diego; then to base at San Pedro, California.

1937 May Exercises off Alaska, Hawaii and Guam.

1938 April–May Exercises off Hawaii.

1939 3 Jan Left San Diego for east coast; exercises off Lesser Antilles; short period at Norfolk Navy Yard.

8 April–10 May Goodwill cruise to South America with *San Francisco* (CA-38) and *Quincy* (CA-39).

6 June Returned to Norfolk.

August With President F. D. Roosevelt aboard observed recovery of submarine *Squalus* (SS-192).

2–11 Sept Neutrality patrol in North Atlantic.

16 Dec Took part in search for German passenger steamer *Columbus;* took on 567 men and 9 women from captured ship.

20 Dec Put Germans ashore at New York; returned to Norfolk.

1940 15 Feb With President F. D. Roosevelt aboard; cruised to Panama and west coast of Central Americas.

March–May At New York Navy Yard.

June Neutrality patrol until autumn.

3–16 Dec President F. D. Roosevelt once more aboard; inspected 50 old destroyers to be ex-changed for British bases.

22 Dec To Portugal with Admiral Leahy, the new Ambassador to Vichy France.

1941 March Scouting patrols on the North Atlantic routes operating from Bermuda.

May Took part in search for the *Bismarck*.

8 August Left Bermuda for Argentia, Newfoundland; *Augusta* (CA-31) joined en route; meeting-point for President Roosevelt and Prime Minister Churchill to sign the Atlantic Charter.

Sept Accompanied first American Marine Corps troop transport to Iceland.

A peacetime photograph of *Tuscaloosa,* exact date unknown. The oblique stroke ('Hashmark') beneath the letter 'E' signifies that this designation is being carried for the second successive year. (USN)

5 Nov War-footing operations in formation with battleship combat group in Denmark Strait; including observation of *Tirpitz* until beginning of January 1942.

1942 8–20 Feb At Boston Navy Yard; then a short period in New York.

March Joined TG 39.1, with *Washington* (BB-56); sailed for England.

4 April Arrived Scapa Flow; exercises with British Fleet units; then escort duties with convoys to northern Russia.

Sept–Oct To east coast for yard refit.

Nov With *Massachusetts* (BB-59) and *Wichita* (CA-45) took part in bombardment of Casablanca (Operation 'Torch'); returned to USA for refit; convoy duties to North Africa.

1943 March–May Exercises off east coast.

May Accompanied *Queen Mary* taking Prime Minister Churchill to New York, then ten days at Boston Navy Yard; escorted *Queen Elizabeth* to Halifax, Nova Scotia.

Sept–Oct Escort for *Ranger* (CV-4), including the first two attacks made by American carrier-borne aircraft on German objectives in Norway 2–6 October.

17 Oct Aided renovation of Allied meterological station at Spitzbergen; then detached from 'Home Fleet'; returned to USA.

3 Dec At New York Navy Yard.

1944 Feb Training exercises and gunnery practise in Casco Bay.

April Installation of electronic equipment at Boston Navy Yard; then Flagship, COMCRUDIV 7.

June–July Allied invasion of Normandy; then sailed to Mediterranean.

August Landings in South of France.

Sept At Philadelphia Navy Yard; then transferred to west coast.

1945 Jan Via San Diego and Pearl Harbor, joined Third Fleet off Ulithi.

16 Feb Bombarded Iwo Jima.

25 March Bombarded Okinawa.

28 June Left Okinawa for Leyte to join Seventh Fleet.

27 August Left for Subic Bay, then to Manchuria and Korea.

20 Sept Left Inchon for China.

Nov 'Magic Carpet' cruise from Shanghai to Hawaii.

4 Dec Arrived San Francisco; short refit.

14 Dec Troop transport from Guadalcanal and Noumea.

10 Jan Arrived San Francisco; transferred to east coast.

13 Feb Decommissioned

△ This photograph was taken some years later, possibly in the second half of 1942. It shows *Tuscaloosa* somewhere in the Atlantic with certain changes: some conversion work has been done around the bridge, there is a lower searchlight platform with only two searchlights, splinter screens for the 5in guns, a half-cap for the forward funnel. She is painted in Measure 22. There are SC-, SG- and Mk 3 radar, but not as yet a Mk 4. A SOC reconnaissance aircraft is on the catapult as there was on the peacetime photograph. (IWM)

▽ *Tuscaloosa,* on 10 November 1944 after two months at Philadelphia Navy Yard. The radar Mk 4 has been replaced by Mk 28. The camouflage is according to Measure 33/13d. The aircraft type is as it was formerly. Near the funnels an extended platform for 20mm guns has been installed. (USN)

△ *Tuscaloosa* viewed from forward on 30 January 1944 in the New York Navy Yard. The most important numbers show the following: (4) former Admiral's Bridge removed to accommodate AA; (5) Mk 33 with Mk 4 radar; (11) SG radar; (12) base for SK radar. There are no tompions in the muzzles of the guns. There is a Mk 3 radar on the Mk 31 rangefinder. (USN)

△ A view of *Tuscaloosa* from aft looking towards the 8in triple turret and superstructure, showing: (1) and (2) 20mm AA mountings; (4) 40mm AA mountings; (11) SG radar; (3) Mk 33 with Mk 4 radar on top of it; (9) Mk 3 radar. (USN)

△ After her transfer to the Pacific Fleet *Tuscaloosa* was painted once again in Measure 22 – presumably at Pearl Harbor. She is seen here in San Francisco Bay on 16 December 1945, probably just before leaving for her second 'Magic Carpet' cruise. (Cas)

San Francisco

1934 10 Feb Commissioned; shake-down cruise including visits to Mexican and Hawaiian waters.

1935 Feb Joined CRUDIV 6 at San Diego; operations in East Pacific until the end of 1938.

1939 Jan Manoeuvres in the area of the Lesser Antilles.

March Flagship, CRUDIV 7.

1 Sept Neutrality patrol from Norfolk.

1940 11 Jan Relieved as flagship by *Wichita* (CA-45); end of February returned to Pacific via Panama Canal, then to San Pedro; joined CRUDIV 6 at Pearl Harbor.

May At Puget Sound Navy Yard.

29 Sept Returned to Pearl Harbor.

1941 May Flagship, CRUDIV 6 at Pearl Harbor.

August Sailed to Long Beach.

27 August Returned to Pearl Harbor.

Sept Divisional Staff left ship.

11 Oct Commencement of yard work at Pearl Harbor Navy Yard.

7 Dec Almost weaponless in yard.

16 Dec Yard work suspended; left for Wake and

Midway with TF 14 in company with *Saratoga* (CV-3).

1941 29 Dec Returned to Pearl Harbor.

1942 8 Jan Left for Samoa with TF 8, later sailed for Gilberts and Marshalls with TF 17.

8 Feb With CRUDIV 6 (TF 11) and *Lexington* (CV-2), operations in New Guinea area.

8–9 March TF 11 and 17 attacked Salamaua and Lae.

26 March Returned to Pearl Harbor.

22 April Escort duties to San Francisco and Australia.

21 June Returned to Pearl Harbor; then sailed as escort to the Fijian Islands.

7 August Flagship, Commander-in-Chief, Cruisers of TF 18 off Guadalcanal-Tulagi.

15 Sept *Wasp* (CV-7) sunk.

23 Sept Making up TF 64 with five other cruisers and DESRON 12.

24 Sept Left for New Hebrides.

12 Oct Battle off Cape Esperance.

30 Oct RADM D. J. Callaghan, CTG 64.4 and his

staff transfer to *San Francisco*; redesignation as TF 65.

31 Oct Departed for Solomons.

10 Nov Flagship, TG 67.4; arrived Lunga Point.

12 Nov After fire control installation put out of action by crashing Japanese aircraft, 15 dead, 29 wounded.

13 Nov Heavily damaged by Japanese surface forces; 45 hits including ones on the bridge which killed RADM Callaghan and all officers except one; a total of 77 dead, 105 wounded.

14 Nov Returned to Espiritu Santo.

23 Nov Sailed for west coast.

14 Dec Yard repairs at Mare Island.

1943 26 Feb Sailed for South Pacific.

20 March Arrived Noumea.

April Left for Aleutians (TF 16); there four and a half months.

July Attacks on Attu and Kiska.

Sept Short yard stop at Pearl Harbor.

5 Oct Joined TU 14.2.1; attacks on Wake and Wilkes.

△ *San Francisco* entering Pearl Harbor on 4 December 1942 following the battle of Guadalcanal where she received many hits. Her Measure 21 camouflage has taken a pounding. (USN)

20 Oct Arrived Makin; fire support for landings.

26 Oct Joined TG 50.1.

4 Dec Attacks on Kwajalein (Marshall Islands); damaged by Japanese aircraft, 1 dead, 22 wounded.

6 Dec Returned to Pearl Harbor.

1944 22 Jan Sailed for Marshall Islands with TF 52.

31 Jan Bombarded Kwajalein and other islands.

8 Feb Joined TF 58 as protection for fast carrier formations.

12 Feb With TG 58.2 off Majuro.

21–28 April TG 58.2 supported landings in area of Hollandia.

30 April Attacks on Satawan.

6 June With TG 53.15 attacks on Saipan.

16 June Attacks on Guam.

19 June Battle of the Philippine Sea.

8 July Bombarded Guam.

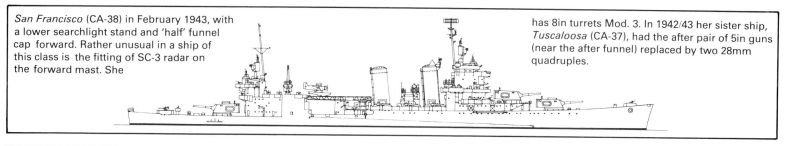

San Francisco (CA-38) in February 1943, with a lower searchlight stand and 'half' funnel cap forward. Rather unusual in a ship of this class is the fitting of SC-3 radar on the forward mast. She has 8in turrets Mod. 3. In 1942/43 her sister ship, *Tuscaloosa* (CA-37), had the after pair of 5in guns (near the after funnel) replaced by two 28mm quadruples.

◁   A close-up of *San Francisco* at Mare Island on 15 December 1942. The effects of three of a total of 45 hits can clearly be seen. She still has the spacious searchlight platform between the funnels. The Mk 33 fire control gear is still without fire control radar. (USN)

△   *San Francisco* on 15 February 1943, after completion of repairs at Mare Island. Some changes are visible; the bridge superstructure has been considerably modified, there is a lower searchlight platform, SC-3 radar on the forward mast, Mk 4 on the Mk 33 and 40mm AA. She is painted in Measure 21. (USN)

▽   *San Francisco*'s next period at Mare Island (August to October 1944) brought about further changes. She is now painted in Measure 33/13d, and has SK air search radar. Note the very high positioning of the Mk 33. (USN)

24 July Bombarded Orote peninsula (Guam).

30 July Left for west coast.

16 August Commencement of yard period at Mare Island.

31 Oct Left for west coast.

21 Nov At Ulithi, Flagship CRUDIV 6.

10 Dec With TG 38.1 to the Philippines.

17–18 Dec Severe typhoon; searched for survivors of three destroyers which had sunk.

1944–45 20 Dec & 5–7 Jan Operations against Luzon.

1945 2–3 Jan & 9 Jan Attacks on Formosa.

Jan South China Sea, Indo-Chinese coast, Formosa, Ryuku Islands, West Carolines.

Feb Honshu, Vulcan and Bonin Islands.

19 Feb Commencement of operations around Iwo Jima.

25 Feb Attacks on Tokyo.

21 March With TF 54 to Ryukyus; bombardment of Kerama, Retto and other targets.

28 March Bombarded Okinawa, for some time with TF 51 and TG 32.15.

July Off Philippines; preparations for invasion of Japanese mainland, but war ends.

Aug–Oct Occupation of Chinese and Korean coasts.

1945 12 Jan Arrived San Francisco.

1946 10 Feb Decommissioned on east coast.

▽▷ Both these detailed photographs were taken in October 1944 at Mare Island. Ammunition is being taken on for the main armament. The Mk 4 has been replaced by Mk 28, the 40mm AA has been increased to 24 barrels. Note the 20mm AA tubs above the anchor. (USN)

NEW ORLEANS CLASS 103

In many respects *Quincy* (CA-39), depicted here as she was in August 1942, differed from most of her sister ships (as could be said of *Vincennes* [CA-44]). There is SC radar on the forward mast, an older version of Mk 33 resting on a tall pedestal. Depth-charge throwers are positioned right aft with smoke generators between them. There is a high searchlight stand.

There are 8in turrets Mod. 3. The bridge is short because neither CA-39 nor 44 had an AA bridge. The barbette of No. 2 turret was approximately 6.5m higher than in the other ships; the funnels were approximately 1m narrower. Contrary to Table B, it can be established from this sketch that she had assorted light AA: only two 28mm quadruples and two 40mm twins aft.

Quincy

1936 9 June Commissioned; CRUDIV 8 in Atlantic.
20 July–27 Sept In Mediterrannean, safe-guarding American interests during Spanish Civil War; relieved by *Raleigh* (CL-7).
5 Oct Returned to east coast; at Boston Navy Yard.
1937 12 April Transferred to west coast; joined CRUDIV 7.

10 May Arrived Pearl Harbor; manoeuvres in Pacific.
1938 At Mare Island Navy Yard.
1939 4 Jan Transferred to east coast.
Feb Manoeuvres within framework of LANTFL.
10 April–12 June Goodwill Cruise to South America.
9 July–24 August Three reservist training cruises; during remainder of year patrol duties in North Atlantic.

1940 April At Norfolk Navy Yard.
May–Sept Cruise to South America.

▽ *Quincy* on 23 May 1942 off the New York Navy Yard, two and a half months before she was sunk. There is a SC radar on the forward mast, the camouflage is that of Measure 12, and the SOC aircraft have their wings folded. (USN)

▷ *Quincy* on 29 May 1942 at New York Navy Yard. A view forward between the two catapults on which four Type SOC reconnaissance aircraft are positioned. Beneath the figure '1' is a 5in loading trainer minus its barrel. (USN)

Oct–Dec Three reservist training cruises.
1941 April–July With TG 2 (*Wasp* [CV-7]) and TG 28 *(Yorktown* [CV-5]); neutrality patrols in mid-Atlantic.
21 July–24 Sept With TG 16, patrols in Denmark Strait and Iceland.
31 Oct Escort duties to Newfoundland.
Nov–Dec Escorted convoy from South Africa to Trinidad.
1942 29 Jan Escort duties to Iceland with TF 15.
March–May At New York Navy Yard, then transferred to west coast.
19 June Arrived San Diego, joined TF 18.
7 August Bombarded Lunga Point, Guadalcanal.
9 August Sunk by gunfire off Savo Island.

Vincennes
1937 24 Feb Commissioned.
19 April Shake-down cruises to Scandinavia, France, England.
1938 Jan Joined CRUDIV 7, Scouting Force; transferred to west coast; operated from San Pedro; at Mare Island until April 1939.
1939 April Returned to east coast.
1 Sept Neutrality patrols off east coast and Caribbean until early 1940; sailed to Azores and French Morocco.
1940 10 June Left Casablanca with cargo of gold for USA; then neutrality patrols.
1941 Jan Short period at Norfolk Navy Yard; operated from east coast.
March Sailed to Brazil and South Africa; transported British troops to Capetown.
1942 4 Jan Returned to Norfolk; short period at the New York Navy Yard.
Jan Operated off east coast with *Hornet* (CV-8).
4 March Left New York for west coast.

▷ Details of the catapults and funnel section are seen in this undated photograph of *Vincennes*. The aircraft is a Type SOC. (USN)

2 April Left San Francisco with *Hornet* (TF 18);
  rendezvous with *Enterprise* (CV-6), TF 16.
18 April 'Tokyo Raid'.
25 April Returned to Pearl Harbor; vain search
  for Japanese Fleet, broken off in neighbourhood
  of Coral Sea.
29 May Left Pearl Harbor for Midway; at Pearl
  Harbor yard until mid-July.
26 July Joined TF 62; Flagship, TG 62.3 off
  Guadalcanal; provided defensive fire against
  Japanese aircraft using even her 8in guns.
8–9 August Battle off Savo Island; sank after
  severe damage by shellfire.

◁▽ Like *Quincy*, *Vincennes* was sunk on 9 August
1942 and photographs from her war period are
rare. Both these attractive photographs show the
ship as she appeared on 2 June 1937 during her
shakedown cruise in English waters. In contrast
with her predecessors, one notes a rather different
bridge. (WL)

BROOKLYN CLASS

These were intended to be heavy cruisers with an 8in main arnament, but, in line with the decisions of the London Fleet Conference, the main calibre was reduced to 6in. In the course of their development the new light cruisers of the *Brooklyn* class turned out very differently. In them were to be seen the effects of the Washington and the first London Fleet Conferences. The latter restricted further the number of heavy cruisers in the apparent conviction that a ship of 10,000 tons standard could be adequately armoured without any thought as to whether its armament was that of a heavy or a light cruiser. The idea was mooted that, in certain circumstances, a ship with twelve 6in guns arranged in four turrets was the equal of (and might even be superior to) a heavy cruiser, because it fired its shells more quickly.

The *Brooklyn*s had nothing in common with the *Omaha*s. There were now more 'firsts'. One of these was the 'flush deck', i.e., ships with a main deck which extended the length of the ship, even inclining upwards a little at the stern. There was also need to have some height aft above the propellers, and to provide an aircraft hangar there; at the sides of the hangar were – also for the first time – two rotatable catapults so that a minimum of four reconnaissance aircraft could be carried. Obviously the type was designed as an answer to the Japanese *Mogami*-class light cruisers. In common with them the *Brooklyn*s had new, quick firing 6in guns arranged in five triple turrets.

There were differences in ships of the class which provide evidence of changes in warship technology at the end of the 1930s. The tripod masts were replaced by lighter, pole masts. In the first seven ships the after superstructure was as compact and tall as the bridge superstructure, which allowed secure installation of the two pairs of fire control installation. It was with the after superstructure and medium armament that differences within the class were most noticeable. For instance, *Savannah* and *Honolulu* had eight new 5in/38 in four twin turrets in place of eight open 5in/25 AA mountings. These were installed during refit work at the end of the war, while the two last ships of the class (*St. Louis* and *Helena*) had the arrangement from the outset. Both these ships showed considerable differences from the seven preceding ships, in that their main superstructure was sited forward and directly aft of the second funnel, and was also lower.

Philadelphia, *Savannah* and *Honolulu* were given hull bulges in 1944. These ships were also modified during the course of the war. This involved changes to the bridge, removal of the armoured bridge and strengthening of the 20mm and 40mm AA machine-guns, the disposition of which can be studied in detail in the data tables.

Helena was the only ship of the class to be lost. What could never have been envisaged at the time was that *Phoenix* would be sold to Argentina after the war and be sunk in May 1982 off the Falklands Islands by two torpedo hits from the British nuclear-powered submarine *Conqueror*.

◁ A midships view of *Brooklyn* in June 1938. Note the short barrels of the 5in/25 AA guns, and the high positioning of the searchlight stand between the funnels. (USN)

△ This undated photograph of *Brooklyn* may date from the beginning of 1942. She has Mk 3 fire control (older model) on the forward Mk 34. Subsequent radar system (SC-1) has not yet been installed. The 5in AA are positioned behind a splinter screen. (USN)

▽ *Brooklyn* in camouflage of Measure 22, on 5 May 1943 after a refit at Philadelphia Navy Yard. Note the modifications to the bridge super-structure, a reduction in the number of searchlights and the addition of SC-2 radar systems and Mk 4. (USN)

Brooklyn

1937 30 Sept Commissioned.

1938 East coast, CRUDIV 8; routine duties.

1939 30 April Took part in opening of World Exhibition at New York.

23 May–3 June Key role in rescue of sunken submarine *Squalus* (SS-192), then transferred to west coast.

1940 18 Feb Participated at 'Golden Gate' Exhibition.

1941 March Goodwill and training cruise to South Pacific.

May Transferred to Atlantic.

1–7 July Accompanied convoy taking USMC troops to Iceland.

Aug–Dec Convoy protection and neutrality patrols.

1942 April Convoy protection between USA and England.

24 Oct Left Norfolk for North Africa.

8 Nov Fire support for landing on Fedhala.

17 Nov Left Casablanca for east coast.

1943 Jan–July Three convoys between USA and Casablanca.

10–14 July Bombardment support for landings in Sicily; remained in the Mediterrranean.
1944 22 Jan–9 Feb Landings at Anzio and Nettuno.
13–23 May Bombarded Formia area.
August Fire support during landings in South of France; remained in Mediterranean.
21 Nov Left Sicily for New York.
1944–45 Dec–May At New York Navy Yard.
1945 May–Sept Operations along east coast.
1947 3 Jan Decommissioned.
1951 9 Jan Handed over to Chile as part of an aid programme; renamed, *O'Higgins*.

Philadelphia
1937 23 Sept Commissioned.
1938 3 Jan Shake-down cruise to the West Indies.
30 April At Charleston.
May President F. D. Roosevelt aboard for several days on Caribbean cruise.
8 May Operated in formation of CRUDIV 8.
27 June Flagship CRUDIV 8, Battle Force.
1939 1 June Sailed through Panama Canal.
18 June Operated with CRUDIV 8 off west coast.
1940–41 April-May Operated from Pearl Harbor; manoeuvres.
1941 May Transferred to Atlantic.

18 June Arrived Boston; neutrality patrol off Bermudas and Nova Scotia.
5 Nov At Boston Navy Yard.
18 Dec Newfoundland, patrol duties.
1942 Feb Two escort passages to Iceland.
16 May Joined TF 22; left Norfolk for A/S patrol in Panama Canal area.
July–Sept Escorted two convoys to Scotland.
15 Sept joined Western Naval Task Force for landings in French Morocco.
7 Nov Landings at Casablanca.
24 Nov Returned to New York; operated from there.

▽ One of the best-known peacetime photographs of *Philadelphia* lying at anchor with *Pensacola*, *Salt Lake City* and *Northampton*. (USN)

◁ A photograph of *Philadelphia* dating from 1943 when she was painted in Measure 22. As fitted out at this time she looks very much like *Brooklyn*. (USN)

△ Following a yard refit in her name-town of Philadelphia this is how CL-41 appeared on 9 May 1945 with SK and SP radar and with a Kingfisher reconnaissance aircraft. Further modifications have been made to the bridge superstructure. (USN)

▷ *Savannah* on 11 August 1942, after eight weeks' refit at Boston Navy Yard. This photograph of the after part of the ship shows the aircraft crane, catapults, after gun turrets and super-structure. Note the rather high after ship which made possible the provision of a below-decks hangar. There is SC radar on the after mast. (USN)

1943 11 Mar Escorted two convoys to Casablanca; then joined TF 85, preparations for landings in Sicily.

8 June Convoy from Norfolk.

1943 9–19 July Bombarded Sicilian coast.

22 July Joined TF 88.

30 July Coastal bombardments, operating from Palermo.

21 August Departed for Algiers.

5 Sept Left Oran for Salerno.

8 Sept Coastal bombardment.

6 Nov Departed with convoy from Oran to east coast.

21 Nov Arrived Norfolk.

1943–44 Dec–Jan At New York Navy Yard.

1944 19 Jan Convoy to Oran.

14 Feb–23 May Fire support at Anzio; yard refit at Malta.

15 August With TG 85.12, fire support for landings in South of France, in Mediterranean until October.

6 Nov At Philadephia Navy Yard until May 1945.

1945 7 July Sailed to Antwerp as escort for *Augusta* (CA-31) which carried President Truman to Potsdam Conference.

2 August Meeting between King George VI and President Truman aboard Augusta.

7 August Returned to Norfolk, Virginia.

6–25 Sept Escorted German passenger ship *Europa*.

26 Oct–25 Dec Two 'Magic Carpet' cruises to Le Havre.

1947 3 Feb Decommissioned.

1951 9 Jan Sold to Brazil, renamed *Barroso*.

Savannah

1938 10 March Commissioned; shake-down cruises to Cuba and Haiti until summer of 1938.

3 June Final fitting-out at Philadelphia Navy Yard.

Oct Sailed to Portsmouth, England.

1939 2 June Left for the west coast via Panama Canal and San Diego to Long Beach.

1940 21 May–Nov Arrived Pearl Harbor; oper-

ated in the Hawaii area, then via Long Beach to Mare Island for refit.

1941 27 Jan Returned to Pearl Harbor; remained in Hawaiian waters.

19 May Sailed for east coast via Panama Canal.

17 June Arrived Boston; Flagship, CRUDIV 8; neutrality patrol North Atlantic; escort for Allied convoys.

7 Dec At New York.

1942 12 Jan Arrived Recife, Brazil; then with *Ranger* (CV-4) patrolled northwards from Bermuda.

9 June–15 August At Boston Navy Yard.

24 Oct Left to join the Western Naval Task Force; landings in French North Africa.

11 Nov Returned to east coast.

30 Nov Arrived Norfolk; then at New York yard.

U.S.S. SAVANNAH. 8/11/42. 3502-42 NYBOS

△ Six months later, *Savannah* as she appeared in January 1943. Note the concentration of MG AA guns to the side of and beneath the wheelhouse. (USN)

▷ *Savannah* in October 1944, just one month after her refit at Philadelphia Navy Yard. She is still painted in Measure 22. The former single 5in/25 guns have been replaced by four twin 5in/38

turrets and the machine-gun AA has been re-sited. SK radar has been fitted and an additional SG. (USN)

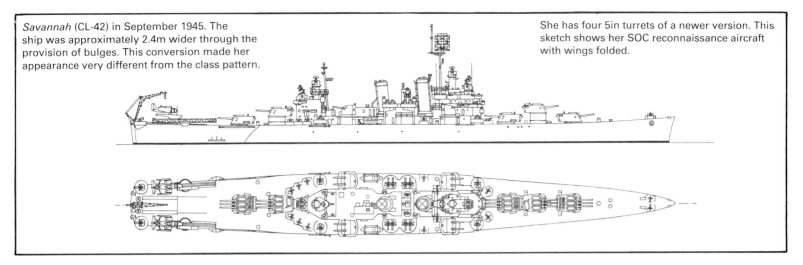

Savannah (CL-42) in September 1945. The ship was approximately 2.4m wider through the provision of bulges. This conversion made her appearance very different from the class pattern. She has four 5in turrets of a newer version. This sketch shows her SOC reconnaissance aircraft with wings folded.

1943 7 Jan Arrived Recife; with escort carrier *Santee* (CVE-29) hunted German blockade-breaker.

28 March Short yard stay at New York.

10 May Left Norfolk for Mediterranean.

23 May Arrived Oran; landings in Sicily after two intermediate stays in Algiers.

8 Sept Landings at Salerno.

11 Sept Heavily damaged by German glider bomb; 197 dead, 15 badly wounded.

12 Sept First repairs at Malta.

7 Dec Left for east coast.

23 Dec Eight months' repairs at Philadelphia Navy Yard.

1944 5 Sept Training cruises.

12 Oct Stand-by training cruises with CRUDIV 8.

1945 Jan With *Quincy* accompanied President F. D. Roosevelt to Yalta Conference.

2 Feb Arrived Malta; President Roosevelt completed journey by air; then to Alexandria.

12 Feb President boarded *Quincy* again.

27 Feb Returned to Norfolk.

8 March Arrived at the new base of Newport, RI.

March–May Training ship for crews about to join new ships; then short period at New York Navy Yard to receive new radar fire control gear for 40mm AA.

June Flagship, Midshipman Training Squadron, operating from Annapolis.

30 Sept Visited Pensacola, Florida, and her name town Savannah.

13 Nov Two 'Magic Carpet' cruises from Norfolk to France.

17 Dec Arrived at Philadelphia Navy Yard.

3 Feb Decommissioned.

U.S.S. CL 42
RFACE VIEW, CLOSE-UP OF BRIDGE.
AVY YARD, PHILA., PA. SEPT. 5-1944
1778-44

◁ Details of *Savannah*'s midships section, 5 September 1944, after conversion at Philadelphia Navy Yard. There is an enclosed 5in/38 mounting on a base, and her 40mm Bofors AA have been given a very high position to improve their field of fire. She has Mk 8 and Mk 12/2 fire control radars. (USN)

△ This detailed photograph of *Nashville* was taken in English waters in September 1938 just before she left with a cargo of British gold for New York. Her four searchlights are on a high platform between the funnels and she has many ship's boats. (WL)

▽ One year after the Japanese onslaught: *Nashville* at anchor in Pearl Harbor on 14 December 1942. The AA guns are provided with splinter screens; an SOC reconnaissance aircraft is suspended from its crane. There is SC radar on the forward mast. She still has her high searchlight platform. (USN)

△ *Nashville* after her Mare Island refit in July 1943. She now has a lower searchlight platform and SK radar on the forward mast. She is painted in Measure 21. (USN)

▷ A historic photograph. General Douglas MacArthur comes aboard *Nashville* from a P7-boat off Leyte on 24 October 1944. One can see the camouflage Measure 16 which was the same on both sides of the ship. It should be noted that the forward fire control Mk 34 is already fitted with a Mk 8 while there is the smaller version of Mk 3 aft.

The former *Nashville* (CL-43), in about 1978 when she was serving in the Chilean Navy.

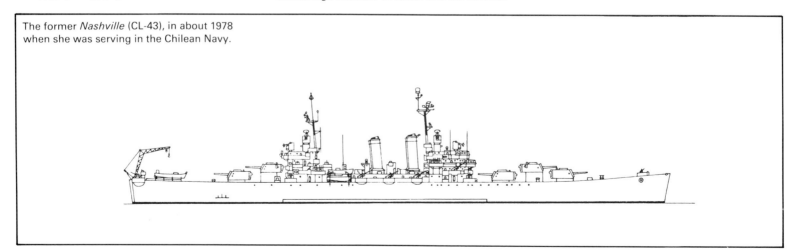

Nashville
1938 6 June Commissioned.
19 July Shake-down cruise to Caribbean.
August Visit to Europe.
21 Sept Transported British gold valued at $25,000,000 from Portland, England to New York.
1939 Cruised to Brazil.
23 June Transferred to PACFL for next two years.
16 July Arrived San Pedro.
1941 Feb Transported USMC troops to Wake.
20 May Transferred from Pearl Harbor to east coast.
19 June Arrived Boston; escort cruise to Iceland.
8 Dec Neutrality patrol, operating from Bermudas.
1942 4 March With *Hornet* (CV-8) transferred to west coast.
20 March Arrived San Diego; proceeded further on
2 April with *Hornet* carrying 16 USAAF B-25 bombers.
17 April 'Tokyo-Raid'.
25 April Returned to Pearl Harbor.
14 May Left for Alaska and the Aleutians as Flagship, TF 8.
June–Nov Patrol duties in North Pacific.
7 August Bombarded Kiska.
22 Nov Arrived Pearl Harbor.
24 Dec Left for Fijian Islands; flagship, TF 67 at Espiritu Santo.
1943 4 Jan Bombarded Munda.

12 May Magazine explosion in forward 6in turret; 18 dead, 17 injured.

22 May Left Espiritu Santo for west coast; repairs to damage and modification at Mare Island Navy Yard.

6 August Left San Francisco.

12 August Arrived Pearl Harbor; two months attacking Wake and Marcus with aircraft carriers.

25 Oct Seven months bombarding targets in New Guinea area and Admiralty Islands.

21 March–4 April Fire protection for the landing on Hollandia, General MacArthur on board.

27 May Attended occupation of Biak.

4 June Superficially damaged by near miss from a Japanese aircraft.

Sept Invasion of Morotai, General MacArthur on board once more.

20 Oct Fire cover for landings on Leyte.

13 Dec Badly damaged by Kamikaze aircraft en route Mindoro; 130 dead, 190 wounded.

1945 12 Jan Repairs at Puget Sound Navy Yard.

15 April Departed for Philippines via San Diego.

16 May Arrived Subic Bay; Flagship, TF 74; in the closing months of the war lent fire support to landings in Borneo; carrier escort duties in Makassar Straits.

19 Sept–17 Nov Sailed to Shanghai with CTF 73 aboard; returned via Pearl Harbor carrying combatants to west coast.

3 Dec Arrived San Pedro; further 'Magic Carpet' cruise to Eniwetok and Kwajalein.

1946 1 Jan Arrived San Francisco.

24 June Decommissioned.

1951 9 Jan Sold to Chile; renamed – *Capitan Prat*.

△ Six weeks later *Nashville* suffered damage from a Kamikaze aircraft which necessitated repairs at Puget Sound Navy Yard. This photograph was taken in San Francisco Bay, probably in January 1946, when she was undertaking her last 'Magic Carpet' cruise. Her fire control gear now has Mk 13 and Mk 28 radar. (Cas)

▷ After her refit at Philadelphia Navy Yard *Phoenix* appeared as in this photograph taken on 30 August 1943. There are SOC reconnaissance aircraft on each of the after catapults. Additions have been made to the radar equipment; on the fire control gear Mk 34 there is Mk 8 Mod. 1 forward, Mk 3 (old) aft. Mk 4 is to be found on the front of the after Mk 33. The ship has been sprayed in a 'Dazzle' pattern – in accordance with Measure 32/5d. (USN)

◁ ▽ Early in 1951 *Phoenix* was sold to the Argentinian Navy where she was to serve for a further 31 years – latterly with the name *General Belgrano* – before she was sunk during the British-Argentinian war on 3 May 1982 by the British nuclear submarine *Conqueror* using conventional torpedoes. These two photographs, which are undated, would be from the ship's last service period. She still carries numerous 20mm twin-barrel AA, and the British Seacat missile launcher near the forward funnel. The 5in/25 AA guns are still housed in protective anti-splinter tubs. The Mk 34 fire control gear controls Mk 13, but only the after Mk 33 remains on board. Otherwise the radar electronic system is of Dutch manufacture (Hollandse Signaalapparaten). The catapults have been removed and numerous portholes have been added below the main deck line. (SoW)

Phoenix

1938 3 Oct Commissioned; shake-down cruise to Trinidad and South America; returned.

1939 Jan Operations along west coast, later from Pearl Harbor.

1941 7 Dec Anchored in Pearl Harbor; remained undamaged; set out with *St. Louis* and *Detroit* in immediate search for Japanese fleet; then convoy escort to west coast and back; sailed for Melbourne; operated in Australian waters until about February 1942; then several months in Indian Ocean; present at evacuation of Java.

1943 July Yard refit at Philadelphia; took Secretary of State Cordell Hull to Casablanca; joined Seventh Fleet in South Pacific.

26 Dec Bombarded Cape Gloucester.

1944 25–26 Jan Bombarded shore installations New Guinea area.

29 Feb Occupation of Los Negros.

4 & 7 March Bombarded Admiralty Islands.

22 April Landings on Hollandia.

25 May Landing on Biak, New Guinea.

4 June Suffered light bomb damage; 1 dead, 4 wounded.

2 July Landings on Noemfoor.

15 Sept Occupation of Morotai, Molucca Islands.

20 Oct Landings on Leyte; Battle of Leyte Gulf, took part in sinking of Japanese battleship *Fuso*.

1945 Jan Invasion of Luzon.

13–28 Feb Bataan, Corregidor.

29 June–7 July Covered mine-clearing operations and landings on Balikpapan, Borneo.

15 August At Pearl Harbor Navy Yard.

Sept Transferred to east coast.

1946 3 July Decommissioned.

1951 9 April Sold to Argentina.

17 Oct Re-named *Desiete de Octubre*.

1956 Renamed General Belgrano.

1982 3 May Sunk during Falklands war by two torpedoes from HM submarine *Conqueror*.

The former *Phoenix* (CL-46) during her service in the Argentinian Navy; this is how she would have looked prior to being sunk in May 1982 off the Falklands.

Boise

1938 12 August Commissioned.
1939 Feb After trials, to West and South Africa
  CRUDIV 9 (Cruisers, Battle Force); at San
  Pedro, California.
1941 Nov Operational cruises between west coast
  and Hawaii.
4 Dec Arrived Manila after escort cruise.
8 Dec At Cebu, Philippines; joined TF 5.
1942 21 Jan Went aground; returned to west
  coast via Ceylon and India.
Feb Repairs at Mare Island.
22 June Escorted New Zealand convoy; returned
  to Pearl Harbor.
31 July–10 August Decoy transport in Japanese
  waters.
August Convoy escort to Fiji and New Hebrides.
14–18 Sept Fire support at Guadalcanal; damaged
  by Japanese hits.
1942–43 19 Nov–20 March Repairs at Philadelphia Navy Yard.
8 June Departed for Mediterranean.
10 July–18 August Landings in Sicily.
Sept Landings at Taranto and Salerno.
15 Nov Arrived New York; transferred to
  PACFL.
31 Dec Arrived New Guinea.
1944 Jan-Sept Operated in New Guinea area.
20–24 Oct Invasion of Leyte.
25 Oct Battle of Surigao Straits.
12–17 Dec Landings on Mindoro.
1945 9–13 Jan Landings on Lingayen; General
  MacArthur aboard.
14–31 Jan Security operation off Luzon.
13–17 Feb Occupation of Bataan and Corregidor.
8–12 March Landings on Zamboanga.
27 April–3 May Borneo; landings on Tarakan.

3–16 June Took General MacArthur to Philippines and Borneo areas; returned to west coast.
7 July Arrived at San Pedro.
3 Oct Transferred to east coast.
20 Oct Arrived New York.
1946 1 July Decommissioned.
1951 11 Jan Sold to Argentina; renamed *Nueve de
  Julio.*

△ *Boise* on 18 April 1939. (Cas)

▽ A photograph of *Boise* dating from January
1945, when she was painted in Measure 21. Much
life-saving equipment is stowed on the 6in turrets,
among other items, mine-clearing gear and 6in
shells. The Mk 33 fire control gear has a Mk 28
radar. On the Mk 34 is Mk 13; and there is an SK
antenna on the masthead. (USN)

Honolulu

1938 15 June Commisioned; shake-down cruise to England.

1939 14 June Arrived at San Pedro; operations along west coast until mid-June then at Puget Sound Navy Yard.

1940 5 Nov Sailed to Pearl Harbor.

1941 7 Dec Suffered minor damage during Japanese attack.

1942 12 Jan Convoy escort to San Francisco.

21 Jan Arrived San Francisco; convoy escort

◁ *Honolulu* in August 1938 during her shake-down cruise in English waters. She still has Mk 31 fire control gear which, to a certain extent, is superimposed on the Mk 33. She has two rows of portholes. The 5in/25s are still under protective awnings. (WL)

▽ *Honolulu* on 30 January 1942 at Mare Island Navy Yard, shows clearly the massive effect of three 6in turrets on the forecastle. Each turret has its own rangefinder, with a periscope on top to survey the turret deck. The lower row of portholes has been eliminated. Note the paddle-wheel steamer in the background. (USN)

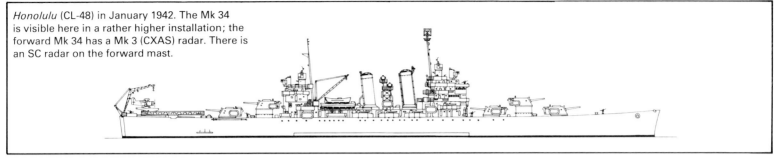

Honolulu (CL-48) in January 1942. The Mk 34 is visible here in a rather higher installation; the forward Mk 34 has a Mk 3 (CXAS) radar. There is an SC radar on the forward mast.

between USA, Australia and Samoa until May 1942.

29 May Departed for Alaska; operated from Kodiak in Aleutians.

7 August Bombarded Kiska.

21 August Fire support at Adak, Aleutians.

Sept–Oct At Mare Island.

3 Nov Convoy escort to Noumea, then to Guadal-canal.

30 Nov Battle of Tassafaronga; *Northampton* sunk, three other US cruisers damaged.

1943 Operations with TF 67 off Espiritu Santo.

May–July Bombarded New Guinea.

4 July Sank Japanese destroyer in Kula Gulf.

13 July Sank Japanese cruiser and destroyer during battle off Kolombangara; hit by torpedo; repaired at Tulagi.

16 August Yard repairs at Pearl Harbor; sailed for Mare Island for completion.

17 Nov Sailed for Solomons.

27 Dec Bombarded Bougainville; long-drawn-out bombardment of Solomon Islands until mid-June.

June Bombarded Guam.

28 June Preparations for occupation of Guam.

6 Sept Fire support off Palau.

12 Oct Left Marcus in preparation for invasion of Philippines.

19 Oct Bombardment in Leyte Gulf.

20 Oct Hit by aerial torpedo.

29 Oct Arrived at Manus, first repairs.

19 Nov Left for Norfolk, Virginia via

20 Dec Pearl Harbor and San Diego; remained at Norfolk until end of the war.

1945 Oct Following last yard refit at Norfolk, underwent trials.

1947 3 Feb Decommissioned.

▷ *Honolulu*, again dating from 30 January 1942: there are now two Mk 34 and only one Mk 3 radar forward. There are 20mm and 28mm AA. In the background one can make out a cruiser of the *Omaha* class. (USN)

△ This photograph of *Honolulu* was taken in November 1943 at the conclusion of her refit at Mare Island Navy Yard when camouflage for Measure 32/2c had been applied. She has new half-caps on the funnels. SK radar and two SG aerials have been fitted as have radar Mk 8 Mod. 1, Mk 3 (old) and Mk 4 (suspended in front). Subsequently *Honolulu* was to be converted as had been *Savannah,* but no photographs showing this conversion seem to be available. (USN)

St. Louis
1939 19 May Commissioned.
6 Oct End of shake-down cruises; neutrality

patrol West Indies until 3 September 1940.
9 Nov To North Atlantic, via the west coast.
12 Dec Arrived Pearl Harbor; fleet manoeuvres.
1941 at Mare Island Navy Yard.
20 June Further operations in Hawaiian waters.
Sept Patrolled between Wake, Midway, Guam and Manila.
28 Sept At Pearl Harbor Yard.
7 Dec Shot down three Japanese aircraft.
10 Dec Unsuccessful search for Japanese fleet; convoy escort between San Francisco and Hawaii.
1942 6 Jan With TF 17 (with *Yorktown* [CV-5]) to Samoa; Gilberts.
7 Feb Returned to Pearl Harbor; resumed convoy escort to and from west coast.
May Accompanied President of Philippines,

▷ This photograph of *St. Louis* taken in March 1942, not long after the USA had entered the war, shows the fundamental differences between the first seven and the last two units of the *Brooklyn* class. One notes differences in the bridge, a different layout of the after superstructure (these serving to some extent as a pattern for what would later be applied to *Savannah* and *Honolulu*) and also her armament of 5in/38 which she had from the very first. The enclosed 5in mountings which she had at the beginning of the war were replaced by mountings of a more modern design. The SC radar antenna which she had at this time cannot be seen here. (USN)

▽ *St. Louis* immediately after her yard refit in October 1944. Very clearly evident are her new camouflage paint of Measure 32/2c; radar equipment: SK-2 and two SG; fire control radar antennae: two Mk 8 Mod. 1 and two Mk 28. (USN)

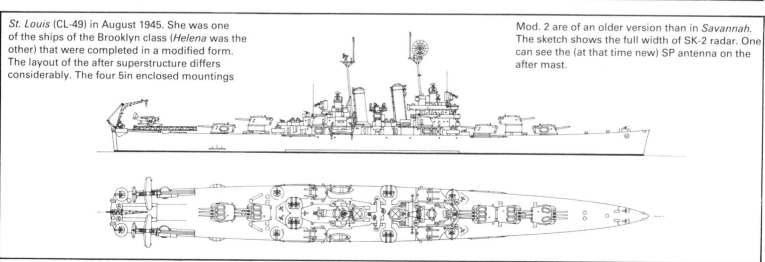

St. Louis (CL-49) in August 1945. She was one of the ships of the Brooklyn class (*Helena* was the other) that were completed in a modified form. The layout of the after superstructure differs considerably. The four 5in enclosed mountings Mod. 2 are of an older version than in *Savannah*. The sketch shows the full width of SK-2 radar. One can see the (at that time new) SP antenna on the after mast.

△ At the end of November 1944 *St. Louis* was badly damaged off Leyte by the impact of two Kamikaze aircraft. Repair work was carried out on the west coast from the end of 1944 to March 1945 and she was painted once again in camouflage Measure 21. She is seen here in San Francisco Bay on 9 November 1945, probably before the commencement of her second 'Magic Carpet' cruise in the Pacific. The worn condition of the 'navy blue' paint shows the effect of sea water. (Cas)

◁ *St. Louis* was handed over to Brazil at the beginning of 1951 and was renamed Tamandaré. This photograph shows the former *St. Louis* with the designation she was then given, C 12. She still has SPS-6 radar on the forward mast. The catapults have been removed.

Quezon (in SS *President Coolidge*) to San
Francisco, then convoy escort to Midway.
25 May To the Aleutians; joined TF 8.
3 August Bombarded Kiska.
25 Oct Left for yard work at Mare Island.
4 Dec Convoy escort to New Caledonia.
1943 Jan To the Solomons; there for five months;
  bombarded various islands.
6 July Battle of Kula Gulf.
10 July Severe bow damage from torpedoes;
  provisional repairs at Tulagi and Espiritu Santo;
  left for Mare Island.
Nov Returned to Solomons.
20–25 Nov Fire support off Bougainville.
1944 Jan–Feb Bombarded Shortland Islands;
  operations in North Solomons, Bismarck Islands
  and New Ireland.
14 Feb Hit by Japanese bombs; 23 dead, 20
  wounded; both ship's aircraft destroyed. Yard
  repair completed end of February; remained in
  Solomons.
May With TF 52.
10 June Left for fire support off Saipan.
19 June Battle of Philippine Sea.
22 June Returned to Saipan.
14 July Left for Marian Islands; bombarded
  Guam until the landing.
29 July Left for west coast via Pearl Harbor; at a
  yard.
Oct Back to Hawaii; sailed to Philippines.
16 Nov Arrived Leyte Gulf.
27 Nov Kamikaze pilot crashed his aircraft on
  after deck; deaths caused among the 20mm gun
  crews; fire in hangar area; second aircraft thrown
  from starboard side of ship; death total 15, 1
  missing, 21 badly wounded.
30 Nov Provisional repairs at San Pedro Bay.
Dec Arrived west coast; yard repairs.
1 March Left west coast.
March Arrived Ulithi; attacks on Japanese mainland until end of March; with TF 54 bombarded
  Okinawa until mid-May.
May Short 'convalescence' at Leyte.
June Bombarded Okinawa.
25 July With TF 95; operations in China Sea and
  against Japanese mainland.
August Joined TF 73, patrol duties in River
  Yangtze area and off Shanghai; anchored in
  Buckner Bay until end of war.
1945–46 Nov–Jan Three 'Magic Carpet' cruises to
  west coast and central Pacific islands.
1966 Feb Transferred to east coast.
20 June Decommissioned.
1951 29 Jan Handed over to Brazil renamed
  Tamandaré.

△   During the Japanese attack on Pearl Harbor
Helena was hit by an aerial torpedo. She was
repaired at Mare Island where this photograph
was taken in June 1942. The portholes, just about
visible in the previous photograph, have been
welded shut. During these first months she has
already received four 40mm quadruples and the
appropriate fire control gear Mk 51, which
together with twelve 20mm Oerlikons and other
guns were fitted in place of various small boats
and the boats' crane. Mk 3 (first version) and Mk 4
(front hanging position) are on the Mk 34 and Mk
33. Note the two mobile conveyor belts behind
No. 3 6in turret which is swung outboard. (USN)

Helena

1939 18 Sept Commissioned for PACFL.
1941 7 Dec Hit by aerial torpedoes at Pearl
  Harbor; repaired there then at Mare Island.
1942 Operated in South Pacific.

Sept Escorted *Wasp* (CV-7) off Guadalcanal.
15 Sept Took on 400 survivors of crew of sunken
  Wasp.
11 Oct Battle of Cape Esperance; sank the cruiser
  Furutaka and the destroyer *Fubuki*.

20 Oct Avoided several torpedoes aimed at her.
11 Nov Convoy escort to Guadalcanal.
1943 Jan Bombarded New Georgia.
11 Feb Took part in sinking of submarine
  RO-102, then yard refit at Sydney.
March Recommenced bombardment of New
  Georgia.
5 July In Kula Gulf; sunk by three torpedoes
  from Japanese destroyers; 168 men lost.

◁ A detailed midships photograph of *Helena*
(CL-50) refitting in June 1941. The 5in twin
mountings are of a type dating from the mid
1930s. She still has one boats' crane and a
considerable number of picket boats on both sides
of the funnels. The mast positioned closely behind
the after funnel is to be found only in the last two
units of the *Brooklyn* class. In the opinion of many
naval officials both these last ships CL-49 and CL-
50 should have been regarded as making up a *St.
Louis* class. (USN)

▽ *Helena* on 1 July 1942 in the Bay of San Pablo
after leaving Mare Island Navy Yard. One can
clearly see the SC radar antenna. One year later
Helena sank in Kula Gulf following three destroyer
torpedo hits. (USN)

WICHITA

Wichita was the last of eighteen heavy cruisers built before the Second World War and conforming to the Washington and London Fleet Conferences. She was the only ship of her class. Although she had been planned as the eighth unit of the *New Orleans* class, she was, in effect, a *Brooklyn* with nine 8in guns arranged in three turrets. She is noteworthy in being the first ship to receive 5in/38 guns: four in single enclosed mountings and four in open turrets. Relatively broad funnel bases were a feature of this ship, and a new version of the 8in triple turret was introduced. With her 'straight-through' main deck, and better positioning of her aircraft aft – which permitted better distribution of the secondary armament – it can be said that *Wichita* was a link between the other 'Washington' cruisers and the war vessels designed subsequently.

Changes prompted by war-time experience were much fewer in this ship than in her predecessors, restricted in effect to the introduction of new electronic gear that was developed and additional AA machine-guns.

It is significant that, at the end of the 1940s, *Wichita* was chosen as the first cruiser to be converted to a guided missile cruiser. Later, however, the preference was given to *Boston* (CA-69) and *Canberra* (CA-70), presumably because they had a longer service life ahead of them.

Wichita
1939 16 Feb Commissioned.
20 April–1 May At Houston, Texas.
May Shake-down cruise to Cuba, Virgin Islands and Bahamas.
25 Sept Joined CRUDIV 7, Atlantic Squadron.
4–9 Oct Neutrality patrol, relieving *Vincennes* (CA-44) then returned to Norfolk.
12 Oct–1 Dec At Norfolk Navy Yard; during the first half of 1940 operated off Cuba and San Juan, Puerto Rico – in the formation 'Caribbean Patrol', with *Vincennes* and five destroyers.
1940 June With *Quincy* (CA-39), showing the flag in South America.
23 Sept Returned to Norfolk.
30 Sept Arrived at New York; three months' training ship for Navy Reservist midshipmen.
1941 Jan–March Operations and exercises in Caribbean.
23 March At New York Navy Yard.
6 April–17 May With *Tuscaloosa* (CA-37) in North Atlantic; yard work at New York.
27 July With TF 16, occupation of Iceland until 20 August.
28 Sept With TG 7.5 (*Wasp* [CV-7], *Mississippi* [BB-41] and four destroyers) around Iceland until December.
7 Dec Anchored in Hvalfjordur, Iceland.
1942 15 Jan Suffered light damage from collision during hurricane.

9 Feb At New York Navy Yard until end of February.
26 March Subordinated to Commander, Naval Forces Europe; with *Wasp* (CV-7), *Washington* (BB-56), *Tuscaloosa* (CA-37) and eight destroyers, sailed for new base at Scapa Flow.
4 April Arrived Scapa Flow, exercises with units of RN Home Fleet.
28 April Convoy escort to Murmansk.
6 May Security patrols from Iceland to Denmark Strait, changing places when necessary with convoy escorts.
6 July Flagship, TF 99.
23 July At yard in Rosyth, Scotland, propeller shaft vibration.
9 August Returned to east coast via Hvalfjordur.
22 August–5 Sept Yard repairs at New York.
24 Oct With TG 34.1 sailed for North Africa on Operation 'Torch'; hit by French coastal batteries, 14 slightly wounded.
12 Nov Departed for USA; at New York Navy Yard then transferred to Pacific Fleet.
1943 29 Jan Battle off Rennell.

▽ *Wichita*, with the British heavy cruiser *London*, during the first half of 1942. The camouflage Measure 12 is clearly visible; she has SC radar and, both seldom encountered, Mk 1 fire control (FA) on both Mk 34s. The open gun mountings are already protected by splinter shields. (IWM)

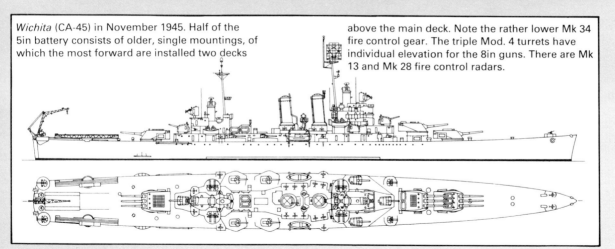

Wichita (CA-45) in November 1945. Half of the 5in battery consists of older, single mountings, of which the most forward are installed two decks above the main deck. Note the rather lower Mk 34 fire control gear. The triple Mod. 4 turrets have individual elevation for the 8in guns. There are Mk 13 and Mk 28 fire control radars.

◁ *Wichita* in San Francisco Bay, on 25 November 1945, on arrival from a 'Magic Carpet' cruise. Mk 13 and Mk 28 fire control radars are now installed. With the exception of SK radar and the 40mm AA, the appearance of the ship has not altered substantially since 1942. To the left of the picture: *Salt Lake City* (CA-25). (Cas)

△ A navy identification photograph of *Wichita* taken in about September 1942 when she was at the New York Navy Yard. She is painted in Measure 22. The flags at both mastheads show that an important personality is on board, in this case the Secretary of the Navy and a Four Star Admiral. (USN)

18 April Via Pearl Harbor to Aleutians; there Flagship, TG 52.10, later TG 16.14.
29 May–18 June Flagship, TG 16.7 off Attu.
22 July Flagship TG 16.21, bombarded Kiska.
4 Sept–3 Dec At Puget Sound Navy Yard.
7 Dec Left San Francisco for Hawaii.
1944 16 Jan Left for invasion of Marshall Islands; there joined TG 58.3; Kwajalein, Eniwetok, Truk.
12 Feb Joined TG 58.2.
20 Feb Accompanied *Intrepid* (CV-11) which had been torpedoed, to Majuro.
4 March At Pearl Harbor, Flagship, CRUDIV 6.
20 March Yap, Woleai, Palau Islands.
13 April New Guinea, Hollandia, Truk, Satawan.
14 June With TU 53.10.8, bombarded Saipan, Guam.
19 June Battle of Philippine Sea.
July–Sept Numerous operations in South-West Pacific.
2 Oct Okinawa, Luzon, Formosa.
18 Oct After a typhoon, joined TF 34; then with *New Orleans* (CA-32) sank Japanese carrier

Chiyoda and destroyer *Hatsuzuki.*
2 Nov Ulithi until mid-November. Operations off Leyte and Luzon; bad turbine vibration.
20 Nov Returned to Ulithi.
27 Nov Left Ulithi, only two propellers functioning, via Eniwetok and Pearl Harbor.
15 Dec Arrived west coast; in yard.
1945 8 Feb Departed for Pearl Harbor.
28 Feb Arrived Pearl Harbor.
6 March Arrived Ulithi.
20 March Joined TU 54.2.3; left for Okinawa; coastal bombardment there.
27 April & 12 May Suffered light damage from gunfire; 12 dead; at the end of the war on
15 August Still in Okinawa area, then occupation of Japan; with formation TG 55.7; 'Magic Carpet' cruise to west coast.
24 Nov Arrived San Francisco.
26 Nov–1 Dec In dry dock at Mare Island; second 'Magic Carpet' cruise to Saipan.
1946 12 Jan Arrived San Francisco, then east coast.
1947 3 Feb Decommissioned.

ATLANTA CLASS

This class was the first to depart fundamentally from all previous cruiser designs. Although developed in peace-time, the design was influenced by two factors: the growing threat posed by aircraft; the construction of increasingly heavily armed Japanese destroyers. The need, therefore, was for a cruiser type which, operating on the perimeter of a battle group, could counter enemy aircraft with a thick curtain of fire while being able at the same time, with an increased number of guns, to take on any destroyer that attempted to engage the central battle group. The only way to achieve this was with the lightest possible ship, having a strong AA component, manoeuvrable and fast enough to lead a destroyer formation. With these requirements in mind, the *Atlanta*s were the true successor of the *Omaha* class. In addition to the heavy 5in dual-purpose AA there were two groups of quadruple torpedo tubes for use against surface ships. The AA component consisted of sixteen semi-automatic 5in/38 in twin turrets which were totally new at that time. Three of the turrets were sited forward and three aft, behind one another on the

highest point of three decks, with one turret on each side of the after superstructure. Such a concentration of anti-aircraft guns on a ship of only 6,000 tons standard resulted in considerable top-heaviness. The 28mm AA was found inadequate and was replaced by 40mm Bofors after the war had begun.

It soon transpired that the AA capability was restricted by the fact that there were only two fire control Mk 37 for the eight turrets, which meant that only a limited number of aircraft could be fought at one time. Barrage fire alone was not sufficient to bring down close-range aircraft. After the beginning of the war all ships were fitted with radar.

From the outset the ships were to have three quadruple 28mm AA and later a further mounting on the quarterdeck. In the two ships that survived, these mountings were later replaced by 40mm twins. These ships were the only US wartime cruisers to have a sonar installation. Top-heaviness was increased by the addition of further AA (20mm and 40mm) during the war.

It is interesting to note that at much the same

time, Great Britain developed a similar cruiser type in its *Dido* class and its main armament was disposed in a similar way to that of the *Atlanta*s.

The relatively low displacement – a consequence of the dictates of the second London Fleet Conference which restricted the building of heavy cruisers – meant that aircraft installation was not possible. The ships were originally designed to make 33 knots, but they never achieved this. As far as is known, the building cost of each ship was approximately 23.2 million dollars.

It is ironic that the first two ships of the class were sunk on the same day off Guadalcanal, not by aircraft (defence against which being the reason for their conception), but by Japanese gunfire and torpedoes.

▽ *Atlanta* (CL–51) off the coast of Maine on 26 October 1941 just before commissioning.

Atlanta

1941 24 Dec Commissioned. accelerated shake-down cruises, then transferred to Pacific; escort duty to New Caledonia.

1942 4–6 June With TF 16 took part in Battle of Midway as escort protection for *Hornet* (CV-8).

7–9 August With TF 16 at Guadalcanal.

24–25 August Battle of East Solomons.

13 Nov Badly damaged in sea battle off Guadalcanal, hit by a torpedo and at least 49 shells; 172 dead, 79 wounded; sank off Lunga Point.

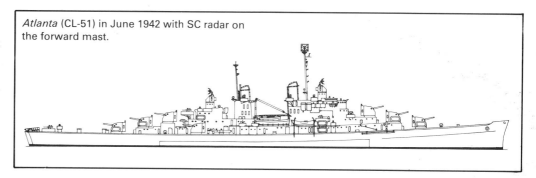

Atlanta (CL-51) in June 1942 with SC radar on the forward mast.

Juneau

1942 14 Feb Commissioned, early in year accelerated shake-down cruise along Atlantic coast.

May Blockade of Martinique and Guadeloupe to prevent take-over by Vichy French Forces; short yard period in New York to complete fitting-out.

1 June–12 August Patrol and convoy duties in Atlantic and Caribbean.

22 August Transferred to Pacific Fleet.

11 Sept Rendezvoused with TF 17, with USS *Wasp* (CV-7) and *Hornet* (CV-8).

15 Sept Rescued survivors from sunken *Wasp* and sailed to Espiritu Santo.

17 Sept Once more with TF 17.

26 Oct Battle off Santa Cruz operating with TF 61 (*Hornet* and *Enterprise*).

8 Nov Convoy escort to Guadalcanal.

13 Dec Hit by two torpedos; after second hit sank within twenty seconds; only ten survivors.

▽   A distinguishing feature of *Juneau* (CL-52) was that two different types of camouflage – both designated Scheme 12 – were applied. This photograph shows the older, mottled pattern. The SC and Mk 4 radar have not yet been fitted.

△ In the later camouflaged version *Juneau* has 'splotches' on the hull which represent a kind of water-line. The ship's electronic systems are visible. The photograph is undated. (USN)

▽ Beginning with *San Diego* all units of the *Atlanta* and the similar *Oakland* class survived the second world war. The above undated photograph of *San Diego* must have been taken in about mid-1942. She is painted in a further variation of Measure 12 camouflage. The patterning of the SC antenna can be seen clearly. (USN)

San Diego

1942 10 Jan Commissioned; shake-down cruise in Chesapeake Bay; transferred to west coast.

16 May Arrived San Diego.

15 June Escort protection for *Hornet* (CV-8); beginning of August landing on Guadalcanal.

15 Sept Witnessed sinking of *Wasp*.

26 Oct Witnessed sinking of *Hornet* (off Santa Cruz).

12–15 Nov Escort protection for *Enterprise* (CV-6) in Battle of Guadalcanal; then operated for several months in the Solomons including a cruise to New Zealand; invasion of Munda and Bougainville with *Saratoga* (CV-3).

1943 5–11 Nov With *Saratoga* and *Princeton* attacked Rabaul and Tarawa.

9 Dec Escorted the damaged *Lexington* (CV-16) to Pearl Harbor; sailed for San Francisco; an operations centre installed and 28mm AA replaced by 40mm Bofors.

1944 Jan At Pearl Harbor; joined TF 58.

31 Jan–4 March Landings on Eniwetok; attacks on Truk; intermediate stop at San Francisco for completion of radar installation.

June Attacks on Wake and Marcus, the Bonins; invasion of Saipan.

△ *San Diego* on 10 April 1944 off Mare Island, in freshly applied camouflage of Measure 33/24d. However, the very dark shade of the darkest surfaces – not solely in comparison with the boot topping – suggests the earlier Measure 32. (USN)

19–20 June Battle of Philippine Sea; invasion of Guam and Tinian; attacks on Palaus.

6–8 August Landing on Peleliu.

21 Sept Attacks in Manila Bay; first attacks on Okinawa with TF 38.

12–15 Oct Attacks on Formosa; escorted damaged cruisers *Houston* and *Canberra* to Ulithi.

17–18 Dec Weathered a severe typhoon.

1945 Jan Attacks on Formosa, Luzon, Indo-China, and South China and Japanese mainland.

Feb Attacks on Iwo Jima.

1 March Bombarded Okino Daijo, landings on Okinawa; attacks on Kyushu.

27–28 March Bombarded Minami Dalto Jima; continued fire support for the landings on Okinawa.

27 August First Allied ship to enter Tokyo Bay; occupied the naval base at Yokosuka.

14 Sept Returned to San Francisco; took part in 'Magic Carpet' cruises.

1946 4 Nov Decommissioned.

1949 18 March Reclassified as CLAA-53.

▷ *San Diego* at Mare Island in April 1944, showing interesting details of the after section. The three after 5in/38 mountings behind one another and stepped, a 40mm quadruple with Mk 51 fire control gear in front of it, a pair of twin Oerlikons, depth-charge racks and smoke-generating equipment. One can clearly see the radar antennae SG and SC-2. (USN)

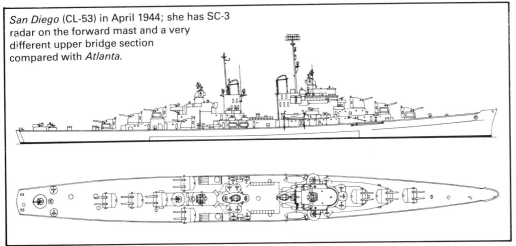

San Diego (CL-53) in April 1944; she has SC-3 radar on the forward mast and a very different upper bridge section compared with Atlanta.

San Juan

1942 28 Feb Commisioned; shake-down cruises in Atlantic.

5 June With formation built around Wasp (CV-7).

30 June Departure of formation from San Diego escorting troop transports to Solomons.

7 August Fire support, Tulagi landing.

8–9 August Battle of Savo Island.

10 Sept Arrived Pearl Harbor with damaged Enterprise (CV-6).

26 Oct Battle off Santa Cruz; damaged by bombs.

30 Oct Arrived at Noumea; provisional repairs; then ten days' repairs at Sydney.

24 Nov Joined Battle Group of Saratoga (CV-3) off the Fijian Islands.

1942–43 Dec–June Operations based on Noumea in Coral Sea, with carrier group and alone.

▷ San Juan at anchor off Norfolk Navy Yard on 3 June 1942, two days before she departed with the battle group based on Wasp (CV-7) in the Pacific. The camouflage is one of the many variations on Measure 12. The SC radar, which can hardly be seen, is positioned behind the after mast. There is an SG on the forward mast. She has 28mm AA and some 20mm Oerlikons. (USN)

▷ San Juan in San Francisco Bay on 14 October 1944. During her refit she received among other items radar antennae SK-2 and Mk 12/22 and was painted in Measure 32/33d. It is clear from this photograph how much the 'dull black' approximates to the black of her boot topping. (USN)

Nov Rabaul and landing on Bougainville, Gilberts and Kwajalein.
6 Dec Left for refit at Mare Island.
1944 19 Jan Returned to *Saratoga* group.
Feb Eniwetok landing.
30 March–1 April With *Yorktown* (CV-10) and *Lexington* (CV-16) attacks on Palaus, Yap and Ulithi.
7 April With *Hornet* (CV-12).
April Landing on Hollandia; Truk.
June Attacks on Iwo Jima and Chichi Jima.
19–20 June Battle of Philippine Sea.
July With *Wasp* (CV-18) and *Franklin* (CV-13); capture of Guam; attacks on Iwo Jima and Chichi Jima.
4 Aug Left Eniwetok with *Yorktown* (CV-10) for west coast; refit at San Francisco.

21 Nov At Ulithi, joined *Lexington* (CV-16) group.
Dec Attacks on Formosa and Luzon; landing on Mindoro.
18–19 Dec Weathered severe typhoon, then to Ulithi for Christmas.
1945 3–9 Jan Occupation of Luzon, attacks on Formosa and Okinawa.
10–20 Jan South China Sea.
Feb With *Hornet* (CV-12) attacks on Tokyo in support of landings on Iwo Jima.
1 March At Ulithi preparing for operations to retake Okinawa.
22 March–30 April With *Hornet* operations around Nansei Shoto, in which *Hornet* sunk by aircraft.
13 June Repairs in Leyte Gulf.

1 July With *Bennington* (CV-20) attacks on Japanese mainland.
27 August Anchorage in Sagami Wan; release of Allied prisoners from Japan.
29 August Anchored in Tokyo Bay.
25 Oct Occupation of Japan.
14 Nov Left for West Pacific; took combatants home.
29 Nov At Pearl Harbor.
2 Dec 'Magic Carpet' cruise to Noumea and Tutuila.
1946 9 Jan Arrived San Pedro with returning troops.
9 Nov Decommissioned.
1949 28 Feb Reclassified as CLAA-54.

OAKLAND CLASS

Just one year after *Atlanta*, *Oakland* left the slipway, the name-ship of an improved class which was very similar in appearance to the *Atlanta*s. Many competent sources do not differentiate between the two and put all eleven ships into one class. The *Oakland* class can be divided into two sub-groups; once consisting of CL-95 to 98; the second, CL-119 to 121 which did not leave the slipway until 1945–46. Both groups owe much to the modifications given to the *Atlanta* class. Common to both is the abandonment of both the beam 5in twin mountings. The original design provided for the fitting of the then current radar installations, but obviously for weight reasons no further Mk 37s were to be added. The 40mm AA had radar-controlled fire direction. All ships of sub-group 1 had quadruple groups of torpedo tubes which were removed in 1945. The light AA was increased to a total of sixteen 40mm and fourteen 20mm guns. Sub-group 2 showed considerable differences. In order to reduce top-heaviness Nos. 2 and 5 turrets, were no longer

positioned one deck higher than the turret just in front or just behind, but were now placed on the main deck. Some of the ships were reclassified as AA cruisers (CLAA) in 1949.

Both the *Atlanta* and *Oakland* classes found themselves at the lowest limit for light cruiser displacement. This precluded the provision of a large fuel supply and made them less useful for operations in the Pacific; their range was insufficient to engage enemy destroyers. They were lightly armoured and their ability to withstand damage was never great.

CL-95 to 98 were components of the Fleet Enlargement Programme of 1940 and, when commissioned, they fitted in closely with the previous *Atlanta* class. They had an open bridge, and the splinter protection for the quick-firing AA was improved. But they, too, suffered from extreme top-heaviness through the massive addition of 20mm and 40mm AA during the war, and this was the main reason that the torpedo tubes were removed in 1945. Initially the 40mm

Bofors were twin mountings, but later additional quadruple mountings or combinations were installed.

After the war, only *Juneau* (II) was left in being until 1955, i.e., somewhat before the beginning of the guided missiles age; all previous ships were struck off between 1946 and 1950. Designs for a new cruiser class to succeed them, which would have used 5in/54 guns, were well advanced when it was realized that future guided missiles would have a great effect on warship deployment, and plans were abandoned.

▽ *Oakland* was the lead ship of the second group of anti-aircraft cruisers. This photograph dates from 29 October 1943 after her first conversion during which among other work the platform on the port side of the second funnel was removed. She saw out the rest of the war in camouflage of Measure 21. She still has her torpedo tubes. (USN)

▷ *Oakland,* on 1 November 1945 after work at the San Francisco yard. (USN)

Oakland

1943 17 July Commissioned; shake-down cruises from San Diego.
3 Nov Arrived Pearl Harbor; joined TG 50.3.
19 Nov Carrier escort off the Gilberts.
26 Nov Marshall Islands.
4 Dec Accompanied the torpedoed *Lexington* (CV 16) to Pearl Harbor.
9 Dec Arrived there; then with TG 58.1 to Marshall Islands.
1944 30 Jan Attacks on Kwajalein.
4 Feb Arrived Majuro.
16–17 Feb Attacks on Truk.

2 March Occupation of Emirau.
30 March–1 April Attacks on Palaus, Yap and Woleai.
April Attacks on Wake, Sawar, Truk and Satawan.
1 May Attacks on Ponape.
11 June Attacks on Guam.
14 June Attacks on Vulcan and Bonin Islands.
19 June Took part in Battle of Philippine Sea.
23–24 June Attacks on Pagan and Iwo Jima.
3–4 July Attacks on Iwo Jima and Chichi Jima.
7 July Attacks on Rota and Guam.
4 Aug Renewed bombardment of Chichi Jima.

6–8 Sept Attacks on Palaus, principally Peleliu.
8–22 Sept Attacks on airfields in Philippines.
10 Oct Attacks on Okinawa.
12–13 Oct Attacks on Formosa and Pescadores.
17–19 Oct Attacks on Luzon.

▽ *Oakland* spent some time at Mare Island Navy Yard at the beginning of 1945 when four 40mm quadruples were fitted and both sets of torpedo tubes removed. She is seen here on 19 October 1945 at anchor off San Francisco, after her return from Okinawa. The radar antennae are SC-2 and Mk 12/22. (Cas)

◁ ▷ After taking part in 'Navy Day' in her name-town of Oakland, *California* spent several weeks at Mare Island Navy Yard where, among other work, as can be seen in both these photographs taken on 1 October 1945, her camouflage had been renewed. The 'orange peel' effect of Mk 22 fire control is very noticeable. (USN)

20 Oct Landing at Leyte; carrier escort in Battle of Leyte Gulf.

Nov–Dec Reconquest of Philippines; departed for west coast.

1945 11 Jan–4 March At Mare Island Navy Yard.

30 March Arrived Ulithi.

2 April Joined TG 58.4; bombarded Sakashima Gunto.

10 April Joined TG 58.3 off Okinawa.

15 April Attacks on airfields on Kyushu.

April Renewed attacks on Okinawa.

13 May Attacks on airfields on Kyushu; in Okinawa area until end of month.

10 July With TG 38.1, attacks on Japanese mainland until end of war.

15 August Occupation of Japan.

31 August Anchored in Tokyo Bay.

3 Oct Left Okinawa with returning military personnel for west coast.

20 Oct Arrived San Francisco.

27 Oct Took part in 'Navy Day' at Oakland, California.

Nov–Dec 'Magic Carpet' cruises to Eniwetok and Kwajalein.

1945 The decommissioning planned for 1945 was cancelled and *Oakland* remained in active service for some years.

1946 Comprehensive refit at Puget Sound Navy Yard.

1946–47 July–Jan Gunnery training ship, operating from San Diego.

1947 Jan–Sept Training cruises in West Pacific.

1949 18 March Reclassified as CLAA-95.

1 July Decommissioned.

Reno

1943 28 Dec Commissioned; shake-down cruise off San Diego.

1944 14 April Left San Francisco for Fifth Fleet (TF 58).

19–20 May Attacks on Marcus.

23 May Wake.

June–July Carrier escort including:

11 June Saipan.

12–13 June Pagan.

15–16 June Vulcan and Bonin Islands.

△▽ These two photographs of *Reno* were taken on 25 January 1944 during trials off the Californian coast. The patterns of both sides of the ship in Measure 31a/24d can be seen. (USN)

19–20 June Battle of Philippine Sea.
20 June–8 July Retaking of Saipan.
17–24 July Landing on Guam.
26–29 July Attacks on Palau Islands.
4–5 August Bonins.
7 Sept Palau Islands.
9–13 Sept Mindanao and other Philippines islands.
15–20 Sept Retaking of the Palaus.
21–22 Sept Attacks on Manila and surroundings.
8 Oct Nansei Shoto.
12–14 Oct Attacks on Formosa; No. 6 turret damaged by Japanese aircraft crash.
24 Oct Attacks on Luzon; stood by badly damaged *Princeton* (CVL-23); this vessel sunk by own forces.
25 Oct Battle of Cape Engaño.
3 Nov Hit by submarine torpedo; towed to Ulithi; provisional repairs there; returned to east coast under own power.
1945 22 March Arrived Charleston Navy Yard; repaired there.
Sept After conversion, sailed to Texas for 'Magic Carpet' cruises to Le Havre.
1946 4 Nov Decommissioned.
1949 10 March Reclassified as CLAA-96.

Flint
1944 31 August Commissioned; to Pacific Fleet.
27 Dec Off Ulithi to join Third Fleet.
1945 Jan With TF 38 for invasion of Luzon.
21 Feb–12 March Iwo Jima.
March–June Carrier escort off Kyushu and Okinawa.
July–August Radar control ship off Nii Shima to aid own transport aircraft.

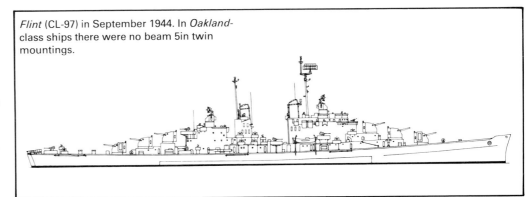

Flint (CL-97) in September 1944. In *Oakland*-class ships there were no beam 5in twin mountings.

△▽ The uppermost of these two photographs of *Flint* was taken in September 1944 and the lower one on 1 December 1944 when she was still undergoing shake-down cruises; both sides of the ship are painted in camouflage Measure 33/22d. Torpedo tubes are fitted but she does not have 40mm quadruples. (USN)

△ *Flint* lying in San Francisco Bay on 29 November 1945, the day after her return from Yokosuka. She was the first cruiser to receive 'ocean gray' camouflage after the end of the war. Signal flags are hanging out to dry. (Cas)

10–15 Sept Tokyo Bay, then 'Magic Carpet' cruise to Honshu and Eniwetok.
13 Oct Left Yokosuka for west coast.
28 Nov Arrived San Francisco; further 'Magic Carpet' cruise to Kwajalein.
1946 11 Jan Arrived Puget Sound.
1947 6 May Decommissioned.
1949 18 March Reclassified as CLAA-97.

Tucson
1945 3 Feb Commissioned; shake-down cruise off San Diego.
8 May Departed for West Pacific.
13 May–2 June Exercises around Pearl Harbor.

16 June Arrived Leyte, joining TF 38 as escort for carriers *Essex* (CV-9), *Ticonderoga* (CV-14), *Randolph* (CV-15), *Monterey* (CVL-26) and *Bataan* (CVL-29).
1 July TF 38 Left for action against Japanese mainland.
10 July & 17–18 July Attacks on Tokyo.
14–15 July Attacks on Hokkaido and North Honshu.
15 August Remained in West Pacific after end of war; occupation of Japan.
27 Sept To west coast via Okinawa and Pearl Harbor.
5 Oct Arrived San Francisco.

27–28 Oct Took part in 'Navy Day' at San Pedro.
1945–46 Nov–August AA (20mm, 40mm and 3in) training ship on west coast.
Sept–Nov Refit at Puget Sound in preparation for detachment to COMDESPAC Command.
1947 24 Feb Left San Diego for manoeuvres off Hawaii.
27 March Returned to San Diego; local operations along west coast until summer.
28 July Arrived in West Pacific.
August–Sept Operations in East China Sea.
20 Oct Left Yokusuka for west coast.
1949 18 March Reclassified as CLAA-98.
11 June Decommissioned.

△   *Tucson* photographed on 18 February 1945 during her trials off the Californian coast. She has both sets of torpedo tubes and 40mm twins. (USN)

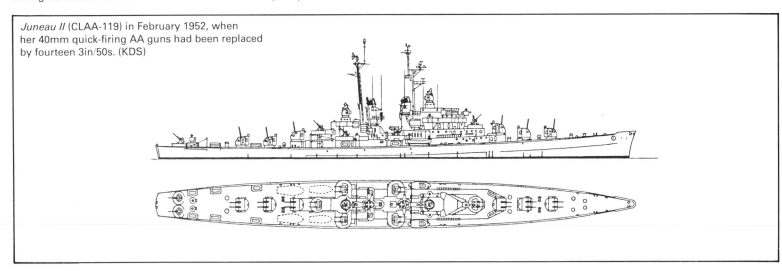

Juneau II (CLAA-119) in February 1952, when her 40mm quick-firing AA guns had been replaced by fourteen 3in/50s. (KDS)

▽ The first of three units of the third group of 'lighter' anti-aircraft cruisers: *Juneau II* (CL-119) seen here in July 1951 off the west coast. As a consequence of the modified disposition of the 5in mountings it was possible to accommodate an additional 40mm AA position in front of the bridge. This meant that a total of six 40mm quadruples were available. None of these ships had torpedo tubes. In place of life rafts a larger number of utility boats were provided. The Mk 37 fire control gear were already equipped with Mk 25 and, on the forward mast, the post-war SG-6 radar antenna, which is rather hard to distinguish in this photograph. (USW)

Juneau II

1946 15 Feb Commissioned; operations along east coast and in Caribbean.

1947 16 April Left with first cruise of Sixth Task Force to Mediterranean.

15 Nov Returned to east coast.

14 June–3 Oct Second Mediterranean cruise.

1949 18 March Reclassified as CLAA-119.

3 May–26 Sept Third Mediterranean cruise.

29 Nov Transferred to Pacific Fleet.

1950 15 Jan Arrived Bremerton; operations on west coast.

22 April Flagship, COMCRUDIV 5.

1 June Arrived Japan, in readiness for Korean operations.

25 June One of first ships off Korean coast.

29 June First coastal bombardment of Korea.

28 July Left Sasebo to sail through Straits of Formosa.

4 August Flagship, 'Formosa Patrol Force' until 29 October, then with aircraft carriers off the Korean east coast; then returned to west coast.

1951 1 May Refit at Long Beach; then operations on west coast and Hawaii.

1952 April Once more off Korea as carrier escort.

5 Nov Returned to Long Beach.

1953 7 April With the Atlantic Fleet.
13 May–23 Oct Operational cruise in Mediterranean; then operations on east coast and
Caribbean.
1953–55 18 Nov–13 Feb Final Mediterranean
cruise.
1956 Decommissioned.

▽ ▷ Both these detailed photographs were taken
at a yard in February 1952 at a time when *Juneau*
had her 40mm Bofors replaced by 3in/50 AA guns.
A twin mounting replaced the quadruple and both
the single 3in guns were fitted aft in the previous
twin housing. Only two Mk 56 fire control gear
were provided for all fourteen 3in guns and they
can be seen near the after mast. As regards radar

antennae, one notes SPS-6B on the forward mast
and SP on the after mast. The ship already had
ECM and other special antennae. Note the bracing
of both masts. (USN)

Spokane

1946 17 May Commissioned.

24 June Left for shake-down cruises off Cuba.

11 Sept Detached to Second Fleet based on Plymouth, England.

7 Oct Left for Europe; operations in North Sea.

1947 27 Jan Left England; manoeuvres off Cuba.

18 March Returned to Norfolk.

22 Sept–14 Oct Refit at New York Navy Yard.

27 Oct Took part in 'Navy Day' at Norfolk.

29 Oct Left for manoeuvres with '2nd Task Fleet' off Bermudas.

8 Nov Left for Plymouth.

16 Nov Arrived Plymouth, under command of CINCNELM.

1948 11 March Returned to Norfolk.

18 March Reclassified as CLAA-120.

27 May–15 Sept Overhauled at New York Navy Yard; throughout remainder of year operations along east coast.

1949 4 Jan With *Philippine Sea* (CV-47) and *Manchester* (CL-83) left for Mediterranean; manoeuvres with units of Sixth Task Fleet.

23 May Returned to Norfolk; during the summer training ship for reservists.

1950 27 Feb Decommissioned.

1966 1 April During her period with Reserve Fleet, reclassified as AG-191. The planned conversion as a sonar test ship did not take place.

△ *Spokane* (CL-120) on the day she was launched, 22 September 1945, at the Federal SB yard at Kearny, New Jersey. The photograph shows clearly the advanced state of construction in which – particularly after the end of the war – ships of this class were launched. (USN)

▽ *Spokane* off Toulon on 28 April 1949, during an operational cruise in the then-designated 'Sixth Task Fleet' in the Mediterranean. The SK-2/SP radar combination stayed with the ship during her entire service life. (MB)

△▽ *Fresno* (CL-121) was in active service for a total period of two and a half years. Both of these photographs were taken in June 1947 in English waters when *Fresno* was operating from Plymouth. She was known for the last few months as CLAA-121. (WL)

Fresno
1946 27 Nov Commissioned; Atlantic Fleet.
1947 13 Jan–7 May Training cruise in Caribbean; visiting cruise to Uruguay and Brazil.
1 August–1 Dec Cruise to northern Europe and Mediterranean.

1948 3 March–19 June Based at Plymouth, England; from there visits to north European ports; then back to east coast; local operations there.
1949 18 March Reclassified as CLAA-121.
17 May Decommissioned.

CLEVELAND CLASS

If the ships of the *Brooklyn* class represented an attempt to make the most of what was allowed by the limits of the Fleet Treaties, the *Cleveland* class owed more to what had been experienced in other countries. The design endeavoured to provide a greater range, and better protection for the anti-aircraft armament on a displacement that was only 300 tons greater. This was achieved by relinquishing the fifth 6in triple turret and by strengthening and improving the disposition of the 5in mountings, which were new at that time and of which only six were installed. At the design stage electronic equipment was enhanced by the provision of control rooms (by enlarging the upper bridge) and, compared to the *Brooklyn* class, the communications installations were improved: new fire control systems, including Mk 37 for the 5in AA and Mk 34 for the 6in armament. Both of these were fitted in duplicate. The light AA was strengthened from time to time during the course of the ships' service. From the point of view of recognition, the first seven ships had a rounded-front bridge; in those that followed the bridge was sharper-angled in front. Unlike the preceding classes, the hull was totally devoid of openings and portholes, which meant that the interior had to be ventilated and illuminated artificially. Very significant was the better sub-division of the hull into many watertight compartments, which is why, although most of the ships saw war service and some suffered severe damage, none was lost.

The emergence of this class was provides a clear proof of the USA's enormous economic capacity. At the planning stage it was thought likely that the USA would be involved in a war with Japan sooner or later. The class consisted of a greater number of ships than, for example, were to be found in the destroyer classes of other large navies. In all, contracts were awarded for 39 units of this: two of these were suspended in 1940, and another one in 1945; 27 of the 36 remaining were actually completed as cruisers. Nine hulls were converted and completed as light aircraft carriers (CV, which from 1943 became CVL). Then, in the mid-1950s, when they had been in existence for an average of fifteen years, six of them were given a comprehensive conversion to guided missile cruisers. It seems to have been the intention to build a total of 52 units of this class, not perhaps because they were especially distinguished in performance (most of them were very top-heavy by the end of the war), but because it was thought that the Fleet urgently required the greatest possible number of units of the same design. At the design stage the superstructures were to have been of light alloys, but there was a shortage of aluminium so ship steel had to be used which did nothing to solve the problems with stability. The building costs amounted to approximately 31,000,000 dollars per ship.

Beginning with CL-64, the ships had an open bridge, dispensing with the citadel. In 1945 an attempt was made in certain ships to reduce top-heaviness; among other measures taken were: removal of one of the two catapults; removal of the range-finder from No. 1 turret; reduction of the electronics system and ammunition stowage.

Twenty-seven ships of the *Cleveland* class were completed. With the exception of *Manchester*, all ships had been taken out of service by the beginning of the Korean War. *Atlanta* alone had a new short period of rebirth as an experimental ship for explosives experiments. Nine units were redesigned and completed as light aircraft carriers. The construction of three further ships was suspended during the Second World War.

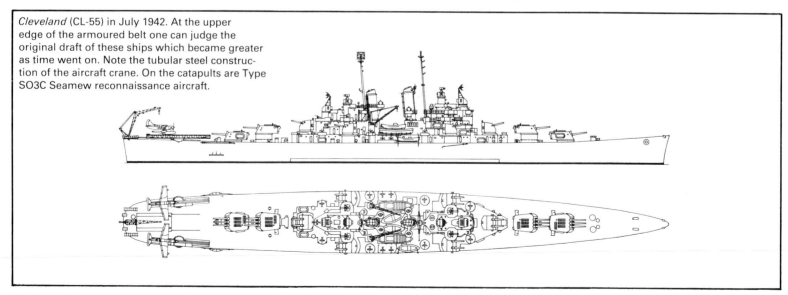

Cleveland (CL-55) in July 1942. At the upper edge of the armoured belt one can judge the original draft of these ships which became greater as time went on. Note the tubular steel construction of the aircraft crane. On the catapults are Type SO3C Seamew reconnaissance aircraft.

CLEVELAND CLASS SHIPS WITHOUT CL DESIGNATIONS WHEN COMMISSIONED

Pennant No.	Name	Fiscal Year	Laid Down	Builder	History
CL-59	Amsterdam	1940	1 May 1941	New York SBdg.	In service as CV-22 Independence
CL-61	Tallahassee	1940	2 June 1941	New York SBdg.	In service as CV-23 Princeton
CL-76	New Haven	1940	11 August 1941	New York SBdg.	In service as CV-24 Belleau Wood
CL-77	Huntington	1940	17 Nov 1941	New York SBdg.	In service as CV-25 Cowpens
CL-78	Dayton	1940	29 Dec 1941	New York SBdg.	In service as CV-26 Monterey
CL-79	Wilmington	1940	16 March 1942	New York SBdg.	In service as CV-28 Cabot
CL-84		1940		Federal	Building suspended 16 Dec 1940
CL-85	Fargo	1940		New York SBdg.	In service as CV-27 Langley
CL-88		1940		Federal	Building suspended 16 Dec 1940
CL-94	Youngstown	1940	4 Sept 1944	Cramp	Building suspended 12 Aug 1945
CL-99	Buffalo	1940	19 July 1940	New York SBdg.	In service as CV-29 Bataan
CL-100	Newark	1940		New York SBdg.	In service as CV-30 San Jacinto

▽ This undated aerial photograph shows *Cleveland* sometime in 1942. The crew are in whites. One can just about make out the SC radar on the after mast. (USN)

Cleveland

1942 15 June Commissioned.

10 Oct Left east coast for invasion of North Africa.

8–12 Nov Supported landiings in French North Africa.

24 Nov Returned to east coast.

5 Dec. Left for Pacific.

1943 16 Jan Arrived Efate, New Hebrides.

27–31 Jan Escort to Guadalcanal.

29–30 Jan Took part in battle off Rennell.

6 March With TF 68 bombarded Vila; helped sink two Japanese destroyers.

30 June Bombarded Shortland Islands.

12 July Landings on Munda, New Georgia; short repair stop at Sydney.

26–27 Oct Preparations for landings on Treasury Islands.

1944 17–23 March Capture of Emirau; repairs again at Sydney.

21 April Returned to Solomons.

8 June–24 August The Marianas.

19–20 June Battle of Philippine Sea, with TF 58.

12–29 Sept Bombarded Palau Islands.

1945 13–14 Feb Bombarded Corregidor.

7 June Left Subic Bay.

10 June Invasion of Brunei, Borneo; then cruise to Manila where General D. MacArthur embarked.

30 June Landing on Balikpapan.

16 July Okinawa and East China Sea.

9 Sept Evacuation of Allied prisoners of war from Wakayama; occupation tasks at Honshu.

28 Oct–1 Nov In Tokyo Bay then sailed for east coast via Pearl Harbor and San Diego.

5 Dec Refit at Boston Navy Yard.

1946 June Reservist training cruise to Halifax and Quebec.

1947 7 Feb Decommissioned.

◁ *Columbia,* painted in Measure 21, on 7 November 1942, two days before leaving Norfolk Navy Yard for the Pacific. There is SC radar on the after mast and there are two peculiarities in the fire control electronics one did not often find: Mk 3 on Mk 34; the Mk 4 is fitted in a very high position and is above the Mk 3. (USN)

◁ This photograph of *Columbia* was taken two years later in November 1944 somewhere in the Pacific when the ship was painted in Measure 33/1d (USN)

Columbia
1942 29 July Commissioned.
9 Nov Departed for Pacific.
10 Dec Arrived Espiritu Santo, New Hebrides.
1943 29–30 Jan Battle off Rennell.
1 Feb Patrols in Solomons.
29–30 June Landings in New Georgia.
11–12 July Bombardment of Munda.
5 Sept Short yard stay at Sydney.
1 Nov Support for landing on Bougainville.
2 Nov Battle in Empress Augusta Bay.
Dec Operations in Solomons.
1944 13–18 Feb Occupation of Nissan.

17–23 March Landing on Emirau.
4 April Left for west coast.
April–August Refit at San Francisco.
24 August Returned to Solomons.
Sept Landings on Palau Islands.
24 Oct Battle of Surigao Straits.
Dec Landings on Mindoro.
1945 6 Jan Landing on Lingayen; heavily damaged by Kamikaze; 13 dead, 44 wounded; both after 6in turrets out of action, continued firing with forward turrets.
9 Jan Hit again by Kamikaze; 24 dead, 97 wounded, six fire control gear and guns out of

action; provisional repairs on Leyte.
Jan–May Repairs on west coast; back to Leyte.
28 June Covered mine-clearing operations off Balikpapan, Borneo.
1 July Occupation of Balikpapan; at end of war cruise to west coast via Guam, Saipan, Iwo Jima.
5 Dec Arrived east coast.
1946 1 July Reservist training cruises.
30 Nov Decommissioned.

▷ Like many others of the first ships of this class, *Montpelier* had a very high positioning for the Mk 4 fire control radar, but fairly early on she was to receive Mk 8 Mod. 1 radar as seen here, on 12 November 1942 in the Atlantic, with the ship painted in Measure 12. The first *Cleveland*-class ships had a bridge superstructure with a rounded front end. Unusually, there is a Type SO3C reconnaissance Seamew on the starboard catapult. (USN)

▷ *Montpelier* in 1945 at about the end of the war, when the starboard catapult had already been removed. The total electronics system was standard practice at that time. (ON)

Montpelier

1942 9 Sept Commissioned; transferred to Pacific.
1943 18 Jan Arrived Noumea, New Caledonia.
25 Jan Flagship, CRUDIV 12 at Efate, New Hebrides.
29 Jan Battle off Rennell.
21 Feb Landings on Russell Islands.
29–30 June & 11–12 July Bombardment of Poporang and Munda in preparation for landing on New Georgia; remained in this area during the following months; then sailed for Sydney.
Oct Flagship, TF 39 in preparation for landings on Treasury Islands and Bougainville.

2 Nov Battle in Empress Augusta Bay.
1944 15 & 19 March Landing on Green Island, Bismarck Archipelago.
March Occupation of Emirau.
14 June Commencement of bombardment of Saipan.
19–21 June Took part with TF 58 in Battle of Philippine Sea; then continued bombardment of Saipan, Tinian and Guam.
2 August Departed for west coast.
August–Nov Refit.
25 Nov Arrived in Leyte Gulf.
12 Dec Landing on Mindoro.

1945 Jan Landing in Lingayen Gulf.
Feb Corregidor, Palawan.
14–23 April Landing on Mindanao.
17 June–2 July Protective cover during mine-clearing operations and for landings off Balikpapan, Borneo.
July–August Three cruises in East China Sea; after end of war, evacuation of Allied prisoners from Wakayama.
18 Oct Landed occupation troops on Matsuyama.
15 Nov Departed for east coast.
24 Jan Decommissioned.

△ ▽ These two photographs of *Denver* were taken in May 1944 during refit at Mare Island. She has just been repainted in camouflage of Measure 33/3d. One can see clearly her fire control electronics, especially the 'porcupine' of Mk 8 Mod. 1 on the Mk 34. The dividing line between the different port and starboard camouflage patterns runs straight through the middle of the bridge. (USN)

Denver

1942 15 Oct Commissioned.

23 Jan Departed for Pacific.

14 Feb Arrived Efate, New Hebrides.

6 March Bombarded Vila.

29–30 June Bombarded Ballale as part of invasion of New Georgia.

1–2 Nov With TF 39, battle in Empress Augusta Bay.

10 Nov Supported landing on Cape Torokina.

13 Nov Hit by aerial torpedo; 20 dead, engines out of action; towed by two fleet tugs to Espiritu Santo, there given provisional repairs.

1944 2 Jan Arrived west coast; repaired at Mare Island.

22 June Arrived at Eniwetok.

4 July Bombarded Iwo Jima.

12–18 Sept Invasion of Palau Islands.

23 Sept Landing on Ulithi.

12 Oct Landing on Leyte.

24 Oct Battle of Surigao Straits.

28 Oct Slightly damaged by Japanese aircraft exploding.

13–16 Dec Landing on Mindoro.

1945 4 Jan Landing on Lingayen.

29–30 Jan Landing on Zambales.

1–7 Feb Convoy escort to Mindoro.

Feb–May Landing on Palawan and Mindanao.

June Landings in Bay of Brunei, and on Balik-papan.

13 July–7 August Operations off Okinawa.

25 Sept–20 Oct Evacuation of Allied prisoners from Wakayama.

20 Oct Left for east coast.

21 Nov Refit at Norfolk.

1946 Jan Reservist training cruise from Newport and Goodwill cruise to Quebec.

1947 7 Feb Decommissioned.

Santa Fe

1942 24 Nov Commissioned; shake-down cruises off east coast, transferred to Pacific.

1943 22 March Arrived Pearl Harbor.

26 April Bombarded Attu, four months' operations in Aleutians.

6 & 22 July Bombarded Kiska prior to landing.

1 Sept Returned to Pearl Harbor; until end of war with CRUDIV 13 as escort for aircraft carriers.

18–19 Sept Tarawa.

5–6 Oct Wake.

Oct–Nov Escort to Bougainville, Gilberts, Tarawa.

4 Dec Kwajalein.

9 Dec Returned to Pearl Harbor.

Dec–Jan Returned to west coast; amphibious exercises operating from San Pedro.

1944 13 Jan Left for Marshall Islands.

Jan–Feb Wotje, Kwajalein, Majuro, Truk, Saipan.

March With *Enterprise* and *Belleau Wood*; Emirau, Palau, Yap and Woleai.

April Landing at Hollandia, attacks on Wake, Sawar, Truk, Satawan, Ponape.

4 May Returned to Kwajalein.

June With *Bunker Hill* attacks on Saipan, Tinian, Guam, Pagan.

July With *Hornet*; bombarded Iwo Jima; attacks on Guam, Rota, Yap, Ulithi.

11 July Returned to Eniwetok; operated with *Essex* until 26 January 1945.

Sept Peleliu, Mindanao, Visayas, Philippines.

Oct Attacked Okinawa, Formosa.

13 Oct protected damaged cruisers *Houston* and *Canberra*.

17 Oct Supported landings on Leyte.

24–27 Oct Operations against Japanese Fleet.

30 Oct Returned to Ulithi.

Nov Manila, the Philippines.

Dec Landing on Mindoro.

18–19 Dec Weathered heavy typhoon and searched for survivors from three sunken destroyers.

1945 Jan Formosa, Okinawa, Luzon, South China Sea.

26 Jan Returned to Ulithi.

10 Feb With *Yorktown*; targets around Tokyo, Iwo Jima.

1 March Returned to Ulithi.

△ This undated photograph of *Santa Fe* may have been taken in the second half of 1943. One notes the strongly increased number of Mk 4 fire control radar. In the background one can discern a *North Carolina*-class battleship. (USN)

▽ *Santa Fe* at anchor in San Francisco Bay towards the end of 1945, with a designation number not quite of the standard pattern (which was either quite small or – later – rather large!). The radar systems are SK-2, two SG, two Mk 13, two Mk 12/22. *Santa Fe* never received a dazzle-pattern paint scheme; from May 1943 she wore Measure 21 camouflage for a longer period than any other US wartime ship. As can be seen, her bridge had been modified after 1943. (Cas)

14 March With *Hancock*; Kyushu.

19 March Took on board 833 survivors from badly damaged *Franklin* (CV-13); accompanied her to Ulithi and Pearl Harbor; returned to west coast.

10 April–13 July Refit at San Pedro.

12 August With *Antietam* sailed to attack Wake.

26 August At end of the war anchored off Okinawa.

20 Sept Arrived Sasebo.

17 Oct–10 Nov Occupation of Northern Honshu and Hokkaido; then two 'Magic Carpet' cruises to Saipan, Guam and Truk.

1946 25 Jan Arrived Bremerton.

19 Oct Decommissioned.

△ While under repair for bomb and aerial torpedo damage, which was completed at Mare Island in February 1944, *Birmingham* received SK and Mk 8 Mod. 1 radar antennae, and was camouflaged to Measure 33/6d. Here she is seen at the end of October 1944, showing the heavy damage above the water-line caused by internal explosions in the light aircraft carrier *Princeton* (CVL-32) whom she was trying to assist. *Birmingham*'s crew sustained many casualties. (USN)

▽ Final repairs of battle damage were carried out at Mare Island. *Birmingham* is seen here at the end of this work on 21 January 1945, painted in Measure 22. The Mk 12/22 radar is now set deeper than previously; Mk 4 and SP radar were added to the after mast. (USN)

Birmingham

1943 29 Jan Commissioned; after shake-down cruises joined Atlantic Fleet.

10–26 July Mediterranean, invasion of Sicily.

5 August Returned to USA, transferred to Pacific Fleet.

18 Sept Tarawa.

5–6 Oct Wake.

8–9 Nov Empress Augusta Bay; damaged by two bombs and one aerial torpedo.

1943–44 Dec–Feb Repaired at Mare Island Navy Yard.

18 Feb Returned to Pacific; joined TF 57.

14 June–4 August Landing on Saipan.

19–20 June Aerial battle in Philippines.

20 July–1 August Landings on Tinian.

21 July Landing on Guam.

9–24 Sept Attacks on Philippine Islands.

10 Oct Attacked Okinawa with TF 38.

15, 18–19 Oct North Luzon and Formosa.

24 Oct Battle of Leyte Gulf; damaged above water-line by explosions in *Princeton*.

1944–45 Nov–Jan Repaired at Mare Island; returned to Pacific.

1945 4–5 March Landing on Iwo Jima.

25 March–5 May Landing on Okinawa.

4 May Damaged by Kamikaze.

28 May–1 August Repaired at Pearl Harbor.

26 August Joined Fifth Fleet off Okinawa.

Nov Sailed to Brisbane, Australia.

1946 22 March Returned to west coast.

1947 2 Jan Decommissioned.

Mobile

1943 24 March Commissioned; shake-down cruises in Chesapeake Bay, transferred to Pacific.

July Training cruises from Pearl Harbor.

23 August Joined TF 15.

31 August Attacked Marcus.

18 Sept Tarawa.

5–6 Oct Attacked Wake with TF 14.

8 Nov Landing on Bougainville with TG 53.3; then with TG 53.7 landing on Tarawa.

20–28 Nov Landing on Betio.

1 Dec Joined TF 50; air attacks on Kwajalein and Wotje; returned to Pearl Harbor.

29 Dec Arrived San Diego.

1944 29 Jan Attacked Wotje.

Feb Occupation of Kwajalein; attacks on Roi, Namur, then from 12 February with TF 58.

12 March TG 58.1 renamed TG 38.1.

20 March Landing on Emirau.

27 March TG 38.1 became TG 58.1 again.

21–22 April Bombarded Wake.

△ Following further damage suffered off Okinawa, repairs were carried out at Pearl Harbor, when she was painted in Measure 21. This photograph shows *Birmingham* riding high in the water of San Francisco Bay in March 1946 following her last return cruise to the West Pacific. (Cas)

▽ *Mobile* commissioned in camouflage Measure 22 and did not receive a 'dazzle pattern' at any time. She is seen here on 14 April 1943 off Norfolk Navy Yard at Portsmouth, Virginia, just before her transfer to the Pacific. At this time she has a very high positioning of Mk 4 radar which can be clearly seen, and one can also see that Mk 8 Mod. 1 and SC-2 had been shipped at her commissioning. (USN)

29–30 April Attacked Truk and Satawan.

1 May Attacked Ponape.

June Saipan, Tinian, Guam, Rota, Vulcan and Bonin Islands.

19–20 June Battle of Philippine Sea.

July Bonin and Vulcan Islands; Guam, Rota, Yap, Ulithi, Fais.

2 August Returned to Saipan.

4 August Chichi Jima.

Sept With TG 38.3 attacked Palaus, Mindanao, the Visayas, Peleliu, the Philippines, including Manila.

Oct Formosa, Pescadores, Visayas, South Luzon.

25 Oct Battle off Cape Engaño.

11 Dec In Philippines.

20 Dec Left for west coast; refit.

1945 29 March At Ulithi.

April With TF 51 off Okinawa, two months there; from the end May transferred to training command TG 95.7 until end of war.

20 August Occupation of Japan and Okinawa.

Sept Several transport cruises with liberated Allied prisoners from Japan and Okinawa.

18 Nov 'Magic Carpet' cruise to San Diego; then a second transport cruise.

1947 9 May Decommissioned.

◁ Just six months later; *Mobile* in October 1943 in the Pacific. It is highly likely that during her stay at Pearl Harbor in July 1943, she was repainted in Measure 21; the number of bridge portholes was reduced and a second SG antenna fitted. Two Kingfisher reconnaissance aircraft are on their catapults. (USN)

▽ *Mobile* in San Francisco Bay on 20 January 1946 after returning from a 'Magic Carpet' cruise. At the end of December 1944 she had been in a west coast yard where, presumably, her radar electronics were modified with SK, Mk 13 and Mk 12/22. The occasion was also taken to fit Mk 63. Seen from this angle one can understand why ships of this class were regarded as beautiful; more acute angles and broadside views give a rather less attractive impression.(Cas)

Vincennes

1944 21 Jan Commissioned.

25 Feb–30 March Shake-down cruises to British West Indies, then Flagship, CRUDIV 14 from 14 April.

16 April Sailed to Pacific via Panama Canal.

6 May Arrived Pearl Harbor.

30 May Off Majuro joined TF 58.

21–13 June Saipan, Pagan.

16 June First attacks on Iwo Jima.

19–20 June Battle of Philippine Sea.

23 June Sailed to Eniwetok for repairs.

7 July Flagship, CRUDIV 14.

14 July With TF 58 again; Guam.

31 July Saipan.

4–5 August Attacked Bonin Islands.

6 Sept Attacked Palaus with TG 38.2.

7 Sept Peleliu.

9–10 Sept Mindanao.

21–22 Sept Attacked Luzon.

1–6 Oct At Ulithi.

10 Oct Attacked Okinawa.

12 Oct Attacked Formosa.

16 Oct Escorted badly damaged cruisers *Canberra* and *Houston*.

24 Oct Battle of Leyte Gulf.

5–6 Nov Carrier escort off Luzon.

18 Dec Weathered typhoon without serious damage (three destroyers sank).

24–30 Dec At Ulithi.

1945 Jan Chinese waters, Cam Ranh Bay; attacked Okinawa.

10 Feb Joined TG 58.1; attacked Japanese mainland.

March–June Attacked Okinawa; then with TG 58.1 against the Kyushus, switching between both several times.

11 June Left for west coast.

8 July Left for refit at Mare Island remaining there until the end of August.

1946 March Several 'Magic Carpet' cruises, including two to New Zealand.

23 March Last arrival at San Diego.

10 Sept Decommissioned.

▷ Beginning with *Vincennes II*, changes made in this class involved the front of the bridge being angular rather than rounded. The positions of Mks 34 and 37 fire control have been transposed. She had SK radar from the start. *Vincennes* entered service relatively late, with the camouflage pattern of Measure 33/3d. The different camouflage, somewhat weathered as a consequence of lengthy service, can be seen. There is no exact date for these photographs, but they may have been taken during the second half of 1944. The darkest camouflage shade suggests Measure 32 rather than 33. (USN)

▽ *Vincennes* went into Mare Island Navy Yard on 8 July 1945 for her first refit since commissioning eighteen months earlier. Although the Pacific war was coming to an end, her fire control electronics were modernised with Mk 8 Mod. 3 and Mk 12/22, and she was camouflaged to Measure 22. She is seen here near San Francisco on 24 March 1946 with two Seahawk aircraft on the catapults. Again, this photograph emphasises the beauty of her lines, focussing as it does on her midships superstructure. (Cas)

△ *Pasadena* was one of the ships to remain in active service for some years after the end of the war. This undated photograph dates from 1946– 48. She wears the light grey peacetime camouflage, but still the small pennant number. In place of SK-2 antenna she now has SR-3 on the forward mast. There is a Seahawk on the sole remaining port catapult. (RPh)

◁△ *Pasadena* came into service in mid-1944, with SK-2 radar and camouflaged in Measure 32/24d, the pattern of which can be seen here. The photograph of her port side was taken on 22 July 1944 during the shake-down cruises off Boston Navy Yard and the undated starboard photograph probably at the same time. (USN)

▽ *Pasadena*, in her 'mothballed' condition, still showing her designation number and with weathered camouflage. This was taken in 1972, that is two years after she had been struck off the Navy List, and very probably destined to be broken up. (LRC)

Passadena

1944 8 June Commissioned; shake-down cruises in summer.

25 Sept Departed for Pacific.

Nov At Ulithi, joined TF 38; attacks on Luzon and Formosa until end of 1944.

1945 Jan South China Sea and Indo-China coast.

Feb Now with TF 58, attacked Japanese mainland and Iwo Jima.

March South Japanese mainland, northerly Ryukyus and Okinawa, serving as Flagship, CRUDIV 17.

28 March–10 May Bombarded Minami Daito.

1 April–10 May Okinawa, Kyushu.

July–August Last attacks on Tokyo, North Honshu and Hokkaido; after end of war occupation duties in Japanese waters.

23 August Flagship, TG 35.1.

1 Sept Entered Tokyo Bay; remained there until January 1946.

1946 19 Jan Left for west coast; refit.

Sept Departed for Central Pacific.

1946–47 Nov–Feb Exercises in Micronesia and fleet manoeuvres off Hawaii; in the summer of 1948 Reserve officers' training cruise.

1948 1 Oct Sailed to West Pacific.

1949 May Operations along Chinese coast.

June Returned to west coast; local operations and exercises.

1950 12 Jan Decommissioned.

◁ In the autumn of 1944 *Springfield* came into service, wearing the camouflage of Measure 33/24d as can be seen from this photograph taken at Bethlehem, Quincy. The electronic system corresponds to what was usual during the last months of the war. (USN)

△ This photograph, also taken at the end of 1944, shows *Springfield*'s starboard camouflage pattern. (USN)

◁ This photograph of *Pasadena* was taken at San Francisco on 10 February 1946, obviously just before the commencement of yard work carried out there. It is not at all certain when 32/24d camouflage was replaced by Measure 22. (Cas)

Springfield

1944 9 Sept Commissioned; shake-down cruises from November off British West Indies.

1945 10–13 Jan Training cruise to Bermudas.

23 Jan Joined TG 21.5 with *Quincy;* sailed with President Roosevelt to Malta; at Azores broke off and returned to east coast.

5 Feb Through Panama Canal.

16 Feb Arrived Pearl Harbor.

6 March Arrived Ulithi.

15 March Joined TF 58.

18–19 March Kyushu and Ryukiu.

23 March–1 April Okinawa.

27–28 March Bombarded Minami Daito Shima; following two months with TF 58 in waters off Okinawa; including

10 May Bombardment of Minami Daito Shima.

13–14 May Attacks on Kyushu.

27 May Fifth Fleet became Third Fleet; period in the Philippines.

13–14 July Hokkaido, North Honshu.

July Attacked Japanese mainland.

27 August With TF 35 at anchorage in Sagami Wan.

30 August TF 31 sailed into Tokyo Bay; occupation of naval base at Yokosuka.

3 Sept *Springfield* arrived in Tokyo Bay.

20 Sept Third Fleet became Fifth Fleet again; remained in Far East until 1946.

1946 9 Jan Left Tsingtau for west coast.

25 Jan Arrived San Pedro; then to Mare Island; operations on west coast.

1 Nov Left for West Pacific; operations mainly in the areas of Guam and Saipan.

1947 19 Feb Departed for west coast – with intermediate stops at Kwajalein and Pearl Harbor.

24 March Arrived San Pedro, then eighteen months' operating off west coast; then sailed to join Seventh Fleet.

1948 3 Nov Arrived Yokosuka.

1949 1 June Return to west coast.

1950 Jan Decommissioned.

1959 March Towed to east coast; converted to guided missile cruiser; reclassified as CLG-7.

△ *Springfield* on 1 May 1946 entering San Francisco harbour after her refit at Mare Island Navy Yard which had begun in January 1946. It seems strange that she is still wearing Measure 22 camouflage so long after the end of the war. (Cas)

◁ As one of the late *Cleveland*s, *Springfield* served as an active fleet ship until the end of 1949 when she was mothballed for the next nine years. This photograph was taken on 9 November 1948 during gunnery practice for which the ship lay at anchor. SR-3 and SP radar have been added and the starboard catapult removed. The hangar cover has just been opened. (USN)

Topeka

1944 23 Dec Commissioned; trials off West Indies.

1945 10 April Left Boston for west coast.

2 May Arrived Pearl Harbor; there became Flagship, CRUDIV 18.

4 June Left Ulithi with TF 38 as escort for *Bon Homme Richard* (CV-31).

June–August Attacked on Ryukyus and Japanese mainland; entered Tokyo Bay mid-Sept 1945.

1 Oct Left Japan via Okinawa for west coast; brought home 259 combatants.

19 Oct Arrived Portland, Oregon.

1945–46 Nov–3 Jan Refit at San Pedro; then left for West Pacific.

1946 24 Jan Arrived Yokosuka; occupation duties in Japan, China and Central Pacific Islands.

20 Nov Returned to San Pedro; yard overhaul and operations on west coast.

1947 22 Sept Sailed to West Pacific.

10 Oct Arrived Yokosuka; joined TF 71; operations mainly in Chinese waters.

1948 7 May Returned to Long Beach.

May–Sept Refit at Pearl Harbor.

Oct Local operations off west coast.

1949 18 June Decommissioned.

△ *Topeka* in March 1945. She was completed three months after *Springfield* and also wore Measure 33/24d camouflage. For this reason she shows a remarkable similarity to *Springfield*. (USN)

1957 Towed from San Francisco to east coast.

15 April Arrived New York Navy Yard; there converted to guided missile cruiser.

23 May Reclassified as CLG-8.

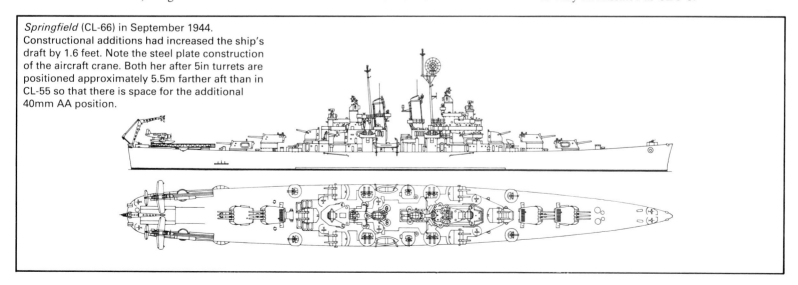

Springfield (CL-66) in September 1944. Constructional additions had increased the ship's draft by 1.6 feet. Note the steel plate construction of the aircraft crane. Both her after 5in turrets are positioned approximately 5.5m farther aft than in CL-55 so that there is space for the additional 40mm AA position.

△ One year later: *Topeka* on 7 March 1946, at
anchor in Manila Bay when she was a unit of Task
Force 77; behind her is a heavy cruiser of the
Baltimore class. On the catapults are two Seahawk
reconnaissance aircraft. (USN)

▷ Construction of the many ships of the
Cleveland class was distributed among several
yards. Hence *Biloxi* (CL-80), although she had a
much higher pennant number than *Topeka*, came
into service almost eighteen months earlier. She
had SK radar, in this case on the after mast, and
was camouflaged to Measure 32/6d. What is not
often seen in photographs is that the after fire
control Mk 8 radar is at an oblique angle. This
photograph was taken on 5 September 1943
during a shake-down cruise off Norfolk Navy Yard
(USN)

Biloxi

1943 31 August Commissioned; joined CRUDIV 13 in Pacific.
1944 31 Jan–8 Feb Landings on Eniwetok.
16–17 Feb Truk.
21–22 Feb The Marianas.
30 March–1 April Palaus, Yap, Ulithi, Woleai.
21–24 April Landing on Hollandia.
29 April–1 May Truk, Satawan, Ponape.
11–24 June Landing on Saipan.
19–20 June Battle of Philippine Sea.
3–4 July Bonins.

12 July–15 August Occupation of Guam.
4 July Bombarded Chichi Jima.
25–27 July Palaus, Yap, Ulithi.
4–5 August Bonins.
31 August–8 Sept Vulcan Islands, Bonins, Yap.
6 Sept–14 Oct Occupation of southerly Palaus.
10 Oct Okinawa.
15, 17 & 19 Oct Luzon.
5, 6, 13, 14, 19–25 Nov Luzon.
24–26 Oct Battle of Leyte Gulf.
14–16 Dec Luzon.
1945 6–7 Jan Luzon.

12–16 Jan China Sea.
15, 16, 25 Feb Honshu and Nansei Shoto.
15 Feb–1 March Invasion of Iwo Jima.
25 March–20 April Okinawa.
27 March Slightly damaged by Kamikaze off Okinawa.
27 April Left for west coast; refit.
July Returned to West Pacific.
18 July Attacked Wake; after end of the war evacuation of allied prisoners from Nagasaki.
9 Nov Occupation of Japan.
1946 29 Oct Decommissioned.

△ *Houston* 11 January 1944 shortly after being commissioned. Her camouflage is Measure 32/1d which she retained until 1945. (USN)

▽ *Houston* on 13 April 1944, three days before she left for the Pacific. The starboard pattern of Measure 32/1d is just about visible. (USN)

▽ Following the severe damage she suffered in October 1944, *Houston* was towed via the Panama Canal to New York Navy Yard where repairs were carried out from March to October 1945. The ship received camouflage to Measure 22 and SP radar; also Mk 13 fire control radars and Mk 12/22. On the other hand, SK radar was replaced by SR which was a fairly rare occurrence. After her refit *Houston* remained in the Atlantic. She is seen here in English waters on 26 August 1946. (WL)

Houston
1943 20 Dec Commissioned.
1944 1 Feb Shake-down cruise in Caribbean; training cruises from Boston.
16 April Departed for Pacific.
31 May Arrived Majuro.
12–13 June Carrier escort in Marianas.
15–16 June Bonins.
19–20 June Battle of Philippine Sea.
26 June Bombarded Guam and Rota.
30 August Left Eniwetok for Palaus.
6 August Bombarded Peleliu and other islands.
17–19 Sept Landing on Peleliu.
10 Oct Okinawa.
12 Oct Formosa.
14 Oct Hit by aerial torpedo in engine compartment, towed with difficulty by *Boston* (CA-69).
16 Oct Taken in tow by ATF *Pawnee*; while being towed hit by another torpedo in stern; first repair in Ulithi.
27 Oct Sailed to east coast.
1945 24 March–11 Oct At New York Navy Yard; remained in Atlantic.
1946 16 April Goodwill cruise to Europe.
14 Dec Returned to east coast.
1947 17 May To Mediterranean with CRUDIV 12.
15 Dec Decommissioned.

Providence
1945 15 May Commissioned.
13 June Shake-down cruises off Cuba.
4 Sept–6 Oct Training of future cruiser and carrier crews.
Nov With *Missouri* (BB-63) Mediterranean.
1946 16 June Left for east coast.
1947 3 Feb Left for short operational cruise to Mediterranean.
Feb Returned to east coast.
1947–48 20 Nov–2 March In Mediterranean.
1949 14 June First decommissioning.
1957 23 May Reclassified as CLG-6.
June Commencement of conversion to guided missile cruiser.

◁▷ *Providence* was also one of the 'late' *Cleveland*s, which did not see action during the war. These two photographs were taken on 14 May 1945, that is to say one day before her official commissioning. The electronic systems corresponded to the standards of 1945, the camouflage was that of Measure 22. This aerial photograph gives an idea of the lines of the ship's hull and the disposition of the various weapons. (USN)

▷ On 9 November 1948 *Providence* was in the Mediterranean when this photograph was taken off Toulon. She was then showing the large standardized pennant number. The SC-2 radar had been replaced by SR-3 and there is a Seahawk reconnaissance aircraft on the sole remaining port catapult. (MB)

△ ▽ *Manchester* (CL-83) was the last unit of the *Cleveland* class which was to remain in active service for almost ten years after the end of the war. These two photographs were taken on 18 April 1948 off Toulon when *Manchester* was making her third visit to the Mediterranean. The forward pennant number – which has a shadowed effect – does not correspond in size with the later standard; the after pennant number corresponded with what was normally carried during wartime. The radar systems corresponded, as previously, with the 1945 standard: SK-2, SP, Mk 13, Mk 12/22. A Seahawk reconnaissance aircraft is on the one remaining port catapult. (MB)

Manchester

1946 29 Oct Commissioned; shake-down cruises in Caribbean.

1947 April–Nov Operational cruise to Mediterranean, interrupted by a fortnight of reservist training in June.

1948 Feb–June, 1949 Jan–March Two further Mediterranean cruises.

18 March Left Philadelphia; transferred to Pacific Fleet.

3 April Arrived Long Beach.

15 May–28 Nov West Pacific; operations in Chinese waters.

1950 Refit at San Francisco Navy Yard in summer.

1 August To West Pacific.

Sept At Sasebo, joining carrier battle group TF 77.

15 Sept Coastal bombardment of Korea.

1952 29 May Returned to west coast.

June Refit at San Francisco.

1953 4 March Commencement of third operational period off Korea with TF 77.

23 July End of Korea operations.

28 July Left Yokosuka for west coast.

1954–55 Operational period in each year with Seventh Fleet in West Pacific.

1956 5 Feb Last arrival at Long Beach.

27 May Decommissioned.

△ This photograph was taken of *Manchester* at anchor in May 1951, probably in the West Pacific. The pennant numbers are now according to regulations. SK-2 radar has given way to SPS-6B and Mk 12/22 has been replaced by Mk 25. (USN)

▽ This detailed photograph of *Manchester* dates from 2 May 1955 when she had SPS-8A radar installed on the after mast at Mare Island. The 40mm Bofors had already been replaced by 3in/50 AA in October 1952 when four MK 56s fire control gear were installed and they can be seen at the side of the bridge superstructure and the after funnel. (USN)

△ *Vicksburg* came into service in mid-1944 when she was painted in Measure 33/6d camouflage, the starboard pattern of which is seen here. The ship is lying rather high in the water, especially forward. (NN)

▷ This is how *Vicksburg* appeared on 19 October 1945, in San Francisco Bay, four days after her return from Okinawa. It is not known why, for a short time after the end of the war, many ships of the US Pacific Fleet had their name in large letters on the side of the hull. The cockpits of both the Kingfishers on their catapults are shut. (Cas)

▷ This photograph of *Duluth* dates from January 1947, during an interval between operational cruises. The second SG radar array has now been replaced by SP and the Mk 8 Mod. 1 by Mk 13.

Vicksburg

1944 12 June Commissioned.
July–August Shake-down cruises in Chesapeake Bay and British West Indies.
11–24 Sept At yard following trials.
5 Oct–15 Dec Training ship for crews destined for large fighting ships.
Dec In yard at Norfolk.
1945 6 Jan Departure for Pacific.
17 Jan Arrived Pearl Harbor; exercises from there until end of month.
5 Feb Left Pearl Harbor.
14 Feb Arrived Saipan.
15 Feb Joined TU 54.9.2; bombarded Iwo Jima with intermediate stops at Ulithi.
March Japanese mainland; bombarded Okinawa.
June Supported mine-clearing operations in China Sea.
24 June–20 August Operations in Philippine waters.
24 August Joined TG 38.2.
5 Sept Entered Tokyo Bay; Flagship, CRUDIV 10.
20 Sept Departed for Okinawa to embark 2,200 combatants for transportation to USA.
4 Oct Intermediate stop at Pearl Harbor.
15 Oct Arrived San Francisco.
27 Oct Took part in 'Navy Day' in Bay of Monterey, California.
1946 17 Jan Refit at San Francisco Navy Yard (Terminal Island).
20 May Short period as Flagship, Third Fleet.
1947 30 June Decommissioned.

Duluth

1944 18 Sept Commissioned.
1944–45 14 Dec–2 March Training cruises out of Newport.

1945 7 April Departed for Pacific via Pearl Harbor.
27 April Escort for aircraft carriers of Fifth Fleet.
5 June Bow damage caused by typhoon; repairs at Guam.
21 July Once again with TF 38; last battles off Japanese mainland.
24 August–16 Sept Radar control ship for own transport aircraft.
16 Sept Entered Tokyo Bay.
1 Oct Departed for west coast.
19 Oct Took part in 'Navy Day' at Seattle.
1946 3 Jan–27 Sept Operational cruise in West Pacific.
1947 24 Feb Special cruise to Pearl Harbor.
May–July Visits to Melbourne, Sydney, Truk, Guam and Manila.
1947–48 22 Sept–19 May Operational cruise in West Pacific.
1948 Reservist midshipmen training cruise to British Columbia.
1949 Feb Took part in cold climate exercises off Alaska.
25 June Decommissioned.

△ ▽ Just a few weeks after being commissioned; *Duluth* seen on 8 October 1944. The camouflage is Measure 32/11a. Clearly visible are the SR-2 radar antenna and both the SG radars; two each of Mk 8 Mod. 1 and Mk 12/22. The aerial photograph was also taken in October 1944. (USN)

Miami

1943 28 Dec Commissioned; shake-down cruises in Caribbean and along east coast.

1944 16 April With sister ships *Vincennes* and *Houston* departed for Pacific.

6 May Arrived Pearl Harbor.

June Attacked Saipan, Tinian, Rota, Guam, Pagan, Bonins.

July Carrier escort to west of Marianas.

August Attacked Iwo Jima and Haha Jima.

7 Sept Attacked Palau Islands, including Peleliu.

12–15 Sept Attacked Philippine Islands.

10–14 Oct Attacked Okinawa.

24 Oct Battle of Leyte Gulf.

Nov Attacked Philippine Islands.

18 Dec Weathered typhoon.

1945 Jan Attacked Formosa, Luzon, French Indo-China, South Chinese coast, Hainan and Hong Kong.

1 Feb Commencement of operations against the Japanese mainland.

March–April Operations east of Okinawa.

24 May Arrived San Francisco for refit.

25 August Sailed to Pearl Harbor.

Sept–Oct Occupation of small island north of Okinawa.

10 Dec Arrived west coast.

1947 30 June Decommissioned.

△ One of the later Casoly photographs of *Duluth* taken on 23 June 1948 at San Francisco, one month after her return from the West Pacific. She still has the small pennant numbers carried in wartime. The starboard catapult has been removed. The ship shows a very clean outward appearance. The presence of fire control radar on the after 40mm gun presupposes the presence of FLG Mk 63. (Cas)

▷ This photograph of *Miami* is dated 9 March 1944 when the cruiser must still have been in the Atlantic. The camouflage is that of Measure 32/1d with which she entered service, but it has weathered badly in just a few months. It is not out of the question that *Miami* had been given Measure 22 camouflage as early as May 1944 at Pearl Harbor. (USN)

△ *Miami* was decommissioned quite soon after the war, after just three and a half years of service. This photograph shows her at San Francisco on 12 February 1946, still painted in Measure 22. (Cas)

◁ This detailed photograph of *Astoria* at Mare Navy Yard dates from October 1944. The texture of the SK antenna, and its relative proportion to the SG can be clearly seen. In the foreground one can see what a relatively small space difference there is between a twin and a quadruple Bofors.

Astoria
1944 17 May Commissioned.
11 Dec With Third and Fifth Fleets as carrier escort until end of war.
14, 16 Dec Attacked Luzon.
1945 6–7 Jan Attacked Luzon.
12–16 Jan Chinese coast.
21 Jan Attacked Formosa.
22 Jan Attacked Nansei Shoto.
15 Feb–5 March Iwo Jima.
17 March–30 May Okinawa.
10 July–15 August Attacks on Japanese mainland.
1948–49 Oct–Feb Operations along west coast and in West Pacific.
1949 1 July Decommissioned.

△ Another late Casoly photograph; *Astoria* on 23 June 1948, passing beneath the Golden Gate Bridge at San Francisco. She is painted in peacetime grey, but has no pennant number. On the foremast she has the short-lived SR-3 radar antenna and on the (during this period) single catapult, a Seahawk. (Cas)

▽ *Astoria* was commissioned in mid-1944 and appeared in camouflage Measure 33/24d, which, as can be seen here, consists of only two shades of colour and, in bright sunlight, makes a very pale impression. This photograph was taken on 21 October 1944 off Mare Island. Both the Kingfisher aircraft are very prominent. (USN)

△ *Oklahoma City* was in service for only two and a half years after commissioning. Following occupation tasks in Japan she returned to the west coast. She is seen here off San Francisco on 14 February 1946. (Cas)

▷ This photograph dated 14 July 1945 shows *Little Rock* very clearly, at Philadelphia Navy Yard just one month after her commissioning. SK-2 and SP radar are aboard together with two Seahawk reconnaissance aircraft on the catapults. (USN)

Oklahoma City

1944 22 Dec Commissioned; after shake-down cruises departed for Pacific.
1945 2 May Arrived Pearl Harbor.
6 June At Ulithi, joining TG 38.1; Okinawa.
June–July Escort protection with Third Fleet.
18 July Attacked Japanese mainland.
10 Sept Entered Tokyo Bay; occupation of Japan.
1946 30 Jan Departed for west coast.
14 Feb Arrived San Francisco.
1947 30 June First decommissioning.
1957 21 May Converted to guided missile cruiser at San Francisco.
23 May Reclassified as CLG-5.

Little Rock

1945 17 June Commissioned; shake-down cruise off Cuba and along east coast.
21 Oct Commencement of cruise to South America.
1946 23 March Returned to east coast.
1946–49 Training cruiser off east coast, alternating with
1947, 1948 Mediterranean cruises in each year.
1949 24 June First decommissioning.
1957 23 May Reclassified as CLG-4; conversion to guided missile cruiser.

△ *Little Rock,* off Toulon on 17 December 1948 during her second Mediterranean cruise. The bow 20mm AA guns appear to have been removed. Six months later she was decommissioned for the first time. (MB)

Galveston
1946 24 April Completion of almost completed ship suspended.
1956 4 Feb Reclassified as CLG-93.
1957 23 May Reclassified as CLG-3.

Amsterdam
1945 8 Jan Commissioned; shake-down cruises until summer 1945.

June Joined CRUDIV 18.
10 July–15 August With Third Fleet, attacked Japanese mainland.
5 Sept Tokyo Bay.
Oct Returned to west coast; until end of 1945 'Magic Carpet' cruises between San Diego and Pearl Harbor.
1947 30 June Decommissioned.

△ There are relatively few photographs of *Amsterdam*. She came to the West Pacific in mid-1945, taking part in the last attacks on the Japanese mainland. She is seen here on 14 October 1945, probably off the west coast after her return from Tokyo. Note the large battle flag. The dividing line between the two paint shades does not run parallel to the water-line and this represents a seldom seen new version of Measure 12. (USN)

▽ This relatively rare and undated photograph of *Galveston* shows clearly that she had been completed with armament when, without having seen service, she was put into reserve, only to emerge ten years later converted to a guided missile cruiser. The photograph was taken presumably in mid-1946; she is very high in the water. (USN)

△ *Portsmouth* was completed in mid-1945, wearing camouflage of Measure 22. Here she is on 22 July 1945 at Norfolk Navy Yard. Note the sponsons on each side of the crane which carry 40mm twins. (USN)

▽ This undated photograph of *Portsmouth* was probably taken in 1947 or 1948. She shows the large standard pennant number and has SG-6 radar in place of SK-2. There is SP on the after mast. *Portsmouth* remained in active service for only four years. (USN)

▷ Although *Wilkes Barre* carried the very high pennant number CL-103 within the *Cleveland* class, she came into service in mid-1944, but was to remain in active service for little more than three years. This photograph was taken on 10 June 1944, i.e., before her commissioning, at the New York Shipbuilding Corporation at Camden, New Jersey. At first sight the colour contrasts might lead one to suppose that Measure 22 has been applied; in fact one is looking at a coat of priming paint; it is known that she was camouflaged in Measure 32/34d when she came into service. (USN)

CONFIDENTIAL
U.S.S. CL-103
TOPSIDE ARRANGEMENT PORT SIDE AT TIME OF INITIAL DEPARTURE
NEW YORK SHIPBUILDING CORP., CAMDEN, N.J.

Portsmouth

1945 25 June Commissioned-shake-down off
  Cuba; attached to 'Operational Development
  Force', until early 1946.
1946 May Goodwill cruise to Africa; brief spell in
  Mediterranean; returned to east coast.
25 Nov Left east coast for Mediterranean.
1947 April Returned to east coast.
1947–48 Nov–Feb To Mediterranean.
1948 11 March Refit at Boston; operations on east
  coast, reservist training cruises in Caribbean.
1949 15 June Decommissioned.

Wilkes Barre

1944 1 July Commissioned; shake-down cruises in
  Chesapeake Bay, and British West Indies.
Oct Transferred to Pacific.
10 Nov Left San Diego.
17 Nov Arrived Pearl Harbor; training cruises in
  Hawaiian waters.
14 Dec Left for Ulithi; joined CRUDIV 17 there.
30 Dec Sailed with TF 38, Formosa, southern
  Ryukyus, Luzon.
1945 9–10 Jan Formosa; South China Sea; landing
  on Lingayen.

12 Jan Detached as TG 34.5; vain search for
  Japanese sea forces Cam Ranh Bay (Indo-
  China); rejoined TF 38.
21 Jan Attacked Formosa.
26 Jan Arrived Ulithi for replenishment; TF 38
  became TF 58.
Feb TG 58.3 with *Essex*.
16 Feb Attacked Tokyo.
19 Feb Attacked Chichi Jima and Haha Jima;
  landings on Iwo Jima.
21 Feb Bombarded Iwo Jima.
23 Feb Rejoined TG 58.3.

1 March Carrier escort during attacks on Tokyo and Okinawa.

14–15 March Exercises with TF 59 based on Ulithi.

18 March Sailed eastward from Okinawa; attacked Kyushu.

23–24 March Attacked targets around Okinawa including Minami Daito Shima.

1 April Beginning of landings on Okinawa; massed attacks on Japanese mainland.

11 May Assisted badly damaged carrier *Bunker Hill*.

12 May Attacked Kyushu.

28 May TF 58 became TF 38.

29 May Left for Philippines.

June Anchored in San Pedro Bay, firing practise off Samar.

1 July TG 38.3 left Leyte Gulf for last attacks on Japanese islands Hokkaido and Honshu.

August Typhoons hindered air attacks.

27 August Anchored in Sagami Wan; occupation of Yokosuka.

3 Sept Entered Tokyo Bay.

9 Sept Flagship, TU 35.7.2 in occupation of Japan.

5 Nov Detached from Fifth Fleet.

9 Nov Departed for Inchon, Korea.

16 Nov Departed for Tsingtau, China; remained at Tsingtau until end of 1945.

1946 13 Jan Left for west coast via Pearl Harbor.

31 Jan Arrived San Pedro.

4 March Departed for east coast via Panama Canal; remained at Philadelphia until summer of 1946.

27 Oct Took part in 'Navy Day' at New Orleans.

1947 17 Feb Departed for Goodwill cruise to England and Norway.

9 Oct Decommissioned.

◁ *Wilkes Barre* off Okinawa in June 1945 when she was part of Task Force 38. It is very clear that she was camouflaged to Measure 32/24d. The photograph was taken from the aircraft carrier *Essex* (CV-9). In the background can be seen a battleship of the *Iowa* class steaming in the opposite direction. (USN)

△ A 'mothballed' cruiser. This 1971 photograph shows *Wilkes Barre* during her period in reserve. The fire control antennae have been left in place for possible future use; the 40mm AA have been given rounded plastic hoods. (LRC)

(CONFIDENTIAL)
U. S. S. CL - 104
PSIDE ARRANGEMENT: STARBOARD SIDE AT TIME OF INCLINING EXPERIMENT
NEW YORK SHIPBUILDING CORP., CAMDEN, N. J.
NOVEMBER 23, 1944

△   This detailed photograph of *Atlanta* was taken on 23 November 1944 at the Camden yard a full week before commissioning. Note the very pale shades of colour of Measure 33/24d. It is rather difficult to make out the Mk 8 Mod. 1 and Mk 12/22 fire control radar antennae, but one can see clearly that there is a walkway around the bridge-house which was not the case with earlier units which had a flat-topped bridge. (USN)

Atlanta

1944 3 Dec Commissioned; operations in Pacific with TF 38.

1945 28 May–11 June &10 July–15 August Attacked Japanese islands, Okinawa and Ryuku Islands; directly after end of war occupation of Yokosuka; occupation of Japan in Honshu coast area.

29 Sept Left Japan.

4 Oct Left Guam taking combatants back to Seattle. Two cruises to West Pacific January–June 1946 and October 1947–April 1948, including visit to Sydney with TF 38 in 1947.

1949 1 July Decommissioned.

1964 May Reclassified as experimental ship IX-304.

Dayton

1945 7 Jan Commissioned; Pacific Fleet.

16 June Arrived Leyte, joined Third Fleet.

1 July Escort protection carrier groups during last attacks on Japanese home islands.

10 Sept Entered Tokyo Bay, occupation of Japan.

7 Nov Left for west coast.

19 Nov Arrived San Pedro.

1946 24 Jan Left for west coast via Pearl Harbor, orders changed en route.

7 Feb Sailed for east coast.

1947 3 Feb Left Norfolk for Mediterranean; Flagship, COMNAVFORMED.

30 Nov Returned to east coast.

1948 9 Feb–26 June Second Mediterranean cruise.

1949 1 March Decommissioned.

△ This undated and rather fuzzy photograph of *Atlanta* may date from 1947/48 when her Mk 12/22 fire control radar had been replaced by Mk 25. (USN)

▽ This undated photograph of *Dayton* may have been taken in 1947 and one notes that, in April 1945, there was nothing new or secret to be censored as regards Mk 12/22 radar. An Admiral's command pennant flies over the SP antenna atop the after mast. Two Seahawk reconnaissance aircraft are on their catapults. (USN)

△ *Dayton,* the last unit of the *Cleveland* class, was commissioned at the beginning of 1945. She arrived just in time to take part in the last actions around the Japanese mainland. This photograph shows her on 23 April 1945 during her period of trials. It should be pointed out that the wartime censor has obliterated only the radar antennae of the two Mk 37 fire control radars. (USN)

▽ This photograph of *Dayton* – with a medium-sized pennant number – was taken on 18 April 1948 off Toulon when the ship was making her second deployment to the Mediterranean, just one year before she was decommissioned. There are no changes in her electronic systems. (MB)

FARGO CLASS

Only two of the proposed thirteen ships of this class were completed. They were a 1942 modification of the *Cleveland* class, in which the two funnels were to be replaced by a single squat funnel so that the heavy concentration of AA would have more advantageous arcs of fire. The armour, weaponry and other features remained as in the *Cleveland*s. The former positions of the Mk 34 and Mk 37 fire control gear were interchanged. The 5in twin mountings on the beam were set deeper, i.e., on the main deck, which made a considerable contribution to stability. As in all newer ships, these two were given radar control equipment for the light AA. Launched just before the end of the war, neither ship saw active service. Although presenting a slightly different appearance and having some different characteristics, the ships were regarded by some as belonging to the *Cleveland* class. The various proposed modifications delayed construction to such an extent that only two units had been completed by the end of the war; the remaining eleven being suspended.

△ *Fargo* the name ship of the tiny class which ended up with only two modified *Cleveland*s. Points of interest are: the single but thick funnel; the rather tightly compressed superstructure; the different siting of Mk 34 and Mk 37, the single catapult on the starboard side with a Seahawk, its wings folded, in position. There is SR-3 radar on the forward mast, SP on the after mast The fire control radar is Mk 13 and Mk 25. This photograph was taken off Toulon on 21 April 1949, during the last operational cruise in the Mediterranean. The command pennant of Vice-Admiral Forrest D. Sherman, flies at the after mast. Less than year later *Fargo* was decommissioned. (MB)

Fargo

1945 9 Dec Commissioned.

1946 15 April Goodwill cruise to Bermuda, Trinidad, Brazil and Uruguay.

31 May Sailed for Mediterranean.

1947 2 March Returned to east coast.

20 May Sailed to Mediterranean, one month as Flagship, COMNAVFORMED.

13 Sept Returned to east coast.

Oct–Nov Manoeuvres in Atlantic as Flagship, Second Task Fleet.

1948–49 Two operational cruises to Mediterranean.

1950 14 Feb Decommissioned.

FARGO CLASS SHIPS LAID DOWN BUT NOT COMPLETED

Pennant No.	Name	Fiscal Year	Laid Down	Builder	History
CL-108	Newark	1942	17 Jan 1944	New York SBdg.	Building suspended 12 Aug 1945
CL-109	New Haven	1942	28 Feb 1944	New York SBdg.	Building suspended 12 Aug 1945
CL-110	Buffalo	1942	3 April 1944	New York SBdg.	Building suspended 12 Aug 1945
CL-111	Wilmington	1942	5 March 1945	Cramp	Building suspended 12 Aug 1945
CL-112	Valleto	1942		New York SBdg.	Building suspended 5 Oct 1944
CL-113	Helena	1942		New York SBdg.	Building suspended 5 Oct 1944
CL-114	Roanoke	1942		New York SBdg.	Building suspended 5 Oct 1944
CL-115		1942		New York SBdg.	Building suspended 5 Oct 1944
CL-116	Tallahassee	1942	31 Jan 1944	Newport News	Building suspended 12 Aug 1945
CL-117	Cheyenne	1942	29 May 1944	Newport News	Building suspended 12 Aug 1945
CL-118	Chattanooga	1942	9 Oct 1944	Newport News	Building suspended 12 Aug 1945

Huntington

1946 23 Feb Commissioned; shake-down cruise off Cuba.

23 July Left to join Sixth Task Force in Mediterranean.

1947 8 Feb Returned to east coast, exercises off Cuba.

20 May Second Mediterranean cruise.

13 Sept Returned to east coast.

24 Oct–14 Nov Reservist training cruise off Bermuda and Newfoundland.

1947–48 Dec–12 April Refit at Philadelphia Navy Yard.

1948 1 June Third Mediterranean cruise.

22 Sept Goodwill cruise to Africa via Suez Canal; Argentina, Uruguay, Brazil, Trinidad.

1949 15 June Decommissioned.

▽ *Huntington* seen in April 1948. (TS)

▷ *Huntington* was completed in February 1946 with camouflage to Measure 22. This photograph was probably taken after commissioning. She still has both catapults aboard. One can see clearly that many AA guns have a larger area of fire as a consequence of the tightly compressed superstructure. (TS)

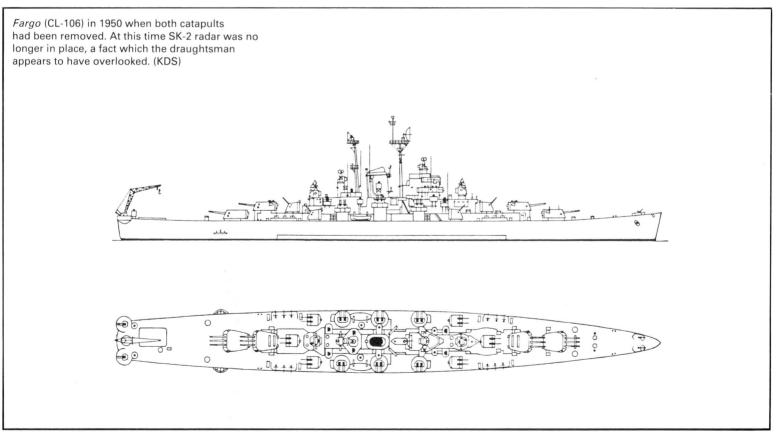

Fargo (CL-106) in 1950 when both catapults
had been removed. At this time SK-2 radar was no
longer in place, a fact which the draughtsman
appears to have overlooked. (KDS)

BALTIMORE CLASS

In appearance the *Baltimore* class, especially when viewed from slightly ahead, looked very much like the *Cleveland*s. They differed from that class chiefly in that they had one fewer triple turret aft and their pair of funnels, positioned quite close to each other, were flattened at the sides (when seen from above), while those of the *Cleveland*s were round. The practised eye notes particularly the fine differences in appearance of the 6in and 8in turrets. The increase in length over the *Cleveland*s was prompted by the need for more light AA guns. These were no portholes. Resistance gunfire was far greater than that of *Cleveland*s. In both classes, the designers sought a higher displacement and therefore a greater range over the previous, treaty-restricted ships. There having been less feverish haste in the construction of these ships than had been the case with the light cruisers, they did not come into service until almost a year later. The *Baltimore* class did not suffer any total losses during the war. Seven of the fourteen ships were converted after the war. Three (CA-73, 75 and 135) were fitted out as fleet flagships, and another four (CA-69, 70, 74 and 136) were converted to guided missile ships (CAG/CG). The construction of two more was suspended at the end of the war. After the war further improvements were made in some ships still in active use; mainly, replacement of 20mm and 40mm AA by 3in/50 guns; temporary installation of Regulus I missiles; continued improvements to radar and other electronics.

Technically, the *Baltimore*s were a development of *Wichita*, just as the *Cleveland*s were a development of the *Brooklyn*s. Time was available to develop the design, because at the end of the war priority was given to the construction of light cruisers. The final constructional design for the *Baltimore* class called for a strong, stable hull, which meant that from the outset certain causes of the topheaviness in the *Cleveland*s were eliminated. The break in number sequence in this class is explained by the fact that all the units of the *Oregon City* class were supposed to slot in from CA-122 onwards. But as that design did not progress as quickly as ships could be built, a further seven ships (CA-130 to 136) were built in accordance with the *Baltimore* design. From this sequence, one more ship, CA-134, was withdrawn to serve as lead ship for the later *Des Moines* class.

Five of the *Baltimore*s served after the war, 1959 to 1973. Of those units that had been mothballed, five were recommissioned during the Korean War and subsequently served from 1955 to 1963.

The number of 20mm and 40mm AA guns varied from ship to ship. The first four ships had two aircraft cranes on the quarterdeck, the remaining ships, one only.

◁ *Baltimore* was the lead ship of the heavy cruiser class bearing her name, which first came into service in April 1943. She is seen here on 9 July 1943. It should be noted that the SK antennae is fitted here on the after mast and that the ship, at a relatively early point in time, had radar Mk 8 Mod. 1. Two Kingfishers are on their catapults. Between the two aircraft cranes is – asymetric with the axis of the deck – a tub to accommodate 40mm quadruple Bofors. The camouflage is that of Measure 21. (USN)

◁ This photograph dates from October 1944 when, during yard work at Mare Island, *Baltimore*'s SK radar was moved to the more forward position and camouflage of Measure 32/16d was applied; the starboard pattern of this can be seen here. (USN)

▽ Details of *Baltimore,* seen at Mare Island on 21 October 1944. The after mast carries only SG radar. Mk 12/22 radar has been newly added. All the 40mm splinter shields are 'dull black'. Ammunition is being loaded. One should take note of the appearance of Mk 8 Mod. 1 radar, the cover of which has been removed for maintenance. Both Kingfishers are in position on their catapults. (USN)

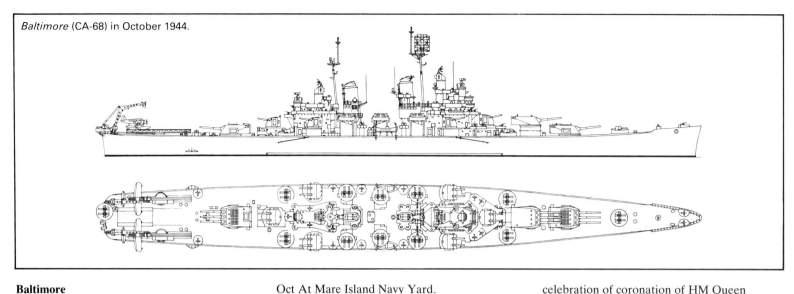

Baltimore (CA-68) in October 1944.

Baltimore

1943 15 April Commissioned; in Pacific.
20 Nov–4 Dec Landing on Makin.
1944 29 Jan–8 Feb Landing on Kwajalein.
16–17 Feb Attacked Truk.
17 Feb–2 March Capture of Eniwetok.
21–22 Feb The Marianas.
30 March–1 April Palaus, Yap, Ulithi, Woleai.
21–24 April Landing in Hollandia, New Guinea.
29 April–1 May Truk, Ponape, Satawan.
19–20 May Air attacks on Marcus.
23 May Air attacks on Wake.
11–24 June Landing on Saipan.
19–20 June Battle of Philippine Sea.
July Returned to west coast; took President
  F. D. Roosevelt to Pearl Harbor for discussions
  with General MacArthur and Admiral Nimitz.
9 August President Roosevelt landed in Alaska.

Oct At Mare Island Navy Yard.
Nov Returned to Third Fleet.
14–16 Dec & 1945 6–7 Jan Attacked Luzon.
3, 4, 9, 15, 21 Jan Formosa.
12 & 16 Jan China coast.
22 Jan Okinawa.
26 Jan With Fifth Fleet.
16–17 Feb Honshu.
19 Feb–5 March Iwo Jima.
18 March–10 June Okinawa; at end of war,
  'Magic Carpet' cruise.
1945–46 29 Nov–17 Feb Occupation of Japan;
  departed for west coast.
1946 8 July First decommissioning.
1951 28 Nov Second commissioning; in Atlantic.
1952, 1953, 1954 Various summer deployments to
  Mediterranean.
1953 June Participation in Fleet Review in

celebration of coronation of HM Queen
  Elizabeth II of Great Britain.
1955 5 Jan Transferred to Pacific.
Feb–August With Seventh Fleet in West Pacific.
1953 31 May Second Decommissioning.

▽   After five and a half years of inaction in the
reserve, *Baltimore* was recommissioned for the
Korean War in November 1951, but remained in
the Atlantic area, being transferred to the Pacific
only at the beginning of 1955. This photograph
was taken on 2 July 1952 off Toulon, during her
first Mediterranean deployment. In place of the SK
antenna one notices SPS-6B, but there is still SG
aft. Both catapults have now been removed, but
the two cranes remained permanently on board.
(MB)

△ Returning from her third Mediterranean deployment, *Baltimore* visited various English ports, at one of which this detailed photograph was taken in September 1954. In the intervening time the Mk 12/22 radar had been replaced by Mk 25 and the after main-topmast was removed to facilitate the fitting of the platform for the SPS-8A height-finding radar. (WL)

▷ *Baltimore* in 1955, once more in the Pacific during the last years of her active service life. She shipped forty-eight 40mm guns throughout her career, and still has both aircraft cranes. (USN)

Boston

1943 30 June Commissioned; in Pacific.
1944 Jan Joined TF 58.
31 Jan–28 Feb Landings on Kwajalein, Majuro, Eniwetok.
30 March–1 April Palaus and West Carolines.
21–24 April Hollandia and West New Guinea.
29 April–1 May Bombarded Truk and Satawan.
11–24 June Landing on Saipan.
15–16 June Attacked Bonin.
19–20 June Battle of Philippine Sea.
12 July–15 August Landing on Guam.

25–27 July Attacked Palaus, Yap, and Ulithi.
15 Sept Landing on Morotai.
6 Sept–14 Oct Capture of South Palaus.
9–24 Sept Attacked Philippine Islands.
10 Oct Attacked Okinawa with TF 38.
11–14, 15, 24–26 Oct, 13, 14, 19, 20 Nov North Luzon and Formosa.
14–16 Dec Attacked Luzon.
24–26 Oct Battle of Leyte Gulf.
1945 3, 4, 9, 15, 21 Jan Attacked Formosa.
6–7 Jan Attacked Luzon.
12 & 16 Jan Chinese coast.

22 Jan Attacked Nansei Shoto.
1 March Returned to west coast.
25 March–6 June Refit at Long Beach; returned to Pacific in about June.
20 July–15 August Attacked Japanese Islands; after end of war occupation of Japan.
1946 28 Feb Returned to west coast.
12 March First decommissioning.
1952 4 Jan Reclassified as CAG-1.
Feb Towed from Bremerton to Philadelphia; converted as guided missile cruiser.

◁ *Boston* off Boston, Massachusetts, on the day she was commissioned, 2 June 1943. Both aircraft cranes and their spreaders have been laid flat on the after deck. This was done if it were desired to give the after deck 8in guns a larger arc of fire. The camouflage is to Measure 21. (USN)

▽ Five days before decommissioning: *Boston,* on 7 March 1946 in San Francisco Bay after returning from Japan. In mid-1945 *Boston* had been given SP radar at Long Beach, and was painted in Measure 22. (Cas)

△ *Canberra* in October 1943 off Bethlehem, Quincy. Camouflage is to Measure 21. Other than two SG there are apparently no larger search radar antennae aboard. Some 20mm AA can be seen beneath the two after fire-control gear. (USN)

▽ *Canberra,* one year later on 10 October 1944, in formation with Task Force Group 38.1. She is painted to Measure 32-18d, although in this photograph, the darkest shade does not give its 'dull black' effect. In the background is a *Fletcher*-class destroyer. (USN)

Canberra

1943 14 Oct Commissioned.
1944 14 Jan Left Boston for San Diego; continued cruise with passengers on board.
1 Feb Arrived Pearl Harbor.
14 Feb Joined TF 58; capture of Eniwetok.
30 March–1 April With *Yorktown* (CV-10) attacked Palaus, Yap, Ulithi, Woleai; then with *Enterprise* (CV-6) attacked Truk and Satawan.

29 April–1 May Renewed attacks on Truk.
May Attacked Marcus and Wake.
June Operations in Marianas; Battle of the Philippine Sea.
August Attacked Philippine Islands and Palaus.
15–16 Sept Landing on Morotai.
2 Oct Attacked Okinawa and Formosa with TF 38.
13 Oct Hit by torpedo in engine compartment;

23 dead; towed by *Wichita* (CA-45) to Ulithi.
27 Oct Towed to Manus, first repairs; sailed to east coast.
1944–45 16 Feb–17 Oct Repaired at Boston Navy Yard.
1945 Returned to west coast.
1947 7 March Decommissioned.
1952 4 Jan Reclassified as CAG-2; towed to east coast for convertion to guided missile cruiser.

Quincy

1943 15 Dec Commissioned; shake-down cruise from Trinidad to Venezuela.
1944 27 March Joined TF 22.
14 May With TG 27.10 to Belfast to join Twelfth Fleet.
6 June–4 July Bombarded coast during Normandy invasion; to Mediterranean.
18–26 July Operated from Palermo.
15 August Landing in South of France.
19 August With TG 86.4, bombarded Toulon and St-Mandrier.
1 Sept Left for east coast.
Sept–Oct At Boston Navy Yard.
1945 23 Jan President F. D. Roosevelt aboard; sailed for Malta Conference.
2 Feb Arrived Malta.
8 Feb In Great Bitter Lake at southern exit of Suez Canal.
14 Feb President F. D. Roosevelt received rulers of Egypt, Abyssinia and Saudi Arabia.
27 Feb Returned to Newport News; transferred to Pacific Fleet.
20 March Arrived Pearl Harbor.
11 April Off Ulithi to join CRUDIV 10; carrier escort.
16–30 April Fire support off Okinawa.
12 May Attacked Japanese islands with TF 58.
5 June Weathered typhoon without casualties; then Flagship, CRUDIV 10.
13 June Returned to Ulithi.
1 July As carrier escort left for second operational period against Japanese mainland.
23 August At end of hostilities, occupation of Japan.
1 Sept Arrived in Tokyo Bay.
20 Sept Joined TF 53 (Fifth Fleet) based in Tokyo Bay.
Oct Sailed to west coast.
1946 19 Oct Decommissioned, Reserve Fleet.
1952 31 Jan Recommissioned.
1953 July–Dec With Seventh Fleet in Korean War.
1954 2 July Decommissioned.

◁ A very attractive yard photograph of *Quincy* in about December 1943. She is still flying her yard flag and is quite high in the water forward. *Quincy* was the last of the four units of the class to have two aircraft cranes aft. (BSt)

△ *Quincy* on the day of her commissioning, 15 December 1943, off Boston. The cranes and the supported tub which accommodated the 40mm quadruple Bofors are very clear. The paint is a relatively dark shade of Measure 21. (USN)

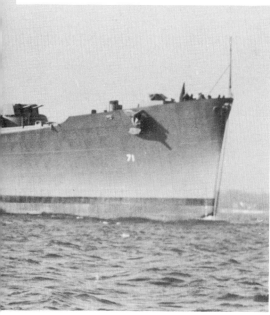

◁ ▷ These two photographs of *Quincy* show both sides of camouflage Measure 32-18d which must have been applied early in 1944. The uppermost photograph is dated 10 April 1944 and was probably taken at Baltimore. The ship is at anchor and signal flags are hanging out to dry. Subsequently she operated for a short time with the Royal Navy and the lower photograph was taken from a British ship during that period. The cranes are lying flat on deck. Note the gun turrets which are swung out, as is the fire-control gear; and the rather large battle flag. (IWM)

▽ Some time after February 1945, when *Quincy* was transferred to the Pacific Fleet, she must have been repainted to Measure 22 as can be seen from this photograph taken in early 1946 off San Francisco. The command pennant of a Commodore flies from the forward masthead. (Cas)

Pittsburgh

1944 10 Oct Commissioned; shake-down cruises.
1945 13 Jan Left for Pacific.
13 Feb At Ulithi to join TG 58.2, with USS
  Lexington.
Feb Iwo Jima, Japanese islands.
March Nansei Shoto, Kyushu.

19 March Towed badly damaged carrier *Franklin*
  (CV-13).
March–May Okinawa.
4 June Lost entire bow section during typhoon, no
  casualties.
10 June Arrived Guam for provisional repairs;
  broken-off bow section later recovered by tug

and brought to Guam.
24 June–16 July Sailed to west coast with temporary bow section; repaired at Puget Sound.
1946 7 March First decommissioning.
1951 25 Sept Second commissioning.
Oct Transferred to Atlantic.
1952 11 Feb–20 May With Sixth Fleet in Mediterranean; operations on east coast and Caribbean.
1 Dec Departed for second deployment to
  Mediterranean.
1953 Jan Goodwill cruise to Indian Ocean as
  Flagship, CINCNELM, Admiral J. Wright.
May–Dec Refit and modernization at Norfolk
  Navy Yard.
1954 19 Jan With Sixth Fleet; cruised with
  Admiral Wright to Indian Ocean.
26 May Returned to east coast.
21 Oct Transferred to Pacific Fleet joined via
  Panama Canal.
26 Nov With Seventh Fleet in West Pacific;
  operations in China Sea.
1955 16 Feb Left for west coast; operations in
  home waters.
1956 28 August Decommissioned.

◁ *Pittsburgh* on 1 November 1944, three weeks
after commissioning. Her camouflage is to
Measure 32/18d. She was completed with SK-2
radar antenna and two SG. One Kingfisher is just
being launched from the starboard catapult.
Pittsburgh was the first ship of the *Baltimore* class
to have only one aircraft crane. (USN)

◁ *Pittsburgh* lost her complete bow section during a typhoon in June 1945 and had to proceed with a jury bow to the west coast where a new one had been fitted by September 1945. This dramatic photograph was taken during a speed trial on 28 September 1945 off Puget Sound Navy Yard. While in the yard she was camouflaged to Measure 21, which shows up here as quite a dark effect. (USN)

▽ After three and a half years in the reserve, *Pittsburgh* was brought back into service at the end of September 1951 during the Korean War, but was transferred to the Atlantic. During her first deployment to the Mediterranean she was photographed off Toulon on 20 March 1952. Both catapults have been removed and SPS-6B radar has been installed. (MB)

St. Paul

1945 17 Feb Commissioned; shake-down cruises in Caribbean.

15 May Left Boston for Pacific.

8–30 June Operations in Hawaii area.

2 July Left Pearl Harbor to join TF 38.

July–August Carrier escort during attacks on Japanese Islands.

27 Aug Sagami Wan, occupation of Japan.

1 Sept Entered Tokyo Bay.

10 Nov Flagship, TF 73 at Shanghai; remained in China until end of 1946 then returned to west coast.

1946 1 Oct Refit at Mare Island.

1947 1 Jan–15 Feb Training cruises off San Diego.

March–Nov Flagship, TF 71 at Shanghai.

▽ *St. Paul* is one of the few *Baltimore*-class ships to serve without interruption for 26 years, during which she carried out many varied tasks. This undated photograph may date from 1947 or 1948 when the SK-2 radar was replaced by SG-6. There is SP radar aft. There are no longer any 40mm quadruples in the forwardmost AA gun tub, nor are there catapults aft. This photograph shows off the attractive lines of the ships of this class. (USN)

1948 April–May Reservist training cruises off west coast.

August–Dec Deployed to West Pacific.

1949 Aircraft replaced by helicopters.

April–Oct Deployment to West Pacific.

1950 Midshipmen training cruise to Pearl Harbor.

June At outbreak of Korean War, midshipmen landed.

July With TG 77.3 patrolled Formosa Straits, remained there until 1 Nov 1950.

9 Nov Carrier escort with TF 77 off Korea; coastal bombardments.

1951 June–Sept Refit at San Francisco.

5 Nov Departed for Korea.

27 Nov Arrived Wonsan.

1952 21 April Off Korea, magazine fire in forward-most 8in turret; 30 dead.

24 June Returned to Long Beach.

1953 28 Feb Left for third Korean operation; escort for *New Jersey* (BB-62) during coastal bombardment.

11 July Hit by coastal gun; one 3in twin damaged, no casualties.

27 July Fired last salvo of Korean War; security cruises off Korean coast.

1954 May Operated in West Pacific.

1954–55 19 Nov–12 July Operated with Seventh Fleet, mainly between Taiwan and Chinese

mainland; during this period a yard stop on west coast.

1955–56 15 August–10 Jan Once more in West Pacific, Flagship, Seventh Fleet.

1956 Feb Refit at Puget Sound.

Sept Flagship, First Fleet.

6 Nov Departed Long Beach for West Pacific via San Diego.

29 Nov Relieved of Flagship, Seventh Fleet by *Rochester* (CA-124).

1957 26 April Departed for west coast.

21 May Arrived Long Beach; operations on west coast.

1958 3 Feb Sailed once more for West Pacific; visited Wellington, New Zealand.

9 March Left Yokosuka.

25 August Returned to Long Beach.

1959 4 May Sailed for West Pacific; became first US warship to be stationed permanently overseas; home port, Yokosuka for 39 months, as Flagship, Seventh Fleet; then in about August 1962, Flagship First Fleet; operations on west coast.

1965 Recommenced yearly deployment to West Pacific, including Vietnam.

1970 Total of five more operational cruises to West Pacific.

1971 30 April Decommissioned.

△ During her lengthy service *St. Paul* was frequently in the Far East. At one time she was the first US Navy ship since the war to be stationed permanently overseas. She is seen here on 27 July 1960 during a visit to Yokosuka as flagship of the Seventh Fleet, after taking President Eisenhower through the Formosa Strait. She now has a pylon mast with projecting platforms and a lattice mast peak. Note the many whip antennae and the fixed radio antenna on No. 2 turret. (SF)

◁ This photograph was taken on 20 September 1951 – probably off San Francisco – when *St. Paul* had just completed a three-months' refit in preparation for Korea. The opportunity was taken to fit twenty 3in/50 in the ten 40mm gun tubs, although this number was reduced on several occasions from this time until the end of her service. Note the asymmetrical arrangement of the AA tub right aft. She still has SPS-6B on the forward mast. (USN)

△ In 1963–64, when this undated photograph was taken, *St. Paul* still had ten 3in guns. The forward 5in mount has been removed in order that its roomy magazine can provide space for the ever-growing fleet staff. A single, side-band antenna is positioned well forward on the forecastle to avoid interference. A TACAN antenna URN-6 is atop the forward mast with radar SPS-37 beneath it. The after mast houses SPS-8A, and Mk 56 controls have been added to the Mk 34 and Mk 37. ECM antennae are to be found on the after funnel. (USN)

▽ ▷ *Columbia* was in active service without interruption for fourteen years until she was decommissioned in 1959 in order to be converted to a guided missile ship. These two attractive photographs show her in English waters in November 1949. The search radar antennae are SR-3 and SP. (WL)

Columbus

1945 8 June Commissioned; Pacific Fleet.

1946 13 Jan Arrived Tsingtau; occupation of China coast.

1 April Took part in sinking of 24 surrendered Japanese submarines.

2 April Left for west coast, remaining there for rest of the year.

1947 15 Jan–12 June Second deployment to West Pacific; operations on west coast; at Puget Sound Navy Yard.

1948 12 April Left for east coast.

19 April Arrived Norfolk.

1948–49 13 Sept–15 Dec, 1950–51 12 June–5 Oct Two cruises as Flagship, CINCNELM.

1951–52 25 August–29 Feb NATO manoeuvres; Flagship, SACLANT.

1952–53 Oct–Jan In Mediterranean; Flagship, Sixth Fleet.

1954–55 Sept–Jan Mediterranean, Flagship, CRUDIV 6; between times training cruises on east coast, manoeuvres in North Atlantic, yard refits.

1955 8 Nov Transferred to Pacific Fleet.

2 Dec Arrived Long Beach.

1956 5 Jan Arrived Yokosuka; operations with Seventh Fleet.

8 July Returned to west coast.

1957–58 Two cruises in West Pacific.

1959 8 May First decommissioning for conversion to guided missile ship.

30 Sept Reclassified as CG-12.

△ *Columbus* in the Mediterranean during the 1950s.

△ This is how *Columbus* looked on 14 March 1959, off Puget Sound Navy Yard, a short time before being decommissioned. Photographic evidence shows that she had six Mk 50 fire control gear by August 1957. The ten twin 3in/50 mounts must also have been fitted at that time and they can be seen here. She has URN-3 TACAN, SPS-12 radar (forward) and SPS-8A (aft). (USN)

◁ This photograph taken from astern of *Helena* is very like one of *Quincy* from the same perspective, except that here both the name of the ship and the pennant number are to be seen, possibly because the ship had been delivered after the end of the war. She is seen here on 4 May 1946 off the French Mediterranean coast, while on her way to China. She still has camouflage of Measure 21; two Seahawk reconnaissance aircraft are on their catapults. Only the first four units of this class had a 40mm quadruple aft. The positioning of the single crane along the ship's centre-line made possible the fitting of two twin Bofors on each side of it. (MB)

◁ *Helena* was one of the heavy cruisers which, from the mid-1950s, were fitted with the Regulus I missile system. This photograph was taken on 28 October 1955 off the coast of southern California and shows a Regulus I being launched from the launching platform near the stern. Three missiles of this type could be stored in the below-decks hangar which can be seen in front of it. The stern sponsons were removed before the missiles' installation. (USN)

▷ *Helena* on 24 August 1954 on arrival at Pearl Harbor during a cruise to Japan. (USN)

Helena

1945 4 Sept Commissioned.

27 Oct Took part in 'Navy Day' off New York; two shake-down cruises off Cuba.

1946 12 Feb Left Boston for world cruise; in England, COMNAVFOR EUROPE and COM Twelfth Fleet on board; three months' training cruises in northern European waters.

1 May Replaced as flagship; to the Near East via Suez Canal.

18 June Arrived Tsingtau.

1947 22 March Arrived west coast; training cruises on west coast.

1948 3 April Departed for West Pacific; operations in Chinese waters.

Dec Returned to west coast.

1949 May Training cruises for reservists.

June At Long Beach Navy Yard where modified to receive helicopters.

July–August Reservist training cruise to Panama and Galapagos Islands.

Nov Amphibious operations off Hawaii; then Japan and Philippines.

1950 Jan Flagship, Seventh Fleet.

21 May Returned to west coast.

June At San Francisco Navy Yard.

6 July Suspension of work at yard and hurried departure for Korea.

7 August Coastal bombardment of Korea.

1950–51 Nov–March Refit at Long Beach.

1951 18 April Joined TF 77 at Sasebo, Japan; coastal bombardment Korea; lightly damaged by shore battery.

20 Sept Returned to Yokosuka: then operations off Korea once more.

8 Dec Refit at Long Beach; all nine 8in gun barrels replaced.

1952 Feb Training cruises and manoeuvres on west coast.

8 June Arrived Yokosuka; operated once more off Korea with TF 77.

24 Nov Relieved of Korea duties, special cruise.

1 Dec Visited by CINCPACFL Admiral Radford and newly elected President Eisenhower; took them to Pearl Harbor.

11 Dec Arrived Pearl Harbor; important personages left.

16 Dec Returned to Long Beach.

1953 4 August Departed for West Pacific.

1954 11 Oct At Yokosuka, Flagship Seventh Fleet; operations mainly in the Taiwan area.

1955 Feb Covered evacuation of Tachen Islands.

July–Dec Operations in home waters off west coast.

1956 25 Jan Arrived Yokosuka; operations mainly in Taiwan area.

8 July Returned to west coast; nine months' operations on west coast, including firing of Regulus-I missiles.

1957 10 April West Pacific; Flagship, Seventh Fleet.

19 Oct Returned to west coast; refit; training cruises; missile-firing until March 1958.

1958 3 August Departed for West Pacific.

21 August Arrived Taiwan; operations mainly in this area.

1959 17 Feb Returned to west coast.

1960 5 Jan With USS *Yorktown* and DESRON 23 in West Pacific, sailed to Korea and Taiwan.

24 June Left Guam for visit to Australia.

June–Nov Refit at Long Beach Navy Yard.

1961 Jan Permanent Flagship, First Fleet.

1961–62 Operations along west coast with diversions to West Pacific.

1963 18 March COM First Fleet transferred to USS *St. Paul*.

29 June Decommissioned.

◁ *Helena* in the Pacific on 12 February 1957, with a Regulus I missile in the stern. The control antenna for the guidance of Regulus was positioned on the after mast. It is a modified SP antenna given the subsequent designation of SPQ-2. The parabolic antenna, however, is rather larger in diameter that that of SP. (Collection LGr)

◁ This is how *Helena* last appeared, probably in 1963 just before decommissioning. The Regulus installation has long been rendered inactive and the SPQ-2 fire control antenna removed. In place there is now SPS-37A antenna on the forward mast which had been converted, as that of *St. Paul*. Note the use of radar antenna SPS-12 (aft) as fire control radar in place of the withdrawn Mk 4. Radio antennae are to be seen on the forecastle and on two of the 8in turrets. (USN)

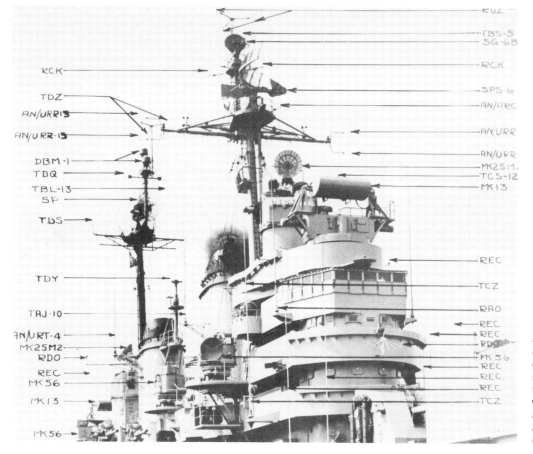

◁ Detailed photographs such as this one of *Helena* taken on 29 July 1953 at Puget Sound, are a veritable gold-mine for spotters of electronic gear dating from the early 1950s. The picture shows also that, as early as 1953, 3in guns and Mk 56 fire control gear were fitted. This was a few weeks before *Helena* sailed for the West Pacific to assume the duties – alternating with *St. Paul* and *San Francisco* – of flagship of the Seventh Fleet. (USN)

▷ *Bremerton,* too, was one of the cruisers brought back into service for the Korean War on account of their long-range 8in guns for coastal bombardment. Here she is seen in February 1952, approximately three months after she re-entered service, carrying the same surveillance and fire control electronics as when she was built, with the exception of SPS-6B. Her armament also remained the same. What was new and remarkable is the fact that, as one can see, she already has four MK 56 fire control gear, although the 40mm AA have not yet been replaced by 3in/50. (USN)

▽ This 'art' photograph of *Bremerton,* possibly at Pearl Harbor, could date from 1955 or rather later. Two Mk 56 have been fitted in the meantime. The 3in/50 are now fitted, but the two AA positions amidships have been removed. Additions are SPS-8A radar and MK 25 gunnery radar. SPS-6B seems to have remained aboard until her decommissioning in July 1960. (USN)

Bremerton
1945 29 April Commissioned.
29 May Shake-down cruises off Cuba in the course of which became Flagship, CINCLANTFL, Admiral Ingram, during an inspection journey he made to South America.
22 July–2 Oct Special tasks in Casco Bay, Maine.
Nov Transferred to Pacific.
15 Dec Arrived Pearl Harbor.
1946 4 Jan Arrived Inchon, Korea; operations with Seventh Fleet.
20 Nov Returned to west coast; then training cruise with Navy reservists.
1948 9 April First decommissioning.
1951 23 Nov Second commissioning, then first operation off Korea with Seventh Fleet.
1952 11 Sept Returned to west coast.
1952–53 Oct–March Refit Long Beach Navy Yard; training cruises, gunnery practise.
1953 5 April Departed for second Korean operation with Seventh Fleet.
Nov Refit at Long Beach.
1954 14 May Departed to join Seventh Fleet in West Pacific.
17 Oct Returned to Long Beach
1955–56 12 July–12 Feb Further operational cruise in West Pacific.
1956–60 Several transfers between First and Seventh Fleet.
1960 29 July Decommissioned.

Fall River

1945 1 July Commissioned.

1945–46 13 Oct–31 Jan Special operations based around Norfolk; joined 'Joint Task Force 1'.

1946 16 Feb–6 March Preparations for use as flagship during atomic bomb tests at Bikini; remained there.

21 May–14 Sept Conveyed Rear-Admiral Fahrion to Marshall Islands; then training operations on west coast.

1947 12 Jan–17 June Flagship, CRUDIV 1, operational cruise in West Pacific.

31 Oct Decommissioned.

▷ *Fall River* had just a little over two years in active service. This photograph shows her camouflaged to Measure 21, on 12 August 1945, a few weeks after she had commissioned. *Fall River* was flagship of the naval forces which took part in the atom bomb tests off Bikini from May to September 1946. During this time the ship carried her name in large letters amidships. (USN)

Macon

1945 26 August Commissioned.

1946–49 Test ship for new installations, AA training ship and training ship for naval reservists.

1948 Cruise to Europe with midshipmen.

1950 12 April First decommissioning.

16 Oct Second commissioning; Flagship CRUDIV 6 in Atlantic; one operational deployment to Mediterranean each year until end of 1959; total of six summer cruises with midshipmen.

1956 In eastern Mediterranean because of Suez crisis.

1957 Jan–March Installation of Regulus I missile installation; then gunnery exercises.

12 June Took part in Fleet Review off Hampton Roads.

1960 Jan Goodwill cruise to South America.

1961 10 March Second decommissioning.

▽ *Macon* off Philadelphia Navy Yard on 14 April 1947. Her three 40mm AA positions are empty and she has only thirty-six 40mm guns aboard. The Seahawk reconnaissance aircraft is clearly visible. (USN)

△ In this photograph of *Macon* taken on 25 July 1948, three empty AA gun tubs are clearly visible. The temporary radar fitted is SR-3. *Macon* was the only ship of the class to receive the raised helicopter platform aft, but the arrangement proved impracticable. Obviously the arcs of fire of the 8in triple turrets aft were greatly restricted and such platforms were, at the latest, removed when ships were brought back into service. *Macon* still has the small pennant number three years after the end of the war. To facilitate aerial recognition the '132' was painted on top of No. 2 turret. (USN)

△ At the beginning of 1956 *Macon* and three other cruisers were fitted with the Regulus I missile system. To accomplish this three aftermost AA gun tubs were removed which reduced the number of 3in guns to fourteen. She is seen here in 1958 after the system had been installed. There is now SPQ-2 on the after mast as guidance radar for Regulus. (USN)

Toledo

1946 27 Oct Commissioned.

1947 6 Jan Departed for two-months' training cruise to West Indies; shake-down cruise off Cuba.

1 April Commenced world cruise via Atlantic, Mediterranean, Suez Canal and Indian Ocean.

15 June Arrived Yokosuka; cruise to Korea.

21 Oct Left Yokosuka via Pearl Harbor for west coast.

5 Nov Arrived Long Beach; remained in Pacific.

1948 3 April With *Helena* departed for Japan.

29 August Arrived Yokosuka; Goodwill cruise in Indian Ocean; in early summer of 1948 operations in Chinese waters while Nationalist Chinese were being evacuated to Taiwan.

16 Sept Departed for west coast.

5 Oct Refit at Puget Sound Navy Yard.

1949 18 Feb Six months' operations on west coast.

14 Oct Departed for eight months' deployment in West Pacific.

1950 12 June Returned to Long Beach.

22 June Left again for West Pacific.

18 July At Yokosuka, Flagship, CRUDIV 5.

26 July First bombardment of Korean east coast as unit of TG 95.5; continued these operations with short supply stops in Japan.

27 Oct Left Yokosuka for west coast.

8 Nov Arrived Long Beach.

1950–51 14 Nov–24 Feb Refit at San Francisco Navy Yard.

1951 2 April Left for west Pacific.

18 April Arrived Sasebo.

26 April Commencement of second operational cruise off Korea.

24 Nov Left Yokosuka via Pearl Harbor for west coast.

8 Dec Arrived Long Beach; seven months' operations along west coast.

1952 16 August Departed for third Korea cruise.

8 Sept Arrived Yokosuka; carrier escort and shore bombardments with intermediate stops in Japan.

1953 28 Feb Left Yokosuka for west coast.

16 April Commencement of five months' refit at San Francisco Navy Yard.

10 Sept Operations along west coast.

20 Oct Left for seventh deployment to West Pacific.

7 Nov Arrived Yokosuka; six months' operations in Japanese, Korean, and East China waters.

1954 16 April Left Yokosuka via Pearl Harbor for west coast.

1 May Arrived Long Beach; five months' operations on west coast.

14 Sept Left for eighth deployment to West Pacific via Pearl Harbor.

7 Nov Arrived Yokosuka.

1955 Jan Supported evacuation of Nationalist Chinese from Tachen Islands.

5 March With *Pittsburgh* departed for west coast.

22 March Arrived Long Beach; operations on west coast.

16 June Refit at Puget Sound to the end of October.

1956 Operations on west coast; during next four years further deployments to West Pacific.

1958 Jan Visited Sydney and Melbourne.

1958–59 9 June–25 Nov Last deployment to West Pacific.

1960 21 May Decommissioned.

▷ *Toledo* was one of the *Baltimore*-class ships that served continuously in the active fleet for fourteen years from the end of 1946 until mid-1960. This undated, broadside photograph was taken in about 1946. She has only thirty-six 40 mm guns; the SK-2 radar antenna cannot be seen. (USN)

▷ This photograph of *Toledo* is said to have been taken in 1951. Again, there are forty-eight 40mm barrels aboard, controlled by at most six Mk 56 fire control gear. The forward mast supports the SPS-68 radar antenna. The pennant number is painted on the upper surface of No. 2 8in turret. (USN)

◁ *Toledo* probably received her Regulus I installation in mid-1955 at Puget Sound. This photograph was taken subsequently and it is clear that the three after AA positions have been removed. The radar equipment is now: SPS-12 and SPQ-2. (USN)

▷ Bridge details of *Toledo,* seen on 12 October 1955 at Puget Sound Navy Yard. Normally the different antennae making up an overall installation would be only generically named, e.g., in this case SPS-12. However there is mention here of the individual designations of various antennae, for example AS-603 – a designation that would not normally be used. (USN)

▽ *Toledo* probably received her 5in/50 AA guns, totalling twenty, at the beginning of 1952 which this undated photograph shows. (USN)

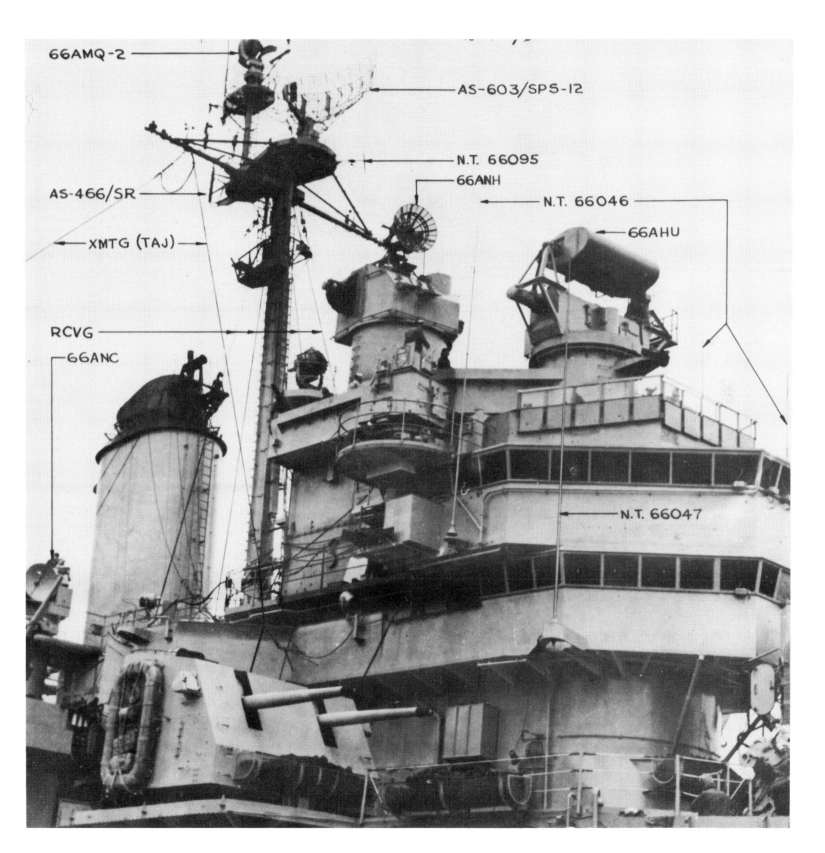

66AMQ-2

AS-603/SPS-12

N.T. 66095

66ANH

N.T. 66046

AS-466/SR

66AHU

XMTG (TAJ)

RCVG

66ANC

N.T. 66047

△ After *St. Paul* and *Helena, Los Angeles* was the third *Baltimore*-class ship to be modified later as a fleet flagship. This photograph was taken in August 1951, supposedly in Korean waters. SPS-6B and SP are among the radar antennae, which are very difficult to distinguish in this photograph. (USN)

▽ During her annual deployments to the West Pacific, *Los Angeles* stayed for a time in 1958 at Yokosuka where this detailed photograph was taken. One assumes she had 3in/50 guns from 1962, but their number declined to fourteen from 1958 to 1963. There are now SPS-12 radar and Tacan URN-3 on the forward mast. (SF)

▷ *Los Angeles* in about 1960, after she had received the Regulus I installation. The SPS-12 on the forward mast has been replaced by SPS-37A. There is a pennant number and radio antenna on No. 2 turret. Right aft can be seen a Regulus I missile on its launcher. (USN)

Los Angeles

1945 22 July Commissioned; shake-down cruises off Cuba.

15 Oct Departure for West Pacific.

1946 31 Jan Arrived Shanghai; operations with Seventh Fleet in 1946.

1947 21 Jan Returned to west coast.

1948 9 April First decommissioning.

1951 27 Jan Second commissioning.

14 May Departed for West Pacific.

31 May Arrived east coast of Korea; Flagship, COMCRUDIV 5.

17 Dec Returned to west coast; refit.

1952 9 Oct Returned once more to Korea.

1953 March–April Lightly damaged by North Korean coastal batteries.

15 May Returned to west coast.

1953–63 Total of eight deployments to West Pacific, mostly as division flagship; including operations along west coast and as far as Hawaii.

1963 15 Nov Second Decommissioning.

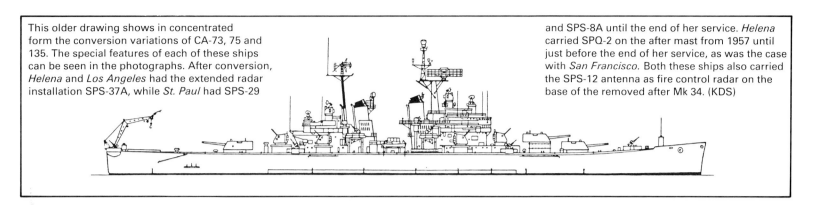

This older drawing shows in concentrated form the conversion variations of CA-73, 75 and 135. The special features of each of these ships can be seen in the photographs. After conversion, *Helena* and *Los Angeles* had the extended radar installation SPS-37A, while *St. Paul* had SPS-29 and SPS-8A until the end of her service. *Helena* carried SPQ-2 on the after mast from 1957 until just before the end of her service, as was the case with *San Francisco.* Both these ships also carried the SPS-12 antenna as fire control radar on the base of the removed after Mk 34. (KDS)

▽   This attractive photograph of *Los Angeles*
may have been taken during her last service
period, in about mid-1962. SPQ-2 is still to be seen
on the after mast although the Regulus installation
has long been abandoned. Note the ECM aerials
around the after funnel. (USN)

▽ During a refit in about 1961, *Los Angeles* was given a forward conical tubular mast with a lattice top. This detailed photograph was taken on 24 October 1961 in a Japanese port. One can see clearly that the after Mk 34 has been removed and SPS-12 has now taken on the function of fire-control radar. One can now see for the first time the SPS-10 radar antenna situated between SPS-37A and Tacan. (TM)

Chicago

1945 10 Jan Commissioned; joined Pacific Fleet.
30 May Arrived Pearl Harbor.
9 August With Third Fleet; bombarded Japanese mainland until end of war, remained in Japanese waters.
7 Nov Left Tokyo for west coast.
23 Nov Arrived San Pedro; yard refit; then deployed to West Pacific.
1946 18 Feb Arrived Shanghai for occupation of Chinese coast.
28 March Departed for Japan.
1947 14 Jan Departed for west coast.
6 June First decommissioning.
1958 1 Nov Reclassified as CG-11; from beginning of 1959 converted to guided missile cruiser.

▽ After a bare two and a half years of active service, *Chicago* was retired in mid-1947 to be converted to a guided missile cruiser in 1959. She is seen here on 7 May 1945, camouflaged to Measure 21. Her equipment corresponds with normal practice for early 1945. (USN)

OREGON CITY CLASS

The *Oregon City* class was to the *Baltimore*s what the *Cleveland* class had been to the *Fargo*s, namely a modified design with one funnel instead of two. Eight ships were planned, but by the end of the war only three ships had been launched, and work on a further ship was suspended during its construction, being rescheduled to enter service in 1951 as CLC-1 (see description of CLC *Northampton*).

The design for the *Oregon*s dated from 1942, and the underlying reasons for its development may well have been similar to those which prompted the design of the *Fargo* class: reduction in top-heaviness; more light AA with increased areas of fire. In order to achieve these aims both funnels were compressed into one and the height of the after superstructure was reduced.

After intensive service use *Albany* was decommissioned in 1958 to undergo extensive conversion to a guided missile cruiser; *Rochester* served with the active fleet until 1961, while the ship giving its name to the class, *Oregon City*, did not even achieve two years of service before being put into the reserve. Only three units completed as heavy cruisers. At the end of the war construction of one ship was interrupted and that of six ships was suspended.

▽ *Albany* was not completed until after the end of the war. This broadside photograph was taken off Boston Harbour one day after her commissioning on 16 June 1946. At that time she still carried the small pennant numbers, it being the opinion that they must be in black to be recognizable as the ship's hull was painted in peace-time light grey. The upper line of the armoured belt can be clearly seen. During her first period of service, *Albany* was active for eleven and a half years. (USN)

OREGON CITY CLASS SHIPS WITHOUT CA DESIGNATIONS WHEN COMMISSIONED OR NOT COMPLETED

Pennant No.	Name	Fiscal Year	Laid Down	Builder	History
CA-125	Northampton	1942	31 Aug 1944	Bethlehem Quincy	Subsequently completed as CLC-1
CA-126	Cambridge	1942	16 Dec 1944	Bethlehem Quincy	Building suspended 12 Aug 1945
CA-127	Bridgeport	1942	13 Jan 1945	Bethlehem Quincy	Building suspended 12 Aug 1945
CA-128	Kansas City	1942		Bethlehem Quincy	Building suspended 12 Aug 1945
CA-129	Tulsa	1942		Bethlehem Quincy	Building suspended 12 Aug 1945
CA-137	Norfolk	1942	27 Dec 1944	Philadelphia Navy Yard	Building suspended 12 Aug 1945
CA-138	Scranton	1942	27 Dec 1944	Philadelphia Navy Yard	Building suspended 12 Aug 1945

▽ This is how *Oregon City* looked in 1973, with the reserve fleet. She still displays the pennant number, but all radar antennae had been removed before she was laid up. All the 40mm Bofors were 'mothballed'. (LRC)

Oregon City

1946 16 Feb Commissioned.

31 March Commencement of shake-down cruises off Cuba.

May Returned to Boston.

3 July Flagship, Fourth Fleet, including training of reservists.

6–19 Oct Reservists training cruises to Bermuda.

1947 Jan Joined Second Fleet; various cruises including a summer cruise with midshipmen to Panama Canal zone and in Caribbean.

15 Dec Decommissioned.

Albany

1946 15 June Commissioned.

1949–56 Alternated on five occasions between operations with Second Fleet along east coast and deployments to Sixth Fleet in Mediterranean; during this period several cruises in the Caribbean, three to South America and one to northern Europe.

1951 Cruise to Rio de Janeiro for inauguration of new President.

1957 Nov Commencement of conversion to guided missile cruiser (CG-10).

◁ Although *Oregon City* was the lead-ship of a small class of only three 'compressed' *Baltimore*s she was only in service for a bare 22 months, that is to say until the end of 1947. She is seen here on 17 June 1946. She was painted in peace-time grey. As with the *Fargo* class, the positioning of the fire-control gear Mk 34 and Mk 37 was changed around from that obtaining in the *Baltimore*s. During her entire service life she had forty-eight 40mm Bofors aboard. (USN)

△ This undated photograph of *Albany* was probably taken between 1949 and mid-1950 during one of her many visits to the Mediterranean. She already has Mk 56; the 3in/50 AA guns replaced the 40mm Bofors from November 1950. Mk 25 has already replaced Mk 12/22 and SR-3 radar replaced SK-2. The command pennant of a Vice-Admiral flies from the after mast. Note how considerably the black funnel cap affects the appearance of the ship. (AB)

This is how *Albany* (CA-123) was envisaged at the time of building; long-range photographic evidence has subsequently corrected certain features. The number of 3in/50 AA installed from the mid-1950 could not have exceeded sixteen, i.e., eight twin mountings. When these guns were installed the radar antenna shown here, SR-3, had already been replaced by SG-6. (KDS)

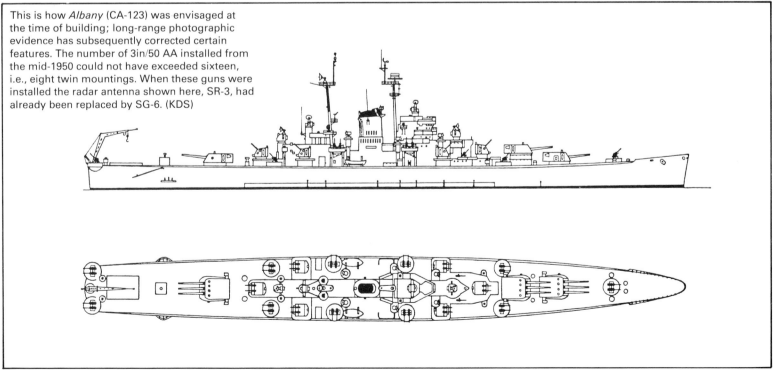

Rochester

1946 20 Dec Commissioned.

1947 22 Feb–April Shake-down cruise off Cuba.

1947–48 April–Jan Total of nine training cruises for reservists.

1948 20 Feb Departure for Mediterranean.

1 March Flagship, Sixth Task Fleet.

14 June End of Mediterranean deployment; replaced as flagship by *Fargo*.

27 June Arrived east coast; reservist training with cruises to Bermuda, New Brunswick and Jamaica; at the beginning of October refit at Boston Navy Yard, including removal of catapults and conversion to receive helicopters.

1950 5 Jan Departed to join Pacific Fleet.

April Left Long Beach for cruise to South Pacific; at Pearl Harbor took on board CINCPACFL Admiral Radford and Vice-Admiral Struble, COM Seventh Fleet; departed for Philippines.

July Carrier escort with TF 57 to Korea; coastal bombardment and landing support; during 198 days at sea off Korea she expended 3,265 8in and 2,339 5in shells.

1951 10 Jan Left Sasebo for west coast.

Feb–May Refit at Mare Island Navy Yard; then training of crews to man ships brought back into service.

27 August Left for exercises off Hawaii; then cruised into West Pacific.

21 Nov Arrived Yokosuka.

28 Nov Once again off Korean coast.

1952 April Returned to west coast.

7 Dec Once more with TG 77.1 off east coast of Korea.

1953 6 April Returned to Long Beach.

4 May–7 Sept Refit at Mare Island Navy Yard, including replacement of 40mm and 20mm AA by 3in/50.

1954 5 Jan Departed for West Pacific; operations with Seventh Fleet.

29 May Left Yokosuka for west coast.

Feb–6 August Fifth deployment to West Pacific.

1955–56 19 Nov–7 March Refit at San Francisco Navy Yard.

1956 29 May–16 Dec Sixth deployment to West Pacific; at beginning of June 1957 Fleet Admiral Nimitz on board; inspected First Fleet.

1958 3 Sept–24 March, 1959 6 Jan–17 June, 1960 5 April–29 Oct Seventh, eighth and ninth deployments to West Pacific.

1961 15 August Decommissioned.

▽   This photograph of *Albany,* said to date from November 1957, has surely been given too late a date. The picture certainly shows the ship as she last appeared in about the mid 1950s. SPS-12 and SPS-8A radar antennae can be seen on both masts with, further forward, URN-3 Tacan. The voluminous AA gun tubs are clearly to be seen and these are arranged asymmetrically aft. She no longer has catapults. (USN)

△ After completion, *Rochester* spent her first three years in the Atlantic, with one deployment to the Mediterranean. After 3in AA had been installed in the autumn of 1953 at Mare Island, she sailed for the West Pacific where this photograph is said to have been taken in March 1954. At the beginning of 1952 the SG-6 radar on the forward mast had been replaced by SPS-6B. (USN)

▽ This August 1960 photograph of the midships section of *Rochester* in a Japanese port, shows ner – one year before being decommissioned – carrying SPS-12 and SPS-8A radar. The after Mk 34 has been removed. Note the slender supports for four of the six MK 56s. ECM antennae can be seen on the after mast. (TM)

DES MOINES CLASS

It can be said that, with this class, the high point and the end of American cruiser development arrived simultaneously. In general terms, these ships had much in common, from an exterior point of view, with their *Oregon City* class predecessors – in the disposition of weaponry and in fire control instruments. This class was the summation of lessons learned in wartime and its ships were (the *Alaska* class excepted!) the largest cruisers ever built. The fact that they were approximately 4,000 tons heavier than *Oregon City* stemmed mainly from the introduction of the world's first fully automatic 8in gun turret. These were capable of a rate of fire 20 shells per gun per minute. Obviously a greater quantity of ammunition had to be stowed which meant larger magazines. A further proportion of the additional displacement was devoted to improved armour. For the first time in heavy cruisers the newly introduced 3in/50 were a standard installation following the experiences of wartime in the Pacific when it was clear that the 20mm AA was relatively ineffective against Kamikaze aircraft, and that even the 40mm Bofors did not always succeed in preventing such aircraft from reaching their target. To improve the performance of the

5in AA, ships of the *Des Moines* class were given two additional Mk 37 control instruments while, for the first time, fire control of the 8in guns was directed by Mk 54.

The 20mm AA – if ever installed – was removed very speedily. Those aircraft catapults that had been installed were removed and the aircraft replaced by helicopters. The after hangar was then used for stowage of ship's boats, the launching and retrieving of which could be carried out by the crane.

With the intention to provide fully-automatic main armament, the *Des Moines* class shows parallels with the *Worcester* class which followed. In 1937 the navy had begun to give the priority to the development of fully automatic twin and triple turrets, and in about 1943 planning began for a cruiser type that would have a main armament of three triple turrets. At that time, development of 8in turrets, able to fire three times as quickly as hitherto available guns, was a breakthrough in gunnery technology. It made the heavy cruiser of much greater value, freeing it as it did from its main drawback – an over-slow rate of fire – a basic reason for the earlier enforced construction of light cruisers with their 6in guns which fired more

rapidly. It is interesting to learn that it had been intended to fit the *Oregon City* class with three twin turrets of the new type, but the navy was anxious to develop a new design of ship to receive these gun turrets, and the idea was dropped in mid-1943.

The class was to have consisted of at least eight ships. Even after the end of the war the navy wished to complete eight, but the growing expectations of the possibilities and effects of guided weapons and cruise missiles made the future of conventional armament problematical. The Korean War, however, had shown that long-range gunnery was of great value in support of troop landings. In this connection the last active ship of the class, *Newport News,* was in fact used for intensive fire support off the Vietnam coast.

The importance of the class showed itself at the beginning of the 1980s when the Reagan Administration re-activated battleships of the *Iowa* class. There had been discussion of a possible alternative, re-activating of *Des Moines* (CA-134) and *Salem* (CA-139) which had been in reserve. For in the quest for ships with adequate armament and adequate accommodation for a unit staff, and with sufficient deck area to accom-

◁ This broadside aerial photograph of the lead-ship of the class, *Des Moines,* was taken on 15 November 1948, just one day before her official commissioning. This was the first American cruiser class to receive 3in/50 AA guns on completion. Obviously there were supply difficulties with this item in 1948: one can see that both the gun tubs near the funnel are empty.

Initially *Des Moines* had SR-3 and SP radar antennae. It should also be noted that – probably for contractual reasons – she was completed with two catapults at a time when, in other ships, one catapult had long been removed. (USN)

△ The elegance of this design is evident from this photograph taken off Toulon on 2 August 1950. The increased fire power of the new 8in Mk 16 guns demanded larger magazines which in turn necessitated a longer forecastle. At this time *Des Moines* had temporarily the maximum allotment of twenty-four 3in/50 guns. The very high bases indicate clearly Mk 54 fire control gear which worked in conjunction with Mk 13 radar. In place of the two catapults one now finds a pad for helicopters which were introduced from the 1950s. SPS-6B radar replaces SR-3 on the forward mast. (MB)

▽ This most attractive photograph of *Des Moines* was taken from a helicopter belonging to the aircraft carrier *Essex* (at that time still CVA-9) on 16 December 1959 in the Mediterranean while the ship was serving for the last time as flagship of the Sixth Fleet. She now has SPS-8A in place of SP radar and there is URN-3 TACAN on the forward mast. Removal of the forward twin mounting reduced the number of 3in/50 guns to 22. (USN)

SHIPS NOT COMPLETED

Pennant No.	Name	Fiscal Year	Laid Down	Builder	History
CA-140	*Dallas*	1942	15 Oct 1945	Bethlehem Quincy	Building suspended 6 June 1946
CA-141		1942		Bethlehem Quincy	Building suspended 7 Jan 1946
CA-142		1942		Bethlehem Quincy	Building suspended 7 Jan 1946
CA-143		1942		Bethlehem Quincy	Building suspended 7 Jan 1946
CA-149		1943		Newport News	Building suspended 12 Aug 1946
CA-150	*Dallas*	1945		New York SBdg.	Building suspended 28 Mar 1946
CA-151 –153		1945		New York SBdg.	Building suspended 28 Mar 1946

modate ship-to-ship missile launchers, the *Des Moines* class were the only serious candidates. Ultimately a navy study demonstrated that, cost-effectively, it was more practical to reactivate battleships than the two heavy cruisers.

Only three ships of the *Des Moines* class were completed. The construction of nine further ships was suspended at the end of the war.

Des Moines

1948 16 Nov Commissioned; then in Atlantic.
1949–57 Series of transfers between operations on east coast, in Caribbean and North Atlantic, with yearly deployments into Mediterranean as Flagship, initially, Sixth Task Fleet, later – from 1950 – Sixth Fleet.
1952 and 1954–57 Yearly summer cruises with midshipmen, including visits to north European ports.
1958–61 Feb–July Flagship, Sixth Fleet for last time.
1961 14 July Decommissioned.

Salem

1949 14 May Commissioned.
July–Oct Shake-down cruises off Cuba, then at Boston Navy Yard.
1949 Nov–Dec Further cruises to Guantanamo; at beginning of 1950 manoeuvres in Atlantic.
1950 3 May First Mediterranean deployment; Flagship, Sixth Fleet.
17 May Replaced *Newport News*.

22 Sept Relieved by *Newport News*; returned to east coast.
1951 3 Jan Three months' intensive gunnery practise off Guantanamo.
20 Jan Commencement of second deployment with Sixth Fleet, relieving *Newport News*; relieved by *Des Moines*; returned to east coast.
1952 1 Jan Refit at Boston.
19 April Third Mediterranean deployment.
28 April Flagship, in place of *Newport News*.
29 Sept Relieved as flagship by *Des Moines*.
9 Oct Arrived Boston.
1953 17 April Further deployment to Mediterranean; relieved *Newport News* as flagship.
9 Oct Relieved as flagship by *Des Moines*.
24 Oct Returned to Boston; refit.
1954 30 April Fifth deployment to Mediterranean.
22 Sept Relieved as flagship by *Des Moines*.
Oct–Nov Manoeuvres in North Atlantic.
1955 Jan–Feb Reservist training cruise to Guantanamo.
2 May Sixth deployment to Mediterranean.
19 May Relieved *Newport News* as flagship.
2 Oct Arrived Boston; four months' yard overhaul.
1956 16 Feb Seventh deployment to Mediterranean; for twenty months permanent Flagship, Sixth Fleet, based on Villefranche; during this period Suez Crisis occurred.
1958 4 July Returned to east coast.
11 August Flagship, Second Fleet, relieving *Northampton* (CLC-1).
2 Sept Ten days' cruise to Mediterranean.
1959 30 Jan Decommissioned.

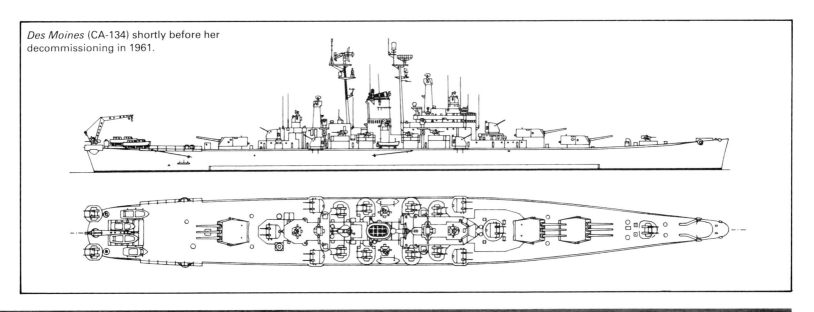

Des Moines (CA-134) shortly before her decommissioning in 1961.

Newport News

1949 29 Jan Commissioned.

1950–61 Yearly deployments to Mediterranean with intervening fleet manoeuvres and midshipmen training cruises in Caribbean and West Atlantic.

1957 Crisis in Syria.

1960 March Rescue work during earthquake in Agadir.

1961 June Crisis in San Domingo.

1962 Wintered at yard for modification as flagship.

August Flagship, COM Second Fleet, Nato manoeuvres and visit to north European ports.

Oct Blockade off Cuba, still as Flagship, Second Fleet.

1963–67 Operations and midshipmen training cruises on east coast and Caribbean.

1965 San Domingo crisis.

June Refit.

1967 19 Sept COM Second Fleet, transferred his flag to *Springfield* (CLG-7).

7 Sept Departure for West Pacific.

9 Oct Arrived Da Nang, Vietnam; Flagship, COMCRUDESFLOT 3.

1967–68 Oct–April Operations and coastal bombardment off Vietnam.

1968 13 May Returned to east coast.

1970 1 June Routine yard work at Norfolk Navy Yard.

6 August Commander, Second Fleet came aboard; for rest of year operations on east coast.

1971 Until summer operations and manoeuvres on east coast.

Sept–Oct Visited Portsmouth, England; Amsterdam, Oslo, Rosyth, Copenhagen, Helsinki and Hamburg.

31 Oct Returned to Norfolk; for rest of year local operations between Norfolk and Newport.

1972 Jan–Feb Operations and exercises on east coast.

March Visited Venezuela and Colombia.

13 April Sailed through Panama Canal to Pacific.

26 April Short stay at Pearl Harbor.

2 May Detached to Commander, Seventh Fleet.

3 May Guam.

6 May Subic Bay.

11 May Operations and coastal bombardment off Vietnam; intermediate stops in Subic Bay and Hong Kong.

10 Oct Explosion in No. 2 turret during coastal bombardment, centre gun barrel destroyed; complete turret out of action for remainder of service.

2 Dec Left Subic Bay for Panama Canal.

24 Dec Arrived Norfolk.

1973 Jan–June Operations on east coast.

17 July–9 August Short dry dock period at Baltimore.

18 Sept Left for visits to Portsmouth, England; Oslo, Copenhagen, Rotterdam and Lisbon.

8 Nov Arrived Norfolk; operations on east coast.

1974 1 Sept Operations and manoeuvres on east coast.

Sept Visited Oslo, Copenhagen, Amsterdam, Portsmouth, England, Lisbon.

30 Oct Arrived Norfolk.

1975 27 June Decommissioned.

◁ *Salem* on 9 June 1954 off Toulon, during her fifth deployment to the Mediterranean. SP radar has been replaced by SPS-8A. The awning extends much further forward. (MB)

▷ *Newport News* was the only ship of the *Des Moines* class to serve continuously for almost 26 years. She is seen here at Hamburg in 1956 when several ships of the Second Fleet were visiting. At this time she had SPS-6B and SPS-8A radar installations and URN-3 TACAN. (Te)

◁ *Newport News* looks quite unchanged in this undated photograph which must, however, have been taken before 1962. Her forwardmost twin 3in/50 guns have been removed. (USN)

△ *Newport News* made several visits to Hamburg and Kiel. She is seen here in the Elbe at the end of a visit to Hamburg in 1966. This is how she appeared after the flagship conversion had been carried out in 1962. At this time she had only eight 3in/50 guns. SPS-37 has displaced the SPS-6 antenna forward, which is now sited on a console beneath the SPS-8A on the after mast. Clearly the

TACAN installation is no longer carried. Note the radio antenna set on the crane. (Te)

▷ This photograph was given to the author on 21 October 1971 by the Commanding Officer of *Newport News* on the occasion of a visit to Hamburg. The date of the photograph was not stated, but it shows the appearance of the ship

some time between the flagship conversion in mid-1962, and 1971. One can see clearly that both lateral 3in/50 AA positions have been replaced by enclosed superstructure in which accommodation for additional fleet staff has been installed. The numerous whip antennae are very evident, particularly the HF Discage radio antenna on the forecastle. (USN)

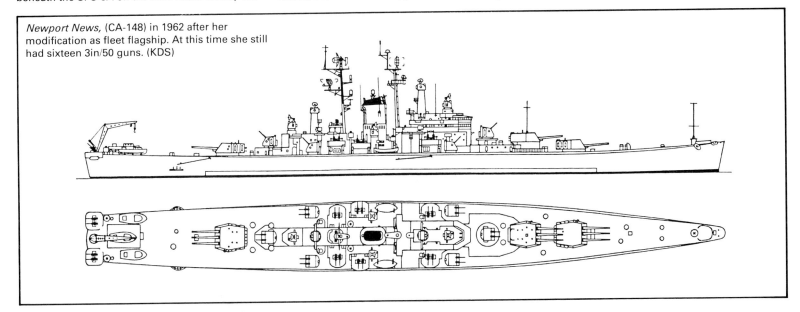

Newport News, (CA-148) in 1962 after her modification as fleet flagship. At this time she still had sixteen 3in/50 guns. (KDS)

△ After completion of 'Farewell' visits to west and north European ports, *Newport News* arrived for the last time in Norfolk at the end of October 1974. Following an explosion on 1 October 1972 off the coast of Vietnam, the centre 8in gun had been removed and No. 2 turret immobilized until the end of her service. The SPS-37, SPS-8A and SPS-6B radar antennae remained aboard, even after the ship had been put in the reserve and, in 1978, struck off the Navy List. (USN)

▽ Approximately ten months before she was retired: *Newport News* in October 1974 somewhere in the Atlantic. The fire control electronics are still well represented by four Mk 37 and four Mk 56, although she no longer has any 3in guns. In the third AA gun tubs, port and starboard, she now has a Mk 28 twin-barrelled Mk 28 launcher for anti-radar class rockets. (USN)

WORCESTER CLASS

The Worcester class represented the last stage in the development of an AA cruiser which had begun before the beginning of the Second World War. The design had several 'firsts'. They were the heaviest light cruisers in the US Navy, heavier than many previous heavy cruisers. This final original design for light cruisers called for the newly developed fully automatic 6in AA turrets, the first and last time they would have been so used, the idea being that they could also be used against destroyers – this representing a clear improvement over the *Atlanta* and *Oakland* classes. The installation of each of two Mk 34 fire controls with Mk 13 and four Mk 37s with Mk 25 radar was an additional improvement, especially if one realizes that these systems could at any time be switched to make use of other weapon systems. Bearing in mind the greater effectiveness of the quicker firing but similar-in-number 6in guns, which would be just as effective against surface targets, both these ships may be regarded as the legitimate successors of the *Cleveland/Fargo* classes. The end of the war prevented these advantages being put into practice.

In appearance only the midships section resembled to some extent the previous *Oakland* class, while the longer (and therefore heavier) 6in turrets necessitated a greater hull length, the turrets being disposed in the same way as in *Oakland*, and because as with the *Des Moines* class it was required to provide a compartment aft to accommodate ship's boats. These various features necessitated a displacement more than twice that of the *Atlanta* class. These were the first and last light cruisers to have installed from the beginning 3in/50 twin mountings.

▷ Fifteen days before she was commissioned: *Worcester* photographed on 11 June 1948 during inclining tests at the Camden, New Jersey yard. The 3in guns are not yet aboard. Mk 37 fire control systems are fitted to direct the fully automatic 6in guns; one can also see here quite clearly that the Mk 11 fire control radar is positioned on a pedestal, although its Mk 34 is absent. (USN)

The *Worcester* class had a total of ten preliminary designs before the eleventh was chosen. Preliminary design J called for ships with only one funnel. The considerable space needed for the six turrets led to a novel arrangement in the engine compartment: the steam turbines were positioned forward in separate compartments with the boilers belonging to them paired. Aft, where the restricted width did not allow this, the conventional layout, i.e., two boiler compartments and one turbine compartment in tandem was used. It transpired that seakeeping was not totally satisfactory, much water coming aboard because of the relatively low midships section. Furthermore, the 6in turrets were much less reliable than the quick-firing 8in triple turrets had been in the *Des Moines* class.

The class had been planned with an increasing fire control development, which was the reason why these ships, in the course of a relatively short period of service, were fitted with a succession of radar installations.

Although having a much greater displacement than the *Cleveland*s, it was still required that the class achieve a top speed of approximately 32 knots, and the engine installation had to be increased to 120,000shp. It is known that they could achieve 15 knots steaming astern with 30,000shp. Only two ships were completed. The construction of a further eight units was suspended at the end of the war. Both ships served for a bare ten years and then had to give way to the new guided missile ships arriving in large numbers.

Worcester

1948 26 June Commissioned; joined CRUDIV 10;
during the first year of service shake-down
cruises and training cruises along east coast.
1949 6 Sept Left for Mediterranean.
10 Dec Returned to east coast.
1950 3 May Left for second Mediterranean
deployment: detached from Sixth Task Fleet; at
the end of July with DESDIV 21 departed via
Suez Canal for Far East.

19 August Arrived Okinawa.
20 August Temporary detachment to Formosa
Patrol Force.
27 August Left to join TF 77 with *Philippine Sea*
(CV-47) and *Valley Forge* (CV-45); operations
off Korean coast.
7–10 Sept Intermediate stop at Sasebo, then
further support of Allied landings at Inchon.
27 Oct Left Yokosuka via Pearl Harbor and
Panama Canal for east coast.

21 Nov Arrived Philadephia.
1950–51 1 Dec–20 March Refit at Boston Navy
Yard.
1951 15 May Left for third Mediterranean deployment; until mid-1950s three further Mediterranean deployments alternating with operations
along east coast and visits to European ports.
1956 Jan Transferred to Pacific Fleet; then a
further two deployments with Seventh Fleet.
1958 19 Dec Decommissioned.

WORCESTER CLASS SHIPS NOT COMPLETED

Pennant No.	Name	Fiscal Year	Builder	History
CL-146	*Vallejo*	1943	New York SBdg.	Building suspended 12 Aug 1945
CL-147	*Garry*	1943	New York SBdg.	Building suspended 12 Aug 1945
CL-154, –159				Building suspended 26 Mar 1945

▽ In 1949, when this photograph was taken,
Worcester still had SG-6 and SP radars. It should
be noted that the after Mk 13 fire control is raised
above the Mk 37, while forward the position is
reversed. (USN)

△ On 3 July 1950, when this photograph was taken off Toulon, *Worcester* was making her second Mediterranean deployment. SPS-6B has now been added to the radar antennae and this has been set up in front of the after funnel. A ship's boat is suspended from the crane. At the end of this month the cruiser was called away urgently to Korea, sailing via the Suez Canal. (MB)

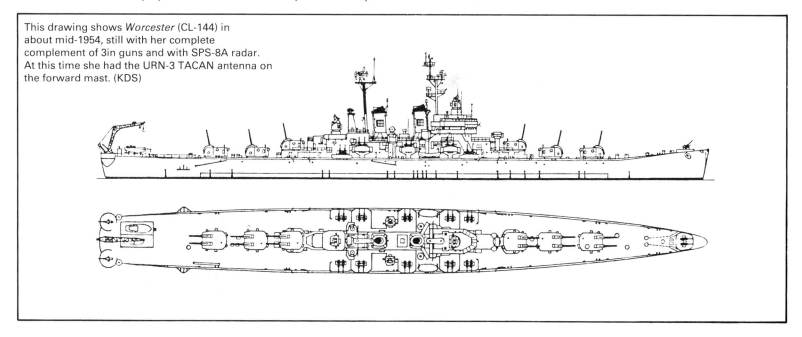

This drawing shows *Worcester* (CL-144) in about mid-1954, still with her complete complement of 3in guns and with SPS-8A radar. At this time she had the URN-3 TACAN antenna on the forward mast. (KDS)

△ In 1956 or 1957, when this photograph was taken, *Worcester* still had twenty-two 3in/50 guns. URN-3 TACAN has been added, as also SPS-8A, while SPS-6 is now on the forward mast. At the end of 1958 the ship was decommissioned. (RPh)

Roanoke
1949 4 April Commissioned; shake-down cruises in Caribbean; remained in Atlantic, training cruises.
1950 6 Jan–May First deployment to Mediterranean; in following years a yearly transfer between operations on east coast and deployment with Sixth Fleet in Mediterranean,

including in summer 1952 midshipmen training cruise to Caribbean and northern Europe.
1955 May End of last Mediterranean deployment.
22 Sept Departed for Pacific Fleet; during next two years a total of nine reservist training cruises from Long Beach.
1956 May–Oct Deployments to West Pacific.
1958 31 Oct Decommissioned.

△ Judging by her radar equipment, this undated photograph of *Roanoke* was taken in the second half of the 1950s. One can see clearly that there is a 3in single mounting in each of the two after gun tubs and these are controlled by fire-control radar. This is to be interpreted as an indication that the fire-control system was a Mk 63, the platform for which is to be seen between the gun tubs and the boats. (USN)

▽ On 24 October 1957, almost exactly one year before her decommissioning, this detailed photograph of *Roanoke* was taken in a Japanese port. A number of 'E' awards are to be seen on the gun turrets, on the fire-control gear and on the bridge. The appearance of the 6in twin turrets is also of interest. In contrast with her sister ship, *Roanake* probably never had TACAN. (HF)

BOSTON CLASS

The first stage in the building of a guided-missile fleet was realized by converting some of the many cruisers which were available at the end of the war. From 1952 both the heavy cruisers *Boston* (CA-69) and *Canberra* (CA-70) were reclassified as CAG-1 and CAG-2. The 'A' in the designation denoted a partial conversion in which the forward third of the ship retained the appearance and qualities of a heavy cruiser, keeping both the forward 8in triple turrets. The tendency at that time was to replace both the thinner funnels by one thicker one; behind the bridge superstructure a new quadrupled lattice mast replaced the pole mast, and the by then numerous antennae for electronic systems were positioned on this. The most important and obvious aspect of conversion was the fitting of two extended guided missile magazines aft, on each of which a Mk 10 twin launcher for the new Terrier I missile was installed. Each magazine could accommodate a total of 144 missiles, a very considerable number for that time. This first missile had a range of only twelve nautical miles.

From the after section of these ships, one 8in triple turret and one 5in twin mounting had to be removed, but as they still had six 8in and ten 5in guns, they were still adequately armed. Only one fire control Mk 34 and one Mk 37 was provided. The number of 3in/50 barrels was reduced from fourteen to ten during conversion, and later to eight, i.e., to four twin mountings.

Many changes were made in the electronics equipment during every year of service. There were no ASW weapons at any time.

Towards the end of their service, both ships, in the light of the increasing obsolescence of the Terrier I system, were used as fire support ships off the Vietnamese coast, during which they were retrospectively reclassified as CA-69 and 70 on 1 May 1968. This marked the suspension of their guided missiled activities, but the installations were not removed. The allegation at one time that *Boston* had been sold to Turkey had no factual basis.

▽ The introduction of the guided missile brought new dimensions and criteria in respect of appearance and recognition details on warships. The growing development of the guided missile cruiser meant a reduction in conventional armament both in numbers and significance in the same measure as the guided missiles were increased. This, of course, was also the case with the electronic systems. *Boston* emerged in the mid-1950s through the partial conversion of Heavy Cruiser CA-69. Her appearance was unchanged from the bow up to and including the bridge superstructure. Most of the rest was new, hence the quadraped lattice mast; the new, single funnel; the missile magazine, the two launchers and the fire control gear. This photograph shows *Boston* on 10 January 1956, two months after her second commissioning. An increase in the antennae can also be established: SPS-6B, SPS-8A, and SPS-10 on the lattice mast, CXRX on the after (pole) mast and SPS-12 on the platform provided behind this. The conversion plan allowed six of the nine 8in guns to be retained, and ten of the twelve 5in guns. With twelve 3in guns, the ship was still well equipped for anti-aircraft deployment. It is interesting to learn that it had been originally intended to place SPS-2 on the after radar platform, and this may be seen on the earlier photographs of models. (USN)

1955 1 Nov Second commissioning, now as CAG-1.
1956 30 Jan Shake-down cruise to Caribbean.
26 Feb Flagship, CRUDIV 6.
15 April Returned from shake-down cruises.
June–Nov Guided missile tests.
25 Oct–16 Nov Manoeuvres off Atlantic coast.
23 Nov Departed for first Mediterranean deployment.
1957 19 March Returned to Norfolk; beginning of June took part in Fleet Review off Jamestown, Virginia.
June–July Midshipmen training cruise to Cuba and Chile.
3 Sept–22 Oct NATO manoeuvres in North Atlantic.
25 Nov At Norfolk Navy Yard.
1958 June–Sept With Sixth Fleet in Mediterranean (second deployment).
Nov Manoeuvres in Caribbean.
1959 Jan–July Operations off east coast.
August Seven months in Mediterranean (third deployment).
1960 27 Feb Five months at Charleston Navy Yard, then operations on east coast and in North Atlantic.
Oct–Dec Fourth cruise with Sixth Fleet.
21 Dec Returned to Boston; operations and

△ Six weeks after commissioning; a detailed photograph of *Boston* taken on 17 September 1955 at the Camden yard. The view is of both the extended Terrier magazines, of the two twin Mk 10 launchers and of the two sole remaining Mk 25 Mod. 7. fire control radars mounted on the Mk 37 which had now lost its purpose. The 3in twins mounted laterally on the main deck were removed in about 1957, either for weight reasons or because when firing they caused interference to the guided missile electronics. To the left of the picture can be seen one of six Mk 56 fire control gear. (USN)

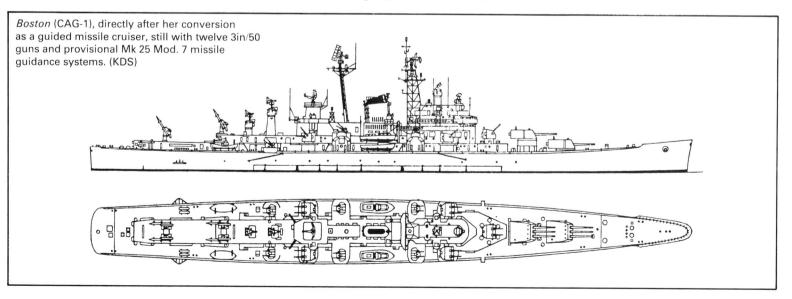

Boston (CAG-1), directly after her conversion as a guided missile cruiser, still with twelve 3in/50 guns and provisional Mk 25 Mod. 7 missile guidance systems. (KDS)

manoeuvres with Second Fleet on east coast.

1961 23 Sept At Charleston Navy Yard.

1961–62 11 Dec–5 March Fifth deployment to Mediterranean; then operations on east coast.

1962 3 August Departed for sixth Mediterranean cruise.

17 Sept Flagship, Sixth Fleet for six weeks.

1963 16 Feb Left for east coast; at Boston Navy Yard for four months (including installation of SPS-30 radar).

July Operations off east coast and Caribbean.

1964–67 Operations on east coast and deployment to Mediterranean; during this period a fire support operation off Vietnamese coast.

1968 28 March Commencement of second Vietnam deployment.

27 April Arrived Vietnam; coastal bombardment.

1 May Reclassified as CA-69.

26 Oct Returned to east coast; yard overhaul.

1969 22 May Left for third deployment to Vietnam.

7 Oct Fired last salvoes.

15 Nov Returned to Boston.

1970 5 May Decommissioned.

△ This aerial photograph of *Boston*, taken on 29 April 1957, shows even more clearly the extent of the conversion measures. After removal of both the 3in/50 twins she now has only eight 3in guns, but six Mk 56 fire-control gear. (USN)

▽ Following the conclusion of NATO man-oeuvres in the North Atlantic *Boston* remained in English waters when this photograph was taken in October 1957. Beneath the CXRX on the pole mast one can see two of the then new ECM antennae; in this photograph they are without the cover that was more usual later. The black boat would seem to be a personal barge of the CRUDIV Commander, a Rear-Admiral. (WL)

△   This photograph was probably taken in 1962 when SPS-12 radar had been replaced by SPS-37A and this was positioned for a short period on the radar platform. At this time the two SWP-5 radar arrays had replaced MK 25 Mod. 7 and there is a HF Discage radio antenna on the forecastle. Although *Boston* could no longer carry any helicopters, there is still a URN-3 TACAN antenna on the after mast. (USN)

▽   A jump of five to six years: *Boston* in the Gulf of Tonkin, bombarding the Vietnamese coast, seen from a helicopter belonging to carrier *Bennington* (CVS-20). The photograph is dated 9 September 1968, but this cannot be accurate because *Boston* had been reclassified as CA on 1 May 1968 and carried her old designation number 69. At this time her Terrier missiles were obsolete and the ship had only her two 8in turrets to thank for not

having been struck off. Considerable changes in the radar electronics can be seen here. SPS-6 and 8A have been removed from the lattice mast, CXRX has been added to the lattice mast as has also the TACAN antenna. SPS-37A is now on the strongly braced pole mast, and, on the platform that has been raised during the intervening time, one sees now SPS-30 and an additional, unidentifiable navigational radar antenna. (USN)

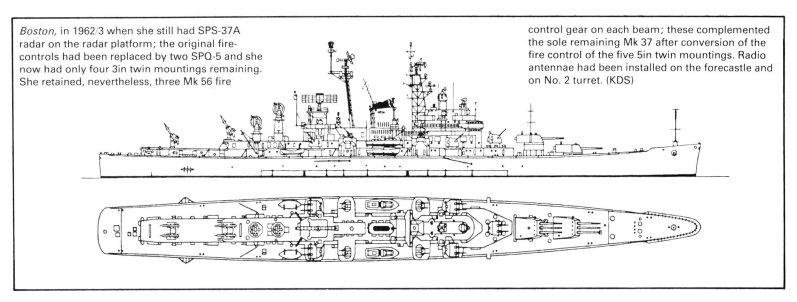

Boston, in 1962/3 when she still had SPS-37A radar on the radar platform; the original fire-controls had been replaced by two SPQ-5 and she now had only four 3in twin mountings remaining. She retained, nevertheless, three Mk 56 fire control gear on each beam; these complemented the sole remaining Mk 37 after conversion of the fire control of the five 5in twin mountings. Radio antennae had been installed on the forecastle and on No. 2 turret. (KDS)

Canberra

1956 15 June Recommissioned, now as CAG-2; operations off east coast until March 1957.

1957 14 March President D. D. Eisenhower aboard; cruised to Bermuda Conference.

12 June Flagship, International Fleet Review in Hampton Roads.

13 June–5 May Midshipmen training cruise to Caribbean and Brazil.

1957–58 3 Sept–9 March Deployment with Sixth Fleet in Mediterranean, then ceremonial flagship at selection and handing-over of Unknown Soldiers from Second World War and Korea, laid to rest in Arlington.

1958 9 June–7 August Midshipmen training cruise to Europe, then yard refit at Norfolk.

1960 3 March Left Norfolk on Goodwill round-the-world cruise; then operations with Sixth and Seventh Fleets.

24 Oct Returned to Norfolk; operations on east coast until end of year.

1963 Oct Transferred to Pacific Fleet.

1965 5 Jan Left San Diego for Vietnam, including radar control station off Da Nang.

1966 Feb Second deployment to West Pacific.

Feb–June Fire support operations off Vietnam.

8 June Returned to San Diego.

11 Oct Third Vietnam deployment.

1967 May Courtesy visit to Melbourne.

1 June Returned to San Diego.

5 Oct Fourth Vietnam deployment.

1968 8 April Left for west coast, there reclassified as CA-70 on 1 May 1968.

18 Sept Fifth deployment to West Pacific, duties included Flagship, CRUDESFORCE, Seventh Fleet.

1969 18 Jan Returned to San Diego.

1970 2 Feb Decommissioned.

◁ A close-up of the stern of Canberra, similar to the one of her sister ship *Boston,* but taken on 5 May 1956 at New York Shipbuilding's Camden yard, shows that the ship had from the very beginning SPQ-5 fire control radar of which one example is to be seen here. She does not have the two 3in twins on the main deck. (USN)

△▽ These photographs, taken on 4 August 1956, show clearly the details of the conversion which *Canberra* had undergone as CAG. The radar electronics correspond with those of *Boston* at that period, of which one can see here very clearly SPS-10 on the port console of the lattice mast. It can be seen, too, how relatively narrow the Terrier missile magazine is compared with the overall width of the ship. The mast on the quarterdeck was only a temporary installation, serving to calibrate the fire control radar. (USN)

◁   Another very clear photograph of *Canberra* dating from 1956. The calibrating mast on the quarterdeck now looks rather different (RPh)

▷   This aerial photograph taken from astern of *Canberra* is dated 19 January 1961, when she was still serving with the Second Fleet in the Atlantic. There are several changes to be observed in the radar equipment. The SPS-12 radar on the platform has been replaced by SPS-13; CXRX has moved to the lattice mast and the pole mast now carries SPS-29 and URN-3 TACAN. (USN)

▽   *Canberra*, 4 August 1956.

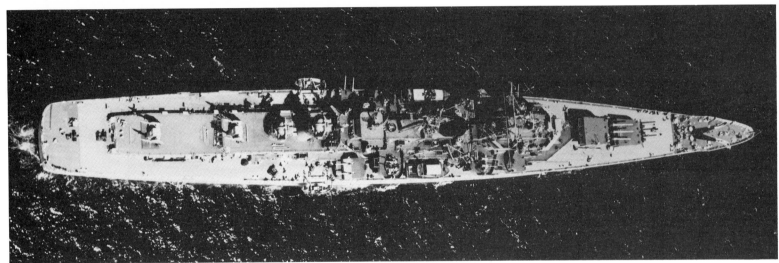

Canberra (CAG-2) at the end of 1964 with the provisional helicopter platform aft, shortly before CXRX radar was removed from the forward mast. (KDS)

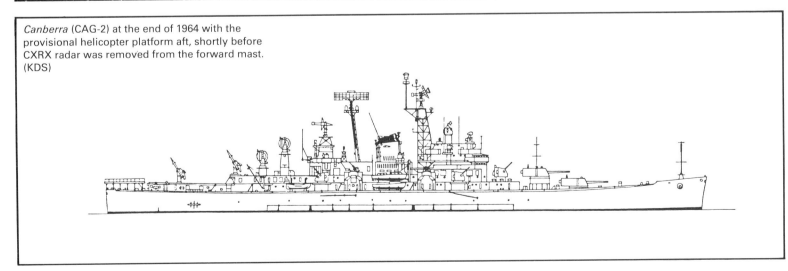

CANBERRA

△ *Canberra* in February 1968, during her fourth Vietnam deployment, shows that CXRX radar is once again in its accustomed place on the lattice mast. In this photograph the marked helicopter platform can be seen more clearly. Two months later, from 1 May 1968, Canberra was reclassified as CA and carried once again the designation '70'. (USN)

▽ *Canberra,* with *Ranger* (CVA-61), on 21 February 1966 in Vietnamese waters as part of TF77. Once again changes are to be seen: a provisional platform has been set up astern for light helicopters; the radar platform has been raised – as was done in *Boston* – with SPS-30 and a surface radar antenna set up on it. The pole mast now carries a test specimen of a satellite antenna.

CXRX has been given a temporary 'between-position' behind the funnel where there could not have been much hope of its efficient operation. There is also TACAN on the forward mast. (USN)

▷ *Boston* in the Mediterranean with the Sixth Fleet.

GALVESTON CLASS

◁ *Galveston* was one of the first guided missile/partial conversions of which — as had been the case with the *Boston* conversion — half of the main and medium armament remained, but no 3in/50 were ever fitted. This photograph was taken on 11 January 1959 during the shake-down period. The fire control electronics for the guns was in line with immediate post-war practice. Mk 34/Mk 13 for the main armament, Mk 37/Mk 25 for the 5in AA. Being fitted with the Talos system, she has in duplicate the combination SPG-49/SPW-2. The radar antenna are readily identified: SPS-10 and SPS-17 on the forward lattice mast, SPS-42 and URN-3 TACAN on the central mast and SPS-B on the raised platform. The custom was invariably followed in all ships fitted with Talos to fit the 3-D radar (here SPS-42) on the highest mast. In this photograph the calibration mast is on the quarter-deck. (USN)

Five years after the introduction of the first guided missile cruiser designation, CAG (*Boston* class), the partial conversion followed of six former light cruisers of the *Cleveland* class, to produce the *Galveston* (two ships) and *Little Rock* (four ships) classes. One *Galveston* and two *Little Rock*s were given the Talos system, the remaining ships receiving Terrier II. The light AA was totally removed during conversion. Of the 5in twin mountings, the *Galveston* class retained three (one in front of and two abeam the bridge superstructure) and the *Little Rock* class retained only the twin mounting in front of the bridge. One each of Mk 34 and 37 fire control systems were retained. The chief feature dating back to the old *Cleveland* class was the slender, tall and closely spaced pair of funnels.

The aft superstructure was completely rebuilt to suit the guided missile systems of the time. The Mk 10 twin starter was positioned aft on the main deck, and the missiles were reloaded from the below-deck magazine behind it. Masting in the two classes differed considerably. The Terrier-armed ships of both classes each received three quadruped lattice masts of which the middle one was the highest. An exception was *Topeka* (CLG-8), the only ship to have a tripod mast forward, and this was because it was required to have mounted on it the heavy Type SPS-37A radar antenna. The three Talos ships were each given a quadruped lattice mast, forward and aft of the funnels with a raised radar platform taking the place of the after mast. From a position ahead, that is to say when the type of launcher or the after superstructure cannot be distinguished clearly, Talos ships can be identified by the fact that they always have their Frescan-3-D radar aerial on the highest possible point, i.e., on the middle mast. On the other hand, the Terrier ships always had the 3-D aerial on the after mast.

All these cruisers functioned as flagships of cruiser/destroyer flotillas, with CLG-4 and 5 serving long years as flagships of the Sixth and Seventh Fleets respectively, with foreign ports as their home bases.

In contrast to the *Boston* class, these ships did not undergo reclassification as CL, but from 1975 the designation of *Little Rock* and *Oklahoma City* was changed from CLG to CG. Neither this nor the *Little Rock* class had ASW installations; in effect they had neither a sonar installation nor A/S weapons aboard. A conversion of both ships took place between 1956 and 1960.

▽   A broadside view of *Galveston,* 16 June 1962, off Philadelphia Navy Yard. In the course of three and a half years almost all the electronic systems have been changed: on the forward lattice mast there are now SPS-10 and SPS-37A. The central lattice mast has been strengthened and reshaped. It now carries the very large SPS-39A antenna and SRN-6 TACAN. On the platform there is now SPS-30. Note the equipment for receiving missiles positioned between the centre mast and the high superstructure for the electronics. The extended Talos missile magazine is all of two decks high and slopes gently to the stern. (USN)

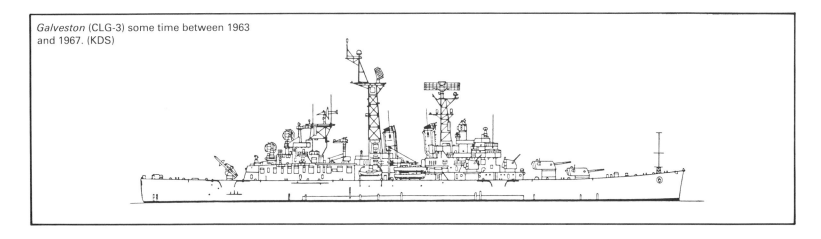

Galveston (CLG-3) some time between 1963 and 1967. (KDS)

Galveston

1958 28 May Recommissioned, now as CLG-3.

30 June Commencement of comprehensive shake-down cruises off Norfolk, including first firing of Talos from a US Navy ship on 24 February 1959.

1959 17 March Special work at Philadelphia Navy Yard.

July Contract-acceptance trial off Norfolk.

1960 4 Jan Operations off east coast.

Feb Explosion tests off Bahamas.

25 March–24 Oct At Philadelphia Navy Yard.

1961 6 Jan–1 March Technical evaluation of Talos for 'Bureau of Weapons'; final acceptance off Cuba.

8 May–21 July Further evaluations of Talos.

30 August–23 Sept Refit at Philadelphia Navy Yard, including modification of Talos launching installation.

1962 23 July Transferred to Pacific; joined CRUDESFLOT 9 on 24 August then operations on west coast.

Oct Flagship, CRUDESFLOT 9 with Seventh Fleet.

1963 16 April Returned to west coast.

1964–65 Oct–Feb Refit.

1965 April Departed for West Pacific; Vietnam, South China Sea; carrier escort protection.

18 Dec Returned to west coast.

1966 Jan Operations off west coast and Hawaii.

31 July–4 Nov Refit at Long Beach Navy Yard.

1967 13 Feb Temporary transfer to Atlantic Fleet; deployment to Mediterranean with COMCRUDESFLOT 10 aboard.

11 March With Sixth Fleet.

30 August Returned to Newport.

10 Sept Returned to San Diego; operations off west coast.

1970 25 May Decommissioned.

Topeka (CLG-8) pre-1967, that is to say before SPS-52 radar had been positioned on the after lattice mast. She was the only CLG with a tripod mast forward. (KDS)

◁ Three years before being decommissioned, *Galveston* was deployed to the Mediterranean where this photograph was taken on 13 May 1967. She now has the amended version of the 3-D antenna, which shows similarities with the SPS-52. On the centre mast flies the command pennant of the Commander, Cruiser-Destroyer Flotilla 10, a Rear-Admiral. (Pa)

▽ *Topeka* photographed in the first years after conversion, certainly before mid-1963. Her conversion corresponded closely with that of the prototype, *Galveston*; what was different was that *Topeka* was given a Terrier guided missile installation. No official reason was given as to why *Topeka* was fitted with a tripod mast forward and no lattice mast. Originally this carried SPS-17,

SPS-10 and URN-3 TACAN. SPS-8B was only in place on the centre mast for a relatively short time. One assumes that there was an SPS-42 aft. (USN)

Topeka

1960 Recommissioned; now as CLG-8.

July Transferred to west coast.

August–Oct Shake-down cruises off southern California coast; following three years two deployments with Seventh Fleet in West Pacific, alternating with refits and local operations along west coast.

1964 March Third West Pacific deployment.

August Commencement of operations off Vietnam.

Nov Returned to Long Beach; twelve months' operations off west coast and manoeuvres with First Fleet.

1965 29 Nov Departed for Vietnam, patrols and coastal bombardment.

1966 28 May Returned to Long Beach; five months' operations off west coast.

1966–67 31 Oct–13 March Refit, including modernization of weapons system and propulsion.

1967 1 August Temporary transfer to Atlantic.

12–13 August COMCRUDESFLOT 12 comes aboard at Norfolk.

14 August Left to join Sixth Fleet in Mediterranean.

22 August Flagship, TG 60.2 replacing *Galveston* (CLG-3).

1968 12 Jan Relieved by *Columbus* (CG-12); end of Mediterranean deployment.

29 Jan Returned to Long Beach.

2 Feb–15 March Refit at Long Beach Navy Yard; final transfer to Atlantic Fleet.

21 March Arrived Mayport.

29 June Left for second Mediterranean deployment; relieved *Columbus* (CG-12).

9 Dec Relieved by Columbus.

19 Dec Returned to Mayport.

1969 5 June Decommissioned.

▽ Being adequately equipped with gun armament, *Topeka* was deployed off the Vietnamese coast to give fire support to US land forces. She was transferred twice from the Pacific to the Atlantic Fleets, and on two occasions was deployed to the Mediterranean. This photograph of her was taken on 1 July 1963 leaving the San Francisco Navy Yard where she had been fitted with the more modern radars, SPS-37A and SPS-30. In about 1967 the antenna appropriate to SPS-52 was fitted in place of SPS-42 aft. It should be noted that – in contrast to the other converted *Cleveland*s – *Topeka* was in service for only nine years. (USN)

LITTLE ROCK CLASS

The four ships of this class can be considered as flagship-conversion variants of the *Cleveland* class, having in common the installation of guided missile systems. CLG-6 and 7 were given Terrier, CLG-4 and 5 Talos. The numbers of missiles carried were 120 and 46 respectively. Distinguishing features were the extended, two-storeyed bridge, with the admiral's bridge being on the lower-deck, and the fitting of only one 6in or 5in turret in front of the bridge. Conversion work was carried out from 1957 to 1960. The two Terrier ships were the first to be decommissioned followed by the Talos units, all before 1980. Care was taken to keep the radar and other electronics as modern as possible during the long service period. A helicopter could be carried aft, but not in the hangar which was used for the stowage of ship's boats. The first converted CLG to leave the fleet was *Topeka* after nine years. The last ship to leave the fleet, *Oklahoma City*, did so after twenty years' service.

Little Rock
1960 3 June Recommissioned now as CLG-4; shake-down cruises to Caribbean; practise firing of Talos.
1961 9 Feb Departed to join Sixth Fleet in Mediterranean.
Sept Returned to east coast.
1962–65 A yearly deployment to Mediterranean (as flagship in 1962) interspersed with operations in North Atlantic and along east coast.
1966 On east coast, including refit.
1967 Jan Recommenced yearly Mediterranean deployment as flagship; home base now changed from Villefranche to Gaeta in Italy.
May Near-East operations.
8 June Israeli forces attacked USS *Liberty* (AGTR-5); *Little Rock* assisted damaged ship and took on wounded.
1968 With Sixth Fleet in Mediterranean.
1970 27 August Left for east coast via Newport and Yorktown, Virginia; cruised to Boston.

1970–71 12 Oct–19 April At Boston Navy Yard.
1971 9 April Operations on east coast and Caribbean.
1 Dec Left Newport for Mediterranean.
9 Dec Arrived at Rota to join Sixth Fleet.
1972 15 April Departed for east coast.
23 April Arrived Norfolk; temporary Flagship, Second Fleet; operations on east coast.

▽ In this sharp, oblique photograph of *Little Rock,* taken on 27 April 1960, after conversion, one can recognize the pattern of the SPS-2 radar (on the platform); the downwards-sloping super-structure deck; the Mk 7 Talos launcher Mod. 0 with training missiles, and the IFF beam Mk X on the SPS-17 antenna. From the outset the large HF Discage antenna had been positioned on the forecastle. Note also the considerable similarity of SPG-49 to the SPQ-5 radar antenna (see *Canberra*). (USN)

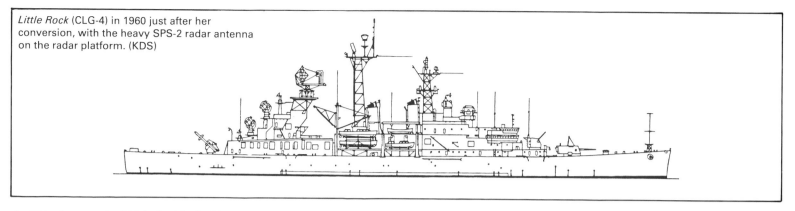

Little Rock (CLG-4) in 1960 just after her conversion, with the heavy SPS-2 radar antenna on the radar platform. (KDS)

◁   This photograph of Little Rock in the Mediterranean, dates from about mid-1962. She shows clearly the very considerable conversion that cruisers selected to be flagships underwent; the two-storeyed bridge has been enlarged forward with the removal of No. 2 6in turret. The bridge superstructure has been enlarged laterally so that there is no longer any room here for 5in AA guns. She still has PS-2 radar on the platform – but this was only for a short time; forward she now has SPS-37A. To aid aerial recognition she shows her designation on top of the 6in turret. (USN)

▽   Little Rock in the Mediterranean in 1974. From 1967 she had operated without 3-D radar antenna which had been replaced by a satellite-receiving antenna. As can be seen, no TACAN antenna is shipped. (P & L)

Sept–Oct With COM Second Fleet aboard, took part in NATO manoeuvres 'Strong Express'.
10–12 Oct At Hamburg.
26 Oct Arrived Norfolk.
8 Dec–15 May Refit at Boston Navy Yard.
1973 16 May At Newport, prepared for overseas operation.
15 August Left for Mediterranean.
26 August Arrived Rota.
29 August At Gaeta, Flagship, 'COM Sixth Fleet' replacing Springfield (CLG-7).
Oct–Nov Special operations with TF 60 in connection with the Near-East crisis; operations in Mediterranean until 27 August.
1976 28 August Relieved as Flagship, Sixth Fleet by Albany (CG-10).
1 Oct Arrived at Philadelphia.
22 Nov Decommissioned; later became a memorial ship at Buffalo, N.Y.

Oklahoma City
1960 7 Sept Recommissioned, now as CLG-5; after shake-down cruises, operations on west coast as first Talos ship in Pacific Fleet; during this period duties included Flagship, CRUDIV 3 and CRUDESFLOT 9.
2 Dec In West Pacific, Flagship, Seventh Fleet.
1961 12 June Returned to west coast.
14 Dec Refit at Long Beach Navy Yard.
1964 7 July West Pacific; Flagship, Seventh Fleet.
1965 June Commencement of fire support duties off Vietnam.
1966 15 Dec Returned to west coast; refit at San Francisco Navy Yard.
1967 July Operations on west coast.
1968 20 Dec Arrived Japan, Seventh Fleet; commencement of permanent operations based on Yokosuka.
1968–74 Operations on west coast, including

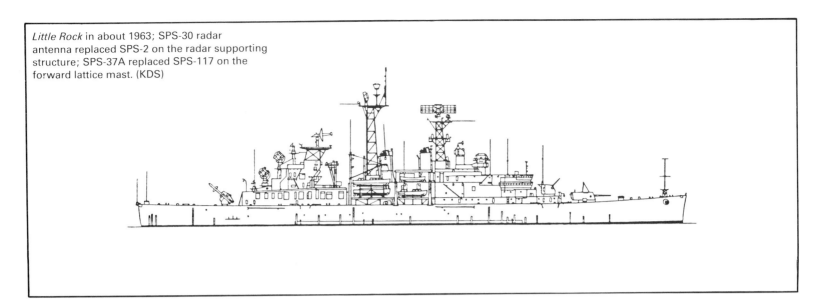

Little Rock in about 1963; SPS-30 radar antenna replaced SPS-2 on the radar supporting structure; SPS-37A replaced SPS-117 on the forward lattice mast. (KDS)

△ *Oklahoma City* was greatly similar to *Little Rock* in appearance and equipment, except that SPS-8B radar was initially installed rather than SPS-2. This photograph, in which one can distinguish Mk 34 fire control gear was taken in the Japanese port of Kobe in February 1962. (TM)

△ At the present time *Oklahoma City* has a noteworthy status. She has been struck off the Navy List, but lies almost complete with weapons and electronics in a state of conservation at Bremerton as the above photograph taken in July 1983 shows. An arrangement between the US Navy and the Bremerton City Council that the ship should serve as a tourist attraction in place of *Missouri* (BB-63) which had been reactivated, never came to fruition.

some off Vietnam.

1975 April–May Evacuation of troops from Vietnam.

1975–78 Operations and manoeuvres in West Pacific.

1978 April–June Courtesy visits to Korea, Guam, Australia, Singapore.

1979 Visits to Korea, Hong Kong, Inchon, Singapore, Thailand.

5 Oct COM Seventh Fleet transferred his flag to Blue Ridge (LCC-19).

18 Oct Arrived Pearl Harbor en route west coast.

31 Oct Visited San Francisco.

6 Nov Last firing of 6in guns and last launching of a Talos in the Navy.

7 Nov Arrived San Diego.

15 Dec Decommissioned.

Providence

1959 17 Sept Recommissioned, as CLG-6; after shake-down cruises off Cuba transferred to Pacific Fleet on 23 July 1960; operations on west coast.

1960–61 Oct–31 March In West Pacific with Seventh Fleet; then operations on west coast.

1962 May Second cruise to West Pacific; Flagship, Seventh Fleet replacing *Oklahoma City* (CLG-5).

1964 August Returned to west coast.

Oct Training cruises on west coast.

△ *Oklahoma City* was based in Yokosuka, Japan from December 1968 to October 1979. This photograph was taken in about 1978 when she had lost the Mk 34 fire control gear some time previously, and the 3-D antenna, in whose place a satellite antenna is now to be seen. There is an SPS-30 on the radar platform and a navigational antenna. (USN)

▽ This photograph of *Providence* off the west coast on 6 June 1966, shows the characteristic appearance of flagship conversions, with a Terrier guided missile system installed. In contrast with the Talos ships, Terrier cruisers had their 3-D antennae on the third lattice mast. From a distance SPQ-5 can be distinguished from SPG-49 only by the fact that the SPQ-5 does not have the two

associated SPW-2 antennae. *Providence* is the only ship of the *Cleveland* conversions never to have had SPS-37A. (USN)

1965 Jan–June Yard overhaul and completion of electronics; remained with First Fleet on west coast.
1966 1 Dec Flagship, Seventh Fleet in Yokosuka replacing *Oklahoma City* (CLG-5).
1967–68 Bombardment off Vietnam visits to Hong Kong, Taiwan, Korea, Thailand.
1968 8 Oct With *New Jersey* (BB-62) bombarded Vietnam.
Nov Visited Australia and New Zealand.
26 Nov Relieved by *Oklahoma City* (CLG-5) as Flagship, Seventh Fleet.
1969 Jan Visited New Zealand and Tahiti.
17 Jan Arrived San Diego; operations off west coast.
7 Feb Flagship, COM First Fleet.
April Exercises in Hawaii area.
1972 11 April Departed for West Pacific.
29 April Coastal bombardment off Vietnam for seven months.
18 Dec Returned to San Diego.
1973 1 July Decommissioned.

Springfield
1960 2 July Recommissioned, as CLG-7.
July-Nov Shake-down cruises off New England and Cuba.
4 Dec Departed for Mediterranean to join Sixth Fleet.

14 Dec Replaced *Des Moines* as Flagship, Sixth Fleet.
1963 11 May–15 Dec At Boston Navy Yard.
1967 Permanently in Mediterranean, based at Villefranche-sur-Mer on French Riviera.
28 Jan Replaced as Flagship, Sixth Fleet by *Little Rock* (CLG-4); sailed for east coast via England.
16 Feb Arrived Boston.
Feb–August Yard overhaul.
1 Sept Replaced *Newport News* (CA-148) as Flagship, Second Fleet; visited European ports.
6 Nov Returned to Norfolk; ten months' operations on east coast.
1968 12 Sept Left for NATO manoeuvres in North Atlantic.
1 Nov Arrived back at Norfolk.
1969 8 July *Newport News* (CA-148) once more Flagship, Second Fleet.
1970 14 Jan *Springfield* once again Flagship, Second Fleet.
August Replaced once more by *Newport News* as flagship.
10 August Departed for Mediterranean.
22 August Replaced *Little Rock* (CLG-4) as Flagship, Sixth Fleet; then for three years permanently in Mediterranean.
1973 1 Sept Replaced as flagship by *Little Rock*.
14 Sept Arrived back at Boston.
1974 15 May Decommissioned.

▷ This close-up was taken in December 1969 from the ammunition transport *Butte* (AE-27) which was in the process of transferring ammunition to *Springfield* while the ships were under way. Question: why are shells being transferred at a point so far aft, when they are destined for the turrets which are situated well forward? Presumably this was the only place where at-sea deliveries could be conveniently received. It would be interesting to learn by what complicated means the ammunition is then taken forward. In this photograph one can see clearly the double-storey frame for housing ship's boats. The boat davit is directly above this. (USN)

▽ After her major conversion *Springfield* operated in the Atlantic and exchanged duties with *Little Rock* and *Newport News* as flagship of the Second and Sixth Fleets. Some two years after her second commissioning, he visited Valletta in Malta where she was photographed on 28 March 1963. (Pa)

240

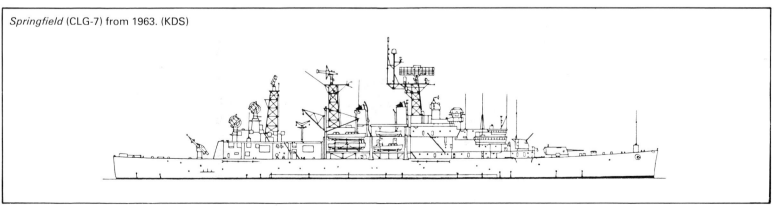

Springfield (CLG-7) from 1963. (KDS)

◁ *Springfield* served for three years as permanent flagship of the Sixth Fleet in the Mediterranean. During this time she was photographed off Toulon on 11 December 1971, two and a half years before her decommissioning. One notes many ship's boats, among them the launch of the Commandant of the Sixth Fleet, near the after lattice mast. As a 'guest' there is a Marine Corps Type UH-1 helicopter on the quarterdeck. One should note that, in this ship, the SPS-10 radar is located in a high position, directly beneath the TACAN installation. (MB)

▽ This detail photograph of *Springfield* was taken in 1967 when the Commandant of the Second Fleet visited Amsterdam. His launch is stowed between the masts on the upper deck. Note the large number of ship's boats. The radar electronics have been changed since 1963: SRN-6 TACAN, SPS-37A and ECM antennae are on the forward mast, SPS-30 on the middle mast as is a new navigational antenna, while on the after mast there is the then new antenna, later a component part of SPS-52, but here coupled to the SPS-39 installation. (Te)

ALBANY CLASS

The conversion of two units of the *Baltimore* class and one of the *Oregon City* class represented a new peak in warship technology. This was a totally new departure from the partial conversions of the *Boston*-class, first-generation of guided missile ships. All weapons and superstructures were removed and completely new superstructures, whose design had been fully tested, were fitted. In effect, these three ships can be seen as the initial stage in the provision of a new class of guided missile cruisers. They were not to appear in service again until 1962–64, whereas *Long Beach* (CGN-9), their (nuclear-propelled) single predecessor, had been completed as early as 1961. Each possessing four guided missile systems, they were the most powerful guided-missile ships in the fleet.

The newly designed superstructures were mainly of light metal alloy. The superstructure block extended for more than two-thirds the length of the ship and was almost two decks in height. The box-shaped bridge, rounded in front, was unusually high and carried the missiles' control system. A radar platform was fitted aft.

Entirely new was the use of two very high mast/exhaust gas funnel combinations, known as 'Mack'. The 'Macks' towered over the very high bridge and carried movable smoke-emission vents, ventilation ducts and radar antennae together with their leads and cables. On each end of the superstructure, forward and aft, was a Talos twin launcher positioned in front of its reload magazine which could accommodate 46 missiles at any one time. Both the Mk 11 Tartar

twin launchers were positioned, unusually, on the beam, one each side of the bridge superstructure. The magazine beneath each of them contained 40 missiles.

The three ships were given an integrated ASW outfit consisting of a SQS-23 hull sonar installation, two triple sets of Mk 32 A/S torpedoes and an eight-cell ASROC launcher.

It is worth mentioning that the ships were originally designed to take eight Polaris ballistic missiles, which were to have been fitted amidships. Later it was intended that Regulus II missiles be fitted in this position. Both ideas were dropped when it became clear that the strategic submarines (SSBN) would be the only Navy ships to carry ballistic missiles. Initially it was not planned to fit these ships in their CG conversion

◁ The conversion of the *Albany*-class ships took place in the early 1960s and represented to some extent a revolution in warship design. Everything above deck on the hulls of these former heavy cruisers was completely new and unfamiliar. The requirements of the fire control electronics necessitated a very high bridge, and the mast/funnel combination had to be correspondingly high; it was known as 'Mack'. Initially, these ships were completed without any kind of gun armament. This aerial photograph taken of the lead ship, *Albany*, was taken on 2 January 1963 during her shake-down period and gives an impression of this major conversion. The platform fitted aft indicates that it had been intended originally to provide SPS-2 radar here. The bulky MK/2 Mod. 0 Talos launcher and its SPG-49/SPW-2 fire control systems behind it show very prominently. Having been conceived as flagships from the start, *Albany* has one bridge deck for the ship's control and one for the formation commander of Admiral's rank. On the forward mast there is 3-D radar SPS-39, and on the after mast search radar SPS-43A, but there are no height-finder antennae aboard. (USN)

with any kind of gun. It took the intervention of the then President, John F. Kennedy, to have each ship fitted for purposes of self-defence with two antiquated 5in/38 singles in open mountings on each side of the after 'Mack', each controlled by a Mk 56.

It had been intended to convert additional ships along the same lines, but only *Albany* (CA-123), *Chicago* (CA-136) and *Columbus* (CA-174) were so converted. The other two were dropped, initially for reasons of economy, and then because it transpired that smaller vessels designed from the onset as guided missile ships had a considerable missile capacity.

As no hangar was provided in these conversions, a helicopter could only be carried on the after deck as a temporary measure. The considerable height of the bridge superstructure and the space between this and the forward group of fire control instruments were necessitated by interference from the two Tartar installations. Space

was provided in the conversions for command staff so that the ships could be used as fleet flagships.

Albany functioned for a year as Flagship, Second and Sixth Fleet, *Chicago* as Flagship, Third Fleet. The decision to abandon the relatively heavy and finally obsolete Talos system was the first consideration in the striking off of these ships. No hasty decision was taken to scrap the last two ships (CG-10 and 11), but *Columbus* was very quickly broken up. *Albany* and *Chicago* were struck off in 1980, only to be put back on the reserve again; it having been realized that still-serviceable ships were being sent too quickly to the breaker's yard.

▽   *Albany* in the Mediterranean, 11 August 1966. It shows well the extent to which the superstructure towers above the narrow hull, made possible only by the use of light metal alloys. As an 'afterthought' *Albany* was given an open 5in/38 mounting and a Mk 56 fire control on each side of the after 'Mack'. Both the bridge and the platform now carry an SPS-30 antenna. It should be noticed that, in this photograph, the SPS-39 aerial is positioned on the after side of the 'Mack' platform, with SPS-10 radar in front of it. (USN)

▷ *Albany* photographed at the end of June 1976 at Norfolk. The after SPS-30 antenna has been removed, replaced by a satellite antenna which she was to retain till her decommissioning. (Te)

△ In February 1967 *Albany* entered the Boston Navy Yard and spent considerable time there while her entire guided missile installation was brought up to date. This photograph was taken some time in 1968. There is external evidence for this in the changes to the upper part of the forward Mack, where she now has SPS-48 radar in front of the yard and in the fact that the SPS-30 antenna has been removed – proof that SPS-48 had taken over many of the height-finding functions of SPS-30. The height of the bridge superstructure is dictated first by the lateral positioning of the Mk 11 Tartar launcher, one of which can be seen, together with both SPG-51 radar antennae. Note the IFF antenna on the upper edge of the SPS-43A. (USN)

▽ *Albany* in mid-May 1975 at Boston where the cruiser, at that time flagship of the Commandant of the Second Fleet, acted as guest ship for the visit of two Soviet guided missile destroyers; on this occasion the Soviet Ambassador Dobrynin came on board. One can see no changes to the ship since 1968. (USN)

Albany

1962 3 Nov Recommissioned, now as CG-10.

1963 Jan–July Refitting period, tests with guided missile installations and electronics systems; shake-down cruises, missile-firing exercises.

August End of period at Boston Navy Yard; operations off east coast and Caribbean.

Oct Acceptance trial cruises.

29 Nov Departed for first Mediterranean deployment.

1964 23 May Arrived Norfolk.

29 June–26 July Operations on east coast.

3–21 Oct Operations on east coast.

1965 24 May Second departure for Mediterranean.

11 Oct Arrived back at Norfolk; operations on east coast.

1966 4 March Third departure for Mediterranean.

25 Oct Arrived Norfolk; operations on east coast and Caribbean.

1967 1 Feb Arrived Boston Navy Yard for AAW modernization.

1969 27 June Changed home base to Mayport; operations on east coast until February 1970.

1970 24 Feb Left for fourth deployment with Sixth Fleet.

16 Sept Returned to Mayport; short cruises around home base.

1971 7 Feb Departed for fifth Mediterranean deployment.

24 July Returned to Mayport; operations and exercises on east coast.

1972 1 Sept Home base changed to Boston.

5 Sept Took part in Arctic Exercise 'Strong Express'.

2–5 Oct Visited Rotterdam.

9 Oct Sixth arrival in Mediterranean, operations with Sixth Fleet.

1973 15 Feb Returned to Boston; short cruises from there.

30 May Temporarily home based at Philadelphia.

6 July Refit at Philadelphia Navy Yard; including modernization of Talos and Tartar.

1974 31 May End of refit; home base transferred to Norfolk; restricted operations on east coast and Caribbean.

16 Sept–3 Dec At Norfolk Navy Yard; modified as fleet flagship.

1975 27 Jan Flagship, COM Second Fleet replacing *Newport News* (CA-148).

11 May At Boston; Soviet Ambassador Dobrynin welcomed aboard as guest of COM Second Fleet.

12–17 May Guest-ship during visit of two Soviet DDGs to Boston.

15 May CNO Admiral Holloway visited *Albany*.

22 May Operations and exercises based on Norfolk.

26 Sept–9 Oct NATO manoeuvre 'Ocean Safari'.

9 Oct–4 Nov Visited Oslo, Hamburg, Rotterdam, Brest, Portsmouth, Rosyth; continuation of 'Ocean Safari'.

10 Dec Arrived back at Norfolk.

13 Dec COM Second Fleet came aboard.

1975–76 1 Jan–5 May Refit at Norfolk Navy Yard.

1976 May–July Local operations on east coast and Caribbean.

10 August Seventh departure for Mediterranean.

7 Sept Replaced *Little Rock* (CG-4) as Flagship, COM Sixth Fleet; change of home base to Gaeta, Italy.

1976–80 Permanently in Mediterranean; operations with Sixth Fleet, interrupted by courtesy visits to ports.

1980 8 May *Puget Sound* (AD-38) arrived Gaeta.

28 May *Puget Sound* Flagship, COM Sixth Fleet.

12 June Left Lisbon for east coast.

21–22 June At New York.

27 June Arrived Norfolk.

29 August Decommissioned.

▷ This very clear and interesting photograph of *Albany* was taken at Messina *circa* 1980, and she does not seem to have undergone any alterations, except that the second SPS-30 has been removed from the platform. The helicopter in the stern is a Sea King, the personal aircraft of the Commandant of the Sixth Fleet. (SP)

△ As had happened with *Oklahoma City, Albany,* after her official decommissioning, was kept in a state of reserve readiness during which, exceptionally, she retained her weapons and sensors (with the exception of SPS-48 and the satellite antenna on the platform aboard. This July 1983 photograph shows *Albany,* high in the water, at her present berth outside the Norfolk naval base. (WD)

△ *Chicago,* photographed on 27 June 1971 at San Diego, shows that, in the meantime, SPS-39 radar has been interchanged with a SPS-52 antenna although one supposes that the SPS-39 remained. (LRC)

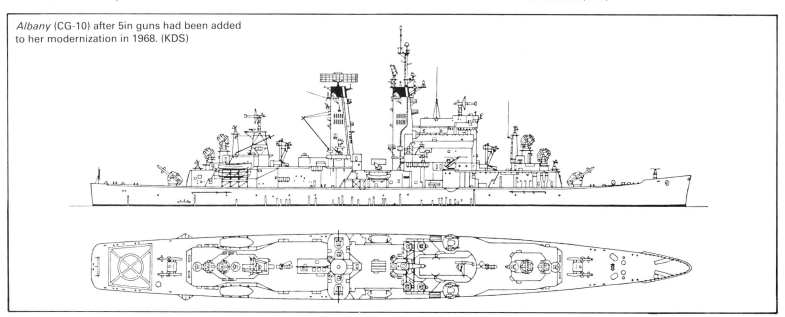

Albany (CG-10) after 5in guns had been added to her modernization in 1968. (KDS)

Chicago

1964 2 May Recommissioned, as CG-11; shake-down cruises; operations on west coast until 1965.

1965 18 Jan–16 April At San Francisco Navy Yard; then training cruises on west coast in connection with special guided missile tests; training cruises for reservists and midshipmen.

Oct Training cruise to Hawaii.

1966 Jan Operations off west coast with First Fleet.

20 April–12 May Preparations for overseas operations.

12 May Left for first deployment in West Pacific.

17 May Arrived Pearl Harbor.

1 June Arrived Yokosuka, COMCRUDESFLOT 11 came aboard.

15 June Operations off coast of Vietnam, in particular service as radar relay ship in connection with the PIRAZ concept; inter-mediate visits to Hong Kong, Subic Bay,

Okinawa, Taiwan, Yokosuka, and Sasebo.

27 Nov–7 Dec Non-stop cruise to west coast, intermediate refuelling from *Sacramento* (AOE-1).

8 Dec Arrived San Diego.

1967 Jan–August Operations off west coast with intermediate visits to Alaska and Canada, temporarily Flagship, First Fleet.

1–27 Sept Preparations for overseas operations.

11 Oct Second departure for West Pacific via Pearl Harbor, Yokosuka, Okinawa, and Subic Bay.

12 Nov On PIRAZ control in Gulf of Tonkin, with intermediate stops at Hong Kong, Subic Bay and Singapore.

1968 Feb Interrupted by PIRAZ stops in Japanese waters, on the occasion of the capture of *Pueblo* (AGER-3) by North Korea.

1 May Sailed for west coast via Guam and Pearl Harbor.

15 May Arrived San Diego; operations off west coast.

1 July–15 Dec Refit at Long Beach Navy Yard.

1969 Jan Operations off west coast.

13 Feb Left Long Beach for third WESTPAC deployment via Pearl Harbor and Subic Bay.

11 March On PIRAZ and SAR control in Gulf of Tonkin, with intermediate stops in Japan, Hong Kong, Okinawa and Subic Bay.

30 August Left Subic Bay for west coast via Guam and Pearl Harbor.

17 Sept Arrived San Diego; operations off west coast.

1970 Jan–August Operations off west coast.

△ Although her pennant number sequence follows immediately after that of *Albany*, the conversion of *Chicago* (CG-11) – in contrast to that of *Columbus* – was not completed until eighteen months after that of *Albany*. This photograph taken in San Francisco Bay in September 1964 shows that in contrast to both her sister ships *Chicago* had from the outset both the 5in guns and both Mk 56 fire control systems and also SPS-30. Evidently the crew has been mustered for quarters. (USN)

◁ This photograph dated August 1980 shows *Chicago* at her final berth in Bremerton, Washington. At that time she had been struck off and, in indication of that fact, the designation '11' was obliterated. The name 'Chicago' was then given to a new submarine of the SSN-688 class, but this measure was later cancelled. As can be seen the after SPS-30 antenna was not removed during her period of service and in fact is still in place at the present time. *Chicago* was officially in the Reserve Fleet until the end of January 1984. (WD)

9 Sept Fourth departure for West Pacific via Pearl Harbor and Guam.

3 Oct Operations in Vietnamese waters; intermediate stops in Yokosuka, Hong Kong and Subic Bay.

1971 24 Feb Left for west coast via Guam and Pearl Harbor.

11 March Arrived San Diego; operations off west coast.

1 July Midshipmen cruise to San Francisco, Seattle and Pearl Harbor.

4 August Arrived San Diego; operations off west coast.

6 Nov Fifth departure for West Pacific with COMCRUDESFLOT 3 aboard; intermediate stops in Guam and Subic Bay.

6 Dec Arrived in Vietnamese waters; operations in Gulf of Tonkin with intermediate stops in Singapore, Subic Bay and Hong Kong.

1972 28 April COMCRUDESFLOT 3 came aboard.

9 May Shot down a Mig aircraft with a Talos missile.

21 June Left for west coast via Guam and Pearl Harbor.

8 July At San Diego.

5 July Home base transferred to Long Beach.

25 August Refit at Long Beach Navy Yard.

1973 30 June Home base transferred to San Diego.

1 Sept End of yard work which had lasted one year.

1975 Jan Operations on west coast.

21 May Sixth departure for West Pacific; intermediate stops at Pearl Harbor, Yokosuka and Subic Bay.

25 June Departed for Indian Ocean and Arabian Sea with visits to Karachi, Mombasa, Mauritius and Singapore.

11–29 Sept At Subic Bay.

30 Sept Operations with Seventh Fleet, including visits to Hong Kong, Manila, Yokosuka.

17 Nov Departed from Subic Bay for west coast via Guam and Pearl Harbor.

14 Dec Arrived San Diego; operations off west coast.

1976 March Manoeuvres with British, Canadian and New Zealand forces.

13 April Seventh departure for West Pacific together with an amphibious group; joint exercises along route.

3 May Arrived Yokosuka; exercises with a carrier battle group including *Midway* (CV-41); operations with Seventh Fleet.

27 Sept Left Subic Bay for west coast via Guam and Pearl Harbor.

16 Oct Arrived San Diego.

Nov Exercises and operations off west coast.

1977 6 Sept Eighth departure for West Pacific.

30 Sept Arrived Subic Bay; operations with Seventh Fleet; visited Taiwan, Hong Kong, Inchon, Singapore and Thailand.

1978 16 March Left Subic Bay for west coast via Guam and Pearl Harbor.

7 April Arrived San Diego; operations on west coast.

24 July–24 Oct Refit at Long Beach Navy Yard, with Talos immobilized, and Tartar overhauled; then operations off west coast.

1979 30 May Ninth departure for West Pacific via Pearl Harbor in company with *Kitty Hawk* (CV-63); exercises in Hawaii area.

4 July Arrived Subic Bay; operations with Seventh Fleet, in between times visited Pusan, Hong Kong, and Sydney.

27 Nov Left Subic Bay for west coast via Pearl Harbor.

17 Dec Arrived San Diego.

1980 1 March Decommissioned.

▷ This rather grainy photograph taken in June 1975 shows that *Chicago* had lost one of the SPS-30 antennae; in the intervening time SPS-48 had been fitted. She is just passing Point Loma on leaving the port of San Diego. (USN)

▽ *Columbus* during the first half of 1963. The two 5in guns and the two SPS-30s were not fitted (at Puget Sound Navy Yard) until November 1963. (USN)

◁ Compared with her sisters, *Columbus* was, to some extent, treated badly. With their installations for flag duties *Albany* and *Chicago* were frequently and for long periods deployed as flagships, but *Columbus* never at any time; nor was any AAW modernization carried out as with *Albany*. This photograph, taken at Genoa on 15 December 1968, confirms that the SPS-39 antenna is still in place on the forward mast. Note also how high the ASROC launcher is placed on the middle deck, a position where it had originally been planned to place Regulus cruise missiles. (LGr)

▷ This attractive aerial photograph of *Columbus* is unfortunately undated. Note the many cars stowed on the roof of the missile magazine. The 5in guns have been swung outboard. (USN)

Columbus

1962 1 Dec Recommissioned, now as CG-12.
1963 March–June Shake-down cruises along west coast.
Nov After installation of SPS-30 radar and two 5in guns, left Puget Sound Navy Yard to be based in San Diego.
1963–64 Dec–March Operations on west coast with First Fleet.
1964 April–May Short stay at Long Beach Navy Yard.
1964–65 5 August–6 Feb Deployment to West Pacific.
1965 March–Dec Operations off west coast.
1966 10 Jan Transferred to Atlantic Fleet.
Feb Flagship, COMCRUDESFLOT 8; operations off east coast.
March NATO manoeuvres in North Atlantic.
15 Oct Replaced *Albany* with Sixth Fleet in Mediterranean.
1967 April Returned to east coast.
Dec Operations on east coast.
1968 3 Jan Second deployment to Mediterranean.
16 July Returned to Norfolk.

July–Oct Refit at Boston Navy Yard.
1 Dec Flagship, COMCRUDESFLOT 10.
2 Dec Departed for third deployment in Mediterranean.
1969 May Returned to Newport; COMCRUDESFLOT 10 came aboard.
13 June–2 Sept Refit at Norfolk Navy Yard.
8 Oct Flagship, COMCRUDESFLOT 2, departed for fourth Mediterranean deployment.
1970 18 March Returned to Norfolk.
17 April–16 July Refit at Norfolk Navy Yard.
6 Sept Fifth arrival in Mediterranean; COMCRUDESFLOT 8 aboard for nine days.
1971 1 March Returned to Norfolk.
12 April–13 Oct Refit at Norfolk Navy Yard.
1971–72 Oct–May Operations off east coast.
1972 17 May Sixth arrival in Mediterranean with Sixth Fleet.
18 Oct Returned to Norfolk; one year of operations off east coast.
1973 2 Nov Seventh trip to Mediterranean.
1974 31 May Return to Norfolk; preparations for decommissioning.
1975 31 Jan Decommissioned.

▷ By the end of the 1960s *Columbus* no longer carried FRESCAN radar, but both SPS-30 antennae remained in place until she was struck off in 1974. She never had SPS-48 radar. Unlike her sisters, *Columbus* was scrapped very quickly. This attractive photograph was taken off the French Riviera on 21 September 1972. (P & L)

LONG BEACH

Long Beach, displacing more than 17,000 tons, was certainly the only 'true' new cruiser of the guided missile era of the 1950s and 1960s, although she was originally to have been a 'frigate' with a displacement of 7,800 tons.

Obsessed by the idea of replacing conventional AA defence with guided missiles, the US Navy sought a high-speed, long-range cruiser type, totally able to escort and protect nuclear-powered aircraft carriers. An atomic reactor suitable for surface ships of 9,000 tons upwards had been successfully developed, so nuclear propulsion was chosen for *Long Beach.*

The ship had a very slender hull, a somewhat rounded transom and a high stem. At the level of the forward missile launcher were collapsible breakwaters. The superstructure was continuous from a point well forward to four-fifths of the ship's length aft. The forward third of the super-structure contained two missile magazines, with a Mk 10 Terrier twin launcher in front of each of them. The two magazines contained a total of 120 missiles of the standard missile SM-1 ER. Up to 1979, the after end of the superstructure was a magazine containing 46 Talos missiles. On this was positioned the comprehensive electronic equipment for fire and guidance control (two each of SPG-49 and SPW-2) with a Mk 12 Talos launcher behind this. An unusual feature was the blockhouse-shaped bridge superstructure whose seven decks were connected by a lift, and whose shape resembled slightly the island in the first atomic aircraft carrier, *Enterprise* (formerly CVAN-65), at the time she completed. The bridge shape was necessitated by the large surface arrays of the SPS-32/33 radar system which were positioned vertically to the sides. The extended mid-section of the superstructure deck was in-tended to receive further weapons systems. Initially a launcher for Regulus II, then eight launching tubes for Polaris; both ideas were abandoned in 1961.

An ASW component of rocket-launcher, three Mk 32 A/S torpedo tubes on each side at bridge height, and a SQS-23 bow sonar was installed. At the beginning of 1963 a single 5in/38 Mk 30 gun was mounted on each side of the superstructure deck. This was said to have been at the instigation of President Kennedy who found it almost unseemly that a powerful and expensive atomic ship should not be able to defend herself against a torpedo-boat. There is a helicopter pad on the stern, but no hangar. The ship was given the computer-controlled command evaluation and information system NTDS.

If the reactor fails or needs to be switched off, an emergency diesel installation enables the ship

△ This aerial photograph of *Long Beach* dates from the first weeks after she was commissioned, that is to say during the last four months of 1961. She does not have the four vertical aerials SPS-33 or the pair of 5in guns. Amidships, behind the ASROC launcher, can be seen the slim funnel of the ship's own waste-burning system. This was how *Long Beach* appeared at the end of 1962 when she paid a visit to Bremerhaven. (USN)

△ *Long Beach,* on 1 April 1963. She is now complete with SPS-33 radar, both the 5in guns and both the Mk 56 fire controls. She has sufficient spare space to stow several cars. One can easily identify SPS-10 radar in front of the TACAN antenna. (USN)

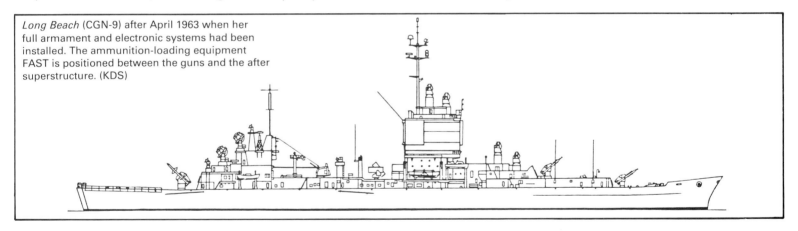

Long Beach (CGN-9) after April 1963 when her full armament and electronic systems had been installed. The ammunition-loading equipment FAST is positioned between the guns and the after superstructure. (KDS)

to proceed, although at a slower speed. The reactors are reported to be similar to those in *Enterprise.* With her first nuclear charge, *Long Beach* steamed for 167,000 nautical miles, the cores being replaced in 1965/66.

Construction costs amounted to 332.9 million dollars which, in the early 1960s, was exceedingly high for a ship other than an aircraft carrier.

In view of her sea-keeping qualities, the Navy intended to keep *Long Beach* in service for at least forty years, i.e., until the year 2002. When it was proposed that 'Strike Cruisers' be fitted with several battle systems, including principally the AEGIS/Mk-26 combination and Tomahawk missiles the Navy decided in 1977 that *Long Beach,* too, be converted as a 'Strike Cruiser' from the beginning of the 1980s (see photograph). For this undertaking the Programmes FY 77, 78 and 79 were to provide a total of 783 million dollars. This scheme was blocked by the Carter administration, who did give an assurance that *Long Beach* would be given a modest conversion between 1979 and 1981, financed by funds from the maintenance and servicing departments. This was, in fact, done in stages. By 1980 the radar had been replaced by SPS-48 and 49. Both SPG-49/SPW-2 fire control installations had been removed and, in place of the Mk 12 launcher, she received two four-tube Harpoon missile launchers Mk 141. Apparently the future fitting of an AEGIS installation is no longer envisaged and both the Mk 10 launchers are still in place. SQS-23 sonar is being replaced by SQQ-23 PAIR.

◁ This is one of the last official photographs of *Long Beach* prior to the first phase of her conversion in 1978. In the stern, the several ventilation outlets are dispersed in such a way, that in front of them – right up to the after Talos launcher – a helicopter pad could be fitted. The ducting for the radar wave guide runs along the after edge of the bridge superstructure. An additional radar antenna is SPS-12 on the peak of the forward mast. The WLR-6 ECCM antennae project from the sides of the bridge yardarms. (USN)

▷ This intermediate-stage photograph of *Long Beach* was taken at San Diego in August 1980. The ship's name is carried on the stern in black letters. (WD)

▷ *Long Beach* at San Diego, August 1980. The pair of Mk 141 Harpoon quadruple launchers fitted before the Talos missile magazine can be seen. Both the hinge-joints for the magazine outlet openings are still in place. (WD)

◁ This photograph of *Long Beach* was taken off the Californian coast in June 1979; after completion of Phase 1 of the 'mid-life conversion'. The complete Talos installation has been removed; otherwise there are no visible changes. SPS-12 radar can clearly be seen. (USN)

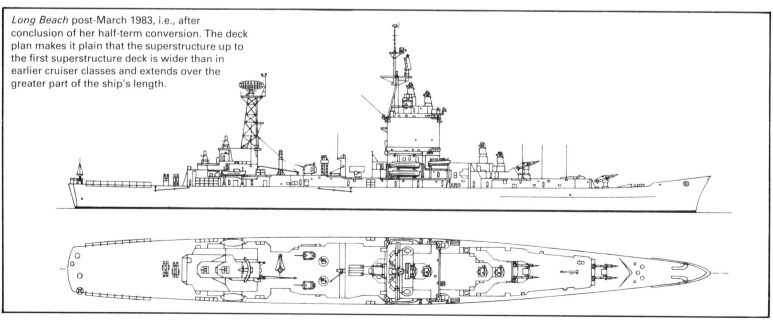

Long Beach post-March 1983, i.e., after conclusion of her half-term conversion. The deck plan makes it plain that the superstructure up to the first superstructure deck is wider than in earlier cruiser classes and extends over the greater part of the ship's length.

◁ *Long Beach* at San Diego in July 1983 after the end of conversion Plase II. The closures for the reload flaps have been removed, and the outlet has clearly been welded tight. The quadruped lattice mast aft is new, and the forward mast has been restructured and given two supporting legs. The ship's name is now carried in a lighter colour. (WD)

▷ Two photographs of *Long Beach*'s blockhouse-style forward superstructure after the fixed-array antennas were removed.

Long Beach

1961 9 Sept Commissioned; in the Atlantic.

2 Oct–16 Dec Shake-down cruises.

1961–62 28 Dec–5 Jan Guided missile firing exercises off Puerto Rico.

1962 15 Jan Visited Bremerhaven, ports in France and in Bermudas.

7 Feb Returned to east coast.

April Manoeuvres as Flagship, CINCLANT, Admiral Dennison; during this period inspection by President J. F. Kennedy and Vice-President L. B. Johnson.

1962 Summer, yard work for final completion of equipment, including SPS-33 radar, both 5in guns and fire control Mk 56.

1963 6 August–20 Dec First Mediterranean deployment.

1963–64 Dec–April Operations off east coast.

1964 28 April Second Departure for Mediterranean.

13 May Formed 'Nuclear Task Force 1' with *Enterprise* (CVAN-65) and *Bainbridge* (DLGN-25). Remained in Mediterranean.

31 July The task force began, via Gibralter, a round-the-world cruise (Operation 'Sea Orbit'), during which *Long Beach* visited Karachi, Melbourne, Wellington and Rio de Janeiro.

3 Oct Returned to east coast.

1965–66 August–Feb Refit at Newport News.

1966 28 Feb Departed for Pacific via Panama Canal; transferred to Pacific Fleet.

15 March Arrived Long Beach; in summer of 1966 operations off west coast.

7 Nov First departure for West Pacific; mainly off Vietnamese coast.

1967 27 April Visited Sydney.

4 July Returned to west coast.

1968 15 April Second departure for Vietnam; duties there mainly radar coverage and controlling own aircraft; shot down two Migs over mainland with Talos missiles.

16 Nov Returned to west coast.

1970–71 March–Dec Refit at Mare Island Navy Yard; then operations off west coast.

1972 March Third deployment to West Pacific; including operations in Gulf of Tonkin until November 1972, then series of transfers between operations off west coast and deployments to Seventh Fleet.

1976 Jan–June Refit at Puget Sound Navy Yard.

Sept Seventh cruise to West Pacific; in this time joint manoeuvres with Australian and New Zealand forces and with *Enterprise* and *Bainbridge* in Indian Ocean.

1977 28 March Returned to San Diego.

1978 4 April Eighth deployment to West Pacific, including operations in Indian Ocean with *Enterprise* and *Truxtun*.

27 Oct Returned to San Diego.

1979 Jan–April At yard in Bremerton, work included dismantling of complete Talos installation and fitting of two Harpoon launchers; then operations off west coast; manoeuvres with Canadian Navy.

1980 7 Jan Departure for ninth deployment to West Pacific.

11 July Returned to San Diego.

30 August Commencement of conversion at Puget Sound Navy Yard ('mid-life conversion').

1981 9 Sept Celebration at yard of 20th year of service.

1982 Nov Once more at sea, following conversion.

1983 March Transferred to San Diego after comprehensive conversion and refitting at Puget Sound.

August Operations off west coast.

△ Taken on the same occasion: the slim bow of *Long Beach* with its raised bulwark. The missile-loading equipment of the upper Mk 10 launcher is raised. Clearly visible are both the newly fitted SLQ-32 (V) 3 ESM installations and SPS-48 radar. (WD)

▽ The most notable change after *Long Beach*'s conversion was in the fitting of the new quad-ruped mast as a base for the SPS-49 radar antenna. SLQ-32 is clearly seen in this photograph. Both the 5in guns and Mk 56 fire control have been retained. (WD)

▽ On no previous US ship was there such a close grouping of the two Mk 15 Phalanx installations as in *Long Beach*. Obviously this greatly restricts the arc of fire which means that there is no scope for defence against an enemy missile approaching from forward. (WD)

ALASKA CLASS

This was a new development in US ship design which owed its origins to a mistake that is to some extent understandable. It had been reported, incorrectly, that the Japanese were planning to build a ship similar in type to the German Deutschland-class pocket battleships. At that time the USN had nothing comparable in terms of high speed, armour and guns, so the FY40 Programme provided for six 'Large Cruisers' which were to be greater than heavy cruisers, in fact more like 'Battle Cruisers', By the time the report was found to be incorrect it was too late to halt construction work on the first two units. *Alaska* (CB-1) and *Guam* (CB-2) were completed so speedily that they were able to take part in war operations with cruisers and carriers. *Hawaii* (CB-3) was suspended in 1947 when 82 per cent completed. CB-4 to 6 *Philippines, Puerto Rico,* and *Samoa*) were cancelled in 1943. In appearance the ships resembled battleships, but in concept they corresponded with what the navy expected of its cruisers, which was why they had only one rudder and why much value was placed on weather-proof storage for aircraft. For design reasons (the after part of the ship was not deep enough), this could only be done by using space amidships (a similarity with the pre-war cruisers) and not in a below-deck hangar as in *Wichita* and the *Brooklyn*s. The 12in/50 triple turrets were designed specially for this class; they were not used in any other ship so their development and maintenance were rather uneconomic.

As *Alaska* and *Guam* were not completed until mid-1944, no large modifications were carried out before the end of the war, and having outlived their purpose they were struck off in 1947.

Alaska
1944 17 June Commissioned; comprehensive shake-down cruises.
1945 13 Jan Joined PACFL at Pearl Harbor.
15 Feb–12 March At Iwo Jima.
15, 16, 25 Feb With Fifth Fleet, attacked Honshu and Nansei Shoto.
17 March–28 May Okinawa.
16 July–7 August Operations with Third Fleet against Japanese mainland.
14 Nov Occupation of Japan, operations off China and Korea.
1947 17 Feb Decommissioned.

Guam
1944 17 Sept Commissioned, shake-down cruise off Trinidad.
1945 17 Jan Departed for Pacific Fleet.
8 Feb Arrived Pearl Harbor.
13 March Joined TF 58 at Ulithi.
18 March Carrier escort protection at Kyushu and Shikoku.
22 March Escort protection for badly damaged carrier *Franklin*.
June Joined TG 38.4.
13 June Okinawa.
16 July–7 August Flagship, TF 95, East China Sea.
7 August Once more at Okinawa; at end of war Flagship, 'North China Force', occupation of Chinese ports.
8 Sept Departed for occupation of Korea.
14 Nov Departed for west coast carrying combatants.
15 Dec Departed for east coast.
17 Feb Decommissioned.

▽   *Alaska* off Philadelphia Navy Yard on 30 July 1944, showing her port side painted to Measure 32/1d. Shortly after she was completed the Mk 4 fire control radar was replaced by Mk 12/22. (USN)

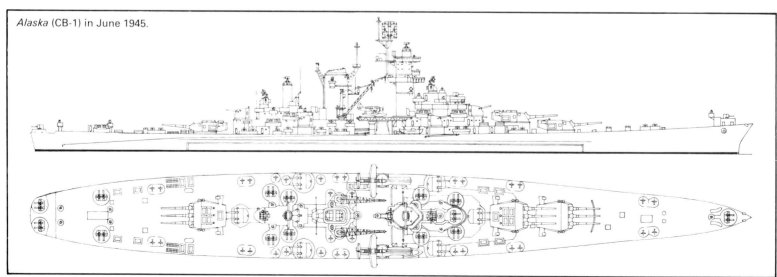

Alaska (CB-1) in June 1945.

◁ The lead ship of both 'Large Cruisers', *Alaska* was only in service for a bare two and a half years; this photograph was taken at Camden, New Jersey during inclining tests on 5 June 1944, twelve days before she was commissioned. She has already been painted in camouflage Measure 32/1d. In this ship a return has been made to catapults fitted laterally. Two combinations of fire control gear Mk 38/fire control radar Mk 8 Mod. 1 are fitted. The Mk 37 fire control system was given initially the Mk 4 fire control radar. SK and SG radar are on the forward yardarm. She has two antennae supports on the funnel, the forward one for SG radar and the after one for radio antennae. The fighting turret has much in common with those on the battleships of that period. (USN)

△ This photograph of the starboard side of Alaska was taken on 28 September 1944; although the ship was still undergoing shakedown cruises the camouflage forward had weathered considerably. There are Kingfisher reconnaissance aircraft on the catapult. (USN)

▽ As can be seen, *Alaska*'s camouflage had been changed to Scheme 22 after her arrival at Pearl Harbor. This photograph was taken on 19 January 1945, presumably in Hawaiian waters. (USN)

SHIPS NOT COMPLETED

Pennant No.	Name	Fiscal Year	Laid Down	Builder	History
CB-3	Hawaii	1940	20 Dec 1943	New York SBdg.	Building suspended 17 Feb 1947
CB-4	Philippines	1940		New York SBdg.	Building suspended 24 June 1943
CB-5	Puerto Rico	1940		New York SBdg.	Building suspended 24 June 1943
CB-6	Samoa	1940		New York SBdg.	Building suspended 24 June 1943

◁ *Guam* on 13 November 1944, still in Atlantic waters, having just completed a sharp turning manoeuvre. One cannot think that the bow AA position could possibly be manned in heavy seas. (USN)

△ *Guam* off Philadelphia Navy Yard on 25 October 1944 during the shake-down period. (USN)

▽ *Guam's* period in service was shorter than that of *Alaska* by three months. The starboard pattern of Measure 32/7c shows clearly how, when viewed from close range, the camouflage effect gives the impression of a ship sinking by the stern. Signal flags are hanging out to dry. The photograph was taken in the last weeks of 1944. (USN)

NORTHAMPTON

Immediately after the Second World War the US Navy made an evaluation of the role played by the Command ships (AGC) from which amphibious operations had been conducted. During the early stages of the war the AGCs had been converted merchantmen whose compartments were made suitable for a Sea Commander and a land Commander, with all their requisite installations. The requirements of spaciousness to house crew plus large numbers of Navy, Army and Marine Corps staff, a multiplicity of electronics, and defence installations were eventually to be embodied in the *Blue Ridge* class.

Eighteen AGCs were used successfully during the war and the Japanese clearly did not realize the extent of their importance, or they would have made greater efforts to destroy these ships, losses among which were extraordinarily low. After the war it was acknowledged that modern command ships were important not only for amphibious operations but, increasingly, for direction of task forces, for example for fast aircraft carrier battle groups.

The choice of a suitable hull to be completed as a Command Ship fell on the fourth unit of the *Oregon City* class, the still incomplete *Northampton* (CA-125). In July 1946 it was decided to continue her construction as a Headquarters Ship with flagship installations.

The construction of CA-125 had been initially suspended on 11 August 1945 when construction was 56.2 per cent complete. Work was resumed on 1 July 1948 to a totally changed design. The ship was reclassified as CLC-1 – the new designation for a tactical command ship. The aim was to provide a headquarters-cum-staff ship which, in the event of war, could receive the President of the USA and the most important command staffs and provide atomic proof accommodation for them. The official abbreviation NECPA was short for 'National Emergency Command Post Afloat'. She was commissioned on 7 March 1953.

While the main bulk of the ship, engine installation and most of the armour were retained, the ship's appearance was completely altered, as compared to her sisters. The entire length of the hull was raised by one deck to provide maximum enclosed compartment space. The high bridge was given a fighting tower mast which accommodated the different radar antennae she received during her service life. Her funnel remained similar to those of her sisters. The after superstructure also had a tower mast to accommodate electronic systems. Many communications antennae were set up on the main deck, and, unusually, a 125-ft antennae mast was positioned between the forecastle and the forwardmost 5in gun.

There were many changes over the years. Until 1963 the forward tower mast had the massive SPS-2 radar antennae which had a horizontal detection range of 300 miles. To complement this the after tower had first the unsuccessful SPS-3 and later SPS-12 and SPS-290. Subsequently various special antennae were tried out on the forward mast, latterly a very large, parabolic antennae, possibly for satellite reception. A further mast, fitted between No. 2 turret and the

◁ The command ship *Northampton* (CLC-1, later CC-1) played an exceptional role during her seventeen active years with the fleet. Main changes throughout this period concerned the combat systems, i.e., weapons and electronics. Since it was intended to keep her equipped with the most up-to-date communications and detection electronics, *Northampton* became virtually a 'laboratory' ship. This, one of the earliest photographs, shows her in 1953, probably a short time before commissioning. She is lying high in the water. She has not yet received her radar equipment. Special features of the ship were the raised main deck level, and the tallest unsupported mast in the fleet, as it was described at that time. (USN)

▷ As Flagship, Commander Strike Force, Atlantic Fleet, *Northampton* spent some time in British waters when this photograph was taken in July 1955. Her complete electronic component can be seen: SPS-2 radar on the lower mast; SPS-3 radar provisionally on the after lower mast; behind this and somewhat deeper SPS-8A height-finder radar; the fire-control combination Mk 67/Mk 25 on the bridge top was to serve all four of the Mk 42 5in guns. There are two 3in/50 mountings on each side, each connected to a Mk 56 fire-control gear. At this time guided missile systems had not yet come into service in the US Navy, so the ship's guns were of great importance. At this time *Northampton* was one of the first ships to receive the newly developed Mk 42 5in/54 guns which were fully automatic. Not until four years later would the 3in/70 be installed, replacing the Mk 22 open mountings. (WL)

bridge, latterly carried a version of the SK-2 antenna, possibly for long-distance reception.

Armament was limited to the current AA guns: four new, fully automatic self-loading Mk 42 5in/54; four 3in/50 twin mountings (later replaced by four 3in/70 twin turrets. Throughout her career, this considerable AA component was reduced: in 1962 the four 3in/70 turrets were removed; in 1968 three of the four 5in/54. At the end of her life she had only a single 5in gun, on the other superstructure deck. Fire control of the 5in guns was from a single Mk 67 on the bridge, but this was eventually removed.

Northampton was the first ship in the US Navy to have weatherproof accommodation for her helicopters, in a hangar aft.

In 1963 the designation was changed from CLC-1 to CC-1, and the official designation now became 'National Command Ship'. As the ship possessed approximately 60 transmitters and receivers and was a fast ship, she could combine with carrier groups.

Northampton

1953 7 March Commissioned as CLC-1, then test ship of 'Operational Development Force' until September 1954, then joined 'Battleship/Cruiser Force Atlantic Fleet'.

1954 Oct–Nov Flagship, COMPHIBLANT.

1954–55 Dec–March Flagship, Commander, Sixth Fleet

1955 1 Sept–22 Oct Flagship, 'Commander Strike Force, Atlantic Fleet' for approximately 15 years, alternating with other tasks.

1955–56 Nov–Jan At Norfolk Navy Yard, then joined CRUDIV 6.

1956 April Six months in Mediterranean with Sixth Fleet; in summer of 1957 began midshipmen training cruises interspersed with NATO manoeuvres in North Atlantic, with visits to European cities.

1961 15 April Reclassified as CC-1, then remained for next ten years with Atlantic Fleet, including deployments to Mediterranean.

1970 14 Jan Decommissioned.

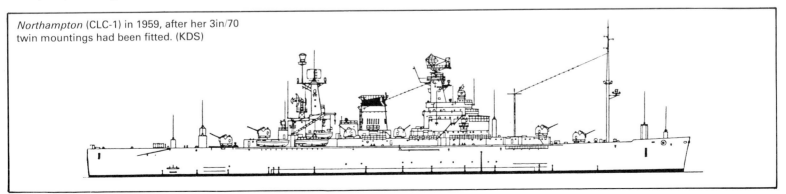

Northampton (CLC-1) in 1959, after her 3in/70 twin mountings had been fitted. (KDS)

△ A photograph taken off Toulon on 14 Aug 1956 shows *Northampton* with the Sixth Fleet in the Mediterranean. An Admiral's barge is abeam the after superstructure. The after tower mast is now painted black. SPS-6B has been removed; SPS-12 on the after tower mast has replaced SPS-3. The new 3in/70 has replaced the 3in/50 guns. (MB)

▽ In September 1957, *Northampton,* following the conclusion of NATO manoeuvres, visited Portsmouth, England, where this photograph was taken. There are no changes to be seen compared with the 1956 appearance. There is SPS-10 radar on the forwardmost antenna mast. (WL)

△ With the Commandant of the Second Fleet aboard, *Northampton,* at the head of a sizeable formation (including *Newport News* and several destroyers) visited Hamburg in 1958 when this photograph was taken. A refuse lighter mars the picture. (Te)

▽ Just one year later: *Northampton* seen in 1959 in English waters. On the after lower mast one sees SPS-29 radar and URN-3 TACAN. Several radio antennas near the after 5in mountings reduce their arcs of fire. (RPh)

◁ This photograph of *Northampton* must have been taken before April 1961 as she still carries the designation 'CLC-1'. On the peak of the after tower mast is positioned either SRN-6 or URN-3 TACAN. (USN).

△ This photograph is dated 7 September 1961 when *Northampton* had already been classified as CC-1. On the forward edge of the funnel is positioned an ECM antenna, and a SRN-6 TACAN on the after tower mast. (USN)

Northampton in about June 1964 when the 3in guns and SPS-2 radar had already been removed. (KDS)

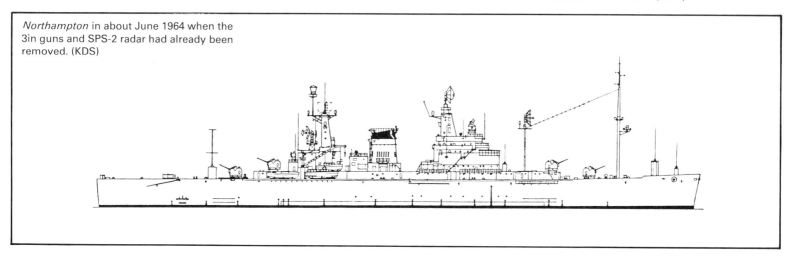

△▽ Up to 28 or 29 August 1963 when both these photographs were taken somewhere in the Atlantic, *Northampton* had undergone several changes which altered considerably certain aspects of her appearance. After ten years the SPS-2 radar has been removed from the forward tower mast. We cannot be certain of what is in its place. It would seem to be an independent IFF installation. A separate radar mast supports a modified SK-2 antenna which is geared to receive signals from the troposphere. To acquire more enclosed compartments from what had been the magazine, the four 3in/70 mountings which she had inherited, and which were difficult to maintain, have been removed. The cruiser operated at all times under the protection of carrier-based aircraft and guided missile ships, so a large number of guns was not required. A Mk 56 fire control appears to have been retained behind the after superstructure, and this would be for controlling the fire of both the after 5in guns. (USN)

△ *Northampton* replenishing at sea from the refrigerator ship *Alstede* (AF-48), 4 June 1964. In place of the IFF instrument on the forward tower mast there is now a second, grained parabolic antenna. Note the very large marked helicopter pad on the quarterdeck. (USN)

▷ During her last years of service *Northampton* underwent further changes in her electronics system and the number of 5in guns was reduced. This photograph is said to have been taken in 1968; it represents the last known appearance of the ship prior to her being decommissioned. Only the after raised gun is still present (in position 'X'). The superstructure deck has been enlarged and raised. The forward tower mast has received a further, new parabolic antenna, the Mk 67 fire control radar having been removed. (USN)

NORFOLK

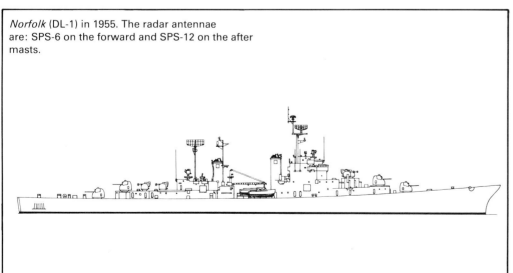

Norfolk (DL-1) in 1955. The radar antennae
are: SPS-6 on the forward and SPS-12 on the after
masts.

△ Norfolk (DL-1 ex-CLK-1) was a 'one-off'. She
was conceived as an anti-submarine cruiser, to be
designated CLK, but the idea of cruisers being
employed for tasks that were properly the role of
destroyers was then abandoned. The designation
'DL', first applied to Norfolk, indicated that a new
category of large destroyer had been interpolated
which resulted in the erroneous designation
'Frigate' being used until 1975. Here Norfolk is
seen on 29 August 1953 off Philadelphia Navy
Yard, five months after commissioning, still in
light condition, relatively high in the water. SPS-6
radar antenna can be seen on the forward mast.
The two Mk L108 A/S rocket-launchers in front of
the bridge are part of the ASW component; they
were never fitted in other cruisers. During the first
years Norfolk carried four 3in/50 twin mountings
Mk 22. One 20mm Oerlikon can be seen beside the
second Mk L108, but there is no official evidence
that she ever received sixteen 20mm AA guns.
Note the heavy crane for ship's boats in front of
the second funnel. (USN)

Experience gained during the Second World War, especially towards the end, revealed the need for a ship with superior ASW capability and with an adequate AA component for the protection of destroyers. Logically, these ships would have to be larger than destroyers built hitherto, but, at that time, anything larger than a destroyer was given the category of cruiser. Therefore, and in parallel with category CLAA among the AA cruisers, category CKL (Light Cruiser, Hunter Killer) was introduced.

On 1 September 1949 *Norfolk* (CLK-1) was laid down, and launched on 29 December 1951. The hull was similar to those of the *Atlanta* class. It is said that some aspects of her design were initiated by the atomic bomb tests at Bikini. The construction of *Norfolk* was carried out to some extent in parallel with that of the four large *Mitscher*-class destroyers which were intended to carry out similar tasks, but were rather smaller, and therefore first designated as destroyers.

As a consequence of the much higher speeds of submerged submarines post-war, it would be necessary to fight them at greater distances than hitherto. As suitable weapons the US Navy was developing: the Mk 108 anti-submarine rocket-launcher (Weapon Able, later known as Weapon Alfa) and the Mk 23 and Mk 24 anti-submarine torpedo tubes, which could discharge wire-directed anti-submarine torpedoes. These were initially the main weapons in *Norfolk*. With four Mk 108 launchers the ship could engage simultaneously several sub-surface targets. The *Mitscher*-class had only two such launchers, and many of the so-called escort destroyers (DDE) were given one or two Mk 108s.

Norfolk was certainly started as a cruiser, but as early as 1951 while building she was moved one stage back as DL-1 (Destroyer Leader), while the four ships of the *Mitscher* class were moved up from DD to DL. Later, in 1955, while retaining the designation DL, the type known as 'Frigates' was introduced. At that time then, *Norfolk* was the only ship that was not a cruiser but which still carried a city name as only cruisers had done hitherto.

On one of the first model photographs made public one could see that *Norfolk* – again like the *Mitscher* class – was to be given four of the new 5in/54 Mk 42 guns. At about this time, however, the newly developed 3in/70 twin mountings became available, although it did not prove practicable, maintenance being uneconomic given the lesser calibre. This gun was therefore fitted in ships only in small numbers, but was to remain in *Norfolk* until she was decommissioned. Before receiving the 3in/70s *Norfolk* had four 3in/50 open twin mountings.

For a while *Norfolk* functioned as E-DL-1 (E for 'Experimental') and for the testing of new weapons. The 20mm AA was removed and the Mk 24 torpedo tubes put out of use. To replace them, six Mk 32 torpedo tubes were shipped, and these are still the standard installation used in A/S ships. In about 1960 the first ASROC launcher was installed and both the after Mk 108 launchers were removed. Much later both the forward pair were removed. In 1958 the SQS-23 hull sonar installation was installed for the first time. It was debated whether this ship and the *Mitschers* should not be converted as guided missile destroyers, and be fitted with launchers and reclassified as DDG.

At the beginning of her service radar antennae SPS-6 and 12 and special SPS-26 antennae were installed. Both the latter were later removed and SPS-6 was replaced by SPS-29.

▽ A photograph, sadly undated, but certainly taken after 1956, shows *Norfolk* now with 3in/70 mounts and SPS-12 radar on the after mast. Directly below the after funnel at the height of the main deck, one can see the exit outlets of four Mk 24 torpedo tubes projecting from the super-structure. It can also be seen that two Mk 56s control the fire of the 3in guns. There is no provision for helicopters. *Newport News* can be seen in the background. (USN)

△ This similarly undated photograph was probably taken in the second half of 1957; it is known that after August 1957 SPS-26, the first FRESCAN installation, was installed: it can be seen here on a sponson behind the after funnel. Two uncovered ECM antennae rest on the funnel mast. It is especially clear in this photograph that the two forward Mk L-108 launchers are not aligned parallel with each other, the one on the port side being set somewhat more forward. Note the relatively high bridge. (USN)

Norfolk

1953 4 May Commissioned as DL-1.

1954 Feb Shake-down cruise in Caribbean, stationed in Atlantic.

1955–57 Flagship, variously of DESFLOT 2, 4 and 6.

1956–57 Flagship, COMDESLANT.

1957 June Took part in international Fleet Review in Hampton Roads.

1959 The eight 3in/50 guns replaced by the new 3in/70s.

1960 Test ship for ASROC; in autumn of 1961 as flagship of a CRUDESFLOT, took part in joint manoeuvres with South American Forces, UNITAS II.

1962 Flagship, COMDESLANT.

1966 Yearly ASW operations with UNITAS, mainly as Flagship COMSOLANT.

28 Nov–16 Dec Flagship during manoeuvres 'LANTFLEX 66'.

1967 Flagship, COMSOLANT with UNITAS VIII.

1968 17 April–15 Oct With 'Middle East Force' in Persian Gulf.

Oct Returned to Norfolk.

1970 Decommissioned.

▷ This photograph of *Norfolk* was taken on 21 August 1964. There are WLR-1 ECM antennae on the funnel mast and Mk 32 anti-submarine torpedo tubes in groups of three near the bridge superstructure; the old Mk 24 torpedo tubes had been taken out of service. (USN)

▷▽ During her 17 years of service, *Norfolk* served as a test ship for weapons and electronics on several occasions. This photograph shows her in 1962, now with SPS-37 radar on the forward mast. Both the outdated after Mk L-108 launchers had been removed after 1960 and the first ASROC eight-cell launcher installed as it was to be in dozens of cruisers, destroyers and frigates during the next 24 years. The outlets of the port Mk 24 torpedo tubes can be clearly seen, with light-coloured tarpaulins in front of them. (USN)

INDEPENDENCE CLASS

The hulls of nine light cruisers of the *Cleveland* class, whose construction had commenced, were replanned and completed as aircraft carriers (CV). In 1943 they were designated CVL (Light Aircraft Carrier). These were:

Independence (CVL-22) ex-*Amsterdam* (CL-59)
Princeton (CVL-23) ex-*Tallahassee* (CL-61)
Belleau Wood (CVL-24) ex-*Newhaven* (CL-76)
Cowpens (CVL-25) ex-*Huntington* (CL-77)
Monterey (CVL-26) ex-*Dayton* (CL-78)
Langley (CVL-27) ex-*Crown Point*, ex-*Fargo* (CL-85)

Cabot (CVL-28) ex-*Wilmington* (CL-79)
Bataan (CV-29) ex-*Buffalo* (CL-99)
San Jacinto (CVL-30) ex-*Newark* (CL-100)
Cabot (ex-CVL-28) is still in active service with the Spanish Navy, serving as the helicopter carrier *Dédalo*. Five units whose construction had been stopped were reclassified in 1959 as AVT (Aircraft Transports) and scrapped in the early 1960s. Two further units (CVL-24 and -27) served for seven and twelve years respectively with the French Navy as *Bois Belleau* and *Lafayette*, before they were handed back to the American

Navy and scrapped.

The completion of these ships reflected the urgent need for carriers, the construction programme of the *Essex*-class heavy carriers being unable to meet the demand. All nine ships came into active service in 1943. Each had two catapults and 45 aircraft. Up to 90 aircraft could be transported in a stowed condition. One unit *(Princeton)* was lost to Japanese aircraft bombing off Leyte.

▽ *Princeton* (CVL-23).

PRINZ EUGEN

After the German heavy cruiser *Prinz Eugen* had surrendered at Copenhagen in May 1945, she was allotted to the United States by order of the Potsdam Conference. The ship was given the US Navy designation IX-300 (standing for 'unclassified vessels') and, under a mixed German-American crew sailed to Philadelphia where six months were spent inspecting comprehensively her high-pressure superheated steam turbines and other installations. In July 1946 she was towed via the Panama Canal to the Marshall Islands where she withstood the atomic bomb tests at Bikini with relatively little damage. Following these the ship was towed to the vicinity of Kwajalein where she capsized and sank in shallow water in December 1946.

◁ The former German heavy cruiser, *Prinz Eugen* was given the American designation IX-300, but retained her name to the end. Here she is seen during preparations for participation in the Bikini Atoll atomic bomb tests. Both the forward 8in guns had been dismantled. Note that additional American devices to assist the tests have been installed on the bridge. The boot topping is carried rather high. The markings on the hull are of interest. (USN)

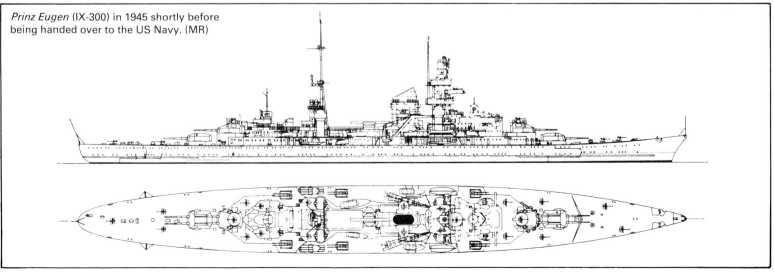

Prinz Eugen (IX-300) in 1945 shortly before being handed over to the US Navy. (MR)

Prinz Eugen (IX-300) photographed in 1945.

ATLANTA

After the light cruiser *Atlanta* (CL-104) had been mothballed in the Reserve Fleet in 1949, with seemingly little chance of being reactivated, she was reclassified in May 1964 as IX-304, brought back into service, and underwent a special conversion. The complete superstructures, funnels and guns were removed to the main deck upon which components and instruments were installed. She was designated 'shock test target ship' and was then subjected to tests involving above- and below-surface explosions. Two complete bridge superstructures, as used in heavy frigates (DLG), and two Macks were installed, and the remaining space was crammed with electronics antennae, weapons and boats. Following a series of shock tests which began in approximately 1965, *Atlanta* was sunk by high-explosive charges in 1970.

◁ The former light cruiser *Atlanta* (CL-104) looked quite remarkable following her conversion as an explosion test ship, when photographed on 1 December 1964. She was ultimately sunk by an explosive charge placed aboard; it lifted her out of the water, she broke in two and sank by the bow and stern. (USN)

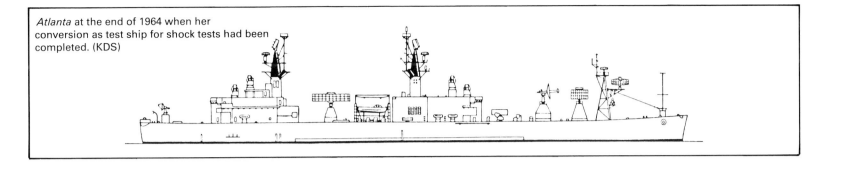

Atlanta at the end of 1964 when her conversion as test ship for shock tests had been completed. (KDS)

SPOKANE

The anti-aircraft cruiser *Spokane* (CLAA-120), which had been mothballed since 1949, was selected in 1966/67 for conversion to a sonar test ship. This involved altering her bows to accommodate a sonar bulge and restructuring her to carry the appropriate display instruments. All guns were removed. The ship could be operated by civilians from the 'Military Sealift Service' and was already reclassified as T-AG-191. The conversion was to have been completed by the end of 1967, but, probably for economy reasons, it was never started, although initial preparations had been made. The ship was then struck off in April 1972.

▽ The former cruiser *Spokane,* now reclassified as AG-191, is seen here in 1973 just before being scrapped. The old pennant number '120' is still visible. To prepare for the intended conversion as a sonar test ship manned by MSC civilian crew, the various weapons and equipment had been removed, probably in 1966. (INRO)

COMPARATIVE TABLES

COMPARATIVE TABLE 1. DISPLACEMENT, DIMENSIONS, COMPLEMENT, ARMOUR AND PROPULSION (BY CLASS)

Pennant No.	Class	Displacement (tons): Standard	Full load	Height (m): Bow	Funnel	Stern	Mast	Dimensions (m): Length overall	Beam	Draught	Complement: Peace	War	Armour (mm): Horizontal	Vertical	Turrets	Conning tower	Propulsion: Power (hp)	Speed (knots)	Endurance /@ knots	Fuel (tons)
CL-4	Omaha	7,050	9,150	10.1	20.7	4.0	33.5	167.8	16.9	6.1	458		76	38	51	51	90,000	34	10,000/15	2,068
CA-24	Pensacola	9,097	11,512	8.8	22.0	5.2	45.5	178.5	19.9	5.9	631		75	51	38 25	203	107,000	32.5	10,000/15	2,116 (max)
CA-26	Northampton	9,006	11,420	10.1	23.2	6.1	42.1	183.0	20.1	5.9	617 29+30+31: 734 + staff		25 51	76	38 57	203	107,000	32.5	10,000/15	1,417-2,108
CA-33	Portland	10,258	12,755	10.1	23.8	5.5	39.1	185.9	20.1	6.4	807 35:917		51 51	102 76	76 51	203	107,000	32.5	10,000/15	1,417-2,125
CA-32	New Orleans	10,136	12,463	8.8	22.9	4.9	35.4	179.2	18.8	6.9	868		76 51	102–127 37	127	165	107,000	32.7	10,500/15	1,241-1,861
CL-40	Brooklyn	9,767 49+50: 10,569	12,207 49+50: 13,300[1]	8.2	20.4	7.0	35.4	185.4	18.8	6.9	868	50: 47/1276	76 51	102–127 38	127	165	100,000	32.5	10,000/15	1,321-1,982
CA-45	Wichita	10,589	13,015	9.2	22.3	7.6	34.5	185.4	18.8	7.2	929		76 51	127 38	127–152 38	203	100,000	33	10,000/15	1,323-1,094
CL-51	Atlanta	6,718	8,340	8.8	20.7	4.0	34.8	165.1	16.2	6.3	26/597	63/785	51	89	38 25	95	75,000	32.5	8,500/15	1,360
CL-95	Oakland	6,718	8,340	8.8	20.7	4.0	34.8	165.1	16.2	6.3	26/597	63/785	51	89	38 25	95	75,000	32.5	8,500/15	1,360
CL-55	Cleveland	11,744	14,131	8.2	23.5	6.7	34.5	186.0	20.2	7.5	54/938	70/1285	76 51	127 38	127	165	100,000	32.5	11,000/15	1,507-2,100
CL-106	Fargo	11,744	14,131	8.2		6.7	32.3	186.0	20.2	7.5	54/938	70/1285	76 51	127 38	127 76	165	100,000	32.5	11,000/15	1,507-2,100
CA-68	Baltimore	14,472	17,031	10.1	26.2	7.6	34.2	205.3	21.6	7.3	59/1083	61/1085 with staff 78/1555	76 51	152	152 76	203	120,000	33	10,000/15	1,200-2,250
CA-122	Oregon City	14,472	17,031	10.1		7.6		205.3	21.6	7.3	59/1083	with staff 85/1660	76 51	152	152 76	203	120,000	33	10,000/15	1,200-2,250
CA-134	Des Moines	17,255	20,934					218.4	23.0	7.9	60/1240	with staff 103/1565	76 51	203 152	152	203	120,000	33	10,500/15	3,006
CL-144	Worcester	14,700	17,997				31.1	207.1	21.5	7.5	70/1286 with staff 99/1302	with staff 1.700	76 51	152 76	102	165	120,000	33	8,000/15	2,400
CAG-1	Boston	13,300	17,500					205.3	21.3	7.6	80/1650						120,000	33	9,000/15	c.2,600
CLG-3	Galveston	10,670	14,600					186.0	20.0	7.8	67/1010						100,000	31.5	7,500/15	c.2,500
CLG-4	Little Rock	10,670	14,600					186.0	20.0	7.8	67/945 with staff 70/1000						100,000	31.5	7,500/15	c.2,500
CG-10	Albany	13,700	17,500					205.3	21.6	8.2	60/950 with staff 85/1120						120,000	32.5	7,000/15	2,500
CGN-9	Long Beach	14,200	17,350					219.8	22.3	9.4	60/950 with staff 80/1080						c.80,000	30+	c.800,000	[Nuclear]
CB-1	Alaska	29,779	34,253					246.4	27.8	9.7	1517		105 57	127 230	127 324	230	150,000	33	12,000/15	3,619
CLC-1	Northampton	13,000	17,204					206.2	21.7	8.1	227/1448[2]						120,000	32		
CLK-1	Norfolk	5,556	8,315					164.7	16.5	7.9[3]	42/504						80,000	34	6,000/20	1,180

[1]CL-50 after refit in 1942: 14,219 tons.   [2]Plus staff: 227/1,448   [3]With SQS-26 sonar dome.

Pennant number, class ship: These give the pennant number of the lead ship of the class and the name of the lead ship (that is to say, of the ship with the lowest pennant number of its class, leaving out of account any other U.S. Navy administrative links there may have been).

Displacement: In tons of 1,016 kilos. The figures on displacement are to be considered only as approximations, as different sources give differing figures.

Height details: These are given in metres and rounded up or down to tenths of metres. These details were taken from an official source; they may therefore be regarded as reliable. The reference line was taken to the waterline.

Dimensions: In tenths of metres rounded up or down. Usually the draught is given for full load condition. It is not known whether (where relevant) the sonar bulges are included in these figures.

Complement: These figures are approximations. Some indicate the maximum possible complement; others the nominal number. In practice however (as was particularly the case in peacetime) the actual number of crew members varied from day to day. Where known, numbers of officers and men are separated by an oblique stroke. Complements were, of course, invariably larger in wartime.

Armour: This was only provided in heavy and light cruisers built towards the end of the Second World War. It is not known whether, in the case of the post-war guided weapon conversions, the vertical armoured bulkheads were removed either partly or completely in the interests of weight reduction. USS *Long Beach* (CGN-9) was completed from higher-specification steel than the cruisers that had preceded her; they had no steel armour plating.

Propulsion: All cruisers mentioned in this book save *Long Beach* had steam turbines. The propulsion unit of CGN-9 consists of two high-pressure water reactors C1W and two sets of geared turbines. The drive consists of two shafts, with an output of 80,000shp. Power and speed figures are mean; in practice they varied considerably according to ship and sea conditions.

COMPARATIVE TABLE 2. CONSTRUCTION

Pennant No.	Name	Fiscal Year	Laid Down	Launched	Commissioned	Decommissioned	Stricken	Builder
CL-4	Omaha		6 Dec 1918	14 Dec 1920	24 Feb 1923	1 Nov 1945	28 Nov 1945	Seattle
CL-5	Milwaukee		13 Dec 1918	24 Mar 1921	20 June 1923	20 April 1944*	16 Mar 1949**	Seattle
CL-6	Cincinnati		15 May 1920	23 May 1921	1 Nov 1924	1 Nov 1945	1946	Seattle
CL-7	Raleigh		16 Aug 1920	25 Oct 1922	6 Feb 1924	2 Nov 1944	1946	Bethlehem, Quincy
CL-8	Detroit		10 Nov 1920	29 July 1922	31 July 1923	11 Jan 1946	1946	Bethlehem, Quincy
CL-9	Richmond		16 Feb 1920	29 Sept 1921	2 July 1923	21 Dec 1945	21 Jan 1946	Cramp
CL-10	Concord		29 Mar 1920	15 Dec 1921	3 Nov 1923	12 Dec 1945	1946	Cramp
CL-11	Trenton		18 Aug 1920	16 April 1923	19 April 1924	19 Dec 1945	1946	Cramp
CL-12	Marblehead		4 Aug 1920	9 Oct 1923	8 Sept 1924	1 Nov 1945	28 Nov 1945	Cramp
CL-13	Memphis		14 Oct 1920	17 April 1924	4 Feb 1925	17 Dec 1945	8 Jan 1946	Cramp
CA-24	Pensacola	1925	27 Oct 1926	25 April 1929	6 Dec 1930	26 Aug 1946	10 Nov 1948*	New York N.Yd.
CA-25	Salt Lake City	1925	9 June 1927	23 Jan 1929	11 Dec 1929	29 Aug 1946	18 June 1948	New York N.Yd.
CA-26	Northampton	1927	12 April 1928	5 Sept 1929	17 May 1930	War loss	13 Jan 1943	Bethlehem, Quincy
CA-27	Chester	1927	6 Mar 1928	3 July 1929	24 June 1930	10 June 1946	1 Mar 1959	New York SB
CA-28	Louisville	1927	4 July 1928	1 Sept 1930	15 Jan 1931	17 June 1946	1 Mar 1959	Puget Sound
CA-29	Chicago	1927	10 Sept 1928	10 April 1930	9 Mar 1931	War loss	22 Feb 1943	Mare Island
CA-30	Houston	1927	1 May 1928	7 Sept 1929	17 June 1930	War loss	8 May 1942	Newport News
CA-31	Augusta	1927	2 July 1928	1 Feb 1930	30 Jan 1931	16 July 1946	1 Mar 1959	Newport News
CA-33	Portland	1929	17 Feb 1930	21 May 1932	23 Feb 1933	12 July 1946	1 Mar 1959	Bethlehem, Quincy
CA-35	Indianapolis	1929	31 Mar 1930	7 Nov 1931	15 Nov 1932	War loss	1 Aug 1945	New York SB
CA-32	New Orleans	1929	14 Mar 1931	12 April 1933	15 Feb 1934	10 Feb 1947	1 Mar 1959	New York N.Yd.
CA-34	Astoria	1929	1 Sept 1930	16 Dec 1933	28 April 1934	War loss	2 Nov 1942	Puget Sound
CA-36	Minneapolis	1929	27 June 1931	6 Sept 1933	19 May 1934	10 Feb 1947	1 Mar 1959	Philadelphia N.Yd.
CA-37	Tuscaloosa	1930	3 Sept 1931	15 Nov 1933	17 Aug 1934	13 Feb 1946	1 Mar 1959	New York SB
CA-38	San Francisco	1930	9 Sept 1931	9 Mar 1933	10 Feb 1934	10 Feb 1946	1 Mar 1959	Mare Island
CA-39	Quincy	1933	15 Nov 1933	19 June 1935	9 June 1936	War loss	2 Nov 1942	Bethlehem, Quincy
CA-44	Vincennes	1933	2 Jan 1934	21 May 1936	24 Feb 1937	War loss	2 Nov 1942	Bethlehem, Quincy
CL-40	Brooklyn	1933	12 Mar 1935	30 Nov 1936	30 Sept 1937	30 Jan 1947	*	New York N.Yd.
CL-41	Philadelphia	1933	28 May 1935	17 Nov 1936	23 Sept 1937	3 Feb 1947	9 Jan 1951*	Philadelphia N.Yd.
CL-42	Savannah	1933	31 May 1934	8 May 1937	10 Mar 1938	3 Feb 1947	1 Mar 1959	New York SB
CL-43	Nashville	1933	24 Jan 1935	2 Oct 1937	6 June 1938	24 June 1946	*	New York SB
CL-46	Phoenix	1934	15 April 1935	12 Mar 1938	3 Oct 1938	3 July 1946	*	New York SB
CL-47	Boise	1934	1 April 1935	3 Dec 1936	12 Aug 1938	1 July 1946	*	Newport News
CL-48	Honolulu	1934	10 Sept 1935	26 Aug 1937	15 June 1938	3 Feb 1947	1 Mar 1959	New York N.Yd.
CL-49	St. Louis	1935	10 Dec 1936	15 April 1938	19 May 1939	20 June 1946	*	Newport News
CL-50	Helena	1935	9 Dec 1936	27 Aug 1939	18 Sept 1939	War loss	15 July 1943	New York N.Yd.
CA-45	Wichita	1934	28 Oct 1935	16 Nov 1937	16 Feb 1939	3 Feb 1947	1 Mar 1959	Philadelphia N.Yd.
CL-51	Atlanta	1938	22 Feb 1940	6 Sept 1941	24 Dec 1941	War loss	13 Jan 1943	Federal
CL-52	Juneau I	1938	27 May 1940	25 Oct 1941	14 Feb 1942	War loss	13 Jan 1943	Bethlehem, Quincy
CL-53	San Diego	1938	27 Mar 1940	26 July 1941	10 Jan 1942	4 Nov 1946	1 Mar 1959	Bethlehem, Quincy
CL-54	San Juan	1938	15 May 1940	6 Sept 1941	28 Feb 1942	9 Nov 1946	1 Mar 1959	Bethlehem, Quincy
CL-95	Oakland	1940	15 July 1941	23 Oct 1942	17 July 1943	1 July 1949	1 Mar 1959	Bethlehem, San Francisco
CL-96	Reno	1940	1 Aug 1941	23 Dec 1942	28 Dec 1943	4 Nov 1946	1 Mar 1959	Bethlehem, San Francisco
CL-97	Flint	1940	23 Oct 1942	25 Jan 1944	31 Aug 1944	6 May 1947	1 Sept 1965	Bethlehem, San Francisco

Pennant No.	Name	Fiscal Year	Laid Down	Launched	Commissioned	Decommissioned	Stricken	Builder
CL-98	Tucson	1940	23 Dec 1942	3 Sept 1944	3 Feb 1945	11 June 1949	1 June 1966	Bethlehem, San Francisco
CL-119	Juneau II	1943	15 Sept 1944	15 July 1945	15 Feb 1946	22 Mar 1955	1 Nov 1959	Federal
CL-120	Spokane	1943	15 Nov 1944	22 Sept 1945	17 May 1946	27 Feb 1950	15 April 1972	Federal
CL-121	Fresno	1943	12 Feb 1945	5 Mar 1946	27 Nov 1946	17 May 1949	1 April 1965	Federal
CL-55	Cleveland	1940	1 July 1940	1 Nov 1941	15 June 1942	7 Feb 1947	1 Mar 1959	New York SB
CL-56	Columbia	1940	19 Aug 1940	17 Dec 1941	29 July 1942	30 Nov 1946	1 Mar 1959	New York SB
CL-57	Montpelier	1940	2 Dec 1940	12 Feb 1942	9 Sept 1942	24 Jan 1947	1 Mar 1959	New York SB
CL-58	Denver	1940	26 Dec 1940	4 April 1942	15 Oct 1942	7 Feb 1947	1 Mar 1959	New York SB
CL-60	Santa Fe	1940	7 June 1941	10 June 1942	24 Nov 1942	19 Oct 1946	1 Mar 1959	New York SB
CL-62	Birmingham	1940	17 Feb 1941	20 Mar 1942	29 Jan 1943	2 Jan 1947	1 Mar 1959	Newport News
CL-63	Mobile	1940	14 April 1941	15 May 1942	24 Mar 1943	9 May 1947	1 Mar 1959	Newport News
CL-64	Vincennes II	1940	7 Mar 1942	17 July 1943	21 Jan 1944	20 Mar 1947	1 April 1966	Bethlehem, Quincy
CL-65	Pasadena	1940	6 Feb 1943	28 Dec 1943	8 June 1944	12 Jan 1950	1 Dec 1970	Bethlehem, Quincy
CL-66	Springfield	1940	13 Feb 1943	9 Mar 1944	9 Sept 1944	31 Jan 1950	see CLG-7	Bethlehem, Quincy
CL-67	Topeka	1940	21 April 1943	19 Aug 1944	23 Dec 1944	18 June 1949	see CLG-8	Bethlehem, Quincy
CL-80	Biloxi	1940	9 July 1941	23 Feb 1943	31 Aug 1943	18 May 1946	1 Sept 1961	Newport News
CL-81	Houston II	1940	4 Aug 1941	19 June 1943	20 Dec 1943	15 Dec 1947	1 Mar 1959	Newport News
CL-82	Providence	1940	27 July 1943	28 Dec 1944	15 May 1945	14 June 1949	see CLG-6	Bethlehem, Quincy
CL-83	Manchester	1940	25 Sept 1944	5 Mar 1946	29 Oct 1946	27 June 1956	1 April 1960	Bethlehem, Quincy
CL-86	Vicksburg	1940	26 Oct 1942	14 Dec 1943	12 June 1944	30 June 1947	1 Oct 1962	Newport News
CL-87	Duluth	1940	9 Nov 1942	13 Jan 1944	18 Sept 1944	25 June 1949	1 Jan 1960	Newport News
CL-89	Miami	1940	2 Aug 1941	8 Dec 1942	28 Dec 1943	30 June 1947	1 Sept 1961	Cramp
CL-90	Astoria II	1940	6 Sept 1941	6 Mar 1943	17 May 1944	1 July 1949	1 Nov 1949	Cramp
CL-91	Oklahoma City	1940	8 Dec 1942	20 Feb 1944	22 Dec 1944	30 June 1947	see CLG-5	Cramp
CL-92	Little Rock	1940	6 Mar 1943	27 Aug 1944	17 June 1945	24 June 1949	see CLG-4	Cramp
CL-93	Galveston	1940	20 Feb 1944	22 April 1945	Completed but never commissioned		see CLG-3	Cramp
CL-101	Amsterdam	1941	3 Mar 1943	25 April 1944	8 Jan 1945	30 June 1947	2 Jan 1971	Newport News
CL-102	Portsmouth	1941	28 June 1943	20 Sept 1944	25 June 1945	15 June 1949	1 Dec 1970	Newport News
CL-103	Wilkes Barre	1942	14 Dec 1942	24 Dec 1943	1 July 1944	9 June 1947	15 Jan 1971	New York SB
CL-104	Atlanta	1942	25 Jan 1943	6 Feb 1944	3 Dec 1944	1 July 1949	see IX-304	New York SB
CL-105	Dayton	1942	8 Mar 1943	19 Mar 1944	7 Jan 1945	1 Mar 1949	1 Sept 1961	New York SB
CL-106	Fargo	1942	23 Aug 1943	22 Feb 1945	9 Dec 1945	14 Feb 1950	1 Mar 1970	New York SB
CL-107	Huntington	1942	4 Oct 1943	8 April 1945	23 Feb 1946	15 June 1949	1 Sept 1961	New York SB

Pennant No.	Name	Fiscal Year	Laid Down	Launched	Commissioned	Decommissioned	Stricken	Builder
CA-68	Baltimore	1940	26 May 1941	28 July 1942	15 April 1943	31 May 1956	15 Feb 1971	Bethlehem, Quincy
CA-69	Boston	1940	30 June 1941	26 Aug 1942	30 June 1943	12 Mar 1946	see CAG-1	Bethlehem, Quincy
CA-70	Canberra	1940	3 Sept 1941	19 April 1943	14 Oct 1943	7 Mar 1947	see CAG-2	Bethlehem, Quincy
CA-71	Quincy II	1940	9 Oct 1941	23 June 1943	15 Dec 1943	19 Oct 1946	1 Oct 1973	Bethlehem, Quincy
					31 Jan 1952	2 July 1954		
CA-72	Pittsburgh	1940	3 Feb 1943	22 Feb 1944	10 Oct 1944	7 Mar 1947	1 July 1973	Bethlehem, Quincy
					25 Sept 1951	28 Aug 1956		
CA-73	St. Paul	1940	3 Feb 1943	16 Sept 1944	17 Feb 1945	5 May 1971	1 Dec 1973	Bethlehem, Quincy
CA-74	Columbus	1940	18 June 1943	30 Nov 1944	8 June 1945	8 May 1959	see CG-12	Bethlehem, Quincy
CA-75	Helena	1940	9 Sept 1943	28 April 1945	4 Sept 1945	29 June 1963	1 Jan 1974	Bethlehem, Quincy
CA-130	Bremerton	1942	1 Feb 1943	2 July 1944	28 April 1945	9 April 1948	1 Oct 1973	New York SB
					23 Nov 1951	29 July 1960		
CA-131	Fall River	1942	12 April 1943	13 Aug 1944	1 July 1945	31 Oct 1947	19 Feb 1971	New York SB
CA-132	Macon	1942	14 June 1943	15 Oct 1944	26 Aug 1945	12 April 1950	1 Nov 1969	New York SB
					16 Oct 1950	10 Mar 1961		
CA-133	Toledo	1942	13 Sept 1943	6 May 1945	27 Oct 1946	21 May 1960	1 Jan 1974	New York SB
CA-135	Los Angeles	1942	28 July 1943	20 Aug 1944	22 July 1945	9 April 1948	1 Jan 1974	Philadelphia N.Yd.
					27 Jan 1951	15 Nov 1963		
CA-136	Chicago II	1942	28 July 1943	20 Aug 1944	10 Jan 1945	6 June 1947	see CG-11	Philadelphia N.Yd.
CA-122	Oregon City	1942	8 April 1944	9 June 1945	16 Feb 1946	15 Dec 1947	1 Nov 1970	Bethlehem, Quincy
CA-123	Albany	1942	6 Mar 1944	30 June 1945	15 June 1946	30 June 1958	see CG-10	Bethlehem, Quincy
CA-124	Rochester	1942	29 May 1944	28 Aug 1945	20 Dec 1946	10 Aug 1961	1 Oct 1974	Bethlehem, Quincy
CA-134	Des Moines	1942	28 May 1945	27 Sept 1946	16 Nov 1948	14 July 1961		Bethlehem, Quincy
CA-139	Salem	1942	4 July 1945	25 Mar 1947	14 May 1949	30 Jan 1959		Bethlehem, Quincy
CA-148	Newport News	1943	1 Nov 1945	6 Mar 1948	29 Jan 1949	27 June 1975	30 July 1978	Newport News
CL-144	Worcester	1943	29 Jan 1945	4 Feb 1947	26 June 1948	19 Nov 1958	1 Dec 1970	New York SB
CL-145	Roanoke	1943	15 May 1945	16 June 1947	4 April 1949	31 Oct 1958	1 Dec 1970	New York SB
CAG-1	Boston		11 April 1952	4 Oct 1955	1 Nov 1955	5 May 1970	6 May 1974	New York SB
CAG-2	Canberra		30 June 1952	1 June 1956	15 June 1956	16 Feb 1970	30 June 1978	New York SB
CLG-3	Galveston		15 Aug 1956	14 Sept 1959	28 May 1958	25 May 1970	21 Dec 1973	Philadelphia N.Yd.
CLG-8	Topeka		18 Aug 1957	14 April 1960	26 Mar 1960	5 June 1969	8 Dec 1973	New York N.Yd.
CLG-4	Little Rock		30 Jan 1957	6 May 1960	3 June 1960	29 Nov 1976	29 Nov 1976	Philadelphia N.Yd.
CLG-5	Oklahoma City		21 May 1957	31 Aug 1960	7 Sept 1960	15 Dec 1979	15 Dec 1980*	Bethlehem, Quincy Coast Steel, San Francisco

Pennant No.	Name	Fiscal Year	Laid Down	Launched	Commissioned	Decommissioned	Stricken	Builder
CLG-6	*Providence*		1 June 1957	3 Dec 1959	17 Sept 1959	1 July 1973	30 June 1978	Boston N.Yd.
CLG-7	*Springfield*		1 Aug 1957	6 Jan 1960	2 July 1960	15 Dec 1973	30 June 1978	Bethlehem, Quincy
CG-10	*Albany*		2 Jan 1959	2 Nov 1962	3 Nov 1962	29 Sept 1980	1984*	Boston N.Yd.
CG-11	*Chicago*		1 July 1959	1 Dec 1963	2 May 1964	1 Mar 1980	31 Jan 1984*	San Francisco N.Yd.
CG-12	*Columbus*		1 June 1959	30 Nov 1962	1 Dec 1962	31 Jan 1975	9 Aug 1976	Puget Sound
CGN-9	*Long Beach*	1957	2 Dec 1957	14 July 1959	9 Sept 1961			Bethlehem, Quincy
CB-1	*Alaska*	1940	17 Dec 1941	15 Aug 1943	17 June 1944	17 Feb 1947	1 June 1960	New York SB
CB-2	*Guam*	1940	2 Feb 1942	12 Nov 1943	17 Sept 1944	17 Feb 1947	1 June 1960	New York SB
CLC-1	*Northampton*	1942	31 Aug 1944	27 Jan 1951	7 Mar 1953	14 Jan 1970	1 Dec 1977	Bethlehem, Quincy
CLK-1	*Norfolk*	1941	1 Sept 1949	29 Dec 1951	4 Mar 1953	15 Jan 1970	1 Nov 1973	New York SB

COMPARATIVE TABLE 3. ARMAMENT

Pennant No.	Name	Year	Main Armament	Secondary Armament	Torpedo Tubes	Catapults	Aircraft	Remarks
CL-4	*Omaha*	1939	Twelve 6in/53	Eight 3in/50, two 3pdr, eight 0.5in MG	6**	2	2	** initially ten torpedo tubes
		1943	Ten 6in/53	Eight 3in/50, twelve 28mm, eight 20mm				
		1945	Ten 6in/53	Eight 3in/50, six 40mm, fourteen 20mm (approx)				
CL-5	*Milwaukee*	1939	Twelve 6in/53	as CL-4	6 ***	2	2	*20 April 1944 to USSR as *Murmansk*
		1943	Ten 6in/53	as CL-4				** returned to USA
		1944	Ten 6in/53	as CL-4				*** as CL-4
CL-6	*Cincinnati*	1939	Ten 6in/53	as CL-4	6 **	2	2	** as CL-4
		1942	Ten 6in/53	as CL-4				
		1944	Ten 6in/53	as CL-4				
CL-7	*Raleigh*	1939	Ten 6in/53	as CL-4	6 **	2	2	** as CL-4
		1942	Ten 6in/53	as CL-4 1945				
		1945	Ten 6in/53	as above				
CL-8	*Detroit*	1939	Ten 6in/53	as CL-4	6 ** ***	2	2	** as CL-4
		1942	Ten 6in/53	as CL-7				*** torpedo tubes removed in 1945
		1945	Ten 6in/53	as 1942				
CL-9	*Richmond*	1939	Twelve 6in/53	as CL-4	6 **	2	2	** as CL-4
		1943	Ten 6in/53	as CL-4 1945				
		1945	Ten 6in/53	as above				
CL-10	*Concord*	1939	Twelve 6in/53	as CL-4	6 **	2	2	** as CL-4
		1945	Ten 6in/53	as CL-4 1945				
CL-11	*Trenton*	1939	Twelve 6in/53	as CL-4	6 **	2	2	** as CL-4
		1943	Ten 6in/53	as CL-4 1945				
		1945	Ten 6in/53	as above				
CL-12	*Marblehead*	1939	Ten 6in/53	as CL-4	6 **	2	2	** as CL-4
		1944	Ten 6in/53	as CL-4 1945				
CL-13	*Memphis*	1939	Twelve 6in/53	as CL-4	6 **	2	2	** as CL-4
		1944	Twelve 6in/53	as CL-4 1945				
CA-24	*Pensacola*	1939	Ten 8in/55	Eight 5in/25, two 3pdr, eight 0.5in MG	6**	2***	4	* sunk after nuclear tests
		1941	Ten 8in/55	Eight 5in/25, sixteen 28mm, nine 20mm				** torpedo tubes removed before the war
		1945	Ten 8in/55	Eight 5in/25, twenty-eight 40mm, twenty-two 20mm				*** starboard catapult removed 1945
CA-25	*Salt Lake City*	1939	Ten 8in/55	Eight 5in/25, two 3pdr, eight 0.5in MG	6**	2	4	** as CA-24
		1944	Ten 8in/55	Eight 5in/25, twenty-four 40mm, twenty-one 20mm				*** as CA-24
		1945	Ten 8in/55	as above, but twenty 20mm				
CA-26	*Northampton*	1930	Nine 8in/55	Four 5in/25	6 **	2	4	* 30 Nov 1942 off Tassafaronga
		1939	Nine 8in/55	Eight 5in/25, two 3pdr, eight 0.5in MG				** six torpedo tubes removed by 1945
CA-27	*Chester*	1930	as CA-26	as CA-26	6**	2***	4	** as CA-26
		1939	as CA-26	as CA-26				1942 also sixteen 28mm
		1945	as CA-26	Eight 5in/25, eight 40mm, twenty-six 20mm				*** from May 1945 only one catapult
CA-28	*Louisville*	1931	as CA-26	as CA-26 1930	6**	2***	4	** as CA-26
		1939	as CA-26	as CA-26 1939				** from April 1945 only one catapult
		1942	as CA-26	Eight 5in/25, sixteen 28mm, ?20mm				
		1945	as CA-26	Eight 5in/25, eight 40mm, twenty-six 20mm				
CA-29	*Chicago*	1939	as CA-26	as CA-26	6**	2	4	* 30 Jan 1943 off the Solomons
		1942	as CA-26	Eight 5in/25, sixteen 28mm, twenty 20mm				** as CA-26
CA-30	*Houston*	1939	as CA-26	as CA-26 1939	**	2	4	* 1 Mar 1942 in the Java Sea
		1942	as CA-26	Eight 5in/25, sixteen 28mm, eight 0.5in MG				** as CA-26
CA-31	*Augusta*	1939	as CA-26	as CA-26 1939	**	2***	4	** as CA-26
		1945	as CA-26	Eight 5in/25, twenty-four 40mm, twenty 20mm				*** 1942 also sixteen 28mm; 1945 catapults removed
CA-33	*Portland*	1934	Nine 8in/55	Eight 5in/25, eight 0.5in MG		2	4	
		1942	Nine 8in/55	Eight 5in/25, sixteen 28mm, twelve 20mm				
		1943	Nine 8in/55	Eight 5in/25, twenty 40mm, eighteen 20mm				
		1945	Nine 8in/55	Eight 5in/25, twenty-four 40mm, twelve 20mm				

Pennant No.	Name	Year	Main Armament	Secondary Armament	Torpedo Tubes	Catapults	Aircraft	Remarks
CA-35	Indianapolis	1934	as CA-33	as CA-33 1934		2**	4	* 30 July 1945 off Savo Island
		1942	as CA-33	Eight 5in/25, sixteen 28mm, twelve 20mm				** 1945 now only one catapult
		1944	as CA-33	Eight 5in/25, twenty 40mm, nineteen 20mm				*** end of 1942 twenty-four 28mm, sixteen 20mm
		1945	as CA-33	Eight 5in/25, twenty-four 40mm, fourteen 20mm				Mid-1945 now only eight 20mm
CA-32	New Orleans	1939	as CA-33	as CA-33 1934		2*	4	* 1945 now only one catapult
		1942	as CA-33	Eight 5in/25, sixteen 28mm, thirteen 20mm				
		1945	as CA-33	Eight 5in/25, twenty-four 40mm, twenty-eight 20mm				
CA-34	Astoria	1939	as CA-33	as CA-33 1934		2	4	* 9 Aug 1942 off Savo Island
		1941	as CA-33	Eight 5in/25, sixteen 28mm, approx. eight 20mm				
CA-36	Minneapolis	1939	as CA-33	as CA-33 1934		2	4	
		1945	as CA-33	Eight 5in/55, sixteen 40mm, approx. eight 20mm				
CA-37	Tuscaloosa	1939	as CA-33	as CA-33 1934		2	4	
		1945	as CA-33	Eight 5in/25, twenty-four 40mm, sixteen 20mm				
CA-38	San Francisco	1934	as CA-33	Eight 5in/25, eight 0.5in MG		2	4	
		1940	as CA-33	Eight 5in/25, four 3in/50 eight 0.5in MG				
		1942	as CA-33	Eight 5in/25, sixteen 28mm, twelve 20mm				
		1944	as CA-33	Eight 5in/25, twenty-four 40mm, twenty-six 20mm				
CA-39	Quincy	1936	as CA-33	as CA-38 1934		2	4	* 9 Aug 1942 off Savo Island
		1942	as CA-33	Eight 5in/25, sixteen 28mm, eight 20mm				
CA-44	Vincennes	1939	as CA-33	as CA-33 1934		2	4	* 9 Aug 1942 off Savo Island
CL-40	Brooklyn	1939	Fifteen 6in/47	Eight 5in/25, eight 0.5in MG		2	4	* 9 Jan 1951 to Chile as O'Higgins
		1945	Fifteen 6in/47	Eight 5in/25, twenty-eight 40mm, twenty 20mm				** End of 1941 also twenty-eight 28mm
CL-41	Philadelphia	1939	as CL-40	as CL-40 1939		2	4	* 21 Aug 1951 to Brazil as Barroso
		1942	as CL-40	Eight 5in/25, sixteen 28mm, ? 20mm				
		1945	as Cl-40	Eight 5in/25, twenty-eight 40mm, twenty 20mm				
CL-42	Savannah	1939	as CL-40	as CL-40 1939		2	4	
		1945	as CL-40	Eight 5in/25, twenty-eight 40mm, twenty-four 20mm				
CL-43	Nashville	1939	as CL-40	as CL-40 1939		2	4	* 9 Jan 1951 to Chile as Prat
		1942	as CL-40	Eight 5in/25, sixteen 28mm, ? 20mm				
		1945	as CL-40	Eight 5in/25, twenty-eight 40mm, eighteen 20mm				
CL-46	Phoenix	1939	as CL-40	as CL-40		2	4	* 17 Oct 1951 to Argentina as General Belgrano
		1945	as CL-40	Eight 5in/25, eight 40mm, nineteen 20mm				(1956)
CL-47	Boise	1939	as CL-40	as CL-40 1939		2**	4	* 11 Jan 1951 to Argentina as Nueve de Julio.
		1945	as CL-40	Eight 5in/25, twenty-four 40mm, eighteen 20mm				** Jan 1945 now only one catapult
CL-48	Honolulu	1939	as CL-40	as CL-40 1939		2	4	
		1942	as CL-40	Eight 5in/25, eight 28mm, twelve 20mm				
		1945	as CL-40	Eight 5in/38, twenty-eight 40mm, twenty 20mm				
CL-49	St. Louis	1940	as CL-40	Eight 5in/38, eight 0.5in MG		2	4	* 9 Jan 1951 to Brazil as Tamandaré
		1942	as CL-40	Eight 5in/38, sixteen 28mm, ? 40mm, ? 20mm				
		1945	as CL-40	Eight 5in/38, twenty-eight 40mm, eight 20mm				
CL-50	Helena	1940	as CL-40	as CL-49 1940		2	4	* 6 July 1943 off Kula Gulf
		1943	as CL-40	Eight 5in/38, sixteen 40mm, twelve 20mm				
CA-45	Wichita	1939	Nine 8in/55	Eight 5in/38, eight 0.5in MG		2	2	
		1945	Nine 8in/55	Eight 5in/38, twenty-four 40mm, eighteen 20mm				
CL-51	Atlanta	1942	Sixteen 5in/38	Twelve 28mm, eight 20mm	8			* 13 Nov 1942 off Guadalcanal
CL-52	Juneau I	1942	as CL-51	as CL-51	8			* 13 Nov 1942 off Guadalcanal
CL-53	San Diego	1942	as CL-51	Sixteen 28mm	8			
		1944	as CL-51	Ten 40mm, fifteen 20mm, previously only eight 40mm				
CL-54	San Juan	1942	as CL-51	as CL-53	8			
		1944	as CL-51	Fourteen 40mm, nine 20mm				
CL-95	Oakland	1943	Twelve 5in/38	Sixteen 40mm, fourteen 20mm	8*			* 1945 removed
		1945	Twelve 5in/38	Twenty-four 40mm, sixteen 20mm				
CL-96	Reno	1943	as CL-95	Sixteen 40mm, sixteen 20mm	8			
		1945	as CL-95	Sixteen 40mm, sixteen 20mm				
CL-97	Flint	1944	as CL-95	Sixteen 40mm, sixteen 20mm	8			
CL-98	Tucson	1945	as CL-95	Sixteen 40mm, sixteen 20mm	8**			** 1945 removed
CL-119	Juneau II	1946	as CL-95	Twenty-eight 40mm				
		1952	as CL-95	Fourteen 3in/50				
CL-120	Spokane	1946	as CL-95	Twenty-eight 40mm				
CL-121	Fresno	1946	as CL-95	Twenty-eight 40mm				
CL-55	Cleveland	1942	Twelve 6in/47	Twelve 5in/38, twelve 40mm, twenty 20mm		2	4	
		1943	Twelve 6in/47	Twelve 5in/38, twenty-eight 40mm, thirteen 20mm				
CL-56	Columbia	1943	as CL-55	as CL-55		2	4	
CL-57	Montpelier	1943	as CL-55	Twelve 5in/38, twenty-four 40mm, seventeen 20mm		2	4	
CL-58	Denver	1945	as CL-55	as CL-57		2	4	
CL-60	Santa Fe	1943	as CL-55	as CL-57, but twenty-one 20mm		2	4	

Pennant No.	Name	Year	Main Armament	Secondary Armament	Torpedo Tubes	Catapults	Aircraft	Remarks
CL-62	*Birmingham*	1943	as CL-55	Twelve 5in, twenty-eight 40mm, twenty-one 20mm		2	4	
CL-63	*Mobile*	1943	as CL-55	as CL-62		2	4	
CL-64	*Vincennes II*	1944	as CL-55	Twelve 5in, twenty-four 40mm, twenty-one 20mm		2	4	
CL-65	*Pasadena*	1944	as CL-55	as CL-64		2*	4	* 1948 now only port catapult
CL-66	*Springfield*	1944	as CL-55	as CL-64		2*	4	* as CL-65
CL-67	*Topeka*	1945	as CL-55	Twelve 5in/38, twenty-eight 40mm, ten 20mm		2	4	
CL-80	*Biloxi*	1943	as CL-55	Twelve 6in/38, twenty-four 40mm, twenty-one 20mm		2	4	
CL-81	*Houston II*	1944	as CL-55	as CL-80		2	4	
CL-82	*Providence*	1945	as CL-55	Twelve 6in/38, twenty-eight 40mm, ten 20mm		2	4	
CL-83	*Manchester*	1946	as CL-55	Twelve 6in/38, twenty-eight 40mm		1*	2	* 1948 port catapult only. By 1951 this had disappeared
		1948	as CL-55	Twelve 6in/38, twenty-eight 40mm				
		1952	as CL-55	Twelve 6in/38, sixteen 3in/50				
		1955	as CL-55	Twelve 6in/38, sixteen 3in/50				
CL-86	*Vicksburg*	1944	as CL-55	Twelve 6in/38, twenty-eight 40mm, ten 20mm		2	4	
CL-87	*Duluth*	1945	as CL-55	as CL-86		2	4	
CL-89	*Miami*	1944	as CL-55	as CL-86		2	4	
CL-90	*Astoria II*	1944	as CL-55	as CL-86		2	4	
CL-91	*Oklahoma City*	1945	as CL-55	as CL-86		2	4	
CL-92	*Little Rock*	1945	as CL-55	as CL-86		2	4	
CL-93	*Galveston*	1946	as CL-55	Twelve 6in/38, ? 40mm		*		* It is doubtful if catapults were fitted
CL-101	*Amsterdam*	1945	as CL-55	as CL-86		2	4	
CL-102	*Portsmouth*	1945	as CL-55	as CL-86		2*	4	* 1946 now only port catapult
CL-103	*Wilkes Barre*	1945	as CL-55	as CL-86		2	4	
CL-104	*Atlanta*	1945	as CL-55	as CL-86		2	4	
CL-105	*Dayton*	1945	as CL-55	as CL-86		2*	4	* 1948 now only port catapult
CL-106	*Fargo*	1946	as CL-55	Twelve 6in/38, twenty-eight 40mm, twenty-one 20mm		2*	4	* 1948 now only port catapult
CL-107	*Huntington*	1946	as CL-55	as CL-106		2*	4	* as CL-106
CA-68	*Baltimore*	1943	Nine 8in/55	Twelve 6in/38, forty-eight 40mm, twenty-four 20mm		2*	4	* Catapults removed in the early 1950s
		1955	Nine 8in/55	Twelve 6in/38, forty-eight 40mm				
CA-69	*Boston*	1943	as CA-68	as CA-68 1943		2	4	
CA-70	*Canberra*	1943	as CA-68	as CA-68 1943		2	4	
CA-71	*Quincy II*	1944	as CA-68	as CA-68 1943		2*	4	* From 1951 no catapults remaining
		1952	as CA-68	Twelve 6in/38, forty-eight 40mm				
CA-72	*Pittsburgh*	1944	as CA-68	as CA-68 1943, but twenty-two 20mm		2*	4	* From 1951 no catapults remaining
		1955	as CA-68	Twelve 6in/38, twenty 3in/50				
CA-73	*St. Paul*	1945	as CA-68	as CA-72 1944		2*	4	* From 1950 no catapults remaining
		1951	as CA-68	Twelve 6in/38, twenty 3in/50				
		1969	as CA-68	Ten 6in/38, twelve 3in/50				
CA-74	*Columbus*	1945	as CA-68	as CA-72 1944		2*	4	* From 1949 no catapults remaining
		1959	as CA-68	Twelve 5in/38, twenty 3in/50				
CA-75	*Helena*	1945	as CA-68	as CA-72 1944		2*	4	* From the early 1950s no catapults remaining
		1953	as CA-68	Twelve 6in/38, twenty 3in/50				
		1957	as CA-68	Twelve 6in/38, eighteen 3in/50, three Regulus I				
		1963	as CA-68	Twelve 6in/38, fourteen 3in/50				
CA-130	*Bremerton*	1945	as CA-68	Twelve 6in/38, forty-eight 40mm, twenty-eight 20mm		2*	4	* From c.1951 no catapults remaining
		1952	as CA-68	Twelve 6in/38, forty-eight 40mm				
		1955	as CA-68	Twelve 6in/38, twenty 3in/50				
		1960	as CA-68	Twelve 6in/38, fourteen 3in/50				
CA-131	*Fall River*	1945	as CA-68	as CA-130 1945		2	4	
CA-132	*Macon*	1945	as CA-68	as CA-130 1945		2*	4	By 1948 catapults had been replaced by a raised helicopter platform (but this was very quickly removed)
		1946	as CA-68	Twelve 5in/38, thirty-six 40mm				
		1954	as CA-68	Twelve 5in/38, twenty 3in/50				
		1958	as CA-68	Twelve 5in/38, fourteen 3in/50, three Regulus I				
CA-133	*Toledo*	1946	as CA-68	Twelve 5in/38, forty-four 40mm, twenty-eight 20mm		2*	4	Catapults removed in about 1950
		1947	as CA-68	Twelve 5in/38, thirty-six 40mm				
		1952	as CA-68	Twelve 5in/38, twenty 3in/50				
		1956	as CA-68	Twelve 5in/38, fourteen 3in/50, three Regulus I				
CA-135	*Los Angeles*	1945	as CA-68	Twelve 5in/38 forty-eight 40mm, twenty-eight 20mm		2*	4	* Catapults removed in early 1950s
		1952	as CA-68	Twelve 5in/38, sixteen 3in/50				
		1958	as CA-68	Twelve 5in/38, fourteen 3in/50, three Regulus I				
		1962	as CA-68	as above, but without Regulus				
CA-136	*Chicago II*	1945	as CA-68	Twelve 5in/38, forty-eight 40mm, twenty-eight 20mm		2	4	
CA-122	*Oregon City*	1946	as CA-68	Twelve 5in/38, forty-eight 40mm, twenty 20mm		2	4	

Pennant No.	Name	Year	Main Armament	Secondary Armament	Torpedo Tubes	Catapults	Aircraft	Remarks
CA-123	*Albany*	1946	as CA-68	as CA-122 1946	2*	4		* c.1949 now only port catapult
		1950	as CA-68	Twelve 5in/38, sixteen 3in/50				1950 no catapults remained
		1957	as CA-68	as above				
CA-124	*Rochester*	1946	as CA-68	as CA-122 1946	2*	4		* From about 1950 no catapults remained
		1953	as CA-68	Twelve 5in/38, twenty 3in/50				
		1956	as CA-68	as above				
CA-134	*Des Moines*	1948	Nine 8in/55	Twelve 5in/38, twenty 3in/50**, some 20mm	2*	4		* From 1949 no catapults remained
		1950	Nine 8in/55	Twelve 5in/38, twenty-four 3in/50				** Four 3in/50 were missing from the very beginning
		1959	Nine 8in/55	Twelve 5in/38, twenty-two 3in/50				
CA-139	*Salem*	1949	as CA-134	as CA-134 1948				
		1952	as CA-134	Twelve 5in/38, twenty-four 3in/50				
CA-148	*Newport News*	1949	as CA-134	as CA-134 1948				
		1962	as CA-134	Twelve 5in/38, sixteen 3in/50				
		1966	as CA-134	Now only eight 3in/50				
		1974	as CA-134	No 3in/50 remaining				
CL-144	*Worcester*	1948	Twelve 6in/47	Twenty-four 3in/50, twelve 20mm	2*			* 1948 catapults removed
		1958	Twelve 6in/47	Twenty-two 3in/50				
CL-145	*Roanoke*	1949	as CA-144	as CL-144 1948				
		1958	as CA-144	as CL-144 1958				
CAG-1	*Boston*	1955	Six 8in/55	Ten 5in/38, twelve 3in/50, four Terrier 2 Mk 10				
		1957	Six 8in/55	as above, but eight 3in/50				
		1970	Six 8in/55	as above, but Terrier inoperative				
CAG-2	*Canberra*	1957	as CAG-1	as CAG-1 1957				
		1970	as CAG-1	Ten 5in/38, eight 3in/50, Terrier inoperative				
CLG-3	*Galveston*	1958	Six 6in/47	Six 5in/38, two Talos 2 Mk 7				
		1970	Six 6in/47	as above				
CLG-8	*Topeka*	1960	Six 6in/47	Six 5in/38, two Terrier 2 Mk 9				
		1969	Six 6in/47	as above				
CLG-4	*Little Rock*	1960	Three 6in/47	Two 5in/38, one Talos 2 Mk 7				Museum ship in Buffalo, N.J. from 21 June 1967
		1976	Three 6in/47	as above				
CLG-5	*Oklahoma City*	1960	Three 6in/47	Two 5in/38, one Talos 2 Mk 7				After being stricken-off, she has been preserved at Bremerton with almost all armament and equipment. Presumably she will be a museum ship
		1979	Three 6in/47	as above				
CLG-6	*Providence*	1959	Three 6in/47	Two 5in/38, one Terrier 2 Mk 9				
		1973	Three 6in/47	as above				
CLG-7	*Springfield*	1960	Three 6in/47	Two 5in/38, one Terrier I Mk 9				
		1973	Three 6in/47	as above				
CG-10	*Albany*	1962		One Talos 2 Mk 12, two Tartar 2 Mk II, One ASROC 8	6 Mk 32			
		1963	Two 5in/38	as above				
		1980	Two 5in/38	as above, but Talos inoperative in 1978				
CG-11	*Chicago*	1964	Two 5in/38	One Talos 2 Mk 12, two Tartar 2 Mk II, One ASROC 8	6 Mk 32			
		1980	Two 5in/38	as above, but Talos inoperative in 1978				
CG-12	*Columbus*	1962	as CG-10	as CG-10 1962	6 Mk 32			
		1975	as CG-10	as CG-10 1963				
CGN-9	*Long Beach*	1961		Two Terrier 2 Mk 10, one Talos 2 Mk 12, one ASROC 8	6 Mk 32			
		1962	Two 5in/38	as above	as above			
		1983	Two 5in/38	Two Terrier 2 Mk 10, two Phalanx 6, one ASROC 8, two Harpoon 4	as above			
CB-1	*Alaska*	1944	Nine 12in/50	Twelve 5in/38, fifty-six 40mm, thirty-four 20mm		2	4	
CB-2	*Guam*	1944	as CB-1	as CB-1		2	4	
CLC-1	*Northampton*	1953	Eight 5in/54	Eight 3in/50				
		1958	as 1953	Eight 3in/70				
		1968	One 5in/54					
CLK-1	*Norfolk*	1953	Eight 3in/50	Eight 20mm, four Weapon Alfa Mk 108	8 Mk 24			
		1957	Eight 3in/50	Four Weapon Alfa Mk 108	as above			
		1960	Eight 3in/50	Two Weapon Alfa Mk 108, one ASROC 8	6 Mk 32			
		1970	Eight 3in/50	One ASROC 8	as above			

COMPARATIVE TABLE 4. ELECTRONICS

Pennant No.	Name	Detection Radar Installations Date	Instruments	Fire Control Installations Date	Instruments
CL-4	Omaha			1940	Mk 16 RF
		Feb 1943	SC-2, SG	Feb 1943	2 Mk 3, several Mk 50/Mk 10 several Mk 44
CL-5	Milwaukee			1940	Mk 16 RF
		1942	SC-1, SG	1942	1 Mk 3, several Mk 50/Mk 10 several Mk 44
		Aug 1943	SK, 2 SG	Aug 1943	2 Mk 3 otherwise as above
CL-6	Cincinnati			1940	Mk 16 RF
		July 1942	CXAM-1, SG	July 1942	1 Mk 3, several Mk 50/Mk 10 or Mk 14, several Mk 44
		Mar 1944	SK, 2 SG	Mar 1944	2 Mk 3, several Mk 50/Mk 10 or Mk 14
CL-7	Raleigh			1940	Mk 16 RF
		July 1942	SC-1	July 1942	1 Mk 3, several Mk 50/Mk 10 or 14, several Mk 44
		May 1944	SK, 2 SG	May 1942	2 Mk 3, several Mk 50/Mk 10 or 14
CL-8	Detroit			1940	Mk 16 RF
		Feb 1942	SC-1	Feb 1942	1 Mk 3, presumably 2 Mk 50/Mk 10, several Mk 44
		Aug 1942	SC, SG	Aug 1942	1 Mk 3 otherwise as above
		April 1944	SK, 2 SG	April 1944	2 Mk 3, presumably 2 Mk 50/Mk 10
		Jan 1945	SK, 2 SG	Jan 1945	as above
CL-9	Richmond			1940	Mk 16 RF
		Nov 1942	SC-1, SG	Nov 1942	1 Mk 3, presumably 2 Mk 50/Mk 10 or Mk 14, some Mk 44, presumably 2
		June 1944	SK, 2 SG	June 1944	2 Mk 3, otherwise as above but without Mk 44
		1945	SK, 2 SG	1945	as above
CL-10	Concord			1940	Mk 16 RF
		Nov 1942	SC-1, SG	Nov 1942	1 Mk 3, presumably 2 Mk 50/Mk 10 or 14, some Mk 44, presumably 2
		1943	SC, SG	1943	2 Mk 3, presumably 2 Mk 50/Mk 10 or 14, some Mk 44, presumably 2
CL-11	Trenton			1940	Mk 16 RF
		May 1943	SC-1, SG	May 1943	1 Mk 3, presumably 2 Mk 50/Mk 10 or Mk 14, some Mk 44, presumably 2
		Aug 1944	SK, 2 SG	Aug 1944	2 Mk 3, otherwise as above but without Mk 44
		1945	SK, 2 SG	1945	as above
CL-12	Marblehead			1940	Mk 16 RF
		Oct 1942	?, SG	Oct 1942	1 Mk 3, presumably 2 Mk 50/Mk 10 or Mk 14, some Mk 44, presumably 2
		May 1944	SK, 2 SG	May 1944	2 Mk 3, otherwise as above but without Mk 44
CL-13	Memphis			1940	Mk 16 RF
		Nov 1942	CXAM-1, SG	Nov 1942	2 Mk 3, presumably 2 Mk 50/Mk 10 or 14, some Mk 44, presumably 2
		June 1945	SK, 2 SG	June 1945	2 Mk 3, otherwise as above but without Mk 44
CL-24	Pensacola			1927	2 Mk 18, 2 Mk 19
		Aug 1940–Jan 1943	CXAM	Aug 1942 + Jan 1943	2 Mk 18/1 Mk 3, 2 Mk 19/Mk 4, presumably 4 Mk 44
	Note. In Oct 1943 there was a total of eight fire control radar Mk 28 in Pensacola.	May 1943 + Oct 1943	SK, 2 SG	May 1943 + Oct 1943	2 Mk 18/2 Mk 3, 2 Mk 33/Mk 4, 6 Mk 51
		May 1944	SK, 2 SG	May 1944	as above but 8 Mk 51
		July 1945 + Oct 1945	SK, 2 SG, SP	June 1945 + Oct 1945	2 Mk 35/2 Mk 28, 2 Mk 33/Mk 28, 4 Mk 63/Mk 28, approx. 5 Mk 51
CA-25	Salt Lake City			1927	2 Mk 18, 2 Mk 19
		May 1943	SK, 2 SG	May 1943	2 Mk 18/2 Mk 3, 2 Mk 19/Mk 4, or several Mk 51
		Jan 1944	SK, 2 SG	Jan 1944	as above
		June 1944	SK, 2 SG	June 1944	as avove but 2 Mk 33/Mk 4 presumably or 8 Mk 51
		Dec 1945	SK, 2 SG	Dec 1945	as above
CA-26	Northampton			1934	2 Mk 24/Mk 3, 2 Mk 19
		June 1941	CXAM		
		Nov 1942	CXAM-1	Nov 1942	presumably 4 Mk 44
CA-27	Chester			1934	2 Mk 24/2 Mk 3, 2 Mk 19
		April 1941	CXAM	Aug 1942	
		July 1943	SC, 2 SG	July 1943	as above, 2 Mk 33/Mk 4
		Oct 1943	SK, 2 SG	Oct 1943	as above but without Mk 44
		Nov 1944	SK, 2 SG	Nov 1944	as above
		May 1945	SK, 1 SG, SP	May 1945	2 Mk 34/13, 2 Mk 33/Mk 28, several Mk 63/Mk 28
CA-28	Louisville			1934	2 Mk 24, 2 Mk 19,
		April 1942	SC	May 1942	2 Mk 18/2 Mk 3, 2 Mk19/Mk 4 some Mk 44
		Dec 1943	SK, 2 SG	Dec 1943	2 Mk 34/Mk 8, 2 Mk 33/Mk 4
		July 1945	SK, 2 SG, SP	July 1945	Mk 34/Mk 8 Mod. 3, 2 Mk 33/Mk 28
CA-29	Chicago			1934	
		Aug 1940	CXAM aft		
		Dec 1942	CXAM forward	Dec 1942	2 Mk 18/2 Mk 3, 2 Mk 19/4 Mk 51
CA-30	Houston	Nov 1941	CXAM	1934	2 Mk 24, 2 Mk 19
				1939	as above
CA-31	Augusta			1938	2 Mk 24, 2 Mk 19
		Aug 1941	CXAM-1	1941	
		April 1942	First set SG, CXAM-1	April 1942	as above Mk 24/2 Mk 3, 2 Mk 33
		Nov 1942	CXAM-1, 2 SG	Nov 1942	Mk 24/2 Mk 3, 2 Mk 33/Mk 4
		1944	SK, 2 SG	1944	2 Mk 34/Mk 8, 2 Mk 33/Mk 4
		1945	SK, 2 SG	1945	as above but instead of Mk 33 2 Mk 37/Mk 28
CA-33	Portland			1935	1 Mk 27, 2 Mk 19
		May 1942	SC, SG	May 1942	2 Mk 27/2 Mk 3, 2 Mk33/Mk 4 several Mk 44
		May 1943	SK, 2 SG	May 1943	as above but without Mk 44
		Nov 1943	SK, 2 SG	Nov 1943	2 Mk 27/2 Mk 3, 2 Mk 33/Mk 4
		July 1944	SK, 2 SG	July 1944	2 Mk 34/Mk 8, 2 Mk 33/Mk 28
		Sept 1945	SK, 2 SG	Sept 1945	as above
CA-35	Indianapolis			1935	2 Mk 27, 2 Mk 19
		April 1942	SG	April 1942	2 Mk 27/2 Mk 3, 2 Mk 19
		Dec 1942	SA, SG		
		May 1943	SK, 2 SG	May 1943	2 Mk 27/2 Mk 3, 2 Mk 33 6 Mk 51
		May 1944	SK, 2 SG	May 1944	as above
		Dec 1944	SK, 2 SG	Dec 1944	2 Mk 34/Mk 8, 2 Mk 33/Mk 28, at least 6 Mk 51
		July 1945	SK, 2 SG	July 1945	as above but Mk 34 with Mk 8 Mod. 3, 4 Mk 63/Mk 28
CA-32	New Orleans			1934	2 Mk 31, 2 Mk 28
		Nov 1942	SC	Nov 1942	2 Mk 31/2 Mk 3, 2 Mk 33
		Aug 1943	SK, 2 SG	Aug 1943	2 Mk 31/2 Mk 3, 2 Mk 33/Mk 4
		Mar 1945	SK, 1 SG, SP	Mar 1945	as above but 2 Mk 37/Mk 28, presumably several Mk 63
CA-34	Astoria			1937	2 Mk 31, 2 Mk 28
		1942	SC	1942	2 Mk 31/2 Mk 3, 2 Mk 28, eventually some Mk 44
CA-36	Minneapolis			1937	2 Mk 31, 2 Mk 28
		Mar 1943	SC	Mar 1943	2 Mk 31/2 Mk 3, 2 Mk 33/Mk 4
		Sept 1943	SK, 2 SG	Sept 1943	as above
		April 1945	SK, 2 SG	April 1945	as above
CA-37	Tuscaloosa			1937	2 Mk 31, 2 Mk 28
		Oct 1942	SC, 2 SG	Oct 1942	2 Mk 31/2 Mk 3, 2 Mk 33, eventually some Mk 44
		Jan 1944	SK, 2 SG	Jan 1944	2 Mk 31/2 Mk 3, 2 Mk 33/Mk 4
		Nov 1944	SK, 2 SG	Nov 1944	2 Mk 31/2 Mk 3, 2 Mk 33/Mk 2
		Dec 1945	SK, 2 SG, eventually SP	Dec 1945	as above
CA-38	San Francisco			1934	2 Mk 31 Mod. 13+14, 2 Mk 28
		Mar 1942	SC-1	Mar 1942	2 Mk 31/2 Mk 3, 2 Mk 33, 4 Mk 44
		Dec 1942	SC-1	Dec 1942	as above
	*One Mk 51 FLG for each 40mm Vierling, plus six extra Mk 51 for 5in weapons.	Feb 1943	SC-3, SG	Feb 1943	2 Mk 31/2 Mk 3, 2 Mk 33/ Mk 4, 4 Mk 51
		Oct 1944	SK, 2 SG,	Oct 1944	2 Mk 31/2 Mk 3, 2 Mk 33/ Mk 28, eventually 12 Mk 51
		Oct 1945	SK, 2 SG	Oct 1945	2 Mk 31/2 Mk 3, 2 Mk 33/ Mk 28, 12 Mk 51*
CA-39	Quincy			May 1940	2 Mk 31, 2 Mk 28
		May 1942	SC	May 1942	2 Mk 31/2 Mk 3, 2 Mk 28

Pennant No.	Name	Detection Radar Installations Date	Detection Radar Installations Instruments	Fire Control Installations Date	Fire Control Installations Instruments
CA-44	Vincennes			Aug 1942	as CA-39
CA-45	Wichita			1939	2 Mk 34, 2 Mk 33
				June 1941	2 Mk 34/2 Mk 1 (FA), 2 Mk 33
		1942	SC	1942	2 Mk 34/2 Mk 1, 2 Mk 33/Mk4
		Nov 1943	SK, 2 SG	Nov 1943	2 Mk 34/2 Mk 1, 2 Mk 33/Mk 4
		Nov 1945	SK, 1 SG	Nov 1945	2 Mk 34/2 Mk 13, 2 Mk 33/Mk 28
CL-40	Brooklyn			1938	2 Mk 34, 2 Mk 28
		Sept 1943	SC-2, 2 SG	Sept 1943	2 Mk 31/Mk 3 (small), 2 Mk 33/Mk 4
CL-41	Philadelphia *First installation of Fire Control Mk 3 (small)			1938	2 Mk 34, 2 Mk 28
				Oct 1941	2 Mk 34/2 Mk 3*, 2 Mk 28
		Aug 1942	SC	Aug 1942	2 Mk 34/2 Mk 3 (small), 2 Mk 33/Mk 4
		April 1943	SC	April 1943	2 Mk 34/2 Mk 3 (small), 2 Mk 33/Mk 4, one Mk 44
		Sept 1945	SK, 2 SG, SP	Sept 1945	2 Mk 34/13, 2 Mk 33/Mk 4
CL-42	Savannah			1938	2 Mk 34, 2 Mk 28
		Aug 1942	SC, 2 SG	Aug 1942	2 Mk 34/2 Mk 3 (small), 2 Mk 33/Mk 4
		April 1943	SC-2, 2 SG	April 1943	as above
		1945	SK, 2 SG	1945	2 Mk 34/Mk 8, 2 Mk 37/Mk 12/22
CL-43	Nashville			1939	2 Mk 34, 2 Mk 28
		Dec 1942	SC	Dec 1942	2 Mk 34/2 Mk 3 (small), 2 Mk 33/Mk 4
		July 1943	SK, 2 SG	July 1943	2 Mk 34/Mk 8, 2 Mk 33/Mk 4
		1945	SK, 2 SG	1945	2 Mk 334/Mk 13, 2 Mk 33/Mk 28
CL-46	Phoenix			1938	2 Mk 34, 2 Mk 33
		Sept 1943	SK, 2 SG	Sept 1943	2 Mk 34/2 Mk 3 (small), 2 Mk 33/Mk 4
CL-47	Boise			1938	2 Mk 34, 2 Mk 33
		1942	?	1942	2 Mk 34/2 Mk 3 (small), 2 Mk 33/Mk 4
		Jan 1945	SK, 2 SG	Jan 1945	2 Mk 34/Mk 13, 2 Mk 33/Mk 28
CL-48	Honolulu			1938	2 Mk 34, 2 Mk 33
		Jan 1942	SC	Jan 1942	2 Mk 34/1 Mk 1, 2 Mk 33
				Oct 1942	as above but 2 Mk 3
		Nov 1943	SK, 2 SG	Nov 1943	2 Mk 34/Mk 8 Mod. 1+3, 2 Mk 33/Mk 4
		Nov 1944	SK, 2 SG	Nov 1944	as above
				Oct 1945	as above but 2 Mk 37/Mk 12/n
CL-49	St. Louis			1939	2 Mk 34, 2 Mk 33
		Mar 1942	SC	Mar 1942	2 Mk 34/Mk 3 (small), 2 Mk 33/Mk 4
		Oct 1943	SC-2, 2 SG	Oct 1943	as above
		Oct 1944	SK-2, 2 SG	Oct 1944	2 Mk 34/Mk 8 Mod. 1, 2 Mk 33/Mk 28
		Nov 1945	SK-2, 2 SG	Nov 1945	as above
CL-50	Helena			1939	2 Mk 34, 2 Mk 33
		July 1942	SC-1, 1 SG	July 1942	2 Mk 34/Mk 3 (small), 2 Mk 33/Mk 4
CL-51	Atlanta	1942	SC-1	1942	2 Mk 37/Mk 4, 3 Mk 44
CL-52	Juneau	1942	SC-1	1942	2 Mk 37/Mk 4, 3–4 Mk 44
CL-53	San Diego	Mar 1942	SC-1, SG	Mar 1942	2 Mk 37/Mk 4, 4 Mk 44
		Jan 1944	SC-2, 2 SG	Jan 1944	2 Mk 37/Mk 12/22, 4 Mk 51
		Oct 1945	2 SG	Oct 1945	as above
CL-54	San Juan	Feb 1942	SC-1, SG	Feb 1942	2 Mk 37/Mk 4, 4 Mk 44
		1942	SC-1, 2 SG	1942	as above
		Oct 1944	SC-2, 2 SG	Oct 1944	2 Mk 37/Mk 12/22, 6 Mk 51
CL-95	Oakland *First installation of Mk 63	July 1943	SC-2, 2 SG	July 1943	2 Mk 37/Mk 4, 8 Mk 51
		July 1945 +Nov 1945	SC-2, 2 SG	July 1945 + Nov 1945	2 Mk 37/Mk 12/22, approx. 2 Mk 63*, 4 Mk 51
CL-96	Reno	Jan 1944	SC-2, 2 SG	Jan 1944	2 Mk 37/Mk 4, 8 Mk 51
		1945	SC-2, 2 SG	1945	2 Mk 37/Mk 12/22 possibly some Mk 63
CL-97	Flint	Aug 1944	SC-2, 2 SG	Aug 1944	2 Mk 37/Mk 12/22
		Nov 1945	SC-2, 2 SG	Nov 1945	as above, possibly some Mk 63
CL-98	Tucson	Feb 1945	SC-2, 2 SG	Feb 1945	2 Mk 37/Mk 12/22, 8 Mk 51, possibly some Mk 63
CL-119	Juneau	1947	SK-2, SP	1947	2 Mk 37/Mk 12/22
		Aug 1948–1951	SG-6, SP	Aug 1948–1951	2 Mk 37/Mk 25, presumably 6 Mk 63
		Feb 1952–1954	SPS-6B, SP	Feb 1952–1954	2 Mk 37/Mk 25, 2 Mk 56/Mk 35
CL-120	Spokane	June 1946	SK-2, 2 SG, SP	June 1946	2 Mk 37/Mk 12/22, eventually some Mk 63
		Aug 1949	SK-2, SG, SP	Aug 1949	2 Mk 37/Mk 25, otherwise as above
CL-121	Fresno	Nov 1946 + June 1947	SK-2, SP	Nov 1946 + June 1947	2 Mk 37/Mk 12/22, eventually some Mk 63
CL-55	Cleveland	1943	SC	Jan 1944	2 Mk 34/Mk 3, 2 Mk 37/Mk 4, eventually some Mk 51
		Jan 1944	?		
		1945	SK-2, 2 SG	1945	2 Mk 34/Mk 13, 2 Mk 37/12/22
CL-56	Columbia	Nov 1942	2 SG	Nov 1942	2 Mk 34/Mk 3, 2 Mk 37/Mk 4
		Jan 1944	SC-2, 2 SG	Jan 1944	2 Mk 34/Mk 3, 2 Mk 37/Mk 4
		Jan 1945	SK, 2 SG	Jan 1945	2 Mk 34/Mk 8 Mod. 1, 2 Mk 37/Mk 12/22
CL-57	Montpelier	Nov 1942	SC, 1 SG	Nov 1942	2 Mk 34/Mk 8 Mod. 1
		June 1944	SC-2, 2 SG	June 1944	2 Mk 37/Mk 4
		1945	SK-2, 2 SG	1945	as above; 2 Mk 34/Mk 8 Mod. 1, 2 Mk 37/Mk 12/22
CL-58	Denver	Jan 1943	2 SG	Jan 1943	2 Mk 34/Mk 3, 2 Mk 37/Mk 4
		May 1944	SK, 2 SG	May 1944	2 Mk 34/Mk 8 Mod. 1, 2 Mk 37/Mk 4
CL-69	Santa Fe	Jan 1943	SC-2, SG	Jan 1943	2 Mk 34/Mk 8 Mod. 1, 2 Mk 37/Mk 4
		May 1943	SK, 2 SG	May 1943	as above
		1945–46	SK-2, SG	1945–46	2 Mk 34/Mk 13, 2 Mk 37/Mk 12/22
CL-62	Birmingham	Feb 1943–Nov 1943	SC-2, SG	Feb 1943–Nov 1943	2 Mk 34/Mk 8 Mod. 1, 2 Mk 37/Mk 4
		Feb 1944–Oct 1944	SK, 2 SG	Feb 1944–Oct 1944	as above
		1945	SK, SG, SP	1945	2 Mk 34/Mk 8 Mod. 1, 2 Mk 37/Mk 12/22
CL-63	Mobile *Received one of the first Fire Control Mk 63 from 1944–45	May 1943	SC-2, SG	May 1943	2 Mk 34/Mk 8 Mod. 1, 2 Mk 37/Mk 4
		Oct 1943	SC-2, 2 SG	Oct 1943	as above
		Jan 1946	SK, SG	Jan 1946	2 Mk 34/Mk 13, 2 Mk 37/Mk 12/22, some Mk 63*
CL-64	Vincennes	Feb 1944	SK, 2 SG	Feb 1944	2 Mk 34/Mk 8 Mod. 1, 2 Mk 37/Mk 4
		April 1945–1946	SK, 2 SG	April 1945–1946	2 Mk 34/Mk 8 Mod. 3, 2 Mk 37/Mk 12/22
CL-65	Pasadena	July 1944–1946	SK-2, 2 SG	July 1944–1946	2 Mk 34/Mk 8 Mod. 1, 2 Mk 37/Mk 12/22
		1947–49	SK-3, SP	1947–49	as above
CL-66	Springfield	Sept 1944-May 1946	SK-2, 2 SG	Sept 1944	2 Mk 34/Mk 8 Mod. 1, 2 Mk 37/Mk 12/22
		1948	SR-3, SP	1948	as above
CL-67	Topeka	Mar 1945	2 SG	Mar 1945	2 Mk 34/Mk 8 Mod. 1, 2 Mk 37/Mk 12/22
CL-80	Biloxi	Sept 1943	SK, 2 SG	Sept 1943	2 Mk 34/Mk 8 Mod. 1, 2 Mk 37/Mk 4
CL-81	Houston	Jan 1944–June 1944	SK, 2 SG	Jan 1944–June 1944	2 Mk 34/Mk 8 Mod. 1, 2 Mk 37/Mk 4
		Oct 1944	SK, 2 SG	Oct 1944	as above but Mk 37/Mk 12/22
CL-82	Providence	May 1945–1947	SK-2, 1 SG, SP	May 1945–1947	2 Mk 34/Mk 13, 2 Mk 37/Mk 12/22
CL-83	Manchester	1945–Oct 1946	SK, SP	1945–Oct 1946	2 Mk 34/Mk 13, 2 Mk 37/Mk 12/22
		Nov 1946–April 1948	SK-2, SG, SP	Nov 1946–April 1948	as above
		May 1951	SPS-6B, SR-3, SP	May 1951	2 Mk 34/Mk 13, 2 Mk 37/Mk 25
		Oct 1952	SPS-6B, SP	Oct 1952	2 Mk 34/Mk 13, 2 Mk 37/Mk 25, 4 Mk 56/Mk 35
		Mar 1955	SPS-6B, SPS-8A	Mar 1955	as above
CL-86	Vicksburg	July 1944	SK, 2 SG	July 1944	2 Mk 34/Mk 8 Mod. 1, 2 Mk 37/Mk 12/22
		Oct 1945	SK, SG	Oct 1945	2 Mk 34/Mk 13, 2 Mk 37/Mk 12/22
CL-87	Duluth	Oct 1944–June 1945	SK-2, 2 SG	Oct 1944–June 1945	2 Mk 34/Mk 8 Mod. 1, 2 Mk 37/Mk 12/22
		June 1947	SK-2, SG, SP	June 1947	as above
CL-89	Miami	Mar 1944	SK, 2 SG	Mar 1944	2 Mk 34/Mk 8 Mod. 1, 2 Mk 37/Mk 4

Pennant No.	Name	Detection Radar Installations		Fire Control Installations	
		Date	Instruments	Date	Instruments
		Feb 1946	SK, 2 SG	Feb 1946	2 Mk 34/Mk 8 Mod. 1, 2 Mk 37/Mk 12/22
CL-90	Astoria	Oct 1944	SK, 2 SG	Oct 1944	2 Mk 34/Mk 8 Mod. 1, 2 Mk 37/Mk 12/22
		1946–48	SR-3, SP	1946–48	2 Mk 34/Mk 13, 2 Mk 37/Mk 12/22
CL-91	Oklahoma City	April 1945–Feb 1946	SK-2, 2 SG	April 1945–Feb 1946	2 Mk 34/Mk 13, 2 Mk 37/Mk 12/22
CL-92	Little Rock	1946–48	SK-2, SG, SP	1946–48	2 Mk 34/Mk 13, 2 Mk 37/Mk 12/22
CL-93	Galveston	1945	SK-2, SG, SP	1945	2 Mk 34/Mk 13, 2 Mk 37/Mk 12/22
CL-101	Amsterdam	Oct 1945	SK-2, 2 SG	Oct 1945	2 Mk 34/Mk 13, 2 Mk 37/Mk 12/22
CL-102	Portsmouth	July 1945	SK-2, SG SP	July 1945	2 Mk 34/Mk 13, 2 Mk 37/Mk 12/22
		1946–47	SG-6, SP	1946–47	as above
CL-103	Wilkes Barre	Aug 1944–July 1945	SK, 2 SG	Aug 1944–July 1945	2 Mk 34/Mk 8 Mod. 1, 2 Mk 37/Mk 12/22
		1946	SK-2, SP	1946	2 Mk 34/13, Mk 37/ Mk 25
		Feb 1949	SR-3, SP	Feb 1949	as above
CL-104	Atlanta	Nov 1944	?	Nov 1944	2 Mk 34/Mk 8 Mod. 1, 2 Mk 37/Mk 12/22
		1946–47	SK-2, 2 SG	1946–47	2 Mk 34/Mk 13, 2 Mk 37/Mk 25
CL-105	Dayton	April 1945	SK-2, 2 SG	April 1945	2 Mk 34/Mk 13, 2 Mk 37/Mk 12/22
		1946–April 1948	SK-2, SP	1946–April 1948	as above
CL-106	Fargo	Dec 1945–April 1946	SK-2, SP	Dec 1945–April 1946	2 Mk 34/Mk 13, 2 Mk 37/Mk 25, spare Mk 55
		April 1949	SR-3, SP	April 1949	as above
		1949	SPS-6B, SP	1949	as above
CL-107	Huntington	Mar 1946	SK-2, SG, SP	Mar 1946	2 Mk 34/Mk 13, Mk 37/Mk 12/22, spare Mk 55
		April 1948	SR-3, SP	April 1948	2 Mk 37/Mk 25, otherwise as above
CL-144	Worcester	June 1948–Oct 1949	SG-6, SR-3, SP	June 1948–Oct 1949	2 FLR Mk 13 (without Mk 34), 4 Mk 37/Mk 25
		Aug 1950	SG-6, SPS-6B, SP	Aug 1950	as above
		July 1951–Aug 1954	SPS-6B, SP	July 1951–Aug 1954	as above but with 4 Mk 56/Mk 35, 9 Mk 51
		July 1955–June 1956	SPS-6B, SPS-8A	July 1955–June 1956	as above
CL-145	Roanoke	April 1949–Mar 1951	SG-6, SP	April 1949	2 FLR Mk 13 (without Mk 34), 4 Mk 37/Mk 25, 4 Mk 56/Mk 35, 9 Mk 51
		Mar 1952	SPS-6B, SP	Mar 1952	as above
		Feb 1953	SPS-6B, SR-3, SP	Feb 1953	as above
		April 1955–Feb 1958	SPS-6B, SPS-8A	Feb 1958	as above
CA-68	Baltimore	July 1943–Aug 1944	SK, 2 SG	July 1943–Aug 1944	2 Mk 34/Mk 8 Mod. 1, 2 Mk 37/Mk 4
		Oct 1944	SK, 2 SG	Oct 1944	2 Mk 34/Mk 8 Mod. 1, 2 Mk 37/Mk 12/22
		July 1952	SPS-6B, SG	July 1952	as above
		June 1953	SPS-6B, SG	June 1953	as above
		Sept 1954	SPS-6B, SPS-8A	Sept 1954	2 Mk 34/Mk 13, 2 Mk 37/Mk 25
		1956	SPS-6B, SPS-8A	1956	as above but now 6 Mk 56/Mk 35
CL-69	Boston	June 1943	2 SG	June 1943	2 Mk 34/Mk 8 Mod. 1, 2 Mk 37/Mk 4
		May 1944	SK, 2 SG	May 1944	as above
		Aug 1945	SK, SP, 1 SG	Aug 1945	2 Mk 34/Mk 13, 2 Mk 37/Mk 12/22
CA-70	Canberra	Oct 1943	2 SG	Oct 1943	2 Mk 34/Mk 8 Mod. 1, 2 Mk 37/Mk 4
		Dec 1944	SK, 2 SG	Dec 1944	as above
		Oct 1945	SK, SP	Oct 1945	2 Mk 34/Mk 13, 2 Mk 37/Mk 12/22
CA-71	Quincy	Dec 1943–April 1944	SK, 2 SG	Dec 1943–April 1944	2 Mk 34/Mk 8 Mod. 1, 2 Mk 37/Mk 4
		1946	SK, 2 SG	1946	2 Mk 34/Mk 8 Mod. 1, 2 Mk 37/Mk 12/22
		1948	SR-3, SP	1948	2 Mk 34/Mk 13, 2 Mk 37/Mk 12/22
		1952–54	SPS-6B	1952–54	as above
CA-72	Pittsburgh	Oct 1944	SK, 2 SG	Oct 1944	2 Mk 34/Mk 8 Mod. 1, 2 Mk 37/Mk 12/22
		Sept 1945	SK-2, 1 SG	Sept 1945	as above
		Dec 1952–April 1953	SPS-6B, SP	Dec 1952–April 1953	2 Mk 34/Mk 13, 2 Mk 37/Mk 12/22
		Oct 1955	SPS-6B, SPS-8A	Oct 1955	2 Mk 34/Mk 13, 2 Mk 37/Mk 25, 4 Mk 56/Mk 35
CA-73	St. Paul	1946	SK-2, SP		
		1947–48	SG-6, SP		
		Sept 1951	SPS-6B, SP	Sept 1951	2 Mk 34/Mk 13, 2 Mk 37/Mk 25, 4 Mk 56/Mk 35
		May 1953	SPS-6B, SP	May 1953	as above
		April 1948	SPS-12, SPS-8A	April 1948	as above
		June 1959	SPS-37, SPS-8A	June 1959	as above
		July 1967	SPS-37, SPS-8A	July 1967	as above
CA-74	Columbus	Aug 1945	SK-2, 1 SG, SP	Aug 1945	2 Mk 34/Mk 13, 2 Mk 37/Mk 12/22
		Nov 1949	SR-3, SP	Nov 1949	as above
		1955	SPS-6B	1955	as above but 2 Mk 37/Mk 25
		Aug 1957	SPS-12, SPS-8A	Aug 1957	as above but now 6 Mk 56/Mk 35
		Mar 1959	SPS-12, SPS-8A	Mar 1959	as above
CA-75	Helena	Sept 1945	SK-2, SP	Aug 1947	2 Mk 34/Mk 13, 2 Mk 37/Mk 12/22
		Aug 1947	SR-3, SP		
		May 1953–Aug 1954	SPS-6B, SP	Aug 1954	2 Mk 34/Mk 13, 2 Mk 37/Mk 25, 6 Mk 56/Mk 35
		Feb 1957	SPS-6B	Feb 1957	1 SPQ-2, otherwise as above
		Jan 1959	SPS-12	Jan 1959	as above but only 1 Mk 34
		1960–Sept 1961	SPS-37A, SPS-12, SPS-10	1960–Sept 1961	as above
		1963	SPS-37A, SPS-12, SPS-10	1963	as above but now without SPQ-2
CA-122	Oregon City	Feb 1946	SK-2, SG, SP	Feb 1946	2 Mk 34/Mk 13, Mk 37/Mk 12/22
CA-123	Albany	June 1949	SK-2, SP	1949	2 Mk 34/Mk 13, Mk 37/Mk 25, 6 Mk 56/Mk 35
		1949	SR-3, SP		
		Nov 1950	SG-6, SP	Nov 1950	as above
		Feb 1956–Nov 1957	SPS-12, SPS-8A	Feb 1956–Nov 1957	as above
CA-124	Rochester	Dec 1946	SP	Dec 1946	2 Mk 34/Mk 13, 2 Mk 37/Mk 12/22
		April 1948	SR-3, SP	April 1948	as above
		Jan 1951	SG-6, SP	Jan 1951	as above
		1952–Mar 1954	SPS-6B, SP	1952–Mar 1954	2 Mk 34/Mk 13, 2 Mk 37/Mk 25, 6 Mk 56/Mk 35
		Feb 1956	SPS-12, SPS-8A	Feb 1956	as above
		Aug 1960	SPS-12, SPS-8A	Aug 1960	as above but only 1 Mk 34
CA-130	Bremerton	April 1947	SK-2, 1 SG, SP	April 1947	2 Mk 34/Mk 13, Mk 37/Mk 12/22
		1951–1957	SPS-6B, SPS-8A	1951	2 Mk 34/Mk 13, 2 Mk 37/Mk 25, 6 Mk 56/Mk 35
CA-131	Fall River	Aug–Oct 1945	SK-2, SP	Aug–Oct 1945	2 Mk 34/Mk 13, 2 Mk 37/Mk 12/22
CA-132	Macon	Oct 1946–April 1947	SK-2, SP	Oct 1946–April 1947	2 Mk 34/Mk 13, 2 Mk 37/Mk 12/22
		July 1948	SR-3, SP	July 1948	2 Mk 34/Mk 13, 2 Mk 37/Mk 12/22, 4 Mk 56/Mk 35
		1950–April 1954	SPS-6B (first operational use), SP	1950–April 1954	2 Mk 34/Mk 13, 2 Mk 37/Mk 25, 6 Mk 56/Mk 35
		1960	SPS-6B	1960	1 SPQ-2, 2 Mk 34/Mk 13, 2 Mk 37/Mk 25, 6 Mk 56/Mk 35
CA-133	Toledo	Dec 1946	SP	Dec 1946	2 Mk 34/Mk 13, 2 Mk 37/Mk 12/22
		Oct 1951	SPS-6B, SP	Oct 1951	2 Mk 34/Mk 13, 2 Mk 37/Mk 25, 6 Mk 56/Mk 35
		Oct 1955–1959	SPS-12	Jan 1955–1959	1 SPQ-2, otherwise as above
CA-135	Los Angeles	Aug 1951–April 1952	SPS-6B, SP	Aug 1951–April 1952	2 Mk 34/Mk 13, 2 Mk 37/Mk 12/22
		May 1954	SPS-6B, SP	May 1954	as above
		1955	SPS-12	1955	1 SPQ-2, 1 Mk 34/Mk 13, 2 Mk 37/Mk 25, 4 Mk 56/Mk 35
		April 1960–Oct 1961	SPS-37A, SPS-10, SPS-12	1960	SPQ-2, 1 Mk 34/Mk 13, 2 Mk 37/Mk 25, 4 Mk 56/Mk 35

Pennant No.	Name	Detection Radar Installations Date	Instruments	Fire Control Installations Date	Instruments
CA-136	Chicago	Jan 1945–May 1945	SK-2, 2 SG	Jan 1945–May 1945	2 Mk 34/Mk 13, 2 Mk 37/Mk 12/22
CA-134	Des Moines	Nov 1948–Oct 1949	SR-3, SP	Nov 1948–Oct 1949	2 Mk 54/Mk 13, 4 Mk 37/Mk 25, Mk 56/Mk 35
		Aug 1950	SPS-6B, SP	Aug 1950	as above
		1953	SPS-6B, SPS-8A	1953	as above
		Dec 1959	SPS-6B, SPS-8A	Dec 1959	as above
CA-139	Salem	1949	SR-3, SP	1949	as CA-134
		1950	SG-6, SP	1950	as above
		May 1951	SPS-6B, SP	May 1951	as above
		June 1952	SPS-6B, SPS-8A, SPS-10	June 1952	as above
		Jan 1957	SPS-12, SPS-8A, SPS-10	Jan 1957	as above
CA-148	Newport News	1949	SR-3, SP	1949	as CA-134
		1950–Sept 1951	SG-6, SP	1950–Sept 1951	as above
		1958	SPS-6B, SPS-8A	1958	as above
		1961–	SPS-37, SPS-8A	1961–	as above
		1975	SPS-6B, SPS-10	1975	
CB-1	Alaska	June 1944	SK, 2 SG	June 1944	2 Mk 38/Mk 8 Mod. 1, 2 Mk 37/Mk 12/22, some Mk 57
CB-2	Guam	Oct 1944	SK, 2 SG	Oct 1944	2 Mk 38/Mk 13, 2 Mk 37/Mk 12/22, some Mk 57
CLC-1	Northampton	Mar 1953	SPS-2, SPS-3, SPS-8A	Mar 1953	1 Mk 67/Mk 25
		Dec 1954	SPS-2, SPS-3, SPS-8A	Dec 1954	1 Mk 67/Mk 25, 4 Mk 56/Mk 35
		July 1955	SPS-2, SPS-3, SPS-6B, SPS-8A	July 1955	as above
		Aug 1956–Sept 1957	SPS-2, SPS-12, SPS-8A, SPS-10	Aug 1956–Sept 1957	as above
		1959–Sept 1961	SPS-2, SPS-37, SPS-8A, SPS-10	1959–Sept 1961	as above
	* Special antenna probably adapted from SK-2	1962	SPS-2, SPS-37, SPS-8A, SPS-10, (SK-2)*	1962	1 Mk 67/Mk 25
		Aug 1963	SPS-37, SPS-8A, SPS-10, (SK-2)	Aug 1963	as above
		June 1964	SPS-37, SPS-8A, SPS-10, (2 SK-2)	June 1964	as above
		1968	SPS-37, SPS-8A, SPS-10, 1 parabolic antenna	1968	Fire-control instruments no longer carried
DL-1	Norfolk	Aug 1953	SPS-6B	Aug 1953	2 Mk 56/Mk 35, Sonar SQG-1
		1955	SPS-6B, SPS-12	1955	as above
		Aug 1957	SPS-6B, SPS-26	Aug 1957	as above, sonar SQS-4
		1962–1965	SPS-37, SPS-10	1962–1965	as above, sonar SQS-26
CAG-1	Boston	Jan 1956–Oct 1957	SPS-6B, SPS-8A, SPS-10, CXRX	Jan 1956–Oct 1957	1 FLA Mk 71/2, Mk 25 Mod. 7, 1 Mk 34/Mk 13, 1 Mk 37/Mk 25, 6 Mk 56/Mk 35
		July 1960	SPS-29, SPS-8A, SPS-6B, SPS-10, CXRX	July 1960	as above but 2 SPQ-5 in place of Mk 25 Mod. 7
	* SPS-37A on a platform	1962–1963	SPS-37A*, CXRX, SPS-6B, SPS-8A, SPS-10	1962–1963	as above
	** SPS-37A on the mainmast	Sept 1964	SPS-37A**, CXRX, SPS-30, SPS-10	Sept 1964	as above
		Sept 1968–	SPS-37A, SPS-30,	Sept 1968–	as above
		Nov 1969	SPS-10	Nov 1969	
CAG-2	Canberra	Aug 1956–April 1957	SPS-6B, SPS-12, SPS-8A, CXRX	Aug 1956–April 1957	1 FLA Mk 71/2, SPQ-5, 1 Mk 34/Mk 13, 1 Mk 37/Mk 25, 6 Mk 56/Mk 35
		June 1957–Jan 1961	SPS-29, SPS-13, SPS-6B, CXRX, SPS-10	June 1957–Jan 1961	as above
		Feb 1965–July 1965	SPS-37A, SPS-30, SPS-10, (CXRX)	Feb 1965–July 1965	as above
		Feb 1968–1970	SPS-37A, SPS-30, SPS-10	Feb 1968–1970	as above
CLG-3	Galveston	Jan 1959	SPS-17, SPS-10, SPS-42, SPS-8B	Jan 1959	1 FLA Mk 77/2, SPG-49/2 SPW-2, 1 Mk 34/Mk 13, 1 Mk 37/Mk 25
		June 1962–May 1969	SPS-37A, SPS-30, SPS-39A, SPS-10	June 1962–Aug 1969	as above
CLG-4	Little Rock	1960	SPS-17, SPS-2, SPS-10, SPS-39	1960	1 FLA Mk 77/2, SPG-49/2 SPW-2, 1 Mk 34/Mk 13, 1 Mk 37/Mk 25
		May 1962	SPS-37A, SPS-2, SPS-10, SPS-39	May 1962	as above
		April 1967–1976	SPS-37A, SPS-30, SPS-10	April 1967–1976	as above
CGL-5	Oklahoma City	Feb 1960–Feb 1962	SPS-17, SPS-8B, SPS-10, SPS-39	Feb 1960	as CLG-4
		1967–1975	SPS-37A, SPS-30, SPS-10	1967	as above but without Mk 34/Mk 13
CLG-6	Providence	Nov 1959	SPS-17, SPS-8B, SPS-10, SPS-42	Nov 1959	1 FLA Mk 73/2, SPQ-5, 1 Mk 34/Mk 13, 1 Mk 37/Mk 25
		July 1965	SPS-29, SPS-8B, SPS-10, SPS-39A	July 1965	as above
		May 1971	SPS-29, SPS-52, SPS-10	May 1971	as above
CLG-7	Springfield	July 1960	SPS-17, SPS-8B, SPS-10, SPS-42	July 1960	1 FLA Mk 73/2, SPQ-5, 1 Mk34/Mk 13, 1 Mk 37/Mk 25
		Mar 1964	SPS-37A, SPS-30, SPS-10, SPS-42	Mar 1964	as above
		1967–Dec 1971	SPS-37A, SPS-30, SPS-10, SPS-52	1967–Dec 1971	
CLG-8	Topeka	1960–61	SPS-17, SPS-8B, SPS-10, SPS-42	1960–1961	1 FLA Mk 73/2, SPQ-5, 1 Mk 34/Mk 13, 1 Mk 37/Mk 25
		July 1963–July 1966	SPS-37A, SPS-30, SPS-10, SPS-42	July 1963–July 1966	as above
		Sept 1967	SPS-37A, SPS-30, SPS-10, SPS-52	Sept 1967	as above
CGN-9	Long Beach	1962	4 SPS-32/33, SPS-10	1962	1 FLA Mk 77/2, SPQ-49/2 SPW-2, 2 FLA Mk 76/4 SPG-55, Sonar SQS-23
		April 1963	4 SPS-32/33, SPS-10	April 1963	as above but still with 2 Mk 56/SPG-35
		June 1966	4 SPS-32/33, SPS-12, SPS-10	June 1966	as above
		1979	4 SPS-32/33, SPS-12, SPS-10	1979	as above but without FLA Mk 77
		1983	SPS-48, SPS-49, SPS-65	1983	as above
CG-10	Albany	Jan 1963	SPS-43A, SPS-10, SPS-39	Jan 1963	2 FLA Mk 77/2, SPG-49/2 SPW-2, 2 FLA Mk 74/2/SPG-51, 2 Mk 56/SPG-35, Sonar SQS-23
		Aug 1966	SPS-43A, SPS-10, SPS-39, 2 SPS-30	Aug 1966	as above
		1970	SPS-43A, SPS-10, SPS-48, SPS41, SPS-30	1970	as above
		1973	SPS-43A, SPS-10, SPS-48,	1973	as above
		June 1976–1980	SPS-41, 1 SPS-30, SPS-43A, SPS-10, SPS-48	June 1976–1980	as above
CG-11	Chicago	May 1964–May 1965	SPS-43A, SPS-10, SPS-39, 2 SPS-30	May 1964–May 1965	as CG-10
		Mar 1971	SPS-43A, SPS-10, SPS-52, 2 SPS-30	Mar 1971	as above
		June 1975–1980	SPS-43A, SPS-10, SPS-48, 1 SPS-30	June 1975–1980	as above
CG-12	Columbus	Mar 1963	SPS-43A, SPS-10, SPS-39,	Mar 1963	as CG-10
		Dec 1964	SPS-43A, SPS-10, SPS-39, 2-SPS-30	Dec 1964	as above
		Oct 1965–Dec 1968	SPS-43A, SPS-10, SPS-52, 2 SPS 30	Oct 1965–Dec 1968	as above
		Sept 1972–1976	SPS-43A, SPS-10, SPS-30	Sept 1972–1976	as above

COMPARATIVE TABLE 5. CAMOUFLAGE

Pennant No.	Name	Date	Camouflage Measure
CL-4	Omaha	Feb 1943	22
CL-5	Milwaukee	Aug 1943	22
CL-6	Cincinnati	July 1942	12 (splotch)
		Mar 1944	22
CL-7	Raleigh	Dec 1941	1
		July 1942	11 or 21
		May 1944	32/1d
CL-8	Detroit	Feb 1942	1 or 11
		Aug 1942	21
		April 1944	33/3d
		Jan 1945	21
CL-9	Richmond	Nov 1942	eventually 14
		June 1944	32/3d
		1945	21
CL-10	Concord	Nov 1942	22
		1943	22
CL-11	Trenton	May 1943	22
		Aug 1944	32/2f
		1945–1946	21
CL-12	Marblehead	May 1942	eventually 14
		Oct 1942	22
		May 1944	22
CL-13	Memphis	1941	eventually 1
		Nov 1942	22
		Oct 1944	22
		+ June 1945	
CL-24	Pensacola	May 1942	11
		Aug 1942	21
		Oct 1943	33/10d
		May 1944	32/14d
		Oct 1945	21
CA-25	Salt Lake City	Dec 1941	3+5
		May 1943	21
		Oct 1943	21
		Jan 1944	21
		June 1944	33/14d
		Dec 1945	21
CA-26	Northampton	Dec 1941	1 + 5
		Nov 1942	21
CA-27	Chester	Aug 1942	11 or 21
		July 1943	11 or 21
		Oct 1943	21
		Nov 1944	32/9d
		May 1945	21
CA-28	Louisville	May 1942	21
		Dec 1943	32/6d
		April 1945	22
CA-29	Chicago	Dec 1942	14 or 21
CA-30	Houston		
CA-31	Augusta	1942	22
		Nov 1942	17
		Jan 1944	22
CA-33	Portland	April 1943	21
		July 1944	33/7d
		Sept 1945	22
CA-35	Indianapolis	April 1942	eventually 11
		Dec 1942– May 1943	21
			32/7d
		May 1944–	22
		Nov 1944	
		Dec 1944	22
		July 1945	22
CA-32	New Orleans	July 1943	21
		May 1945	22
CA-34	Astoria	July 1941– Aug 1942	21
CA-36	Minneapolis	1942	21
		Sept 1943	Special camouflage as DD
CA-37	Tuscaloosa	1941	12 (?)
		Oct 1942	12 (splotch)
		Nov 1944	33/13d
		Dec 1945	22
CA-38	San Francisco	May 1942	11
		Feb 1943	21
		Oct 1944	33/13d
		Oct 1945	22
CA-39	Quincy	May 1942	12
CA-44	Vincennes	1942	12 (splotch)
CA-45	Wichita	1942	12
		Nov 1943	22
		Nov 1945	22
CL-40	Brooklyn	May 1943	22
CL-41	Philadelphia	1942	12
		April 1943	22
		Jan 1945	22
CL-42	Savannah	Jan 1943	22
		1945	22
CL-43	Nashville	1942	12
		1943–1944	16 (Thayer)
		1945–1946	21
CL-46	Phoenix	1944	32/5d
CL-47	Boise	Oct 1944	22
		Jan 1945	21
CL-48	Honolulu	Nov 1943	32/2c
CL-49	St. Louis	Oct 1943	21
		Oct 1944	32/2c
		Nov 1945	21
CL-50	Helena	July 1942	21
CL-51	Atlanta * Measure 12: hull single colour; upper works dappled.	1942	12*
CL-52	Juneau Measure 12 at first; April 1942, dappled overall; end of 1942, hull with patches, upper works dappled.	1942	12*
CL-53	San Diego	Jan 1942	12
		Jan 1944	21
		Oct 1944	33/24d
		Oct 1945	21
CL-54	San Juan	June 1942	12
		Oct 1944	32/22d
CL-95	Oakland	1942–1945	21
CL-96	Reno	Dec 1943	31a/24d
CL-97	Flint	Aug 1944	33/22d
		Nov 1945	peace-time grey
CL-98	Tucson	Feb 1945	21
CL-119	Juneau		
CL-120	Spokane		
CL-121	Fresno		
CL-55	Cleveland	May 1942	12 (splotch)
		1943– Mar 1946	22
CL-56	Columbia	1942	12
		Nov 1942	21
		Jan 1944	22
		Oct 1944	33/1d
		May 1945	22
CL-57	Montpelier	Aug 1942	12 (splotch)
		+ Nov 1942	
		June 1944	22
		Oct 1944	32/11a
		1945	22
CL-58	Denver	1942	21
		Nov 1942– May 1944	33/3d
CL-60	Santa Fe	Jan 1943	12 (splotch)
		May 1943– 1945	21
CL-62	Birmingham	Feb 1943	22
		Nov 1943	21
		Feb 1944	33/6d
		Oct 1944– Jan 1945	22
		1945	21
CL-63	Mobile	April 1943–	22
		Oct 1943– 1946	21
CL-64	Vincennes	Jan 1944	33/3d
		April 1945– 1946	22
CL-65	Pasadena	June 1944	32/24d
		Feb 1945	32/24d
		Feb 1946	21
CL-66	Springfield	Sept 1944	33/24d
		May 1946	22
CL-67	Topeka	Mar 1945	33/24d
CL-80	Biloxi	Sept 1943	21
		April 1945	32/6d
CL-81	Houston	Jan 1944– Oct 1944	32/1d
		Aug 1946	22
CL-82	Providence	May 1945	22
CL-83	Manchester	1946	13
CL-86	Vicksburg	July 1944	33/6d
		Oct 1945	22
CL-87	Duluth	Oct 1944	32/11a
		June 1945	22
		Jan 1947	21
CL-89	Miami	Mar 1944	32/1d
		July 1945– Feb 1946	22
CL-90	Astoria	Oct 1944	33/24d
CL-91	Oklahoma City	April 1945– Feb 1946	22
CL-92	Little Rock	July 1945	22
CL-93	Galveston	1945	22
CL-101	Amsterdam	Jan 1945	31a/10c
		Oct 1945	12 mod.
CL-102	Portsmouth	July 1945– May 1946	22
CL-103	Wilkes Barre	July 1946	32/24d
		July 1945	21
CL-104	Atlanta	Nov 1944	33/24d
		1945	21
CL-105	Dayton	April 1945	22
		1946	22
CL-106	Fargo	April 1946	22
CL-107	Huntington	Mar 1946	22
CL-144	Worcester		
CL-145	Roanoke		
CA-68	Baltimore	June 1943	21
		Oct 1944	32/16d
CA-69	Boston	June 1943	21
		May 1944	21
		May 1945– Mar 1946	22
CA-70	Canberra	Oct 1943	21
		Dec 1944	32/18d
		Oct 1945	22
CA-70	Quincy	Dec 1943	21
		April 1944	32/18d
		1946	22
CA-72	Pittsburgh	Oct 1944	32/18d
		Sept 1945	21

Pennant No.	Name	Date	Camouflage Measure
CA-73	St. Paul		
CA-74	Columbus	Aug 1945	21
CA-75	Helena	1946	21
CA-122	Oregon City	1945–Feb 1946	22
CA-123	Albany		
CA-124	Rochester		
CA-130	Bremerton		
CA-131	Fall River	1945	21
CA-132	Macon		
CA-133	Toledo		
CA-135	Los Angeles		

Pennant No.	Name	Date	Camouflage Measure
CA-136	Chicago	May 1945	21
CA-134	Des Moines		
CA-139	Salem		
CA-148	Newport News		
CB-1	Alaska	June 1944 / Mar 1945	32/1d / 22
CB-2	Guam	Sept 1944 / Mar 1945	32/7c / 22
CLC-1	Northampton		
DL-1	Norfolk		
CAG-1	Boston		
CAG-2	Canberra		

Pennant No.	Name	Date	Camouflage Measure
CLG-3	Galveston		
CLG-4	Little Rock		
CLG-5	Oklahoma City		
CLG-6	Providence		
CLG-7	Springfield		
CLG-8	Topeka		
CGN-9	Long Beach		
CG-10	Albany		
CG-11	Chicago		
CG-12	Columbus		

BIBLIOGRAPHY

E. Bagnasco / G. Giorgerini: *Navi in Guerra*, Bramante Editrice, Milan, 1974

R. V. B. Blackman: *The World's Warships*, Macdonald, London, 1958, 1963

A. Bredt / G. Albrecht: *Weyers Flottentaschenbuch*, Verlag J. F. Lehmanns bzw. Bernard & Graefe, Munich; various editions

R. V. B. Blackman / J. Moore: *Jane's Fighting Ships*, Jane's, London; various editions

W. H. Cracknell: Warship Profile 28, *CA-35 Indianapolis*, Windsor, Berkshire, 1973

P. C. Cocker: *Building Warship Models*, Charleston, S.C., 1974

Conway's All the World's Fighting Ships 1922–1946, Conway, London, 1980

Conway's All the World's Fighting Ships 1947–1982, Conway, London, 1983

C. D. Corse, Jr.: *Introduction to Shipboard Weapons*, Naval Institute Press, Annapolis, 1975

L. Davison: *United States Cruisers*, II. Pensacola, Fla., 1975

C. Ellis: *Warship Camouflage 1939–1945*, Kristall Productions, Henley-on-Thames, 1975

N. Friedman: *Naval Radar*, Conway, London, 1981

— *U.S. Naval Weapons*, Conway, London, 1983

— *Modern Warship*, Conway, London 1979

J. C. Fahey: *The Ships and Aircraft of the U.S. Fleet*, Naval Institute Press, Annapolis, Md.

G. Giorgerini: *Gli Incrociatori della Seconda Guerra Mondiale*, Ermanno Albertelli, Parma, 1974

— *Storia della Marina, Profili*, Fabbri Editori, Milan, 1978

M. Hori: *U.S. Navy in 1961*, Tokyo, 1961

Ch. Hansen: *USS Francisco, a technical history*, 1978

B. Ireland: *Warships of the World, Major Classes*, Ian Allan, Shepperton, 1976

P. Klepsch, S. Breyer: *Die fremden Flotten im 2. Weltkrieg und ihr Schicksal*, J. F. Lehmanns Verlag, 1968

Leeward Publications: *Battle Damage Report CL-50, Helena*, Annapolis, 1979

H. T. Lenton: *American Battleships, Carriers and Cruisers*, II. Macdonald, London, 1970

Maru Graphic: *U.S. Cruisers*, Tokyo, 1976

S. E. Morison: *History of United States Naval Operations in World War II*, vols I–XV.

Naval History Division: *Dictionary of American Naval Fighting Ships*, 8 vols, Washington, D.C., 1959–81

Naval History Division: *Offizielle Gliederung der Seestreitkräfte 1939–1945*, Washington, D.C.

Office of Naval Intelligence: *O.N.I. 54, U.S. Cruisers*, Washington, D.C., 1943

— *O.N.I. 222*-US, Washington, D.C. 1945

M. D. van Orden: *The Book of the United States Ships*, Dodd, Mead & Co., New York, 1969

R. T. Pretty: *Jane's Weapon Systems*, Jane's, London; various editions

Rapidfire! Final Edition; CA-148 Newport News, Norfolk, Va., 1974

J. S. Rowe, S. L. Morison, N. Polmar: *Ships and Aircraft of the U.S. Fleet*, Naval Institute Press, Annapolis, Md., various editions

J. Rohwer, G. Hümmelchen: *Chronik des Seekrieges 1939–1945*, Stalling-Verlag, Oldenburg and Hamburg, 1968

L. Sowinski: *USN Camouflage*, The Floating Drydock, Philadelphia, Pa., 1976, 1977

P. H. Silverstone: *U.S. Warships in World War II*, Ian Allan, Shepperton, 1965

S. Terzibaschitsch: *Die Kreuzer der U.S. Navy 1942–1975*, Stalling-Verlag, Oldenburg and Hamburg, 1975

— *Seemacht USA*, Verlag Bernard & Graefe. Munich, 1982

F. Uhlig: *Naval Review*, Naval Institute Press, Annapolis, Md., various editions

A. Wetterhahn: *Flotten-Revue 1948*, vols I and II, USA, Paul Schmalenbach, Bremen, 1948/9

B. Weddertz: *Dictionary of Naval Abbreviations*, Naval Institute Press, Annapolis, Md., 1970

JOURNALS

U.S. Naval Institute *Proceedings*, Annapolis, Md.

Ships of the World. Tokyo

Surface Warfare Magazine, Washington, D.C.

Warship, Conway, London

Warship International, USA

INDEX

PHOTOGRAPH ACKNOWLEDGEMENTS

Abbreviations of photograph credits in the captions represent the following photographers and institutions to whom the author extends his thanks. AB, Arrigo Barilli, Bologna, Italy; AP, Associated Press; BSt, Bethlehem Steel Corp., Quincy Yard, Quincy, Mass., USA; Cas, Sammlung Casoly, San Francisco, Cal., USA; GP, Giovanni Peditto, Messina, Italy; HF, Haime Fukaya, Japan; INRO, International Naval Research Organization, USA; IWM, Imperial War Museum, London, England; LRC, Lary R. Cote, San Diego, Cal., USA; LGr, Luciano Grazioli, Messina, Italy; MB, Marius Bar, Toulon, France; NN, Newport News S. B. & D. D. Co., Newport News, Va., USA; ON, OUR NAVY, USA; Pa, Pavia, Malta; P&L, Pradignac & Leo, Nice, France; RPh, Real Photographs, England; SF, Shizuo Fukui, Japan; SoW, Ships of the World, Tokio, Japan; Ta, Tailhook Association, Bonita, Cal., USA; Te, Verfasser; TM, Teruo Makino, Osaka, Japan; TS, Tedd Stone, USA; USN, United States Navy, official photograph; WD, Will Donko, Schärding, Austria; WI, Warship International, USA; WL, Wright & Logan, Portsmouth, England; WN, Dr. Wolfgang Noecker, Lübeck, Germany. Abbreviations of line-drawing credits represent: KDS, Klaus Dieter Schock; MR, Frank Mrva. Others were drawn by Eberhard Kaiser.